THE DEVELOPMENT
of VIRGIL'S ART

THE UNIVERSITY OF CHICAGO PRESS
CHICAGO, ILLINOIS

—

THE BAKER & TAYLOR COMPANY
NEW YORK

THE MACMILLAN COMPANY OF CANADA, LIMITED
TORONTO

THE CAMBRIDGE UNIVERSITY PRESS
LONDON

THE MARUZEN-KABUSHIKI-KAISHA
TOKYO, OSAKA, KYOTO, FUKUOKA, SENDAI

THE COMMERCIAL PRESS, LIMITED
SHANGHAI

THE DEVELOPMENT
of VIRGIL'S ART

~~~~~~

By HENRY W. PRESCOTT

~~~~~~

THE UNIVERSITY OF CHICAGO PRESS
CHICAGO ⋅ ILLINOIS

COMPOSED AND PRINTED BY THE UNIVERSITY OF CHICAGO
PRESS, CHICAGO, ILLINOIS, U.S.A.

TO MY FRIENDS

NOW OR FORMERLY IN THE COMMUNITY
OF
THE UNIVERSITY OF CALIFORNIA

PREFACE

A growing interest in the larger cultural aspects of antiquity has led to the production of many manuals and a multitude of translations from ancient authors. The Loeb series of translations would be even more useful if it were accompanied by interpretations of the various authors which indicated their place in the history of literature and in the development of literary types. In the present volume I have attempted this task for Virgil. I have also had in mind teachers and students of Virgil in our high schools and colleges to whom Virgil's *Aeneid* is often too largely a means of learning the Latin language rather than a literary masterpiece worthy of their best appreciative power. For such an audience documentation and pretentious learning are out of place. And the size of the book has led to the omission of bibliography and erudite footnote, which more learned readers can easily supply from their own resources.

So far as any definite theses are involved, I am interested in presenting the Romans, like the Hellenistic Greeks, as adapting and continuing the literary forms of the Greeks of the Classical period, with obvious limitations in respect to originality. The development of Latin poetry is the story of a gradual emergence from the processes of translation and adaptation to a higher continuative process in which a certain kind and degree of originality are manifest. Individual Latin poets sometimes pass through this development as they mature in power. Virgil's development is the development of Latin poetry in miniature. And in Virgil's ultimate achievement there is something superior to the accomplishment of Hellenistic Greece. He organizes old material into an inimitable whole and completely Romanizes Greek stuff. He regulates the riot of feeling in late Greek poetry and chastens it with the restraint of Classicism.

It is now just fifty years since Mr. W. Y. Sellar wrote his critical appreciation of Virgil, and his work, both in style and in content, is unsurpassed. I have avoided any such comprehensive treatment as Mr. Sellar undertook, and have limited myself to certain aspects of Virgil's art which the studies of the last half-century have illuminated. Poetic diction, imagery, and versification are rarely and casually mentioned, and in general only those features of the poet's art are treated which can be appreciated without a knowledge of the poem in its Latin form. The result is a perhaps undue emphasis upon literary technique.

In recent years the poems of the *Virgilian Appendix* have been a hotbed of controversy, and I regret that I have not been able to agree with the convictions of many American scholars that almost all the poems are from the hand of Virgil; though some of them may be later than Virgil's time, I find in them evidence of the early literary environment of the poet which impelled him, in his early manhood, to follow the vogue of the preceding generation, the age of Catullus and the New Poets. In the *Eclogues* the studies of Leo and of Skutsch have been suggestive and valuable. In both the *Eclogues* and the *Georgics* the scattered studies of Virgil's sources by P. Jahn have been serviceable, although my interpretation of the results in some points differs from his. In the chapters on the *Aeneid* I owe the discussion of Virgil's political and social environment largely to Norden's study in the *Neue Jahrbücher für das klassische Altertum* (VII [1901], 249 ff., 313 ff.), and the chapter on the sixth book of the *Aeneid* is an attempt to make a synthesis of the material which Norden has scattered through his learned commentary on that book.

My chief indebtedness in the account of the *Aeneid* is to the epoch-making work of Richard Heinze, *Virgils Epische*

Technik. The first part of his book, which analyzes the *Aeneid* with the exception of Book vi, I have paraphrased, rearranged, condensed, and expanded, and the pages on character treatment in the second part have been used for the final chapter of my book. For the liberty to use Professor Heinze's work so freely I am greatly indebted to the generous courtesy of his publisher, B. G. Teubner, of Leipzig and Berlin.

I have felt that the readers for whom I have chosen to write would wish to know the content of the poems under discussion, and in general I have included the material as well as the form in my discussion. Out of regard for the practical needs of teachers and students of the *Aeneid* I have adopted an analytical rather than synthetic method. In the analysis of the *Aeneid*, however, the natural order of the books of the poem is interrupted. It is desirable to present Virgil's relation to earlier epic at the outset; for the comparison of the *Aeneid* with Homeric and Hellenistic epic reveals at once Virgil's artistic aims and principles, and provides criteria for the appreciation of other parts of the poem which are independent of Greek epic.

To improve the appearance of the printed page I have printed the translations into verse without attaching the names of the translators. I am greatly obliged to my colleague, Professor Frank J. Miller, for his translation of the passage from *The Gnat,* on pp. 28–29. The translation of the same poem on pp. 28, 31 is by Edmund Spenser. The translation of *The Cabaret Girl,* on pp. 55–56, is by the late Professor Kirby Smith, from the volume entitled *Martial the Epigrammatist and Other Essays,* published by the Johns Hopkins University Press. The verses of *The Salad,* on p. 67, are by William Cowper. The translations of passages from the *Eclogues,* the *Georgics,* and the *Aeneid* are by Theodore C. Williams, published by the Harvard University Press (*The*

Georgics and Eclogues of Virgil) and by Houghton Mifflin
Company (*The Aeneid of Virgil*). The latter work is used by
arrangement with, and special permission of, Houghton Mifflin Company; and to them and all the other publishers I am
grateful for allowing me to quote from their publications. The
translations of Apollonius' *Argonautica* are from the hand of
A. S. Way, as published by J. M. Dent and Co. in the Temple
Classics.

It remains to thank most heartily my friend, Mr. George
R. Noyes, for suggesting the work, encouraging it, and help-
fully criticizing some of the earlier pages, and the University
of Chicago and its press for undertaking the publication.

HENRY W. PRESCOTT

UNIVERSITY OF CHICAGO
September, 1926

CONTENTS

xi

VIRGIL'S LITERARY HERITAGE

Latin poetry is part of a continuous stream that rises in Greece and finds its way through Italy to modern Europe. There is no need of denying to the Romans a certain kind and degree of originality. They were not only translators and adapters and transmitters of Greek literature. They often continued the flow of Greek ideas in new and improved channels, and contributed Roman elements to the current. Though they were imitators rather than creators, their imitation was generally superior to the achievements of the Greeks in the centuries just preceding the Christian era, who themselves accomplished hardly more than the perpetuation of earlier Greek form and substance modified by the conditions of a new age. The Romans were legatees of a vast literary inheritance. They cherished and developed their patrimony, but they were dependent upon it for their own growth and progress.

This Greek heritage was not altogether uniform and homogeneous. Down to the end of the fifth century B.C. the Greeks had cultivated and perfected those qualities which have ever since been comprehended under the term Classicism, a feeling for beauty realized with due sense of proportion and fineness of taste. But during the four centuries immediately preceding the birth of Christ, in the period variously called Alexandrian and Hellenistic, the Greeks, however devoutly they admired the epics of Homer and the dramatic poetry of the fifth century, quite naturally and inevitably encouraged new tendencies which in many respects anticipate modern Romanticism.

In the fourth century the Greeks yielded rapidly to the cosmopolitan tendencies incident to an enlarged experience in the new lands now open to them by Alexander's conquests. Greek art of the fifth century had developed in city states, and to a large degree in one city state, Athens. The peculiar endowment of the Athenians liberated them from the disadvantages that in theory at least attend the development of art within the limited horizon of a city state. Indeed, there are some obvious blessings in the close-knit organization which binds the individual to his family, his clan, and, through them, to his native city. In such a society the limitation imposed on individual initiative may be offset by a fine sense of responsibility, and this sense in turn may help to develop a feeling for proportion and a general conservatism which individualism, with its inherent vices of introspection and emotionalism, constantly endangers. We are not, however, concerned with abstractions and theories of government or art. The essential point is that Hellenistic poetry differed from the poetry of the fifth century, and that difference was largely an inevitable result of changes in the external world.

Even in the fifth century the seeds of revolt were sown at Athens. In so conservative a literary type as tragedy the poet Euripides shocked the conservative Athenians. Hampered by the tradition which limited his rôles and his situations to divine and superhuman characters and their entourage he gratified his own impulses by approximating such rôles to the patterns of ordinary human contemporaries by lapses from the elevated diction of tragic style and by portrayal of the commonplace activities of his fellow-citizens. Later, an orator and rhetorician, Isocrates, advocated a cosmopolitan outlook. These seeds grew to full fruition when the conquests of Alexander emancipated the Greeks from their absorption in the affairs of small city states into a world-wide interest promoted by increased opportunities of travel and business activity. The alert Greek mind reacted quickly upon the new experiences.

In literature, as in life, the individual pushed himself into the foreground. In those types of poetry which did not of themselves prompt a personal revelation the poet used prologue and epilogue and parenthetical aside in which to obtrude his private history, parade his own convictions, or register his emotions. So far as this appears in epic it is the style of Hesiod rather than of Homer. In other types better adapted to the free play of his self-consciousness the poet portrayed his own experiences, real or imaginary. This self-consciousness brought with it an introspective habit and a constant emphasis upon feeling rather than action, a zest for the analysis of emotions, but seldom with a view to explaining action as an issue from spiritual conditions, and in general a somewhat shallow psychological interest. The devoted advocate of fifth-century ideals is surprised and offended by the riot of unregulated emotion, the immediate outpourings of distressed souls which, whether of the poets themselves or of literary characters, seem to have lost the sanity and self-restraint currently attributed to the Greeks. Even the outward-turned eye was content to photograph, rather than interpret artistically, what it saw. The immediate realities of the new world must have been overpowering, and any disposition to idealize may well have been retarded by the number and variety of new experiences and phenomena. Drastic portraiture, a choice of gruesome and sensational themes and situations, and an enjoyment of repulsive aspects of life as literary topics sharply differentiate this later Greek age from that of Sophocles and Phidias.

The old Greek sensitiveness in matters affecting structure and style changed appreciably in the new epoch. Athens was no longer the center of Greek culture. The steadying effects of its conservative standards did not prevail always in the new intellectual centers of Africa, Egypt, Asia Minor, and Syria. Especially toward the end of the period oriental influences broke down all sense of proportion. Much of the sentimentality, in its extreme form, was peculiar to poets of the farther East. These same influences promoted the extravagant use of rhetorical embellishments which, though taught and practiced in Athens at the end of the fifth century, were there for a long time employed with some degree of taste and restraint. Sentence structure lost the simple effectiveness of direct Attic style, and individual poets in the less realistic types of poetry often resorted to lumbering periods that dragged interminably over a number of verses. On the other hand, a contradictory phenomenon sometimes appears: a striving for pithy epigrammatic expression results here and there in short and jerky sentence structure. Similar weaknesses emerged in the larger formal elements. The general interest in emotional appeal encouraged a lavish attention to feeling and a corresponding neglect of the important stages of action, or a brief dismissal of them. Frequent digression broke down the orderly progress of both narrative and emotional poetry. These vices do not obtrude themselves in all *genres* or in all poets. Not a few Hellenistic poets perpetuate the taste and general sense of proportion characteristic of the best Greek art, but the defects are sufficiently common to mark a departure from earlier standards.

The difficulty of defining the poetry of this later Greek age is itself significant of the complexity and the contradictory qualities of the period. Any one of the various poets cultivated, not one *genre,* but many literary types; each type had features differentiating it from other types, but not infrequently the *genres* lost distinctive individuality by blending one with another. Neither artist nor artistic product submits easily to definition. Furthermore, the age was much given to whimsical novelties and startling eccentricities.

The modern reader, however, cannot trust himself to appreciate the eccentricities, though he may observe the contradictory qualities. The pedantry which permeated Hellenistic elegy and epic and, less frequently, the other poetic types is a glaring contrast to the riotous indulgence in feeling. It is abhorrent to the modern reader, unless he be a devoted follower of Robert Browning, but it is not one of the whims and eccentricities of the age.

The academic standpoint is revealed in various ways. The poet, often a student of philology, resorts to obsolete words and other peculiarities of diction and usage that his scholarly studies have unearthed. Even in the selection of themes a scholarly interest is manifest. Antiquarian studies of cities and towns had brought to light a mine of folk-tales and legends to which poets gladly turned as a relief from the trite versions of old heroic saga; but often in using these legends for literary purposes the poet showed his pedantic point of view by telling the tale in hard, unsympathetic fashion, much in the manner of the antiquarian from whom he derived it, and on occasion he concluded his narrative with a formal statement of the author and book whence his material had come, in the dry pragmatic style of a university professor. In general, out-of-the-way versions of old myths or quite unused new legends, particularly of a sentimental and gruesome sort, supplied much of the material of poetry, and in either case the poet easily appears to be somewhat erudite, and often requires the sympathetic intelligence of a sophisticated and esoteric circle of listeners. Somewhat allied to this bookishness, but deeply rooted in the conservatism characteristic of all antiquity, is the emphasis upon the link that binds the present to the past. A bit of narrative, itself often presented effectively, is stimulated by a desire to explain an existing custom or institution by the facts of the narrative, and this causal nexus is reinforced by a dry conclusion, like a tag from an *Encyclopedia Hellenica*, which prosily records that owing to these events of a remote past the custom of the present has arisen.

An index of defects and limitations naturally does scant justice to many admirable features of Hellenistic poetry. Some types suffered more than others. Epic and elegy, artificial and traditional, suffered more than other *genres,* such as mime, epigram, and comedy, that touched more immediately contemporary experiences and the actualities of Greek life. Even in the artificial types there are poems of exquisite finish; of prettiness too studied to match the more virile beauty of earlier poetry, but none the less winsome, especially to the modern eye and ear; of nice feeling that stops short of sentimentality, portrayed with rare delicacy and sympathy; of rich sensuousness of sound and situation; and the more realistic types have a natural vigor in the dramatic expression of universal experience in comedy or in the outbursts of momentary personal feeling aroused in epigram by love and enmity, by domestic tragedy and happiness, by the amenities of convivial life, and by aesthetic satisfaction in art and literature.

The period during which poetry developed at Rome, from its beginnings in the third century to the time of Virgil, roughly coincides with the last two centuries of the Hellenistic period in the Greek world. The Romans, imitators of the Greeks from the start, might very naturally have sought their models among the Hellenistic poets who were contemporary with the earliest Latin poets. But with few exceptions the early period of Roman poetry is marked by a constant resort, in the types of epic and tragedy, to the older Greek models, Homer and the tragic poets of the fifth century. Plautus and Terence, to be sure, because the license which inspired the lampooning burlesque of Aristophanes in the fifth century in Greece was not granted to Roman comic poets, adapted the pathetic comedies of intrigue and manners by Menander and his contem-

poraries in Hellenistic Greece. Ennius, however, is ambitious
to be a Roman Homer, and in tragedy adapts the plays of
Aeschylus, though his favorite is the precursor of the Hellenistic period, Euripides. In his minor works he reveals many
points of contact with somewhat whimsical Hellenistic types
of poetry. It was during Ennius' activity, in the early part of
the second century B.C., that Rome, by its conquest of the
Greek world, came into more immediate touch with Hellenistic ideas, and by the middle of that century, Hellenistic
thought had become familiar to educated Romans through
visits of notable rhetoricians and philosophers from Greece.
Ennius' nephew, Pacuvius, is the first tragic poet who reveals a distinct leaning toward the Hellenistic tragic poets
rather than the great triad of the fifth century. During this
second century there is a constantly growing number of educated Greeks who find their way to Rome, largely owing to
the vicissitudes of war. The immediate effect was a strong
reaction against Greek influence which centered about the
strong personality of Cato the Censor just before the middle
of the century. But the resistance was futile. In the second
half of the second century feeble efforts were made to Ro
manize the comic drama, to develop indigenous Italian dramatic types, and even Accius, though adapting Greek tragedies, was regarded by later generations as no mere trans-
lator, but, like Ennius in epic, as the producer of something
genuinely Roman. The poet Lucilius, in his miscellanies, is
pre-eminently Roman, although the fragments of his work
indicate that he has read widely in Hellenistic literature and
that it has appreciably affected him. Such phenomena, however, are temporary. The floodgates are open for the tide of
Hellenistic influence which sweeps in at the beginning of the
first century in the age that politically is marked by the name
of the first great Roman autocrat, Sulla.

To some extent the influence of Hellenistic thought and

literary practice is immediately revealed in Sulla's own procedure. His chief literary work takes the form of memoirs in
prose, a record not so much of the history of his time as of his
own personality. This autobiography was edited and published by a freed Greek slave in Sulla's household, an educated Greek who might easily have assisted in the composition of the book. The work itself was dedicated to Lucullus
and was definitely intended to provide material for a history
of the Social War, which Lucullus was writing in his leisure
moments. This history by Lucullus was written, not in Latin,
but in Greek. Atticus, the friend of Cicero and an authority
on Greek idiom and style, in reviewing Lucullus' work found
some barbarisms and solecisms, violations of good Greek
usage. To Atticus' criticisms Lucullus neatly and wittily responded that he had departed just enough from the Greek
idiom to prove that his work was really that of a Roman. All
these conditions are symptomatic: the literary activity of
men of affairs, the emergence of autobiography as a literary
genre, the effort to rival the Greeks in the use of their own
language, the existence of an educated Roman competent to
criticize even the niceties of Greek usage, and in the background the educated Greek freedman editing and publishing
the memoirs of the leading Roman of the day.

The poetry of these early decades of the first century was
ephemeral. Little of it endured even into the next generation.
Yet the political terrorism of the day promoted, probably,
rather than retarded, literary activity. Characteristic of the
new interests of Sulla's generation and of the general tendencies which culminate in the poetry of Virgil's boyhood is
the work of Laevius. In a collection of poems in not fewer
than six volumes, under the Greek title *Erotopaegnia,* or
"Amatory Trifles," he presented an array of long and short
poems which in their content, general style, and amazing
variety of metrical forms probably illustrated the most mod-

ern developments in Hellenistic poetry. The fragments of this
work suggest that the style was little short of sensational. His
diction is marked by new formations, forced extensions of
earlier usage or new inventions, by Greek words and Grecized
compounds of Latin words, and by the perversion of familiar
words into new meanings. In sentence structure he runs to
short independent sentences, with an almost complete neglect
of subordinate clauses; his interest is in the word, novel and
sensational in form or meaning, rather than in the sentence.
His meters are lyrical, the song measures either of early
Greek lyric poets or of the manifold adaptations and re-crea-
tions of them by Hellenistic poets; and his forms of verse are
often whimsical, as in "The Phoenix' Wing," the lines of
which, as they appeared on the page, probably marked by
their varying lengths the outlines of the bird's wing, a *tour de
force* cultivated by Greek poets early in the Hellenistic period. The content of his poems was largely sentimental; the
titles of separate poems point to the love stories of mythology, of Helen, Alcestis, Laodamia, and there is a tantalizing
trace of his own amatory experiences. In general this miscel-
laneous collection was an exact reproduction, in Latin dress,
of a Hellenistic edition of Greek poems such as we have today
in the extant collections of Theocritus' poems, or, vaguely
outlined, in the new discoveries of Callimachus' work. In its
external appearance it anticipated, probably, the similar collection of long and short poems in divers meters from the hand
of Catullus in the next generation.

In the second quarter of the first century, the period of
Virgil's boyhood, the lines between conflicting interests were
somewhat sharply drawn. Every generation has its new
poets. But the new poets of Virgil's youth, Catullus and his
associates, were regarded by older men of their time, such as
Cicero, with a mild aversion not unlike the conservative attitude toward imagists and writers of *vers libre* today. It is un-

fortunate that we cannot as yet clearly define all the objections of the older generation toward the new movement; we may only vaguely discern the controversy in passages of Cicero's works, in scattered comments elsewhere, and in its later issues, perhaps, in certain satires of Horace. The poetry of this period, except for the work of Lucretius and Catullus, exists only in very scanty fragments. At the outset it should be observed that there is no controversy in one respect. By implication, at least, everybody is now agreed that dependence upon Greek models is inevitable and desirable. The conservative opinion of the day, however, seems to have been that the practice of Ennius and Accius was quite different from that of Catullus and his associates: Ennius and Accius had assimilated their Greek models and made some headway toward a national Roman literature. Catullus and other New Poets, in varying degrees, were Grecizing Latin poetry. Against what particular details this hostile criticism was directed we are not fully informed. But certainly some of it was aimed at the constant transliteration of Greek words, the fondness for the musical sounds often produced by Greek patronymics and other Greek vocabulary, and the development of new Latin formations oftentimes on the analogy of Greek forms, the total effect of which seemed to be a flagrant violation of pure Latinity. Some dissatisfaction was expressed with metrical details. Probably it is safe to add to these indictments some of the novel features of the new poetry as we see it best in Catullus and as we have seen it in Laevius. New Greek *genres* are represented, which earlier Roman poets failed to cultivate: the short epic, the sentimental elegy, the court poem, the epithalamium, the epigram. In general the sources of inspiration are no longer Homer and the Greek tragedians, but Hellenistic poets. There is a bewildering diversity of meters, many of which were not easily taken over into Latin poetry. In addition to no small number of Greek words there is a general preciosity of diction, at least in the artificial poems. And in these same poems, despite many virtues, there is a strained sentimentality and that contradictory pedantry which we have identified as characteristic of many Hellenistic types. Yet these defects are perhaps more than counterbalanced in Catullus' case by the simple directness and easy grace (Greek qualities reinforced by his own animated personality) with which, particularly in his shorter poems, he conveys to the reader his passing moods and registers the experiences, not of Greek mythological heroes and heroines, but of himself in the exciting social and political life just before the outbreak of the Civil War.

Catullus was only one of many. Closely associated with him were a number of young men whose figures are much more shadowy and vague because their poems have not survived. But they were all linked together by a community of political, social, and intellectual interests, and their ideas gained considerable impetus through the close interaction of the various members of the group. And not only were they bound to one another, but through individual members of the group they had immediate points of contact with the sources of Greek culture at Rome in the second quarter of the century and later.

Politically, their sympathies were in many cases directed against the rising autocrat, Julius Caesar. At him Catullus, Calvus, and Furius Bibaculus aimed their invectives in bitter epigrams. Toward some of these opponents Caesar adopted a conciliatory policy. Several of the group were rivals of Catullus in his love for Clodia, the Lesbia of his poems, and through the rascality of her brother, Clodius, they were more or less involved in the social and political turmoil of the day. However much Cicero may have frowned upon the new movement in literature, he must often have found himself aligned with these New Poets through a common antipathy toward Clodius. Cicero had himself translated into Latin the most popular didactic poem of the Hellenistic period, Aratus' treatise on astronomy, and his mild hostility in literary matters must have been prompted more by a proud concern for pure Latinity than by any such unreasonable opposition to things Greek as had animated the censorious Cato in the middle of the preceding century.

Intellectually, the activities of the group may have been furthered and unified by the teacher, scholar, and poet, Valerius Cato, a characteristically Hellenistic figure in the range of his interests. As scholar he edited Lucilius; as teacher the extent of his influence is quite unknown; but either as teacher or professional critic he is credited in a Latin epigram with "making poets," a delightfully ambiguous phrase which might cover the inspiration furnished in the schoolroom and in public readings or the destructive agency of a professional bard and reviewer. He was most closely associated with two other poets of the group: with Furius Bibaculus, pronounced foe of Julius Caesar and Octavian, and possibly the Furius of Catullus' poems, and with Helvius Cinna, companion of Catullus in his trip to Bithynia and author of a laborious and pedantic epic, in Hellenistic style, on the illicit love of Zmyrna, the outcome of nine years' effort and the occasion for equally laborious commentary in explanation of its obscurities.

Through Helvius Cinna, possibly, these New Poets came into immediate contact with the most fruitful source of Hellenistic ideas and literary forms at Rome in this period. In the year 73 B.C., shortly before Virgil's birth, the Hellenistic poet, Parthenius, a native of Bithynia in Asia Minor, was brought to Rome as a military captive when his native town of Nicaea was besieged by Roman forces. He fell into the hands of a man named Cinna as the spoils of war, and this man Cinna may have been the father of the poet, Helvius Cinna. Recognized as a person of education and refinement, Parthenius was freed and unquestionably came into close relations with the literary Romans of the day. His poem in Greek, a *Bon Voyage* (*Propempticon*), may well have been the model of Helvius Cinna's *Bon Voyage* to Asinius Pollio. Even upon the young Augustans of the next generation his influence was immediate. Virgil, who is reported to have learned Greek from Parthenius, knew his work and occasionally appropriated his verses. Parthenius' version of the story of Scylla may be the background of the *Ciris* of the *Virgilian Appendix*, and a Renaissance scholar guessed, plausibly enough, that the *Moretum* of the same *Appendix* was based on Parthenius' Greek poem on a salad. Even more sugges tive of the wide scope of this Hellenistic poet's effect upon later Roman poetry is the fact that he gathered from Greek sources a collection of the gruesome tragic love stories favored by the modern Greek poets, and from them prepared in Greek a plot book of such tales, that Virgil's friend, Cornelius Gallus, might use them as material for Latin epics and elegies. So the New Poets of Catullus' generation and the young Augustans were bound together by a common attachment to a potent intermediary between Hellenistic Greece and Rome.

Parthenius himself, in his Greek poems, was much under the influence of an earlier Hellenistic poet, Euphorion, remarkable for his enigmatic and pedantic style. When Lucian, a late Greek essayist, wished to satirize some of the defects of Hellenistic poetry, he bracketed, as representatives of its qualities, Callimachus, Euphorion, and Parthenius. Cicero, sadly admitting that the old Roman worthy, Ennius, is no longer properly esteemed, contemptuously dubs the New Poets "the singers of Euphorion." This choir of Cicero's contemporaries that responded to the leadership of Euphorion and of Parthenius inspired the group of young Augustans whom Horace in one of his satires caustically describes, with reference to one of its members, as "singing naught save Calvus and Catullus." But whatever antipathy in the next generation Horace may have momentarily felt toward the New Poets, it was they who determined the trend of things in the days of Virgil and Horace, in the Augustan period. Horace himself, and Virgil, particularly, paid their tribute in abundant imitations of Catullus. Ovid and Propertius even more submissively fell in with the tide of Hellenistic influence. Some of these Augustan poets are not outspoken in their appreciation of the New Poets of the previous generations. Closely associated with Augustus himself and with Maecenas, they could hardly afford to approve openly earlier adherents of the enemies of Julius Caesar, or else they happened to cultivate types of poetry which did not suggest recognition of Catullus' achievements in mythological epic, elegy, and epigram. Neglectful or contemptuous as Horace may sometimes have been, Virgil and lesser contemporaries were long under the spell of Catullus and others of the group. Born and educated in northern Italy, Virgil was in his boyhood never far from Cremona, the birthplace of Furius Bibaculus, or from Verona, the home of Catullus. Valerius Cato is said to have been a Gaul, which presumably means that his home was in the same general region. The effects, however, of breathing the same atmosphere as some of these New Poets are quite incalculable, and the later associations of Virgil, at Rome or Naples, may equally well explain his early attachment to the group that was most zealously promoting the cultivation of modern Greek types of poetry.

In general the differences between the New Poets and the next generation of Augustans are a matter of degree and method. All are committed to the perpetuation of Greek types. Consciously or unconsciously, they vary only in their ways of assimilating or adapting their Greek models. The ultimate goal, which they themselves may not always clearly discern, is the complete Romanization of these exotic *genres*.

The half-century (70–19 B.C.) covered by Virgil's life is marked by tense civil strife, which relaxes only when the poet has almost reached his fortieth year. His boyhood and youth fell in the years of Catiline's conspiracy and Cicero's famous consulship, of Pompey's emergence to power, of Caesar's conquests in Gaul, and of the struggle between Pompey and Caesar for supreme control. The murder of Caesar found the poet well matured, a young man of twenty-seven, and his three important works, the *Eclogues, Georgics,* and *Aeneid,* follow this catastrophe. His nature poems, if we may roughly so call the pastorals and the didactic treatise on husbandry, were written in the decade when Octavian, the future Augustus, was occupied with conquests in the Far East and, later, with the frustration of Antony's ambitious designs. His national epic was composed in the following decade, after the battle of Actium, when Octavian, secure in his position as first citizen of the state, was endeavoring to restore the lost vigor of the Roman republic. The poet's literary activity, therefore, aside from some juvenile efforts, falls in the last two decades of his life: his nature poems, when the poet was in his thirties and Octavian was gradually getting control of the government; his epic, when the poet had reached his prime, and Octavian, now Augustus, had brought about permanent peace and could begin a reconstruction of the shattered remnants of his empire.

Nor should we fail to note Virgil's relation, in time, to the great men, especially the literary men, of his century. He was a boy of about fifteen when Lucretius and Catullus died, the great poets of the older generation. He was himself five years older than Horace, seven years older than Octavian, eleven years older than the historian, Livy. For a quarter of a century, if his observation had been abnormally acute in his infancy, he might have watched the careers of Cicero and of Caesar. The younger poets of the day, Tibullus and Propertius, were beginning their work when Virgil had undertaken his last poem, the *Aeneid*, though Tibullus died, prematurely, in the same year as Virgil. Ovid saw Virgil, but did not know him. Virgil, then, is a link between the older poets, Lucretius and Catullus, and the young elegists, Tibullus, Propertius, and Ovid. He might have seen all of them.

The reaction of Virgil to the personal and intellectual influences of his youth and early manhood was more immediate than to any of the external events of this stirring period. Temperamentally perhaps reflective and studious, he yielded readily to the literary currents of his boyhood, following the New Poets, Catullus, and others in the cultivation of epigrams and probably other minor types of the more modern Greek poetry, expressing his emotions and his experiences in the Northern Italy of his boyhood days, and also continuing the fashionable cultivation of artificial poems in Greek manner after the style of the New Poets. Throughout his youth, as later, he was devoted to philosophical studies, and these may have stimulated, or may have been stimulated by, his admiration for Lucretius, whose diction and phrasing Virgil delights to refashion for his own purposes whenever occasion calls for it. Even through the period of the Civil War there is little, if any, positive evidence that he was diverted from purely intellectual interests by the tense political situation. But personal experiences in the issues of that war drew him more directly into the main current of events. His pastoral poems, artificial as they are, frequently reveal his personal contact with men of affairs, who happen often to be active in the intellectual life of the period. Thus gradually he comes to co-operate in the political and patriotic movements of the two decades that center about the battle of Actium. A cultivation of merely artificial themes and a reproduction of Greek material are no longer satisfying to an intimate associate of Octavian and Maecenas. The *Georgics* is perhaps not untouched by a sympathetic interest in the difficulties of Italian husbandmen after decades of civil dissension. Certainly it breathes a patriotic fervor that in the *Eclogues* is limited to a single poem, and that finds no counterpart in the didactic treatises of the later Greeks. A thoroughly developed national interest and patriotic endeavor combined with a matured skill in poetic art contributed to make his final work, the *Aeneid*, the proper culmination of his career, in which at last the literary heritage of the Greeks is fused with a truly Roman spirit and a truly Roman power of effective organization.

THE ATMOSPHERE OF VIRGIL'S YOUTH AND EARLY MANHOOD

The biographies that have come down to us from antiquity are often untrustworthy. Although details in the lives of men of affairs were recorded in official documents, the modern machinery of registration and record and the outlet furnished by the modern newspaper for a natural interest in the doings of both humble and prominent personages are not paralleled by any ancient methods. A biographer of Virgil, writing a generation after the poet's death, would have at his disposal the works of the poet and a mass of material that had drifted down through oral and written communication from the poet's own time. Virgil's close association with the court circle may lend greater credibility to certain facts in the ancient tradition than would be the case if he were a relatively obscure person, but the means of transmission leaves the way open for considerable tittle-tattle and exaggeration in the mouths of gossips. This possibility is greatly increased by the fact that the poet is hardly dead before rival factions of devotees and detractors examine the available material with a view to exalting or depreciating the subject of their critiques and biographies; in this conflict of hostile forces facts are distorted to suit the critics' special purpose. The resort of his biographers and critics to the poet's own works supplied a sounder basis of judgment, but unfortunately in Virgil's case his own poems were easily misinterpreted. The artificial pastorals which he wrote in his early manhood were specially adapted to the expression of double meanings. Explicit references to contemporary men and events that violated the pastoral illusion led to a view, not always incorrect, that in these same poems there were subtler and more covert references to the poet's own experiences; as time went on, this view gained, rather than lost, in strength, and from century to century the *Eclogues* yielded more and more material to biographers as the allegorical interpretation of the pastorals was elaborated by successive generations. By the fifth century the poet's name came to be spelled Virgilius, instead of Vergilius, and fanciful etymologists connected the name with *virgo,* "maiden," furnishing the poet's admirers with further evidence of his virginal qualities, or with *virga,* "magician's wand," which gave impetus to the constantly increasing mystical interpretation of the poet's work and to the medieval conception of the poet himself as a wizard. The issues of this long tradition, a curious mixture of plausible fact with positive fiction or distorted truth, appear today in a number of ancient *Lives* of Virgil, attached to the names of various worthies, Donatus, Servius, Probus, Philargyrius, Phocas, or anonymously transmitted in different manuscripts and in Latin commentaries on the poet's work. It is a perilous task to extricate the truth from this mass of material that accumulated between the first century after Christ and the early Renaissance.

In this difficulty the modern, like the ancient, biographer turns to Virgil's own works for correction or corroboration of the ancient tradition. The tradition is suspiciously ample when it deals with persons and events of the period covered by Virgil's *Eclogues,* and here it is possible, by a reasonable interpretation of the pastoral poems, to discriminate in the biographical tradition, on occasion, fact from fancy. But the difficulties are by no means solved. For at the outset we are confronted by a group of poems of which the authorship is seriously questioned. These poems, if by Virgil, offer a rich supply of material for the understanding of his early environment and of his apprenticeship in the art of poety. The group includes *The Gnat (Culex), Ciris, The Salad (Moretum), Curses (Dirae), The Cabaret Girl (Copa), Aetna,* and a collection of shorter poems entitled *In Lighter Vein* (*Catalepton*). With the exception of *The Salad* and *The Cabaret Girl*, these poems are ascribed to Virgil in the account of his life attached to the name of Donatus, which is itself probably an amplification of a biography written by Suetonius in the early part of the second century after Christ. In extant texts of the *Life* the authorship of the *Aetna* is admitted to be a subject of dispute, but it is not clear whether the doubts arose in early or late antiquity. Servius, both in his *Life* and in his commentary on the *Aeneid*, includes it among Virgil's poems without reservations. The authenticity of *The Gnat* is vouched for as early as the first century after Christ by competent witnesses: Lucan, Statius, and Martial. Suetonius probably included it in his list of Virgil's genuine poems at the beginning of the second century A.D., and definitely stated that it was written by Virgil at the age of sixteen. Modern scholars contend that Virgil could not have written *The Gnat* until he was twenty-one or twenty-six.

Many facts included in the poems of *In Lighter Vein* square with credible and specific details in the *Lives* and with the conjectural environment of a youth in Northern Italy. The last epigram in the collection is an epilogue by the editor, and in it the poems of the collection are referred to as the work of a poet when his Muse was still unskilled. If we could be sure that Virgil's literary executors, who published his *Aeneid*, were responsible also for this collection of short poems, the proof of Virgil's authorship would be appreciably strengthened. As it is, one of them (ii) is referred to as Virgil's by Quintilian, a century after Virgil's death, and another (xii) is similarly attributed by a grammarian of the fourth century. *Ciris* is ascribed to Virgil in the expanded commentary of Servius on *Eclogues* vi. 3. *The Cabaret Girl* is not cited as Virgil's until the fourth century A.D., but it is included in the list of Virgilian poems in Servius' *Life*. The

Salad had found its way into collected editions of Virgil's work by the ninth century, though its position in such collections militates against, rather than for, its authenticity, and none of the ancient *Lives* of Virgil records it among the poet's works. *Curses* is vouched for by Donatus and Servius in their biographies.

Certainly by the ninth century all these poems, and others manifestly not by Virgil, were incorporated in editions of the poet's works. Nowadays they are roughly relegated to a so-called *Virgilian Appendix,* and they have become a fencing ground for the adroit interplay of nimble wits. Scholars thrust and parry over the minutiae of manuscript tradition; the peculiarities of diction, syntax, and meter; the resemblances in phrasing to other poems by Virgil himself, or by his predecessors, contemporaries, and successors; the identification of individuals ambiguously referred to in the poems, and all the other evidence that may tend to support or disprove the authorship of Virgil. The general trend today favors the authenticity of *The Gnat* and of most, if not all, the poems *In Lighter Vein; Ciris* gains adherents now and then; the charm of *The Cabaret Girl* wins that poem an occasional vote; but *The Salad, Curses,* and the philosophical poem, *Aetna,* are championed only by the boldest advocates. In general, nothing can safely be said except in the form of a pedantic double negative: few, if any, of the poems can be proved not to be from Virgil's hand. But whether Virgil's or not, many of them reveal, more clearly than any other evidence, the influences that affected the poetry of his boyhood and youth.

Virgil's grave at Naples was an object of veneration a century after his death. Upon his tombstone one read that the poet was a Mantuan. Virgil himself, in *Georgics* iii. 10–12, implies as much. Some of his ancient biographers, perhaps only more specifically, locate his birthplace near Mantua, at Andes, which in Dante's time had been identified with the modern Pietole; it is possible, however, that this narrower limitation is due to false inferences from the first and ninth eclogues, in which later scholars found a more precise reference to Virgil's personal history than is warranted by the poems; and even the identification of Andes with Pietole is at least questionable. His tombstone may also have contained the date of his death. Both his birth and death are quite consistently and precisely dated in the ancient authorities, the former as October 15, 70 B.C., the latter as September 22, 19 B.C. The uncertainty that must have prevailed regarding his parentage and minor details of his family history is revealed by the variant reports in the earliest biographical material. His parentage was humble. According to one tradition the father was a potter, and the making of pottery in Northern Italy in the poet's time was certainly a very general and profitable occupation. A variant report, which numbered more adherents, accounted for the father as the hired man of a minor public official, a courier; Virgil's father is said to have married the courier's daughter, Magia, and the poet was their offspring. This story, with the fanciful tale of circumstances attending the poet's birth that represents the mother, on the night before the event, dreaming that she had given birth to a laurel branch which, on touching the ground, immediately developed into a fruitful tree, smacks of late invention. The mother's name, Magia, and that of her father, Magius, though they are possible names of Etruscan origin, are so closely related to the Latin noun, *magus*, "a magician," that one may suspect the whole story is part of the later interest in establishing Virgil's credit as a wizard. It is, of course, equally possible that the names Magius and Magia are authentic, and stimulated the fancy that the son and grandson inherited the virtues of a magician. The story of the laurel branch can hardly be separated from the fifth-century spelling of the poet's name as Virgilius, with consequent associations of that

form of the name with the Latin noun *virga,* "branch." In
any case the pains taken with the poet's early education suggests that his father had come to be a man of some means, and
the biographical tradition furnishes an explanation of this
situation in the statement that the father bought up woodland
and devoted himself to bee culture. Not only might this
activity have increased the father's income, but it may well
have provided a degree of acquaintance with agriculture and
the care of cattle and bees, which, in the poet's *Georgics,* seems
to rest on some personal contact with the problems of husbandry. On the whole, however, it is not very likely that
Virgil was the typical country boy. He spent most of his time
during the plastic period of boyhood in small cities, where, in
the course of his elementary education, his earlier environment served only to induce a sympathetic interest in the literature of the schoolroom which was redolent of country life.

The family moved to Cremona when Virgil was still a lad.
There at least he assumed the *toga virilis,* an outward indication that he had reached maturity. Probably he attended
school at Cremona. And a subsequent stay in Milan was
doubtless prompted by a desire to avail himself of the best
educational facilities in Northern Italy. The course of study
that Virgil followed at Cremona and Milan is not easily reconstructed. There was no formal school system in Italy such as
we are familiar with today; there was considerable variation
in different localities. But from the more explicit information
that we have of schools in the time of Quintilian, at the end
of the first century A.D., we may suspect that in Virgil's boyhood education was being transformed under Greek influence,
and that this involved a large amount of attention to early
Greek literature. It is probable also that in literary studies
the interpretation of poetry was emphasized in the classroom
to the disadvantage of prose. Such a curriculum would include perhaps Homer, Hesiod, the early Greek lyric poets,

and the dramatists of the fifth century; and on the Roman side, the poets of the third and second centuries B.C., such as Ennius, Naevius, Plautus, and Terence. There is sufficient evidence in Virgil's own youthful confessions that the study of rhetoric, conducted in a curiously artificial fashion and taught largely in connection with abstract and bookish themes rather than with any vital topics of contemporary life, was already regarded as the crowning feature of the school curriculum. To these courses in literature and rhetoric were added mathematics, astronomy, medicine, music, but the whole was not harmoniously fused together as it had been in Greece, where the system originated.

As evidence of Virgil's precocity his biographers quote a commonplace elegiac couplet that celebrates the death of one Ballista and his burial beneath a mountain of stones. The safety of travelers was thereby insured. Ballista was apparently a brigand, and, if we are to accept tradition, also a school teacher. The credit of the teaching profession is secured if we suppose his school was only for gladiators. Very likely the author was playing with the name of a rocky mountain near his home, and he may have been at the same time demolishing a school teacher whose name lent itself to the conceit that the epigram suggests.

Another youthful poem, *The Gnat,* in the hexameter measure of heroic epic, is a much more significant document. A prœmium of forty verses dedicates the poem to a boy named Octavius, who is dignified by the somewhat exalted epithets *sanctus* and *venerandus.* The identity of this boy is much disputed. In most of the recent discussions he is supposed to be the future Octavian and Augustus, ultimately Virgil's patron. But if Virgil wrote the poem at the age of sixteen, this Octavius would have been only nine years old; the difficulty of course is lessened if Virgil wrote *The Gnat* at the age of twenty-one or twenty-six. We have, however, no trustworthy

evidence that Virgil came into contact with Octavian until
the poet was nearly thirty years old, and it is idle to speculate
regarding the possibility that Julius Caesar's activities in the
north brought his nephew, Octavian, into any earlier relations with the poet's family in that region in the year 50 B.C.
or thereabouts. Nor, without some such intimate relations,
is it easily conceivable that Octavian, simply as the recognized
heir of his uncle, was so prominent as to attract the attention
of ambitious poets at the early age to which the Latin word
puer properly applies. A conservative conclusion is that if
Virgil wrote the poem, and if he wrote it at the age of sixteen,
the boy cannot be Octavian, although the identification becomes more plausible if the poem was written when the poet
was in his early twenties. Since there is an Octavius Musa
whom Virgil celebrates as his friend in other poems (*Catalepton* iv and xi) it seems almost perverse to deny the likelihood
that it is he whom Virgil, with youthful enthusiasm, adorns
with the qualities somewhat extravagantly expressed in the
epithets *sanctus* and *venerandus,* suggestive of moral purity
and the high respect accorded to it.

In his opening verses the poet clearly indicates that his
epic measure and diction are not to be taken too seriously.
His Muse is slender; his poem as tenuous as a spider's web.
Such accord as there may seem to be with epic arrangement
and epic style is mere playful exercise. He postpones to a
later season a more serious theme and style, more worthy of
his friend Octavius. Thus we are prepared for the mock heroic
treatment of a trivial situation. We need expect no explicit
jests. The humor lies simply in the sober narrative, with all
the parade of elevated epic diction, of a gnat's philanthropic
service and unmerited death and ultimate reward. From this
announcement of a *jeu d'esprit* the poet turns to a formal epic
invocation of Phoebus and Pales, the former as god of music,
the latter as a pastoral goddess, and from them passes to a

further address to his friend Octavius in which he expresses his abnegation of the high epic themes of mythology and history; his verses are not the sturdy heroic sort, but, he reiterates, the soft and slender verses of playful toying with epic narrative. And he concludes his prooemium with lavish prayers for his friend's fame and happiness.

The narrative that follows in nearly four hundred verses might easily be dismissed in a few sentences. A herdsman, falling asleep, is threatened by a snake. A gnat sees his danger, stings him, and so saves his life. The herdsman, waking, in ignorance of the service rendered, kills not only the snake, but the gnat. The gnat then appears to the herdsman in a dream and plaintively describes the horrors of the underworld to which the shepherd has ungratefully banished him. A grave and epitaph are the gnat's ultimate reward.

In the choice of theme and manner of treatment the poem illustrates the influence of modern Greek poetry as it reached Virgil directly or as it filtered through the work of the New Poets. Of a definite Greek background there is no evidence. The closest approach to the subject matter is a fable, in one of the by-ways of Greek literature, of a herdsman whose flocks suffered annually from the attacks of a serpent; the herdsman killed the animal; the serpent appeared to him in a dream and demanded burial; failing to carry out the request, the herdsman was punished by the loss of his own life and the destruction of his family. This story takes a different turn from that of the gnat, and we do not know that it ever was used for literary purposes. It might be noted, in passing, that the elaborate burial at the end of *The Gnat* would be more inevitable if it were not merely an act of gratitude, but a pious fulfillment of duty such as Aeneas performed for Palinurus in Virgil's epic. But it is more the manner of the narration than the theme that suggests Greek background. The extravagant parody of Homeric style attempted in a Greek poem, *The Battle of the Frogs and Mice,* is, to be sure, far from the tone of this "easy running verse with tender feet," but the ample diffuse handling of a fable of service done to a human being by an insignificant animal and the elegiac plaint of this "nursling of the humid air" are characteristic of the whimsical and emotional trend of late Greek poetry.

The essential facts of the story so concisely outlined above are of course quite justifiably adorned for poetic treatment. One misses simply that sense of proportion in the use of decorative and pathetic material that characterizes the older classical style. In one respect the copious detail has value of a purely economic sort. The action covers an entire day and part of a night, and the intervals of time are marked off by epic descriptions of the early morning, noon, and evening. The ornamental digressions, describing the blessings of pastoral life and the individual trees that form the grove in which the shpeherd's flocks refresh themselves after the noonday heat, by their very length serve to make more plausible the considerable lapse of time during the forenoon and part of the afternoon before the catastrophe takes place. The gnat's complaint occupies nearly half of the entire narrative, and the relatively brief dismissal of the serpent's attack and of the gnat's rescue of the herdsman indicates that the poet is interested chiefly in the elaborate description of the other world which forms the penultimate chapter of the poem.

These three sections of the poem which occupy so disproportionate an amount of space—the blessings of pastoral life, the description of the grove, and the gnat's lament—all foreshadow the interests of the author of the *Eclogues, Georgics,* and *Aeneid.* The whole setting of the poem is pastoral. The shepherd at dawn drives his flocks to their feeding ground, a high mountain top, where they wander free through the woods, thickets, and valleys,

> Some on the soft green grass feeding their fills,
> Some, clamb'ring through the hollow cliffs on high,
> Nibble the bushy shrubs, which grow thereby.
>
> Others the utmost boughs of trees do crop,
> And brouse the woodbine twigs that freshly bud;
> This with full bit doth catch the utmost top
> Of some soft willow, or new growen stud;
> This with sharp teeth the bramble leaves doth lop,
> And chaw the tender prickles in her cud,
> The whiles another high doth overlook
> Her own like image in a crystal brook.

Having left the flock to graze at will in this brief but acute observation of their picturesque activity, the poet abruptly bursts forth into an apostrophe on the happiness of shepherds, which harks back to the splendid picture of philosophic contentment with the simple life near the beginning of the second book of Lucretius, and looks forward to the more compact statement of the farmers' case in *Georgics* ii. 458 ff. Virgil's youthful exercise in the theme is diffuse and repetitious. The general scheme of his opening sentence is curiously identical with that in the passage of the *Georgics,* but it is longer and more involved. He sows with a sack, whether it be a matter of concrete details to illustrate his thought or of rhetorical ornament; the repetition of the same word at the beginnings of phrases and clauses, temperately employed in the shorter version of the *Georgics,* is tediously reiterated in *The Gnat.* Yet the verses are agreeably rich in pleasing sounds.

> O shepherds' joy (if one, with mind foretaught,
> Should not disdain the poor man's way of life,
> And, scorning these, turn him to dreams of wealth),
> Unknown to cares, in hearts unfriendly hid,
> Which constant rack the greedy souls of men!
> Though his no fleece, twice dipped in Syrian dye,
> Bought with Attalic wealth; nor glint of gold
> Beneath the panelled ceiling of his home,

Nor beauteous paintings, tempt his soul to greed;
Though gleaming gems be of no worth to him;
Though Alcon's cups, Boethus' cunning work,
Bring him no joy; though pearls of Indies' seas
Are valueless—yet he, with soul unsoiled,
Oft lies full length upon the sward's soft bed,
While blossoming earth, with budding herbage decked,
In spring's sweet time shows all the fields picked out
With various hues. As there, glad in the song
Of rustling marshy reeds, he takes his ease,
Afar from envy's tricks, strong in himself,
Tmolus' leafage, with green boughs agleam,
Wraps him about with his own cloak of vines.
His the sweet goats that drip with milky dew,
Groves too, and Pales, bounteous to his flocks;
While deep within the vales are shady grots
Forever trickling with fresh springs for him.
Who in the longed-for age could be more blest
Than he who, pure of soul and tired of sense,
Dwelling afar, knows not the greed of wealth,
Fears not grim wars, the deadly clash of fleets,
Nor yet, but to adorn with glittering spoils
The holy fanes of gods, or, high upraised,
To overpass the record mark of gain,
With folly risks his life 'gainst savage foes?
His is a god shaped by the pruning knife,
Smoothed by no artist's hand; his fane the groves;
For him the simple flowers of the field
Give myrrh Panchaean from their varied blooms.
His, too, is sweet repose, unsullied joy,
Free joy, with simple cares. Toward this he strives;
Toward this aims every sense; this is the thought,
Deep hidden in his heart, that in repose,
Content with any fare, he may abound,
And that with pleasant sleep he may knit up
His weary frame. O flocks! O rustic Pans!
O vales most sweet with wood nymphs' fountain set!
In whose poor worship, each one for himself,
The shepherds, vying with the Ascraean bard,
With hearts at ease live out their care-free lives.

As yet the poet has not set the action of his story in any definite place. But when he brings the herdsman and his flocks to a grove for refreshment in the heat of noonday, it is a specific grove, not near Mantua or Cremona, but in the Greek world of myth and mythical associations. Here Agave, daughter of Cadmus, stained with the blood of her own son whom she had killed in the frenzy of religious zeal, fled for refuge from Bacchus. This condensed reference to a familiar myth enabled a Greek, and possibly a Roman, reader to localize the grove in Northern Greece, and such a reader easily filled in the missing links of the story of Agave's slanderous attack upon the mother of Bacchus, Bacchus' punishment of Agave in leading her, in the enthusiasm of her own advocacy of his worship, to murder her own son, and the god's continued pursuit of her after the tragedy. This grove, sacred to Artemis, is peopled with the fairies of Greek mythology, Pans, satyrs, wood nymphs, and water nymphs. The grateful shade that it offers to the herdsman and his flocks is furnished by a dozen varieties of trees and shrubs, painfully listed in the style of a formal catalogue, and the tedium of the catalogue is hardly relieved by the mythical history of each tree. The lotus recalls the luring of Odysseus' comrades. The poplars are the grieving sisters of Phaethon. Demophoon's disloyalty toward Phyllis gives pathetic significance to the almond tree. The oracular oak supplied the food of primitive life. From the pine the good ship Argo was built. Descriptive epithets briefly characterize the ilex, cypress, beech, and myrtle, and the ivy binds fast the arms of the poplar tree lest she, the sister of Phaethon, should lash herself in excess of grief for the loss of her brother. Not even the birds, frogs, and shrill cicadas can persuade us of the naturalness of this grove. Much as we may enjoy the happy fancy that invests the trees with all the pathetic experiences of human beings, we are too conscious, if we are familiar with the trend of late

Greek poetry, that these are the favorite transformation stories of the modern Greek age, and the emphasis upon the pity-compelling features in the elaboration of details is thoroughly Hellenistic. It is a highly artificial and literary grove.

The trees of this grove, however, are not the particular trees that passed through these pathetic experiences and transformations. The mythical stories which they recall serve only to reinforce the atmosphere of fairyland. And into this fairyland creeps a veritable dragon, a huge speckled serpent, brandishing his tongue and rolling his scaly coils. He lifts up his glittering breast, holds aloft his scarlet-crested head, and flames flashing fire from his stern eyes. The sleeping shepherd is saved by the philanthropic gnat. With all the exactness of Homer in describing the part of the anatomy reached by the hostile weapon on the battlefields of Troy, the poet indicates the precise spot where the friendly sting of the gnat pierced the herdsman and roused him from his slumber:

> A little nursling of the humid air,
> A gnat, unto the sleepy herdsman went,
> And marking where his eyelids, twinkling rare,
> Shewed the two pearls which sight unto him lent,
> Through their thin coverings appearing fair,
> His little needle there infixing deep,
> Warned him awake, from death himself to keep.

The shepherd fatally bruises the gnat, lays about him with the branch of a tree, and kills the serpent. Thus briefly, as compared with the surrounding decorative passages, the critical action is dismissed, but the fable is adorned even here with all the grandiloquence of epic.

The complaint of the gnat, when he returns to the shepherd as a ghost in the vision of the subsequent evening, is a tedious catalogue of the horrors of Tartarus and the everlasting bliss of heroes and heroines in the Elysian Fields. The description is justified by the gnat's proper resentment, but the choice of details is prompted only by the very general thought that the horrors offend the little animal, and that the happiness of the more fortunate, like the easy slumber of the thoughtless shepherd, contrasts unwarrantably with the fate attached to the gnat's philanthropic service. The poet, if he be Virgil, as yet reveals no promise of the dramatic power with which he organized similar material in the sixth *Aeneid*. It is an aimless wandering and a haphazard choice of mythological figures. The topography is simple. There is no elaborate classification of souls. The whole revelation lacks altogether the high moral earnestness and the inspiring grandeur of philosophical theory which in Virgil's epic redeem the triteness of the theme. Such qualities would be inappropriate in the resentful plaint of the gnat. There is, however, full recognition of the pathetic possibilities of such a description, notably in the selection of women punished for their vices or rewarded for their devotion. The commonplaceness of Tantalus, Tityus, and Sisyphus, and of the heroes of the Trojan War is somewhat relieved by the pictures of domestic infelicity and happiness in which the cruel wives, the Danaids, the vengeful mother, Medea, and the pitiless Procne and Philomela are set over against the loyal wives, Alcestis, Penelope, and Eurydice. This is the same feeling, pervasively Hellenistic rather than peculiarly Virgilian, which provided the Fields of Sorrow and the pathetic figures of heroines who died prematurely for love's sake in the sixth *Aeneid*. The arid catalogue of heroines in the eleventh *Odyssey* is a significant contrast, and the contrast brings out sharply in *The Gnat* the modern Greek appreciation of emotional appeal. But the youthful poet has none of the organizing power that later, in the *Aeneid*, leads to the massing of incidental heroines from the midst of whom the figure of Dido emerges into the foreground with dramatic as well as pathetic effect. The story of Eurydice leads to an elaboration of her experience in which

Orpheus naturally becomes the prominent actor, and through him a loose transition is made to the heroes of the Trojan War. Here the poet manages to list several of the events of the Homeric story, curiously exalting Ajax at the expense of Achilles, and using Odysseus to furnish a catalogue of the episodes of the *Odyssey*. Agamemnon concludes the Greek list and provides the text for the dolorous fate of the Greeks themselves on their return, with a spirited digression on the storm at sea that wrecked the Greek ships. To this thoroughly Greek, and modern Greek, picture of the other world is attached one Roman element: a notably brief and bare list of the heroes of the Roman republic, the feeblest imaginable foreshadowing of the splendid muster-roll at the end of the sixth *Aeneid*.

The gnat's plea is effective. The herdsman, by way of reparation, builds the little animal a grave and plants eighteen varieties of flowers about it, eighteen at least that are duly named and catalogued with brief characterizing epithets, and others loosely grouped as all that the spring supplies. The account of the herdsman's grave-digging is wordy and diffuse; the catalogue of flowers is monotonously marked by the same recurrent introductory word; and the poet apparently restrains himself with difficulty from enlarging upon the mythical associations of the various flowers, indulging only in a brief summary of the story of Narcissus. The gnat's epitaph rounds off the end of the poem.

Neither in the choice of theme nor in the elaboration of it, so far as the larger elements of structure are concerned, is there any clear evidence of immaturity in this poem. The general scheme and the digressory ornamental and pathetic embellishments are in accord with the formal practice of Greek poetry of the Hellenistic period, and the possibility of a definite Greek background is always open. Nor, on the other hand, need we allow the Greek elements to blind us to the poet's sincerity in his praise of the simple life of herdsmen, to his nice observation and his patent enjoyment of nature, to the significance of his choice, if only for a playful purpose, of epic narrative and manner; both the pastoral setting and the tourist's picture of the other world, with the passing glimpse of Roman heroes, are promising indications of more mature accomplishments in bucolic poetry and in epic. The youthfulness of the author is revealed only to readers of the poem in its Latin form. Such readers are troubled by striking variations from Virgil's practice in his later work. His vocabulary contains words that Virgil never employs in his maturer poems, but many of these are from the storehouse of Lucretius. His diction and phrasing often lapse from the urbane to the colloquial and vulgar. He delights in accumulating adjectives and adjectival participles in his descriptive phrases without any of the restraint that marks Virgil's use of the same liberty in later days. In metrical details there are some vagaries. In these features we may perhaps recognize a youthful poet who has not yet settled down to the sober and steady gait of manhood.

The atmosphere of unreality and poetic artifice in *The Gnat* is agreeably changed in the group of short poems, *In Lighter Vein*. Here alone in all his poetry Virgil, if he be the author, found an easy outlet for the expression of personal experiences and emotions. Here, consequently, are revealed many sides of his nature that are either altogether hidden or only faintly indicated in most of his mature work. After reading some of these poems we may well believe that Virgil might easily have become proficient in satirical or genial criticism of his fellow-beings and of society in general. We get grateful glimpses of his personal friends, of his predilections and aversions, of a sense of humor that is only latent in his more dignified poems, of a drastic wit that the pastoral and the didactic treatise and the epic necessarily tend to repress. It may also be the case, of course, that some of these qualities were subdued and softened by maturing years, but many of them are racial. Italian animation and fervid passion emerge momentarily in these brief records of personal feeling and experience.

The caption *Catalepton* is a mere transliteration of the Greek κατὰ λεπτόν, already employed by a Hellenistic poet, Aratus, as a title to cover short poems of a nugatory character. The title, however, is not demonstrably of Virgil's choosing. The collection covered by it in most of our texts includes three poems on the scarecrow god, Priapus, usually grouped under a separate title, *Priapea,* and fifteen other poems, numbered separately and, with one exception (No. ix), appropriately styled epigrams. It should not be forgotten that if these poems are Virgilian few of them can be definitely dated. Some of them the poet may have composed as an avocation when he was more seriously engaged in the heavier labors of middle life. But many of them help us to construct the somewhat shadowy outlines of a formative period in his career.

The epigram had been fully developed in Greece before Latin poets at the beginning of the first century B.C. began to cultivate it. Intended originally to mark a burial place and honor the deceased, or to celebrate the occasion of a votive offering, it was limited in this practical service as an inscription by the hard material upon which it was engraved and by the small space into which it had to be compressed. Brevity, therefore, and suggestive, rather than explicit, style were distinguishing qualities; and in the hands of Greek artists such as Simonides a noble simplicity of thought and restraint of feeling gave dignity and effective pathos to the inscription. Soon the purely utilitarian purposes of the inscriptional epigram became only a part of its service. Detached from tombstone and votive offering it was a purely literary *genre,* and the mold of the inscription was then filled with a new and varied material. As a vehicle for the expression of all kinds of transitory emotion and for the celebration of any occasion, it increased slightly in length, and in time lost much of its restraint and dignity. Often devoted to convivial and amatory themes and to the events of ordinary life, it was quite easily and immediately Romanized when Catullus and his contemporaries, keeping the metrical form of the elegiac couplet and of a variety of Greek lyrical measures, filled it with the record of their own experiences. The poems of this type that Virgil may have written are full of easily audible echoes of Catullus.

A special type of epigram was suggested by the figure and function of Priapus, in origin a Greek god. He was supposed to protect the orchards, and rude images of wood, often painted red, were set up in gardens to represent him; to these images rustic offerings were made, and the god was fancied as exercising protective power against thieves. As a vegetation deity his generative function was emphasized in these rude icons and easily gave rise to indecorous suggestions in the epigrams, so that in modern usage Priapean has acquired a special connotation. The three poems, however, attributed to Virgil are singularly free from any indecency, and in that respect contrast strikingly with the small *corpus* of Latin *Priapea* from other hands, most, if not all, of which are later in composition than the time of Virgil. Virgil, indeed, may have introduced the type into Latin poetry. His first Priapean is a conventional pair of elegiac couplets in which the four seasons are briefly characterized; the god rejoices in the offerings that spring, summer, and autumn bring him, but fears the winter lest the lazy farmers use him for firewood. In its play on the Latin words for "wooden" (*ligneus*) and "fire" (*ignis*) the poet echoes the soberer idea of Lucretius' philosophy (i. 911–14) that, etymologically as well as physically, the seeds of fire (*ignis*) are inherent in the wood (*lignum*). But, aside from this play of wit and pretense of learning, the

poem lacks the grace and vigor of the later handling of the
same theme in the description of the old man of Corycus, in
Georgics iv. 134–48:

> The rose of spring and autumn's apples red
> He was the first to pluck. When winter's chill
> Still split the rocks with frost and laid cold curb
> Upon the frozen stream, already he
> Was toving with some soft-tressed hyacinth,
> Chiding slow summer and the laggard spring.

The second Priapean poem, in a long series of impetuous
iambic verses and with a rich harmony of melodious sounds,
describes the god's image, the gifts that are brought him, and
concludes with a jovial admonition to the passer-by to hold
up his hands, while passing through the orchard, apparently
not only as a worshipful attitude, but also as a preventive
against temptation to thievery; the farmer himself is approaching, and may use the god's equipment as a club to
punish the thief. In the style inherited from the early inscription the god in all these epigrams addresses the passer-by, and
the poems have consequently a dramatic effect and a charm-
ing informality. And this poem is nicely adorned. The dimin-
utives, so favored by Catullus, enrich the liquid sounds,
which, in combination with staccato dentals, contribute to an
intricate pattern of agreeable assonances. The gifts are listed
in catalogue style, but with poetic variations. The seasons
again appear in connection with the offerings, each season set
off by a recurrent word at the beginning, and the thought of
the whole poem falls into orderly stanzas. Not only is the
style worthy of Virgil, but one verse (13), in which the fat
lamb sent to market brings home the farmer's hand heavy
with money, seems to anticipate Virgil's description of Tityrus in his first eclogue (35), whose hand, in the spendthrift
days when Galatea was his sweetheart, never returned home
from market heavy with money. The third Priapean poem

varies further the metrical form. In a measure which Catullus
had already used for a different theme, the god again describes
his own image and the offerings brought to him. There is a
longer list of offerings than in the second poem, and a fuller
picture of the idyllic surroundings of the orchard god. The
boys of the neighborhood are gently advised to refrain from
thievery, and genially directed to the garden of the next-door
neighbor; for he is rich and his Priapus is not so watchful a
guardian. The swampy surroundings of the god of this poem
may have been suggested by characteristic features of the
valley of the Po, near Virgil's own home.

Such restraint as Virgil may have exercised in the *Priapea*
was wholly abandoned in three epigrams, xiii, xii, and vi, in
all of which the spirit and diction of Catullus' most drastic
invective are employed to demolish examples of the prevailing debauchery of the day. Catullus had attacked in merciless iambics, published shortly after 55 B.C., a favorite of
Caesar and Pompey. In this poem, No. xxix in the collection
of Catullus' verse, not only Mamurra, the favorite in question, was assailed as a debauchee and spendthrift, but his
powerful patrons, Caesar and Pompey, were made to wince
under the poet's venomous abuse as the father-in-law and the
son-in-law who had ruined everything. Caesar's daughter,
Julia, had married Pompey, and this unholy political alliance
had lavished the rich profits of foreign conquests upon the
wastrel Mamurra for the indulgence of his lust. If these three
virulent epigrams of the collection are Virgil's, they are interesting as echoes of Catullus. And they bridge a gap between
the invective poems of Catullus and the epodes of Horace that
breathe the bitterness of personal animosity in imitation of
the early Greek poet, Archilochus. Nos. xii and vi, written in
the same measure as Catullus xxix, attack one Noctuinus,
obviously a nickname, perhaps suggesting the night owl
(*noctua*), whose vision is clear only at night and whose ac-

tivity consequently tends toward nocturnal pleasures. In xii, Noctuinus is ironically congratulated on his marriage to the daughter of Atilius; Atilius, however, has two daughters: not only the bride, but his wine-jug, and Noctuinus, in marrying the one, has unwittingly wedded the other. In vi the same Noctuinus and his father-in-law are associated in licentious practices, and the poet stings them with the lash of Catullus' concluding verse: "O son-in-law and sire-in-law, you've ruined all." Such a poem must have been written when the memory of Catullus' tirade was still fresh. Nor need we endeavor to protect Virgil's reputation by assuming that in this temporary preoccupation with somewhat repulsive themes he is masquerading rather than reporting the realities of his own experience. The artificiality of a literary exercise is quite wanting. The high seriousness of Virgil's later poetry is not necessarily in conflict with these records of familiarity with, and participation in, the loose living of Italian society in its most degenerate days. It is, however, true that the third poem of this group, No. xiii, so far as it seems to report the poet's own experiences, reveals facts that are not covered by any material in the ancient biographies of Virgil. The ancient *Lives*, on the other hand, are in general altogether vague regarding any incidents of Virgil's life before the date of the *Eclogues*. If we accept the poem as Virgil's, the opening verses apparently attest that the poet had been a soldier, and had even crossed the water in such service, before the poem was written, and now is open to the charge of being a slacker. The military service might have been imposed upon him at the outbreak of the Civil War in 49 B.C., in connection with the general levy raised by Caesar, and his later inability to serve would accord with the ancient tradition that he had symptoms of tubercular trouble. But the poem is concerned only incidentally with the poet. It sketches, in iambic couplets of the sort that Horace employed in his first ten epodes, the portrait of a spendthrift and voluptuary, and records the scandalous chronicle of his doings at home and abroad. A sister is not proof against his greed. A brother feels the pinch of poverty now that the patrimony is wasted. Pederasty, lascivious dances at orgiastic festivals, the smelly haunts of the sailors by the river Tiber, low taverns occupy his time, and after fully indulging his vices he comes home to a fat wife for whom he has nothing but wanton kisses. Poverty and starvation are in store for him, and for domestic comfort only his lazy brothers, an angry Jove, and an uncle as licentious, bibulous, and famine-stricken as he is himself. Unlike Catullus' Mamurra, his practices may expect no encouragement from Caesar. The uncertainty of the text (vs. 35) leaves the identity of the wastrel in doubt. Whether he is Lucius, or Luccius, or Lucienus, he is of the same kidney as Noctuinus in the other two epigrams. It is clear that the poet has been charged by this debauchee with being a slacker, and that this charge prompts the violent retort. And inasmuch as the poet, in the course of the poem, declares that he will no longer follow the voluptuary to his dissolute haunts, we may return to the opening verses with the suggestion that they are not to be taken literally of previous military service and subsequent withdrawal from active warfare. The conventions of sentimental poetry represent active service in warfare as the direct antithesis of the inactivity of the honest and earnest lover. We may suspect that the speaker in this poem, after some adventures, perhaps under the tutelage of Lucienus, with light o' loves such as Lucienus evidently favors, has settled down to sincere devotion to a single sweetheart. Taunted by Lucienus with a conventional charge that as an honest and earnest lover he is no longer a potential soldier, but a slacker who prefers the idleness of love to energetic service as a soldier, he retorts that at least he will no longer follow Lucienus in his infamous adventures with many sweethearts, and the burden of the poem becomes a doubtless exaggerated revelation of the private life of a new Mamurra.

The aggressiveness of such verses may seem at odds with the quieter strength and dignity of Virgil's other compositions. The passionate tone is not due to Hellenistic influence. In part the virulence is inseparable from the literary *genre,* to which Archilochus, a Greek poet of the pre-classical period, had long since given the bitterness of his tense personal feeling. But the excitable Italian, as Catullus' similar poems suggest, is temperamentally disposed to these invective iambics; it is not merely a literary heritage. In like manner and in the same meter, though with more genial and kindly humor, the poet in *Catalepton* x satirizes a parvenu who must have been a notorious character in Virgil's home country. As Quintio, a name peculiar to the proletariat, he had driven a mule-cart, perhaps a rural express wagon, out of Cremona to the neighboring towns of Mantua and Brixia. He had rivals. Trypho and Ccrylus—their names suggest hungry Greeklings —kept livery stables, perhaps, and competed for the inter-urban trade. But Quintio prospered, and with prosperity came social and political recognition. The poet does not say so explicitly. According to him Quintio has changed his name to Sabinus, and has dedicated to Castor and Pollux a picture, or statue, of himself sitting on an ivory chair. This chair is easily taken to be the curule chair, the prerogative of certain magistrates both at Rome and in Italian municipalities. But it may equally well be the case that the muleteer, without ever having attained any local prominence as a magistrate, has celebrated the end of a prosperous career as a mule-driver by dedicating a picture of himself somewhat sumptuously seated, and the poet has been inspired by the votive offering to lampoon the pomp and circumstance of the parvenu's self-glorifying gift.

At all events the poem provides a vivid picture of a social

type rarely found in ancient literature, though no doubt common in the life of Greece and Italy. The humor is broad, but there is none of the cutting sarcasm of the Greek poet Anacreon's scathing attack upon the Greek parvenu, Artemon, in the sixth century B.C. The actuality of the type is interestingly attested by the facts of contemporary history in Virgil's own day. Ventidius Bassus, a native of Picenum in Northern Italy, was the ancient example of a self-made man. Starting as a sort of stage-driver who conveyed Roman officials through his district, he was intrusted with the transportation of supplies for Caesar's army and gradually rose through the prescribed series of official positions until he became a consul, provincial governer, and triumphant general, and after his death was honored with a public funeral. His enemies, among them Cicero, sneeringly referred to him as a mule-driver. From Cicero we also learn that candidates for office who lacked a distinctive surname arbitrarily added such surnames to improve their chances of election, and Sabinus is definitely mentioned by Cicero as an example of such fictitious surnames, apparently with reference to some politician of the time. It is indeed tempting, if unwise, to regard Ventidius as the individual who took the surname Sabinus for political purposes, and to identify this parvenu with the subject of the epigram, assuming the ivory chair of Quintio-Sabinus to be the curule chair which Ventidius Bassus-Sabinus acquired when he was elected to a praetorship. But a more conservative view leaves us simply with an entertaining skit on a local character, satisfying particularly as a glimpse of the poet's environment in his early life at Cremona.

Of more importance than any conjectural identification of the muleteer is the form of the caricature. The poet has parodied the fourth poem of Catullus. In this poem, Catullus, in the style of the votive epigram, pretends to stand before the model or picture of a ship and narrates to imaginary

passers-by the achievements of his yacht. Written as if to
be inscribed probably beneath a model or picture of the boat
in which Catullus sailed from Bithynia to Italy, the poem of
Catullus sets forth the speed of the yacht, its success in passing all competitors, as attested by all the regions through
which the boat has traveled, even by its own home in Pontus,
where it was originally a tree on a mountain top. There in
Pontus, according to the testimony of the yacht itself, it stood
when a tree, and then as a boat carried Catullus over stormy
seas, regardless whether the wind blew starboard, port, or
astern. It was so seaworthy that it never needed to offer
prayers and vows to the divinities of the sea for its safety,
but now, all danger happily passed, resting from its labors in
the peaceful content of old age, it dedicates itself to Castor
and Pollux, the twin gods who protect sailors from the perils
of seafaring. Virgil, adopting the same iambic meter, but
neatly changing the tone from sympathetic appreciation to
genial ridicule, similarly stands before the picture of Quintio-
Sabinus in his ivory chair and recounts to imaginary spectators the career of the muleteer whose mule-wagon was never
passed by any rival car, as the competing livery men, Trypho
and Cerylus, can testify; especially Cerylus, in whose stable
Quintio, now Sabinus (just as the tree in Catullus' poem is
now a yacht), once sheared the manes of the animals to protect their necks from the chafing of the yoke. Cold Cremona
and swampy Gaul were Quintio's home; there in his early
days he stood in a swamp, stuck in the mud, unpacked his
mule wagon, and bore the yoke himself over the corduroy
roads, no matter whether it was the starboard or the larboard
mule that refused to budge. Nor did he ever need to offer
prayers and vows to the gods of the road. But now, at the
end of his career, he dedicates his reins and currycomb, the
tools of his trade handed down as an heirloom in the family,
and a picture of himself in an ivory chair to the twin gods,

Castor and Pollux, who perhaps are humorously transformed into fresh-water divinities presiding over the swamps and floods of the low marsh lands near Cremona and Mantua. No paraphrase, however, can fully reproduce the skill with which Virgil perverts words and phrases of Catullus and, without any essential disturbance of the sequence of thought in the original, blends votive inscription with pungent satire.

A smaller group of epigrams in elegiac couplets introduces us to a few of Virgil's friends. In iv, with the exuberance of Catullus' hearty appreciation of his friends and a suggestion of Catullus' phraseology, he addresses Musa, celebrating his youthful accomplishments in poetry. In xi the death, real or imaginary, of Octavius is humorously attributed to strong drink, a charge which the dead friend promptly denies, avowing that his death was natural and fated. These opening verses are a mere appropriation of an epigram by the Hellenistic poet, Callimachus, in which he similarly reproached his friend, Menecrates. After this jesting quatrain Virgil concludes his epitaph with a conventional eulogy of Octavius' literary work, including a Roman history. It is likely that the Octavius of xi and the Musa of iv are one and the same person, and that this Octavius Musa is the Octavius to whom *The Gnat* was dedicated. As a citizen of Mantua he may have become known to Virgil in the poet's school days, and as playing some rôle in the distribution of land near Mantua to the soldiers at the end of the Civil War he may have come into contact with Virgil in the trouble over the proposed allotment of Virgil's family estate to soldiers in 43 or 42 B.C. Certainly it was a lasting friendship, if the Octavius of Horace's *Satires* i. 10. 82 is the same person; for that satire indicates that Octavius was still living in 35 B.C. It may well be doubted, however, whether Virgil's epigram celebrates the actual death of his friend. Octavius may have been temporarily dead to the world in the excessive hilarity of a drinking party.

A much closer and longer friendship developed among
Virgil, Plotius Tucca, and Lucius Varius. These two friends
ultimately became Virgil's residuary legatees and literary executors. The passage of Horace's *Satires* groups them with
Octavius so closely that we may easily fancy all three of them
as constituting, with Horace and Virgil, the protégés of Maecenas, whom Horace includes in this list of critics whose
praise he values. The intimacy of the friendship with Plotius
Tucca and Varius is suggested by the fact that the two epigrams addressed to them contain the only possible evidence
that we have, outside some unreliable chronicles of scandal in
the ancient *Lives* and in ancient commentary on the *Eclogues*,
of Virgil's amatory adventures. In *Catalepton* i, addressed to
Tucca, a married woman's return to town fails to console
the poet, for her husband keeps her under lock and key. In
vii, with considerable feeling, he confesses to Varius his passion for a boy. Such poems probably furnished some justification for the charges of immorality in the ancient tradition,
which, however, were easily exaggerated in the bitter quarrel
between his friends and detractors that ensued after his death.
No doubt, also, the defense of his character to which this
quarrel gave rise was stronger than the facts warranted, and
we may best adjust the difficulty by admitting that the poet
was probably no better than many of his contemporaries. His
maturer work, however, is remarkably free from any indications of interest in the sensational erotic themes that attracted
Hellenistic poets in their choice of subject matter from myth
or legend or supposedly personal experience.

A detail in this last epigram throws some light upon Virgil's relation to earlier and contemporary disputes that arose
naturally when Greek poetry was imitated by the Romans.
In the second verse of the epigram, if we accept an attractive
emendation, he refers to the boy as his sweetheart, using a
Greek word for the idea, but in the following couplet he sug-

gests that the rules (and they may be rules set down by his friend, Varius) require him to use a Latin word. This sudden intrusion of what seems a purely academic question into the midst of an amatory epigram reveals Virgil perhaps as taking a somewhat moderate position in the argument over the use of transliterated Greek words. Laevius, Catullus' predecessor, had strewn his poems with Greek vocabulary. Catullus, too, especially in his longer poems, indulged in them. Cicero's aversion to the New Poets, on the other hand, was probably stimulated to some extent by his interest in protecting the purity of Latin diction. Virgil's juvenile work indicates close dependence upon Catullus and Lucretius, and Greek words, whether proper names or transliterated common nouns, are profusely employed in the poems of this *Virgilian Appendix*. Except, however, for a reasonable enjoyment of musical Greek proper names, Virgil's later work is not conspicuously marked by any such indulgence. The humorous tone, therefore, in which Virgil seems to twit contemporary purists in this epigram regarding the propriety of Greek diction in Latin verse perhaps represents his youthful allegiance to Catullus and the New Poets before he had been won over by Varius, Horace, and others to the cause of pure Latinity and possibly to other features of Romanizing propaganda.

If, however, in epigram vii we accept the reading of the manuscripts, *putus,* instead of the emendation to the Greek word, *pothos,* Virgil will be making a humorous concession to Latin stylists who regarded *putus* as a vulgar synonym of *puer* and unfit for poetry.

His attitude on other matters of style is trenchantly expressed in two epigrams in which he returns again to invective iambics, though now not the impetuous throbbing measure of his attacks on Noctuinus, Lucienus, and Quintio, but the heavier form used similarly by Catullus, in which long syllables drag out the end of the verse. The text of *Catalep-*

ton ii is quite uncertain, and the meaning of almost every word and phrase is disputed. The background of the poem is historical. T. Annius Cimber, at some time before the year 43 B.C., murdered his brother. For this act Cicero grilled him in a punning reference in his *Philippics*. The essential thought of Virgil's epigram is covered by Quintilian, who quoted it in connection with his own assault upon those who cultivate archaic and obsolete diction. Cimber, in the epigram, is amusingly charged, as a rhetorician, with having mixed a poisonous brew of antiquated words for his brother. In accord with this thought he is dubbed a Thucydides, the Greek historian, who, in the view of Greek literary critics, used obscure, archaic, and strange diction. So much is clear. Beyond this lies much plausible conjecture and some misdirected effort to relate the thought of the poem to larger problems of literary style which occupied the attention of theorists in Virgil's day. But however interesting such speculation may be to students of the history of style, the epigram contains no evidence of Virgil's subscribing to one rather than another theory of style. At most it protests against a mannerism or affectation; the examples are chosen from Greek, and Cimber may have been a teacher of Greek rhetoric and of Greek origin himself. It may, indeed, be questioned whether Quintilian rightly used the epigram as confirmation merely of his own attitude toward archaisms. For the ingredients of Cimber's brew include the Greek words *min* and *sphin,* which, in Greek epigrams after Virgil's time, are stock examples to illustrate the wearisome minutiae run down by pedantic scholars and exploited in the lecture-halls of the grammarians and the rhetoricians. No antagonist of similar modern practices could express himself more testily than the Greek epigrammatists assailing the "grammarians . . . . hunters of melancholy conjunctions, who take delight in *min* and *sphin* and in inquiring if the Cyclops kept dogs," or the teacher of oratory and rhetoric who, along with tags from Demosthenes and other ancient orators, teaches the children *min* and *sphin*. It is this same general abuse of standardized schoolroom practice that Virgil voices in *Catalepton* v; here, in my understanding of the verses, he bids farewell to two kinds of teachers who, however, had much in common: the rhetoricians, whose bombast he deplores, and the tribe of dull-witted pedants, both of whom are nothing but clashing cymbals dinning empty sounds into the ears of their youthful listeners. Virgil mentions in his poem several of the pedants, only two of whom can be identified, somewhat dubiously, as antiquarians of his own day. Both of these epigrams seem to express primarily the resentment of an artistic temperament toward the pedantic interest in rhetorical flourishes and in grammatical and antiquarian details on the part of contemporary teachers of literature and oratory. In so far as the bombast of the rhetoricians in epigram v is described as "not Greek," there may be a special animus against the extremely florid oriental style known as Asianism, which stood in sharp contrast with the simple effectiveness of Attic Greek style. But Virgil is not thereby primarily aligning himself with the devotees of Attic style. In both epigrams, with precisely the same vocabulary and bitterness of tone that Greek epigrammatists employ in general diatribes against grammarians and rhetoricians, he is assailing the meticulous exploiting of language and style characteristic of Greek and Roman lecture-halls. And the aversion to formal rhetoric accords with the stories, in the ancient tradition to which we have already referred, of his failure in prose composition and in court practice.

Virgil's acquaintance with rhetorical teaching may have begun at Milan and was continued at Rome. His juvenile poems are oftentimes marked by a less restrained use of rhetorical artifices than his maturer poems. It would be helpful if we could date precisely the time when his aversion found expression in this fifth epigram. For the poem is composed of two stanzas: one, his scornful valedictory to teachers of rhetoric (or possibly his fellow-students) and to the noxious pedantry of the schoolroom; the other, an announcement of a new program. The new program provides positively for an intensive study of philosophy under Siro, and negatively excludes further writing of poetry. Or, as he puts it, the Muses are to return—he cannot resist their attractions—but *pudenter et raro*. It is a general view that *pudenter*, "modestly," in this phrase indicates that Virgil had previously indulged in licentious poems, which he now forswears, and of course the invectives against Noctuinus and Lucienus might well come under this rubric; the younger Pliny later includes Virgil in his list of devotees of the unchaste Muse. But it is more likely that Virgil is inviting the Muses to visit him rarely and not to stay too long. The self-restraint in *pudenter* may qualify the poet's hospitality rather than his choice of poetic themes. In any case it is clear that we must find room in the poet's life for a period of some length devoted to philosophy and only rarely interrupted by poetic composition. And since his later life, from 41 B.C. to his death, seems to have been occupied quite continuously in the writing of his three great works, for this and other reasons which will shortly appear, the period of absorption in philosophical study must fall within the decade 52–42 B.C. Obviously, any further clue to the time and the nature of his studies is likely to be provided by such information as we can gather regarding the person, Siro, who is announced in Virgil's imagery as the haven of rest toward which he is sailing from the stormy seas of grammarians and rhetoricians.

Siro was an Epicurean philosopher. His master, Epicurus, had promulgated the doctrines of the school in Hellenistic Greece at the beginning of the third century. Contemporaneously a rival school of Stoics had come into prominence under the leadership of Zeno. Broad generalizations regarding these two rival philosophies are as dangerous as definitions of socialism today. In the considerable time intervening between their first establishment and the importation of their doctrines into Rome, their views were exposed to constant criticism from within and without their circle of adherents. There were radical and conservative wings of both parties. There were essential variations from orthodoxy which individuals here and there ardently supported.

Broadly speaking, the two schools had some points of view in common. Both were issues of an individualistic age, and as such each inclined to emphasize the individual man, not as a member of a city state, but as having an inherent right to live for himself. Each school, therefore, regarded ethics as the goal, and ethics that conserved the interests of the individual. A serene and independent life was their ideal. Each school was interested in attaining certainty in the processes of thought. They shared the conviction that the real is what is touched and seen. Both schools were materialistic.

Outside this common platform they were at odds with each other. The Stoics were more practically minded than the Epicureans. Within certain limitations, variously defined, the Stoic, without surrendering his energetic self-consciousness, admitted the necessity of founding a family and participating in the activity of the commonwealth. He was disposed to maintain, on the whole, the existing social order. He endeavored to justify the religious dogma, to save popular mythology by a rationalized explanation of it. He devoutly believed in performing the duties of that situation in life in which he found himself placed by a material divinity whose creature and subject he confessed himself to be. He was frankly dependent upon the general order of the universe, and to that extent a quietist and fatalist.

The Epicurean, on the other hand, believed in enjoying at

every instant the possible pleasure of the moment. He stood
aloof from public life and business. He was his own master.
He rejected popular mythology, except possibly as a means of
literary ornament. He found a place for the gods of orthodoxy only as disinterested observers, not as regulators, of the
affairs of men. To the Stoic notion of dutifully working out
the potentialities of our being the Epicurean opposed as an
ideal the full enjoyment of all that the conditions of human
life permit.

In the first half of the second century Epicurean philosophers were resident at Rome, but their creed did not attain
popularity until the time of Virgil's boyhood. Then the poem
of Lucretius gave sublime expression to their physical theories, and Lucretius' ardent devotion to the person of his master, Epicurus, as well as to the doctrines of the school was
doubtless contagious. When Virgil had reached the age of
twenty-five, the fortunes of the sect at Rome were in the
hands of two Greek representatives, Siro and Philodemus. To
Siro three brief allusions are made by Cicero in writings of the
year 45. Evidently at that time he was uppermost in Cicero's
mind as a leader in Epicurean thought. In one of these references Philodemus is bracketed with Siro. It is suggestive, if
accidental, that the two philosophical treatises in which Cicero alludes to Siro have for their dramatic setting the immediate vicinity of Naples.

The buried city of Herculaneum, near Naples, after
eighteen centuries of concealment beneath the volcanic accretions from eruptions of Mount Vesuvius, in our own modern times has thrown no little light on the activities of Siro
and Philodemus in this neighborhood. By piecing together
the data derived from these discoveries and other information contained in the ancient biographies of Virgil and commentaries on his works, we are able, however dimly, to see
the outlines of intellectual intercourse that was pregnant with

important results, not only for Virgil's development, but for the whole course of literature and thought in the Augustan period.

In the year 1750 a shaft sunk into the mass that overlay the city of Herculaneum brought the explorers into the garden of an extensive villa. Eventually the surrounding rooms were excavated, and in one of them were found portrait busts of notable Epicurean philosophers and hundreds of papyrus rolls, some quite disintegrated, others charred and caked together. Much patient ingenuity has been devoted to unrolling and deciphering the rolls of the library in this household. By skilful mechanical and chemical processes the material has in part been unfolded, read, and transcribed, but the work is still far from complete, and future discoveries may vastly extend our knowledge. The bulk of the rolls proves to be crabbed philosophical treatises from the hand of Philodemus. In one of these rolls Philodemus expresses an intention to return to Naples to "our Siro" and to the social intercourse that centers about him and to engage in philosophical discussions at Herculaneum. The society that gathered about Siro may be partially recovered from other rolls. In one, a tract by Philodemus on flattery, four Romans are addressed and apparently urged to welcome the treatise because they have listened to fragmentary discussions of the theme and of other similar topics before the present essay was completed. Two of the names of these four Romans are plainly Varius and Quintilius. The other two names are partially destroyed, but the remains of one contains what might be the first letter of Virgil's name in its Greek form, and the other might be the end of the name either of Plotius (Tucca) or of Horace. The names of Varius and Quintilius are easily decipherable in another papyrus, but unfortunately the context is not intelligible.

These dry facts acquire more significance when we learn from the *Life of Virgil*, by Probus, that the poet spent several years of gentlemanly leisure in the society of Quintilius, Tucca, and Varius studying the tenets of the Epicurean sect. Quintilius, under his other name of Varus, is described also by the commentary of Servius on the *Eclogues* as a fellow-student of Virgil's under Siro. These three young friends of Virgil, therefore, were associated with him in intimate intellectual and social intercourse under the leadership of Siro and probably of Philodemus. Of them Lucius Varius Rufus, somewhat older than Virgil, was a writer of tragedy and epic; his didactic poem, *De Morte,* perhaps reflected the teachings of Siro and Philodemus as well as the earlier poem of Lucretius; with Virgil he introduced Horace to Maecenas; with Plotius Tucca he edited and published the *Aeneid* after Virgil's death. Of Plotius Tucca we know little except his co-operation with Varius in publishing the *Aeneid.* But all three of those friends, Varius, Tucca, and Virgil, are celebrated by Horace as the purest souls in the world. The last of the company, Quintilius Varus, was a native of Cremona and may have known Virgil in earlier days. Horace describes him as an ideal critic, and in 23 B.C. commemorates his death in a eulogy of his purity, honesty, and general uprightness of character, remarking that nobody mourns his death more than Virgil. It is not certain that Horace himself was one of the group at Naples, but his early allegiance to the doctrines of Epicurus may have been due to his intimacy with this circle.

The harbor, therefore, that Virgil sought was not altogether figurative. For Siro's activity centered about the Bay of Naples. Of Siro himself we know practically nothing. His light is dimmed by the greater splendor of Philodemus, whose influence upon Virgil is less tangible and evident. A Syrian Greek, philosopher and epigrammatist, he was patronized by a Roman patrician, Calpurnius Piso, a member of a family whose intellectual interests for many generations led them to cultivate the friendship of literary artists. To Cicero's speech against Piso, delivered ten years before these young Romans gathered about Philodemus and Siro, we owe a vivid picture of the life of a Greek dependent in an influential Roman family which indicates how Greek culture was often communicated to Roman patricians. Cicero, for his immediate purposes, probably overdraws the dissolute life that Piso led in this companionship of the Epicurean philosopher. Philodemus, according to the orator, was demoralized by the association, and excusably entangled in a friendship from which he could not easily withdraw. For the Greek dependent Cicero hardly conceals his admiration. He compliments him upon his general intellectual interests, unusual in Epicureans, and praises his epigrams as neat, witty, and clever, though often licentious. And the extant remains of these epigrams bear out Cicero's estimate, contrasting favorably with the crabbed style of Philodemus' philosophical essays. To Piso Philodemus was doubtless indebted for his livelihood, and it is not unlikely that the very villa at Herculaneum which has disclosed so many treasures of Epicurean thought was the property of Piso, and lent by him to Philodemus. One may only conjecture how much of Greek thought and Greek literature was here disseminated from the two Greek teachers, Siro and Philodemus, and became, through Virgil, Lucius Varius, Plotius Tucca, and Quintilius Varus, part of the warp and woof of Augustan poetry.

Virgil's early interest in Lucretius' presentation of Epicurean doctrine, evinced in occasional echoes of Lucretian phraseology in *The Gnat* and other youthful poems, probably prepared him to receive with zest the technical exposition offered by Siro and his associates. Among the poems of the *Virgilian Appendix* is one, *The Cabaret Girl,* that breathes the spirit of Epicureanism and concludes with the familiar admonition to neglect the morrow and live fully in the present.

If one approaches the poem after reading the Greek epigrams of Philodemus there is no essential change in atmosphere, but the same frank enjoyment of riotous pleasure and the same easy fluency of expression. Pleasure, as Epicurus defined it, was a distinctly noble and ennobling pursuit. But Philodemus, brought up in the luscious sensuousness of a Syrian home, does not hesitate in his epigrams to revel in the lower pleasures that, in Cicero's stern indictment, perverted Calpurnius Piso and his associates. It may be accidental that the heroine of *The Cabaret Girl*, like Philodemus, is a Syrian. It is more to the point that the lush detail is oriental in its extravagance. Yet we must qualify the suggestion of Philodemus' influence with the further observation that the shepherd's music, cool groves, sparkling water, rich stores of fruit and flowers are in the manner of Theocritus' seventh idyl. Pastoral and epigram are fused in a graceful and seductive picture of the attractions of a wayside tavern:

'Twas at a smoke-stained tavern, and she, the hostess there—
A wine-flushed Syrian damsel, a turban on her hair—
Beat out a husky tempo from reeds in either hand,
And danced—the dainty wanton—an Ionian saraband.
"Tis hot," she sang, "and dusty; nay travelers, whither bound?
Bide here, and tip a beaker—till all the world goes round;
Bide here and have for asking wine-pitchers, music, flowers,
Green pergolas, fair gardens, cool coverts, leafy bowers.
In our Arcadian grotto we have some one to play
On Pan-pipes, shepherd fashion, sweet music all the day.
We broached a cask but lately; our busy little stream
Will gurgle softly near you the while you drink and dream.
Chaplets of yellow violets a-plenty you shall find,
And glorious crimson roses in garlands intertwined;
And baskets heaped with lilies the water nymph shall bring—
White lilies that this morning were mirrored in her spring.
Here's cheese new pressed in rushes for every one who comes,
And, lo, Pomona sends us her choicest golden plums.
Red mulberries await you, late purple grapes withal,
Dark melons cased in rushes against the garden wall,

Brown chestnuts, ruddy apples. Divinities bide here,
Fair Ceres, Cupid, Bacchus, those gods of all good cheer,
Priapus too—quite harmless, though terrible to see—
Our little hardwood warden with scythe of trusty tree.
Ho, friar with the donkey, turn in and be our guest!
Your donkey—Vesta's darling—is weary; let him rest.
In every tree the locusts their shrilling still renew,
And cool beneath the brambles the lizard lies perdu.
So test our summer tankards, deep draughts for thirsty men;
Then fill our crystal goblets, and souse yourself again.
Come, handsome boy, you're weary. 'Twere best for you to twine
Your heavy head with roses and rest beneath our vine,
Where dainty arms expect you and fragrant lips invite;
Oh, hang the strait-laced model that plays the anchorite!
Sweet garlands for cold ashes why should you care to save?
Or would you rather keep them to lay upon your grave?
Nay, drink and shake the dice-box. Tomorrow's care begone.
Death plucks your sleeve and whispers: 'Live now, I come anon.' "

The rollicking tone of this poem is not altogether at odds with
the shorter elegiac poems, *In Lighter Vein,* however much it
may seem to depart from the dignity of Virgil's later verse. It
is notably Greek in setting and atmosphere. The picture of
the Syrian dancer and castanet player in the opening verses
appears in one or two Greek epigrams; so, for example, in the
epitaph by an unknown Thyillus on Ariston, the castanet
dancer, "who used to toss her hair among the pines in honor
of Cybele, carried away by the music of the horned flute, who
could empty one after another three cups of untempered
wine, delighting in love and the fatigue of the night-revels."
Philodemus himself in one of his epigrams celebrates a similar riotous wanton associated with the worship of Cybele. In
The Cabaret Girl, however, the dancer is not a religious fa-
natic, but a cabaret artist. Her only interest in the religious
cult of Cybele is betrayed in the invitation addressed to the
traveling priest of the goddess, "the friar with the donkey,"
to turn aside and enjoy the privileges of the wayside inn, an

invitation which mendicant priests of oriental divinities in these later days were not always loathe to accept. The Greek background is again visibly patent in the profusion of trans- literated Greek words. The metrical technique and the ap- parent imitation of some of its phrasing by Propertius carry the composition of it to a date at least as early as the decade in which Virgil was writing his *Aeneid,* whether or not Virgil himself wrote *The Cabaret Girl.*

Into this same period of preoccupation with philosophy the prœmium of another poem of the *Virgilian Appendix, Ciris,* seems at first sight to fit perfectly. The author of this poem avows that, "although surrounded by the green shade of the blooming tree of Philosophy," and having girt himself for far loftier tasks than mere poesy, he will complete a poem in which he hopes to bring to a peaceful end his efforts as a poet and henceforth relinquish his love for the Muses. Ob- viously this is the same mood of abnegation that marked the conclusion of the fifth epigram. *Ciris* very easily becomes the fruit of one of those rare and short visits of the Muses which Virgil somewhat inhospitably invited when he was about to enter the garden of Epicurus. Later in his prœmium the au- thor gives us more detail. He would much prefer to compose a philosophical poem in honor of the learned young friend (no less a person than Messalla) to whom the poem is dedicated, but his sinews are not yet hardened for such a trying task; as a makeshift he offers this poem on which he spent the years of his youth before his Muse had acquired any degree of skill. *Ciris,* therefore, if Virgil wrote it, was practically completed before he began his study under Siro. It was a work that cost many midnight hours, as the poet himself admits. And prob- ably some special reason for dignifying Messalla led to refur- bishing it in the midst of the distracting and alluring shade of the garden of Epicurus.

But it is by no means immediately clear that Virgil can be

the author of this proœmium. For the garden in which the tree of philosophy grows is called "Cecropian"; this should mean Athenian, or at least Greek. Now the term "garden" in ancient literature is technically applied to the school of Epicurus, but if the author describes himself as in the "Cecropian garden" he should mean that he is studying Epicurean philosophy at Athens. With such a residence in Athens the subsequent description of the robe woven for Athena at the Panathenaic festival would aptly accord as a personal reminiscence. Furthermore, the author's interest is not exclusively in Epicurus; he has a comprehensive interest in those whom he calls "the four ancient heirs," meaning, presumably, Plato, Aristotle, Zeno, and Epicurus. Such phrasing suggests the university career at Athens which young Romans generally sought at this time if they could afford it. And among these young Romans was Messalla himself, who, about the age, probably, of nineteen, in the year 45 B.C., went to Athens and remained there until after the murder of Caesar. It is conceivable that the poem was written by some young Roman who was a fellow-student of Messalla's in that period. The opening couplet describes the author as previously ambitious for fame and now disgusted at the rewards that come from the approval of the mob. Whether the writer sought fame through literary achievement or a political career is not clear, but there is no evidence that Virgil concerned himself about political office; and if success in literature is meant, *The Gnat* and the epigrams, in bulk at least, seem to be a rather feeble output for a truly ambitious poet. Virgil's philosophical studies under Siro may have whetted his interest and may have prompted further studies at Athens, but it is difficult to believe that the "Cecropian garden" is loosely applied to the association of young Romans under Siro and Philodemus on the shores of the Bay of Naples.

The diction, meter, and general style of the poem have

been cited for a variety of contradictory purposes, be it a matter of date, or authorship, or both. The outstanding fact is that it is the most characteristic example in ancient literature of the Hellenistic epyllium, or short epic, more richly illustrating the possible features of this literary *genre* than any extant Greek examples. Invented by the Hellenistic Greek poets as a reaction from the long epic, the epyllium undertook the narration of heroic adventure or sentimental experience in a few hundred verses. Its brevity often encouraged, in the hands of the better artists, a nicety of finish and meticulous attention to detail that gave to the short epic all the qualities of fine miniature work as contrasted with the broader fresco effects of the older Homeric poems.

In a characteristically long prologue, occupying one-fifth of the entire work, the author of *Ciris*, like the author of *The Gnat*, exploits himself and explains his choice of theme. There seems indeed to be a reference to *The Gnat* in vs. 19, in which, repeating the diction of the prologue to *The Gnat*, he admits a previous indulgence in playful verse and in the soft tenuous style. Messalla receives scant attention. The author digresses, with the usual pedantry of late Greek style, into a discrimination of the two Scyllas, who, in Greek legend, are often confounded, the Scylla of the *Odyssey*, and the Scylla, daughter of Nisus, king of Megara, heroine of a sentimental tale that is to be the theme of *Ciris*. Into this digression of forty verses he weaves an amazing amount of learned detail. This same confusion of heroines which the author of *Ciris* here learnedly indicates and avoids Virgil himself, in his sixth eclogue, as did Ovid later, perpetrates without apology. Yet one must not on that ground deny the possibility that Virgil wrote *Ciris;* for consistency in the choice of confused or variant forms of the same legend is not accounted a virtue either by Hellenistic poets or by their Roman imitators.

The story of Scylla is one of the pathetic and sentimental

tales much favored by the modern Greek poets. The daughter of Nisus, king of Megara, she falls desperately in love with Minos, king of Crete, when he is waging war against her native city and her father, an early example of the fatal fascination exerted by the gallant soldier—*toujours le militaire*. Her father's power of resistance depends upon a single strand of red hair conspicuous among his white locks. Shorn of this, like Samson, he loses his strength. The girl is willing to betray her father and native city out of love for Minos, and makes a compact with her soldier lover accordingly. But Minos, after the fulfilment of her bargain, cruelly binds her to his ship and sails away. The gods intervene and change her into the bird known as *ciris*. As such, however, she is condemned to a life of solitude, and her father, himself transformed into another bird, the *haliaetos*, becomes a pronounced enemy of the *ciris* and pursues her. The metamorphosis, therefore, in true Hellenistic fashion, forms a conclusion quite as important as the sentimental incident, and with the usual pedantic interest in etymology the heroine becomes a "shearer" (the meaning of the Greek bird-name *ciris*), having shorn her father's hair; nor does the poet fail to make this point clear. But for this tragic love story this hostile pair of birds would never have existed. That is the fanciful and playful implication of the tale.

The conclusion of the poem is as disproportionately long as the prologue. For one hundred and fifty verses the poet lingers over the description of Scylla's precarious plight, putting in her mouth a pathetic monologue that must have been difficult to deliver in her position of quite literal suspense, and carefully listing the geographical points of interest that she passes while hanging to the ship. The metamorphosis is described with all the detail of Ovid's corresponding stories of transformation, but unrelieved by any of his witty conciseness.

The poet has left himself only slightly more than half his poem for the main narrative. In this narrative he subordinates the logically important stages of the action. The essential fact that Minos demanded the red lock of hair as a condition of requiting the love of Scylla is dismissed in a single verse. The actual cutting of the hair, the consequent fall of Megara, the brutal treatment of Scylla by Minos—all this, though it is the main catastrophe, is dismissed in five verses. Nor do we ever learn where and how the heroine first saw and fell in love with her soldier hero. On the other hand, the poet describes in great detail her love frenzy, with the usual interest of the modern Greek in pathological symptoms. Scylla wanders about the city in a crazed condition, forgets her work and the care of her person; her bosom heaves with sighs; she climbs the city wall at night to get a sight of the watchfires of the enemy. With some consciousness of the value of dramatic suspense the action is desirably retarded when Scylla's nurse, Carme, catches her in her first attempt to steal her father's lock of hair. The two women engage in contentious and somewhat diffuse dialogue. The usual pedantic digression appears here and there. The author intrudes an antiquarian interest in the founding of Megara, in the ancient Athenian brooch that adorns the head of Nisus, and in variant versions of the legend of Britomartis. Rhetorical question, exclamation, apostrophizing, hysterical interjections combine with lumbering sentence structure to annoy a reader who is sensitive to the proprieties of style. Yet, open to criticism as such a structure and style may be, all the rhetorical devices, the pedantry, and the copious detail should not blind us to the recognition of the poet's skill in vivid description, his keen analysis of the physical and psychical effects of love. The delicate portrayal of the girl's timid approach to her father's chamber, of the nurse's tender care and sympathy, is worthy of a youthful Virgil.

Nor do the long disorderly sentences and the subordination of action to feeling militate against the view that Virgil wrote the poem. These features are characteristic of the Hellenistic epyllia and of Roman imitations such as Catullus had already attempted in his story of the wedding of Peleus and Thetis. The plot of *Ciris,* indeed, bears a marked resemblance to the version of the story, current probably in Virgil's youth, which Parthenius had turned into Greek verse. The style of *Ciris,* therefore, is likely to be the style of the Greek model from which it was copied, and apparent departures from the manner of Virgil's later or contemporaneous work are immaterial as evidence against his authorship. There are manifest echoes throughout the poem of phrases from Lucretius, Catullus, and Calvus. These imitations accord with features of the other poems that we have been considering, with *The Gnat* and many of the epigrams. Even more significant is the fact that *Ciris* contains no small number of phrases which, only slightly modified, recur in Virgil's *Eclogues, Georgics,* and *Aeneid.* These point to the conclusion that Virgil later imitated the author of *Ciris;* but whether in so doing he was imitating himself or another is not clear. For it is a striking characteristic of Virgil's mature poems that he both frequently refashions phraseology already used earlier by himself, and also appropriates, sometimes for complimentary purposes, the phrases of contemporary friends and poets. Thus the authorship of *Ciris* becomes a very complicated problem, and the solution must remain uncertain. One fact, however, emerges from the complications: the poem must have been written when Messalla could properly have been styled a *iuvenis,* and when extensive imitation of Catullus and Calvus was the literary vogue. The date of composition, therefore, is probably earlier than Virgil's *Eclogues,* and the poem, regardless of the question of authorship, becomes at least an important document for the recovery of the literary tastes that prevailed in the decade between 52 and 42 B.C.

The Messalla to whom *Ciris* is dedicated is probably M. Valerius Messalla Corvinus. Born in 64 B.C., if not a few years earlier, he studied at Athens in company with Horace and the younger Cicero for several years, from 45 B.C. on, but returned to Rome after the murder of Caesar. A sturdy advocate of republican forms of government and vigorous opponent of all autocrats, he first joined Brutus and Cassius, then, after the second battle of Philippi, submitted to Antony. Ultimately reconciled to the supremacy of Octavian, he never swerved from his republican principles. After minor military achievements in the decade between 40 and 30 B.C., he won special renown in Aquitania in 29–27, celebrating a triumph on his return to Rome in 27. His influence on literature, through direct contributions of his own and literary patronage of young poets such as Tibullus, Lygdamus, and Sulpicia, was considerable. Among the poems *In Lighter Vein,* No. ix is a panegyric of this republican hero. Modern scholars are less ready to grant that Virgil is the author of this encomium than of any other poems among the epigrams. If Virgil is the author of it, it becomes easier to admit that he is the author of *Ciris,* also addressed to Messalla. Following the practice of Hellenistic poets in addressing somewhat stiff and formal encomia to their patrons, whether of royal or lesser degree, the author of ix very prosily recounts some of Messalla's military successes, both realized and prospective, but devotes more space to his literary accomplishments. The poem was written just after a conspicuous military victory, and the language points to a triumph as consequent upon Messalla's success. Encomiastic writers are doubtless prone to exaggeration, but it is difficult to believe that Messalla's somewhat notable attack upon Octavian's camp in the first battle of Philippi is the text of the opening verses, and the only record

of a triumph in Messalla's career is attached to the year 27
B.C. Nor may we deny that Virgil could have written such a
prosy poem in the decade when he was composing the *Aeneid*.
One might as well deny that Theocritus could write pane-
gyrics on Hieron and Ptolemy and some of his more graceful
pastorals contemporaneously. It is characteristic of Hellenistic poets and of their Roman imitators to cultivate a variety
of styles in accord with a variety of *genres*. Somewhat positive evidence of Virgil's authorship seems to be furnished by
the statement in the poem that Messalla has written certain
poems in Greek which the author of this *Eulogy of Messalla*
has to some extent appropriated in his own Latin compositions. And upon this statement there immediately follows a
quatrain in which, apparently, Messalla's writing of pastoral
poems is celebrated, possibly the Greek poems referred to in
the previous verses. This celebration of Messalla's pastorals
is couched in terms familiar to readers of Virgil's own pastorals. Meliboeus and Moeris, characters of Virgil's own pastoral poems, in Messalla's verse rested comfortably *patulae
. . . . sub tegmine fagi,* "in the wide-branching beech tree's
shade," precisely the phrase of the opening verse of Virgil's
first eclogue. It is certainly a natural inference that Virgil
himself, writing this panegyric, here implies that some of his
own pastoral compositions were imitations of Messalla's pastoral poems in Greek. In any case the fact that *Ciris* and the
Eulogy of Messalla are by the same hand is somewhat weakly
substantiated, not only in so far as both poems are addressed
to Messalla, but by the occurrence in both poems of the same
phrase, Greek in origin, but unusual, if not positively rare, in
Latin, *communis deus*, applied to Mars as an impartial god of
war. And the concluding verses of the eulogy, in which the
author expresses a desire to emulate Callimachus, the greatest
of Hellenistic poets, might easily refer to *Ciris*, for the epyl-

lium, in Hellenistic Greece, was specially associated with Callimachus' name.

The author of *Ciris* was eager to write a philosophical poem in Messalla's honor; *Ciris* itself was a temporary concession to the author's undeveloped skill. Physical explanations of the creation of the universe and of various natural phenomena were essential to philosophical creeds. It is tempting to find in *Aetna* the ultimate realization of this poet's ambition. Though not addressed to Messalla, the poem explains the physical processes which accompany, and account for, the eruptions of the famous Sicilian volcano. Easily suggested by the sixth book of Lucretius' more comprehensive philosophical poem, and full of the catchwords and of some more significant phrases of the Lucretian didactic epic, it accords very well with the interests of the author of *Ciris* and of the youthful Virgil as a student of philosophy at Naples. Yet there is nothing clearly and consistently Epicurean in the doctrines of the poem; Stoic theory may form the groundwork of the physical explanation of Aetna's eruptions. It is, indeed, always possible that the poem is merely a translation or loose adaptation of a Greek original. In this case the arguments regarding date and authorship derived from style and content are hardly valid. Nor can one profitably compare the style of *Aetna* with Virgil's supposedly contemporary or later work. The didactic presentation of physical phenomena carries with it a style peculiarly its own. In spite of its drily scientific material, however, the poem, like Lucretius' *De rerum natura* and Virgil's *Georgics,* is redeemed by the author's ardor and enthusiasm. We can hardly with safety regard it as anything more than an interesting document, perhaps illustrating the intellectual tendencies of a period when Lucretius was a dominant force, although even the date cannot be established beyond peradventure.

However uncertain the authorship of *The Cabaret Girl,*

Ciris, and *Aetna* may be, Virgil's preoccupation with philosophy in and about the year 45 B.C. is beyond question. It would appreciably strengthen the authenticity of these poems if any of them clearly reflected Epicurean doctrine. *The Cabaret Girl,* with its graceful and easy style and its frank enjoyment of the pleasures of the passing moment, is in its general manner more readily Virgilian than either of the other poems. But for the tangible effects of this early absorption in the higher and soberer doctrines of physical philosophy we must look to Virgil's more mature work, to the sixth eclogue, in which Silenus sings:

> . . . . How gathered from the vast inane
> The seeds of earth, of waters, and the winds
> Were mixed with flowing fire; how sprung from these
> The primal elements began, and shaped
> One soft conglomerate ball, the new-born world.
> Then the worlds hardened, and the seas' confine
> Was given for Nereus' dwelling, till earth wore
> Diversity of slow-grown shapes; at last
> Earth's fields looked up in wonder and beheld
> The unfamiliar sunshine, and the rains
> That from a loftier welkin now dropped down.
> Then mighty forests rose; and things that breathe
> Roamed few and fearful o'er the pathless hills.

Or to the song of Iopas at the banquet scene in Dido's palace at the end of the first *Aeneid:*

> . . . . Of the moon
> He sang, the wanderer, and what the sun's
> Vast labors be; then would his music tell
> Whence man and beast were born, and whence were bred
> Clouds, lightnings, and Arcturus' stormful sign,
> The Hyades, rain-stars, and nigh the Pole
> The great and lesser Wain; for well he knew
> Why colder suns make haste to quench their orb
> In ocean-stream, and wintry nights be slow.

These are the themes that Virgil's mind may well have dwelt upon in those years at Naples when philosophy for a time made the visits of the Muses few and brief.

From any modern reader's standpoint, the visit of the Muses that inspired *The Salad*, another poem of the *Virgilian Appendix*, was singularly ungracious. Nothing, certainly, could be farther from the style that we associate with Virgil's later work. Simylus, a humble farmer, gets up in the early morning, starts his fire, and grinds the grain for his bread. He rouses his servant:

> From Afric she, the swain's sole serving-maid,
> Whose face and form alike her birth betrayed;
> With woolly locks, lips tumid, sable skin,
> Wide bosom, udders flaccid, belly thin,
> Legs slender, broad and most misshapen feet,
> Chapped into chinks, and parched with solar heat.

She keeps the fire going and sets the water boiling while he finishes the preparation of the bread and leaves it on the hearth, covered with tiles and embers, to bake. Meantime, he repairs to his garden to gather the makings of a salad:

> Four plants of garlic, large, and rooted fast;
> The tender tops of parsley next he culls,
> Then the old rue-bush shudders as he pulls,
> And coriander last to these succeeds,
> That hangs on slightest threads her trembling seeds.

He calls for his pestle and mortar, and grinds up the ingredients, adding salt and cheese:

> His nostrils oft the forceful fume resent;
> He cursed full oft his breakfast for its scent,
> Or with wry faces, wiping as he spoke
> The trickling tears, cried: "Vengeance on the smoke!"

Olive oil and vinegar flavor the mixture. The bread is now baked. He satisfies his hunger, and, incased in farmer's togs, which the poet humorously dignifies as puttees and a helmet, he yokes his steers and starts the day's ploughing.

Such a prosily detailed account of the trivial and commonplace may seem unworthy of poetic treatment. But the
poem has merit. As a bit of narrative it has a homely directness in keeping with the simple living which it describes. The
humor is fetching. The commonplace activities are neatly
dignified by elevated diction, which, however, is not pitched
too high and stops short of broad caricature. It is an excellent
example of a rare type of *genre* picture which Hellenistic
poetry resorted to more frequently than our scanty remains
of it attest. The casual note in one late manuscript, to the
effect that Parthenius had written a poem in Greek which Virgil imitated in *The Salad*, probably has no more value than a
modern conjecture, but it is none the less a very plausible
conjecture. Sueius, an obscure poet of the age of Sulla, had
written a Latin poem with the same title. Both Sueius and
Virgil might have known Parthenius personally. In any case
the mildly humorous treatment of such a theme is thoroughly
in accord with the style in which Callimachus probably described, as part of *Hecale*, the humble environment of the
aged woman who entertained Theseus on his way to slay the
bull at Marathon; a style which the fragments of the Greek
poem only feebly suggest, but which is clearly demonstrated
by Ovid's corresponding picture of the household of the aged
couple, Philemon and Baucis, who similarly entertained un-
awares the divinities, Jupiter and Mercury. Ovid's realistic
sketch of the humble home and its furnishings is more explicitly humorous. But all three poems, *Hecale,* the narrative
of Ovid's *Metamorphoses,* and *The Salad,* are primarily evidences of the Hellenistic interest in realistic pictures of the
simpler phases of lowly life, possibly part of a reaction from
the vicious aspects of sumptuous living which led to an appreciation of "the little hut for shelter, warmed by a little fire, a
poor cake of no fine meal kneaded by your own hands in a
stone trough, mint or thyme for a relish, or even coarse salt

not unsweetened," as the Hellenistic poet, Leonidas of Tarentum, quite devoid of sense of humor, delights to express it in his brief epigrammatic sketches of many personages in the humbler walks of life. Nor is it at all unlikely that Virgil, later drawn to celebrate the simple life of herdsmen in his pastorals, among early experiments with various types of Hellenistic poetry may have found special pleasure in adapting this sketch of the poor farmer, Simylus, and the swarthy negress, Scybale, and of their scantily furnished house and more richly dowered garden. Whoever the author was, he was toying with a Hellenistic theme, as Catullus' contemporaries were prone to do.

It is somewhat easier to credit Virgil's authorship of the last of these dubious poems of the *Virgilian Appendix, Dirae,* or *Curses.* The first and ninth eclogues, as reasonably interpreted with the help of ancient commentators, provide a picture of stormy times in the district round Virgil's home at Mantua. After the battle of Philippi, in 42 B.C., the veterans of the Civil War were given allotments of land in Northern Italy, and the present owners were ejected to meet the needs of the soldiers. Even in the year before, if we are to believe the *Life* by Probus, similar confiscations were made. That Virgil's home was endangered in these troublous times is probable from the content of the two eclogues. Nor is it improbable that the eighth epigram refers to the threatened loss of his home property and the necessity of finding a refuge for his parents from the vicissitudes of these strenuous years; from this poem it appears that he had acquired the villa of his friend and teacher, Siro, as a new home for his parents, replacing Mantua and Cremona. Into such general circumstances the situation of *Curses* fits admirably. The author, deprived by a soldier of his farm lands, in a series of stanzas interrupted by a varied refrain visits a succession of imprecations upon the property of which he has been dispossessed.

The crops are to become sterile, the woods blasted, and by a
reversal of nature, the sea is to overflow the land. To his
sweetheart, Lydia, and to his beloved farm the poet bids a discouraged farewell. The framework of the poem is curiously
artificial. Instead of pronouncing his curses for the first time
the speaker calls for the repetition of them, inviting in his refrain a friend, Battarus (a foreign, if not a Greek, name), to
accompany him upon the flute. A considerable number of
phrases in the poem recur, with slight modifications, in Virgil's *Eclogues,* and these parallel passages seem to some to indicate that *Curses* was composed earlier than the *Eclogues.*
Again, as in *Ciris,* we are confronted by the alternatives, between which it is difficult to choose, that Virgil in his *Eclogues*
is refashioning his own earlier phraseology or that he is appropriating by way of compliment the phrases of some contemporary or earlier poet. Against Virgil's authorship can be
brought only a few bits of internal evidence. The speaker
visits the curse of sterility upon what he calls the "joys of
Sicily." This phrase may set the scene in Sicily rather than in
Northern Italy; but it may also be taken as a poetic periph-
rasis for grain, for which Sicily was a great productive center.
The impious act through which the speaker suffers is attributed to one Lycurgus. This Greek name, whether it be intended to suggest the Spartan lawgiver or the fabulous king
of Thrace, or nobody in particular, seems to have no special
relevance to anyone who was concerned in the confiscations of
the year 42. Finally the heroine, Lydia, faintly indicated in
the background of *Curses,* emerges into the foreground of another poem, which for many centuries was regarded as part of
Curses and has only in modern times been set apart from it as
an independent poem under the title *Lydia.* In this second
poem the general style and situation are different. The keynote of the poem is envy. The poet has not lost his estate, but
for some unrevealed reason he is separated from it and from

his Lydia. The strain is morbidly pathetic, only momentarily humorous, when he bids Jove turn away his ears as he praises Lydia in terms that make her a fit consort for the king of gods, and throughout he is cloyingly sweet in his portrayal of the well-mated animals or gods and of his own less fortunate love. It is very easy to say that *Lydia* is un-Virgilian, and that *Curses* and *Lydia* cannot be by the same hand. It is equally easy to assert that the two poems became accidentally united through the possession of a common heroine, Lydia. But it is as probable that the common heroine points to a common authorship, and that such difference as there is in style between the two poems arises from the difference in situation and from that versatility which characterizes Hellenistic poets and their Roman imitators. Certainly there are phrases of *Lydia,* as of *Curses,* that anticipate the *Eclogues* and *Georgics* of Virgil; in that respect the two poems differ only quantitatively. And if Valerius Cato, as is known to be the case, lost his inheritance in the days of Sulla's confiscations in the earlier part of this same century, and if he, as tradition states, celebrated a Lydia in verse, we can never be very positive that he is not the author both of *Curses* and *Lydia.* The sound evidence for Virgil's authorship of *Curses* is largely external, in the statement of the *Lives* by Donatus and Servius; the relevance of the content to Virgil's own experiences may be accidental.

Again, as in the case of most of these disputed poems, what emerges from the obscurity that hides both date and authorship is the certainty that *Curses* is merely a Hellenistic mold, in this instance somewhat fuller of Italian material than *Ciris, The Cabaret Girl,* or *The Salad.* The occasion is undoubtedly furnished by a bit of purely Italian experience. But the form of curses visited upon the farm which its owner has lost is a palpable reproduction of a modern Greek type of poetry, best illustrated by the work of the same Euphorion who furnished Cicero with his caustic epithet applied to Catullus and the other New Poets. A recent papyrus discovery contains some verses of Euphorion's poem, but they hardly convey more than we gather from the title, *Curses, or the Cup-Thief;* such Greek poems were the expression in literature of a superstitious belief in the efficacy of curses.

One may readily sympathize with the growing tendency, among recent interpreters of the *Virgilian Appendix,* to regard all or most of these pieces as so many documents of the poet's slowly developing genius. But a conservative review of the evidence can hardly result in anything but the moderate assertion that *The Gnat* and most, if not all, the epigrams of *In Lighter Vein* are more surely attested as Virgil's work than the rest; that of the remainder the external evidence of authenticity is never earlier than the second century A.D., if the list of works in Donatus' *Life* goes back to Suetonius; and that some of them are not clearly stamped as Virgil's until the ninth century. The internal evidence for and against authenticity is extremely complicated and correspondingly difficult to analyze and evaluate. It is, however, altogether probable that many of the poems illustrate the general trend of Latin poetry between the years 55 and 42 B.C. If not by Virgil, they are by his contemporaries and possibly his friends. And we may with some security infer the probable range of his interests and the initial developments in his career from these examples of the literary products of his youth as well as from the actual facts in the biographical tradition.

By the accident of birth Virgil was nurtured in an atmosphere that some of the New Poets of the previous generation may well have impregnated with their new ideas and literary practices. By the continuity of literary tradition which linked Catullus and his associates to the young aspirants who ultimately became notable figures in the Augustan epoch, Virgil was attached indissolubly in his early years to the great poets of his boyhood, Catullus and Lucretius. The phrases of Catullus and the spirit and form of Catullian epigram, if not of the epyllium, he had made his own. The diction of Lucretius and an ardent enthusiasm for the high themes of philosophy and for the noble expression of them are reflected in his youthful phraseology and in the active interest which prompted him to abandon poetry for the society of Siro and Philodemus at Naples. The effect of this interlude of philosophical study was probably deep and lasting. From it may well have come, not only technical knowledge, but the high seriousness which gives occasional dignity to the *Eclogues* and *Georgics* and more consistent elevation of thought and sublimity of style to the national epic. But as documents of progress in literary art these poems of the *Virgilian Appendix* point mainly to a complete subservience to contemporary fashion. This fashion impelled the poet, not merely to echo phrases of Catullus and Lucretius, but to adapt the various literary *genres* of Hellenistic Greece, reproducing probably the versatility of these modern Greek poets in handling a variety of literary types and themes in a corresponding diversity of styles and often with an interfusion of Grecized diction. There is little likelihood that in these earlier years he made any considerable effort to free himself from the bonds of this now established dependence upon modern Greek models. Of individual predilections that later found less trammeled expression we may discern possible traces. The pastoral coloring of *The Gnat* and *The Cabaret Girl*, the rural background of *The Salad* and *Curses*, more or less certainly foreshadow the general interests of the author of the *Eclogues* and *Georgics*. There are intimations, too, that epic narrative, of the genially humorous sort in *The Gnat*, possibly of the sentimental type in *Ciris*, attracted Virgil even in his youth. Of this attraction there is further, though dubious, evidence in the *Life* by Donatus and in the amplified version of Servius' commentary on *Eclogues* vi.3. Here we are told of a youthful attempt at epic, either an early essay on the theme of the *Aeneid* or an account of the deeds of the Alban kings, from which the poet was deterred by difficulties variously reported. Perhaps, then, in this early period the dissensions of his countrymen were stirring him to patriotic purposes, the realization of which was happily deferred.

But of personal experience, unless *Curses* is genuine, and of national Roman or Italian material, positive traces are conspicuously wanting except in the epigrams, *In Lighter Vein*. In the main the *Virgilian Appendix* reveals a poet, or group of poets, sedulously engaged in making over Hellenistic themes, Hellenistic literary types, and even some Greek vocabulary for assimilation by an audience that apparently is dulled, in its appreciation of poetry, to any keen sense of national consciousness by the civil conflict that rages continuously in the outer world. It is Virgil's gradual emergence from this undue subservience to the established vogue of close imitation or adaptation of modern Greek models that we shall discover as he grows to maturity of power.

The impulses that stirred him as he approached the age of thirty could hardly have been very different from those which inspired him to write the personal creed at the end of the second *Georgics* a few years later:

> My fondest prayer is that the Muses dear,
> Life's joy supreme, may take me to their choir,
> Their priest, by boundless ecstasy possessed.
> The heavenly secrets may they show, the stars,
> Eclipses of the sun, the ministries
> Of the laborious moon, why quakes the earth,
> And by what power the oceans fathomless
> Rise, bursting every bound, then sink away
> To their own bed; why wintry suns so swift
> Roll down to ocean's streams: what obstacle
> Opposes then the lingering wheels of night.

But if to such mysterious domain
Nature debar my entrance, if the blood
Flows not so potent in my colder breast,
Make me true lover of the field and farm,
Of streams in dewy vales, of rivers broad
And lonely forests, far from pomp and fame.

His overpowering ambition to write a philosophical epic in the style of Lucretius had to give way to the more modest indulgence of his love for the field and farm in the pastoral eclogue and the *Georgics*.

THE POETRY OF THE FIELD AND FARM

I. THE ECLOGUES

The pastoral today is practically an abandoned type of poetry. Nothing in literature, perhaps, seems so remote after the disaster of a European war as this peaceful *genre*. Yet it was after a violent civil strife, in the years immediately following the battle of Philippi in 42 B.C., that Virgil, himself a sufferer from the issues of that war, found in the pastoral a means of expressing the art that had begun to mature as he approached the age of thirty. His juvenile efforts were mere experiments, and if some of the poems of the *Virgilian Appendix* represent even approximately his early promise, they do not encourage us to hope for any great accomplishment. In his pastoral poems he is still groping. He arrives, to be sure, however feebly, at a slightly advanced stage of development in so far as his pastorals are in part stimulated by personal experience, colored by Italian material, and marked by constant allusion to contemporary men and events. But the result is not an artistically fused whole.

His choice of this particular type of poetry again illustrates the strong force of literary tradition. Any instinct that he may have had to strike out into new paths is effectually clogged by his intellectual environment. He still allows himself to be pressed into the service of the propagators of later Greek forms of poetry. After amateurish struggles with epigram and, possibly, short epic, he turns now to a third Hellenistic type, the pastoral.

The pastoral emerges suddenly in Greek literature in the third century B.C., and at once attains its highest and best form in the hands of Theocritus. By what progressive stages, if any, the perfection of Greek pastoral was achieved is somewhat mysterious, at least to the modern reader. But much of the mystery is caused by the fact that the term "pastoral" conveys to us today a sharply defined literary type of which the classical poet and reader were quite unconscious. Theocritus and his contemporaries did not recognize as a distinct kind of poetry the ten poems which, in our present collection of the Greek poet's work, deal primarily with the experiences of country folk. On the contrary, the ten pastoral poems of Theocritus (Nos. 1, 3, 4, 5, 6, 7, 8, 9, 10, 11) are, in content and essential features of form, all of a piece with three other poems (Nos. 2, 14, 15) which, in the same brief scope and in the same realistic and dramatic style, reveal aspects of the life of city folk. We do not know what common term Theocritus would have applied to these two groups of poems, but our understanding and appreciation of the beginnings and development of the sort of poetry that issues in the pastoral is enhanced if we think of all these poems as mimes, differentiating the larger from the smaller group as country and city mimes, respectively, but recognizing the essential oneness of the two divisions in so far as all the poems are brief, dramatic, realistic portrayals of the life of the lower and middle classes in both the city and country. It is purely accidental that a large majority of these poems are concerned with country life, and that of these ten rural poems, all but one have herdsmen as their main characters. From this accidental circumstance, and the further fact that later imitators of Theocritus usually emphasized the rural setting of such poems and gave herdsmen the prominent rôles, the modern term "pastoral" has arisen with its special connotation.

In Greece before the fifth century there were probably rude popular performances in which a person or group of persons presented on a stage brief scenes from everyday life. The text of such scenes might be in prose or verse. Though crude at first, these dramatic pieces may have acquired literary finish and a modest measure of artistic form by the fifth century, when Sophron, to the admiration of the philosopher Plato, cultivated them in prose. Sophron, like Theocritus, was a Sicilian, and his influence upon Theocritus' city mimes is well established. It is probable that Sophron's mimes were dramatically recited rather than acted. So, too, although it is a matter of some dispute, the mimes of a contemporary of Theocritus, Herondas, recovered as recently as 1891, were probably recited by a single performer somewhat as the monologue artist of today plays various rôles in his dramatic recitations. Herondas, by his limping iambic verse and drastic photography, perhaps reflects more closely than anybody else the cruder form of earlier dramatic mime. In Theocritus' hands the recited mime undergoes a formal change: perhaps because of the great vogue of Homeric epic in public recitations, the meter of epic becomes established in the literary mime, and henceforth the dactylic hexameter is regularly used by Theocritus and his imitators. The essential facts are that the country and city mimes of Theocritus, though intended for recitation, probably developed out of short plays, and they owe to such beginnings their distinguishing qualities of brevity, realism, and dramatic form.

A rural setting is only faintly suggested by a very few of the titles and of the scanty fragments of Sophron's works. Herondas, with the possible exception of one allegorical mime, is primarily interested in the life of the city or small town. It is therefore impossible to say whether Theocritus' rural or pastoral mimes mark any originality on his part in the choice of material. Earlier poetry, epic, lyric, the drama, and the epigram, here and there have pastoral coloring. It is quite likely that Theocritus' environment in the island of Sicily led him to give prominence to herdsmen and reapers, although ancient theory, with many fanciful details, ascribes the introduction of pastoral poetry into Greek literature to the time of the Persian Wars, at the beginning of the fifth century, and for aught we know the activities of the herdsman as he watched his flocks in the mountain pastures of Arcadia in Greece proper or in the western island of Sicily may have appealed to composers of the dramatic mime before Theocritus modified it into an artistic recitation. Through him, in any case, and Virgil's imitations of him, the pastoral emerged as a form of country mime.

Our delight in the artful artlessness of the Theocritean pastoral is not seriously impaired by our ignorance of the precise stages through which ruder dramatic mimes slowly passed on their way toward a highly sophisticated and finished form. In a compass, usually, of fewer than a hundred verses, the Greek poet sets before us the active characters conversing together in dramatic dialogue. Sometimes there is no narrative introduction. Often, however, the rôles and situation are introduced by narrative in the poet's own words. Occasionally this narrative is addressed to a friend of the poet, and the pastoral then becomes an epistle in outward form. Otherwise the dramatic elements of the earlier mimes are retained. There is often movement such as we should expect on a stage; seldom is it a stationary picture. Through this dramatic dialogue Theocritus, when at his best, succeeds in conveying naturally a wealth of information and suggestion from which the thoughtful reader visualizes the characters of the speakers, their immediate and more remote environment—the details of flowers, richly colored; of murmuring trees and babbling brooks; the outlines of the deeper background—and all the rustic activities, sentimental adventures, poignant experiences of the herdsmen themselves. The poem has no dramatic unity in any large sense but it has distinct beginning, middle, and end. The language of the speakers, like their experiences, is real and natural. It reveals the colloquialisms of their speech, their proverbial forms of utterance, their fondness for moralizing, and occasionally, with drastic realism, their penchant for frank indecency. Nor may we deny that some flights of fancy and poetic images discovered in this pastoral discourse are well within the range of Sicilian peasantry. Seldom are there thoughts or experiences that would not be appropriate to a herdsman. In this perfect naturalness, particularly of the fourth and fifth poems, Theocritus is a master.

In other poems, however, such as the first, sixth, and eleventh, we seem to be getting away from the realities of the countryside, or at least to find them presented through a medium that contradicts rustic reality. In these poems the material of the herdsmen's songs is drawn from legend, and this interest in the legends of Daphnis and of Polyphemus reminds us of the stock material of the more elevated types of poetry, epic and elegy. This choice of theme does not entirely spoil the illusion. The particular legends are distinctly rural. Daphnis is the neatherd par excellence, a pastoral hero. Polyphemus is a mock-heroic herdsman. Both are natural themes of the countryside, and the herdsmen may well have had their store of legendary narratives along with their own amatory and bucolic adventures. But, granting the naturalness of the legendary themes, the poet's handling of them drifts a bit from the strictly realistic reproduction of rural life. For example, instead of choosing a simple form of the folk-tale of Daphnis, which herdsmen might have known, Theocritus presents in his first idyl a form of the tale that betrays conscious literary rehandling of the popular story. And the song of the herdsman in which the tale is set forth reveals a finished technique far above the capacity of a rustic singer. A refrain, in itself characteristic of popular ballad, sets off very artistically units of varying thought and mood, and in one case artfully interrupts the thought, with striking advantage to dramatic suspense. The narrative, by the poet's ingenious method of letting the last tragic chapter of Daphnis' fatal experience naturally reveal all the earlier presuppositions, betrays the skill of the poet, Theocritus, rather than any untutored art of the pastoral singer. In two other poems, on Polyphemus, although the one-eyed gigantic herdsman of the *Odyssey* is humorously sentimentalized and given a degree of naïveté that may seem to smack of the homely wit of rural invention, these amusing and winsome qualities attached to the repulsive and impious giant of the Homeric epic are an issue from earlier lyrical and comic modifications traditional in literature; they are not the happy creations of a Sicilian peasant's fancy.

These manifestations of conscious art become positive artificiality in Theocritus' seventh poem. Beautiful as the "queen of the idyls" is, analysis reveals that we are not in the presence of actual herdsmen. The pastoral mime has become a means of celebrating contemporary poets and musicians, and even of criticizing contemporary methods in literary composition. It is not impossible that the throne of Zeus (vs. 93) is a covert allusion to the throne of Ptolemy, the reigning king of Egypt. To some extent the text on its surface reveals this artificiality. The description of Lycidas (11 ff.) suggests not a real herdsman, but a counterfeit. The account of Aristis (99 ff.) awards extravagant praise if a mere rustic singer is celebrated. The person called Aratus must be identical with the Aratus of the sixth poem, and if so, he is clearly a friend of Theocritus, and not a rustic. Palpably, without any attempt at masquerade, Philetas, an older contemporary poet, appears under his own name in vs. 40, and in the same verse, under the pseudonym of Sicelidas, a contemporary epigrammatist, Asclepiades, emerges, easily identified by ancient commentary on the passage and other references to him under the same pseudonym. The same ancient commentary informs us that the Simichidas who plays one of the two prominent rôles in the scene is no less a person than Theocritus himself. That the other active rôles, and the other persons incidentally alluded to, are poet friends of Theocritus is altogether probable, even if modern scholars have failed convincingly to identify them. Once the disguise is removed, the herdsmen of the poem become a company of poets and musicians gathered in the island of Cos for the pursuit of literature and music. Of this bucolic masquerade there can be no question. Nor is it surprising if, with this patent evidence of an artificial and allegorical pastoral before them in the seventh poem, modern scholars have suspected that, even in such apparently realistic poems as the fourth and fifth, there might be lurking, behind the masks of herdsmen and rustic singers, real contemporaries of the Greek poet. Especially in such a highly artistic product as the song of the first poem the singer may have been, in the minds of an esoteric circle of Theocritus' friends, a distinguished poet of the day, masked as Thyrsis.

Even if we must limit the artifice to the seventh poem, it has a far-reaching import. For here lies the tangible starting-point of Virgil's intrusion into pastoral of contemporary poets and courtiers and of Octavian himself, and of double meanings and various covert allusions. Out of Virgil's practice, much exaggerated by the interpretations of later Latin commentaries, developed the artificial pastoral of the courts of Nero and of Charles the Great. And the early Renaissance, with its criticism of contemporary politics, religion, and life, and its masquerade of courtiers, priests, poets, and what-not in the form of the pastoral eclogue, perpetuates the classical tradition without serious change except in so far as contemporary environment modified the masqueraders and the material of their pseudo-rustic dialogue. Through Italian, Spanish, and French intermediaries the type became general in Europe, and in English countries gained currency from the time of Spenser's *Shepherd's Calendar* down into the eighteenth century, when it became "a plague in every European capital."

Thus the initial step was taken toward that toying "with a Corydon in ruffles and knee-breeches piping to a Phyllis with patched cheeks and a ribbon on her crook, or a Marie Antoinette playing the shepherdess in the gardens of Trianon, while the real peasants were dying upon their nettle-broth outside." But Theocritus, at least, was quite innocent of any substantial offense. The herdsman in the realistic pastoral was pre-eminently singer and musician, and an identification of pastoral singer and contemporary poet was consequently a very simple diversion on Theocritus' part. It arose easily in an age of late Greek thought which stimulated such masquerading. For it was at the same time that contemporary kings were identified with gods. Ptolemy and Zeus were equivalent terms. Alexander the Great was Dionysus. And if Theocritus chose to disguise himself as the herdsman, Simichidas, there was the happy common possession of musical and poetic skill to justify the fusion, just as the divine right of kings was happily expressed and ratified by the deification of contemporary monarchs.

The Theocritean pastoral not only introduced the pastoral masquerade; it initiated other typical features of bucolic poetry that later became conventionalized. Partly, perhaps, as a reflection of a natural melancholy in the mood of actual herdsmen, partly as the result of Hellenistic interest in the sentimental and pathetic, the pastoral at times became almost elegiac in tone and temper. It had a special predilection for the dirge and for the lover's complaint. The dirge beautifully illustrated in Theocritus' first poem, celebrating the death of the legendary pastoral singer, Daphnis, has a history quite apart from the pastoral. Imitated by a later Greek poet, Bion, in his *Lament for Adonis,* and by a pupil of Bion's in his *Lament for Bion,* the poem of Theocritus, with the later imitations, inspired Milton's *Lycidas* and Shelley's *Adonais,* and, to a lesser degree, Arnold's *Thyrsis.* But in the narrower range of the pastoral itself the dirge and the plaintive theme of unrequited love, whether in the serious vein of Theocritus' third poem or in the deliciously humorous setting of the sixth and eleventh poems, in which Polyphemus ineffectually woos his Galatea, modulate the themes of bucolic poetry in a dominant minor key.

Another outstanding feature of the Greek pastoral, more or less inevitably recurrent in all the later developments of the type, seriously affects the form, as well as the content, of the poetry. Greek religious rites and a variety of social customs express a pervasive interest in competition. Doubtless Sicilian herdsmen gave vent to their feelings and experiences in song, and in their songs this competitive interest easily found expression. The singing-matches of pastoral poetry are probably in some measure realistic. Responsive song became almost inseparably attached to the pastoral as early as Theocritus, and not infrequently is the nucleus of a given poem. Sometimes, as in the first and third poems of Theocritus, a single song makes up the substance of the piece, but in these cases there is a symmetry and balance in the structure of the single song that are only superficially less evident than when a pair of singers engage in a responsive duet. In the fullest form of competitive responsive song, two pastoral singers, after preliminary conversation, in which gradually their competency in music becomes a subject of discussion, determine the prizes, the scene of the singing-match, the umpire, and other details. The competition follows. It may take the form of two long songs, sometimes of equal length, or of shorter songs or stanzas, alternately recited. In the latter case the alternating distichs or quatrains, or whatever they may be, not only correspond in length, but develop an elaborate balance in thought. One singer introduces a theme, in one or more stanzas, which the other singer is obliged to resume and improve upon in similar stanzas. And this broad responsion in theme is accompanied oftentimes by a minute responsion in details of phrasing and of meter and of rhythm. A theme properly elaborated develops neatly a natural transition to a new topic. The poem ends with the umpire's decision on the merits of the competition. Nicely handled, this internal and external symmetry, with infinite variations and deft transitions, affords no little opportunity for clever technique. But obviously, in spite of considerable flexibility, such an intricate responsion in form and thought tends to harden and stereotype and to fix in a rather stiff mold the rustic realities of the pastoral poem.

These distinguishing qualities of the Greek pastoral—the pastoral masquerade with all the consequent possibilities of direct or covert allusion and double meanings, the melancholy strain of the dirge and lover's plaint, and the various forms of the responsive singing-match—were the literary heritage bequeathed to Virgil, and bequeathed chiefly by Theocritus. One may, however, in reading Virgil's pastorals, discover traces of a larger Greek background. The proper names that the Roman poet attaches to his herdsmen are consistently Greek, and the bulk of them are those already used by Theocritus; but a minority, still Greek, are not found in Theocritus. The Greek pastoral was cultivated after Theocritus by Bion and Moschus, of whose work we have scanty fragments. Pastoral coloring intrudes itself into other types of late Greek poetry, somewhat noticeably, for example, in the epigrams of an Arcadian poetess, Anyte. Arcadia, in Greece proper, is notably a pastoral region. Shut off from the seacoast, its mountain pastures afforded desirable facilities for grazing, and its local myths and religious cults reflect the pastoral interests of its people. Pan, the peculiar property of pastoral legend and religion, is closely associated with Arcadia and its mountain peak, Maenalus. The herdsmen of Theocritus, except in the artificial setting of the seventh poem, are thoroughly Sicilian, although the poet, of course, refers to Pan incidentally as a god of Maenalus in Arcadia. Virgil's scenes are sometimes distinctly Sicilian. His settings are sometimes also Italian, but seldom with any precise individualizing of characters and scenes as realistically Italian. In a few poems, however, there are faint glimpses of an Arcadia as the proper habitat of herdsmen, and vague hints that this region, perhaps through earlier literary tradition, had become conventional, and its people typical of somewhat idealized herdsmen. This is particularly noticeable in Virgil's tenth eclogue, with its Arcadian setting and its oft-quoted allusion to Arcadians as skilful singers:

> Arcadian shepherds, in these hills some day
> Ye will make verses on my love and tears.
> Who but Arcadians have a voice to sing?

Even if the Arcadian coloring in this poem comes from the poems of Virgil's friend, Gallus, whose poetry he celebrates in the eclogue, it still remains likely that some Greek pastoral poetry, now lost to us, presented clearer pictures of a pastoral Arcadia. Virgil's dependence upon Theocritus is patent, but further acquaintance with lost Greek material is quite possible. And in particular these hints in Virgil of Arcadia as a paradise of herdsmen are suggestive to those who know the elaboration of this conception of Arcadia as it was worked out in the Renaissance by Sannazaro and Sir Philip Sidney.

To this Greek pastoral Virgil was attracted, doubtless, by his early life in rural surroundings, but we may well suspect that even without such an environment in his boyhood and youth, the intellectual atmosphere of his maturing years would have drawn him to these experiments in pastoral poetry. The ninth epigram of the collection *In Lighter Vein,* as we have seen, represents Messalla as writing pastorals in Greek that were the prototype of Virgil's in so far as they contained the Virgilian characters, Meliboeus and Moeris, and the Virgilian picture of herdsmen "in the wide-branching beech tree's shade." How much more Virgil owed to Messalla we have no means of knowing. It may well have been the influence of Messalla's pastoral poetry that led Tibullus, and others of Messalla's coterie of protégés, to introduce so much pastoral coloring into their elegiac poems. These elegics, however, were published a decade and more later than Virgil's eclogues. So, too, if the pastoral elements in Virgil's tenth eclogue reflect the pastoral coloring of Cornelius Gallus' elegies, we have further evidence that before Virgil cultivated such poetry the pastoral was established in the repertory of the young Augustans.

At the conclusion of his *Georgics*, Virgil attests his authorship of the eclogues:

> I that erewhile, when youthful blood was bold
> Played with the shepherd's muse, and made my song
> Of Tityrus beneath the beech tree's shade.

Internal evidence points to the years 41–39 as marking the period in which he indulged in this poetic *genre*, and with these dates the statement of Donatus that he spent a triennium on the bucolic poems is in satisfactory accord. The title, *Eclogae*, or *Selected Pieces*, is probably not of his choosing, but the invention of an editor. This title, perverted in spelling and meaning by early Italian humanists, ultimately emerges in early English pastoral as *Aeglogues*, as if it were related to the Greek word for "goat," and could mean the dialogues of goatherds. The arrangement of the poems, however, is probably Virgil's. For the final tenth poem is announced in the opening verses as his last effort, and the opening eclogue, in which Octavian is a prominent figure, probably owes its position to the poet's desire to dignify the man who already gave promise of becoming the ruler of the Roman state. Such a manifest dedication as that intruded in vss. 6–13 of the eighth eclogue may indicate an earlier publication, perhaps only in the circle of the poet's intimate friends, either of individual poems or of the collection as a whole, in which Asinius Pollio was specially honored. The chronological order of the poems cannot be fully recovered, but references from one eclogue to another establish in some cases that one poem is earlier than another, and in a few cases precise dating is attainable.

Among the earliest of the pastorals are the second and third eclogues. Demonstrably earlier than the fifth, they are more slavishly dependent upon Theocritus than any of the others.

In the second eclogue a herdsman, Corydon, laments his unsuccessful love for a boy, Alexis. Ancient commentary on the poem, prone to find the pastoral masquerade everywhere in Virgil, asserts that Alexis is Alexander, a slave boy beloved by Virgil and a gift to him from his friend, Asinius Pollio. The truth of the assertion we are unable to test. But of the person, Virgil, or any personal experiences of the poet himself there is no visible trace in the poem, however much some amatory adventure of his own may have prompted the composition. The melancholy lover begins his plaint at high noon, and though it occupies fewer than seventy verses, at the end of it the oxen are dragging home the ploughshare, and the setting sun is doubling its shadows. Evidently the poet cared little for a plausible indication of the lapse of time, or else time passed more quickly then than now for heartsick lovers. In form a brief narrative introduction followed by a long monologue, the poem resembles Theocritus' third idyl, in which similarly a goatherd addresses to Amaryllis his futile appeal. But the details are largely drawn from the solo songs of Theocritus' eleventh, and to a less degree, sixth, poems, the naïve yearnings of the sentimental Cyclops for his nymph, Galatea, with random echoes from other Greek pastorals.

If one is not troubled by reminiscences of the humorous sentimentality of Theocritus' Polyphemus, in effective contrast with his gigantic stature and physical repulsiveness, Virgil's poem is mildly successful. But inevitably these qualities of Polyphemus lose most of their force when transferred to a quite ordinary boorish herdsman. Plaintively scolding Alexis for his cruelty, and threatening suicide, Corydon begins to doubt whether he has wisely chosen the object of his love. Amaryllis was sulky and disdainful, Menalcas, darkskinned, but Alexis' fair complexion and less tempestuous disposition promise little advantage over these sweethearts of earlier days. Calmly appropriating from Theocritus all the items of Polyphemus' wealth and his naïve self-satisfaction, Corydon endeavors to soften the heart of Alexis by the alluring prospect of a rich, accomplished, and handsome lover:

> . . . . Thy proud looks
> Despise me, and of my estate and name
> Seek not to know—how rich in herds I be,
> What flowing milk I get, and how I own
> Wide-pastured o'er the slopes of Sicily
> A thousand ewes; their sweet, fresh milk is mine
> In parching summer and the wintry cold.
> I can sing also: . . . .
> Nor think me quite uncomely. By the shore
> Where the sea lay untroubled by the breeze,
> I saw my mirrored shape; nor do I fear,
> Even in thine eyes, to rival Daphnis' mould,
> If such a glass be true.

Peevishly complaining that Alexis will not share the simple delights of rural life and the privileges of instruction in music, Corydon offers enticing gifts, the various items of which are drawn from Theocritus' third and eleventh poems. But the bouquet of flowers is elaborated independently of the Greek poet, and the style of the description marks a distinct advance in artistic massing of details over the unorganized listing of plants that grew about the insect's grave in *The Gnat* (400 ff.). Nor can any translation reproduce the music of the Latin sounds in the following description:

> . . . . Come hither, loveliest boy.
> The wood-nymphs bear thee lilies heaping high
> In osier baskets; and a naiad white,
> Plucking pale violets and poppies tall,
> Wreathes scented fennel with narcissus bloom,
> And lavender with all sweet herbs she binds,
> And bids sad-vestured hyacinth look gay
> Mated with sprays of saffron marigold.

Fruits blended with flowers fail to win Alexis, and Corydon reproaches himself for wasting gifts on such an unappreciative boy. Momentarily disposed to depreciate himself as a boor and no fit competitor of richer rivals in the bestowal of gifts, he quickly recovers self-esteem and finds heroic precedent in Trojan Paris for the dignity of rural life and for the romantic aspirations of a mere herdsman. But dejection is the pervasive and final note. The waning sun marks the end of day, but the flame of his love burns steadily on—the same contrast that led the love-stricken heroine of Theocritus' brilliant second poem to note the calm sea and gentle winds when her own soul was in the turmoil of love. Hopelessly he resorts to Polyphemus' final source of consolation: there are chores to do, and if Alexis disdains him, there may be another Alexis somewhere, less disdainful.

Corydon's plaintive strain excites a measure of pity in the reader that is happily tempered with amusement at his naïve conceit. The third eclogue is more consistently merry in tone, and provides a more comprehensive and varied picture of the occupations and experiences of herdsmen. It illustrates fully the conventional scheme of the pastoral singing-match, and at the same time the peculiar nature of Virgil's imitation of Theocritus. The theme and the general arrangement of the action are based on Theocritus' fifth poem, but the details are derived from various pastorals of the Greek poet. So, for example, the herdsmen meet at the outset and open their conversation in a couplet that closely translates the initial verses of Theocritus' fourth poem. In the raillery of their subsequent dialogue Virgil returns to the fifth poem of Theocritus for most of his material, but when the talk begins to drift toward the proposal of a singing-match and the selection of prizes, instead of using the phrasing ready to his hand in the fifth poem, he resorts to Theocritus' eighth idyl, casually appropriating, however, as prizes the pair of cups described more fully and effectively in the first poem of Theocritus. When the umpire is chosen there are faint echoes again of the fifth idyl. In the course of the singing match, aside from two passages in which there is no trace of any Greek background, the poet shifts back and forth from one Greek idyl to another, starting with large thefts from the fifth, then a cento of phrases from the fifth, fourth, and eighth, a close adaptation of the fourth, and concluding with the umpire's decision, which, instead of following the close of the fifth idyl, is rather freely invented. And among these larger appropriations there are scattered shorter themes and phrases suggested by other Greek idyls, so that the result may seem, to an unsympathetic student of imitation, to be a patchwork of Theocritean themes and motives derived not only from almost all the Greek pastorals, but, in one or two cases, even from those poems of Theocritus that are not primarily pastorals at all.

If all these evidences of imitation, and others that cannot be appreciated without full knowledge of both the Greek original and the Latin version, were listed in deadly parallel columns, as modern scholars delight to assemble them, one might easily picture the Roman poet as thumbing his copy of Theoc-

ritus and constructing a mosaic of Greek ideas and phraseology. But the picture would be quite unfair to Virgil. Close
as the imitation is, and undoubted as the proof must be of his
lack of creative imagination and originality, it is quite clear,
from his later work and from a more sympathetic analysis
even of his accomplishment in pastoral poetry, that Virgil's
procedure was not mechanical, and in kind, though not in degree, was hardly different from the practice of many modern
artists. Like Tennyson, for example, he had a very sensitive
ear and a very retentive memory. Having once completely
absorbed his Theocritus and having set himself to the composition of Roman pastorals, his quickness in the associating
of ideas and his overflowing store of Theocritean motives and
phrases led him to produce, naturally enough, a bit of poetic
tapestry in which the strands of Greek thought and situation
are intricately woven into a pattern only faintly marked by
threads of original invention. One cannot strongly object to
the process if the result does not, except by careful critical
analysis, reveal a clumsy patchwork and an inferior work of
art. In Virgil the result is in this case a well-organized and
mildly effective whole, but the unfortunate feature is that by
thus combining elements from various idyls of Theocritus he
has not succeeded in achieving a poem that bears comparison
for a moment with either the fourth or fifth idyls of the Greek
poet. He cannot escape comparison, and the comparison is
fatal. The strikingly strong individuality, for example, of the
two herdsmen of Theocritus' fourth idyl and the convincing
realism of the talk and action of the characters in the fifth
idyl are blurred and weakened in Virgil's poem by the interfusion of various details from other sources that destroy unity
of character and action. It is a matter of small moment that
in this curious process of imitation unity of occupation is destroyed; in Theocritus, throughout any single poem, a goatherd is always a goatherd, a shepherd always a shepherd; but

by Virgil's promiscuous appropriation of phrases from various different Greek idyls, a given herdsman becomes a keeper, at one and the same time, of various animals. Even if this should happen to contradict the realities of rural life, no modern reader is specially disturbed by this minor issue of Virgil's peculiar procedure. But it seriously impairs the value of such poems as the second and third eclogues if, in his selection and combination of Theocritean motives and situations, Virgil never approaches such fine characterizations as those of Theocritus' Cyclops, or of the keen-witted, bantering Battus of the fourth idyl sharply contrasted with the dull and gawping Corydon; or if, in choosing to take hints from the description of the cups in the first idyl, he eliminates all the animated art of that Greek portrayal of the coquettish maiden directing her thoughts and glances now to one lover, now to another, of the ancient fisherman with his straining muscles, and of the sly foxes lurking in the vineyard with malicious designs upon the lunch-basket of the small boy who sits on the garden wall, carefree, and idly weaving a trap for locusts.

Yet it may not be denied that, with diminished force, Virgil in his third eclogue has succeeded in drawing a fairly vivid picture of the rough wit, the rustic idiom, the varied interests of herdsmen, their sentimental adventures, and the details of their pastoral activity. The scene is not definitely set. There is only a vague background of grassy green farmland and blooming orchard. Rustic raillery leads to sly hints of careless shepherding and emaciated flocks, of thievish appropriation of the animals' milk, of neighborhood scandals (with neat ellipses of the facts to tease the imagination), and of knavishness of various sorts. The singing-match is worked out in balanced stanzas, couplets symmetrically interwoven in the larger mass of triads. It opens with formal prayers to patron divinities, passes quickly to sentimental themes, the girl sweetheart, Galatea, the boy love, Amyntas, and to the

gifts each lover brings his love. Such sentiment, indeed, is the
note most often struck. The symmetry of the larger composition often recurs within the smaller units of the individual
stanzas. Much of it is lost without the Latin original and the
rhythmical and metrical structure of the Latin hexameter, but
the balanced phrases of these two stanzas may suggest the
extreme of this balance, not only between stanzas, but within
each stanza:

> Menalcas: Wolves are a shepherd's bane: the heavy showers
> Our ripening harvest spoil, and storms the trees;
> 'Tis angry Amaryllis troubles me.
> Damoetas: Sweet to the thirsty corn is falling dew,
> Buds to a weanling, willows to its dam;
> To me the fair Amyntas, only he.

So the two herdsmen play battledore and shuttlecock with
their chosen themes until the umpire charitably declares the
game a draw and bids them close the floodgates of song.

Today nobody, unless he shares Virgil's knowledge of
Theocritus, is disturbed by the patchwork of Theocritean
phrases and motives which close analysis reveals. But the
continuation, in the Virgilian eclogue, of the pastoral masquerade and the considerable extension of Theocritus' rather
limited violation of the pastoral illusion by direct references
to contemporary poets and musicians mar considerably one's
enjoyment of the rural setting and characters. Doubtless by
Virgil's time these had become accepted conventions. The
pastoral masquerade, of course, is revealed only by ancient
commentators on the poems, who often misrepresent the
poet's intention and disagree among themselves in identifying
the rustics of the poems with certain contemporaries of Virgil.
Many such identifications are the issue probably of town talk
in Virgil's day, and correspondingly unreliable. But the existence of such masquerading is hardly to be doubted, however
exaggerated and pernicious in its effect upon later pastoral
the allegorical interpretation in ancient commentaries may be.

More disturbing are direct references by the herdsmen of the pastorals to Virgil's contemporaries, friends, and patrons, occasionally personal foes or persons with whom he has less immediate associations. Such allusions in the poet's own mouth in a few preludes or interludes are relatively inoffensive, but intruded among the rustic realities of the poems, they abruptly recall the reader from the dramatic setting to the actualities of life at Rome in the poet's day. Nor is it more than a moderate offset to this disadvantage if from such personal references we gather some knowledge of Virgil's surroundings and human relations in his early contact with intellectual circles at Rome.

The uncertainty regarding the date and authorship of *Ciris* and of the ninth poem of the collection *In Lighter Vein* makes it doubtful whether or not Virgil had already come into any intimate connection with Messalla, but by 42–39 B.C., when he was twenty-eight years of age and more, he had formed attachments to other men of affairs. Of these the most important was C. Asinius Pollio. Six years older than Virgil, Pollio was favorably known to Catullus as a lad of personal charm and wit, and his departure to Athens for study and recreation won a *bon voyage* from Helvius Cinna. Thus associated in his youth with the new poets, Pollio seems never to have lost his interest in literature and art. The earlier years of his manhood brought success in the law courts and in public life. A partisan of Julius Caesar and later of Mark Antony, he was active in the Civil Wars. According to the somewhat perplexed and dubious tradition regarding Virgil's early life, Pollio was legate of Antony in the province of Gallia Transpadana at the time when Octavian distributed territory in the neighborhood of Virgil's home to the soldiers of the Civil Wars, and managed to protect Virgil's family estate. Such intervention may have led to the kind of intimacy which prompts Virgil in his eighth eclogue to say that he is writing pastoral verses at the command of Pollio. But Pollio's combination of intellectual interests with no small influence as a man of affairs may well have drawn Virgil to him at Rome before the year 42. In the year 40 Pollio attained the consulship, and the Messianic eclogue was written in that year with the hope that it might be worthy of such a consul. Then Pollio, as representative of Antony, had just arranged a peace with Octavian through Maecenas. In the next year he won a triumph over the Parthians. His later activity leaves no perceptible mark on Virgil's poetry. He withdrew from public life and became a patron of literature and art, and a writer himself of no slight distinction. Establishing the first public library at Rome and a collection of works of art, introducing the practice of reading literary works in public, a literary critic of some discernment, he lent consistent aid to the development of intellectual interests. Tragedies and a history of the Civil Wars were his own chief contribution to the literature of the period.

Uncertain as Pollio's interference in Virgil's behalf may be, there can be no reasonable doubt that another official, Alfenus Varus, was actively concerned in these distributions and did protect Mantua and Cremona from violent inroads by the veterans of the Civil War. An ancient tradition represents Varus as legate of Octavian, dispossessing Asinius Pollio and supervising the distribution of farm lands. Whatever the facts are, Virgil in his ninth eclogue celebrates Varus as the savior of Mantua and Cremona. Though Varus may be identical with an author of a juridical treatise, he is otherwise not credited with any literary work or intellectual interest. He must be distinguished from the poet and associate of Virgil's youthful studies under Siro, the Quintilius Varus of Horace' eulogistic ode. The very possibility of confusion of these two men affects the interpretation of Virgil's sixth ec-

logue, dedicated in the prologue to a Varus. This prologue indicates that the Varus addressed had won some distinction in
military service, and Virgil, in his prœmium, declines to record Varus' achievements in an epic naturally demanded by
such exploits, but promises a pastoral poem, written, as he
says, under orders, presumably from Varus himself. This
phrasing corresponds to the words of the eighth eclogue, in
which, similarly, Pollio is celebrated as triumphant over the
Illyrians, and as having ordered a poem from Virgil's hand.
Such a description in the sixth eclogue clearly fits better Alfenus Varus than the poet, Quintilius Varus, of whose martial
exploits we have no record. The part of the sixth eclogue,
however, in which the promise of the prœmium is realized
represents Silenus, the mythical teacher of the wine god,
Bacchus, as caught and chained by two rustics, and singing,
under duress, of the creation of the world, a theme briefly expounded in accord with Epicurean doctrines, and then following it with a succession of mythological ballads, most of which
are stories of metamorphoses. In the midst of this series are
inserted a tribute to Virgil's friend, the poet Cornelius Gallus,
and, probably, a modified quotation from Gallus' own handling of a mythological theme. An ancient comment on the
poem finds in Silenus the Epicurean philosopher, Siro, the
teacher of Virgil and Quintilius Varus; and in the whole setting, and in the exposition of philosophical theory and mythological themes which were subject to literary treatment by
Cornelius Gallus and others, there is some tangible support for
modern conjectures that the poem is either a joyous souvenir
of earlier days when Virgil and Quintilius Varus were associated under Siro in the study of philosophy and literature, or
a special commemoration of the achievements in poetry of
their friend, Cornelius Gallus. In either case it is tempting to
identify the Varus of the prœmium with Quintilius, rather

than with Alfenus Varus, but the mention of military prowess in the prologue is as yet an obstacle to this theory.

Of Virgil's close intimacy with Cornelius Gallus there can be no question, and probably Gallus' quick rise to prominence in public affairs and his early accomplishments in the field of letters made him a singularly influential friend in any effort that Virgil may have been making at this time toward connections with those circles of men who seem to have divided their time between active engagement in the political affairs of the day and the cultivation of literature and art, either as intelligent critics or creators. A year or two younger than Virgil, born just north of the Adriatic Sea, not far from Virgil's home and in a region that may have been susceptible to the influence of Valerius Cato, one of the earliest propagators of Hellenistic style and methods, Gallus was in his youth acquainted with the New Poets of Catullus' generation, and perhaps more closely attached to them than our extant evidence enables us to demonstrate. It is at least clear that Parthenius, from whom certainly emanated much of the material and stimulus that directly affected Catullus and his contemporaries, wrote in Greek a plot book of Hellenistic love stories, dedicating it to Gallus and expressly indicating that he intended Gallus to use the material for Latin elegies and epics. It is not without significance that Virgil, whose early absorption in the materials and methods of Hellenistic poets is manifest, is intimately acquainted with this young poet, so closely identified with the main current of literary ideals during Catullus' generation. With Pollio and Alfenus Varus, Gallus played some part in the distribution of lands to soldiers in 42 B.C., but only a minor rôle as collector of money from communities whose property was not involved in the confiscation. His elegies on his sweetheart, Lycoris, must have been published before the tenth eclogue, in which Virgil praises them and probably quotes from them with complimentary intent.

From the sixth eclogue and Servius' comment on it we learn that Gallus had translated poems, probably short epics, of the Hellenistic writer, Euphorion, or was planning such a translation at the time when the eclogue was composed. In his later years Gallus seems to have become diverted into political life. He fought against Antony, and after the battle of Actium held a post in Egypt. In 30 B.C., when Egypt became a Roman province, he was made prefect, but fell into disfavor with Octavian and was so severely punished that he committed suicide in 26 B.C. Virgil's consistent devotion to him is attested not only by the sixth and tenth eclogues, but by the eulogistic tribute originally forming the conclusion of the fourth book of the *Georgics,* but deleted when Gallus' fall from grace made it unwise to commemorate publicly their friendship.

It is apparent that this triumvirate of influential friends must have served Virgil well, both in the material difficulties relating to his family estate in Northern Italy, and in the realization of any social or intellectual ambitions he may have cherished during his residence in Southern Italy, at Rome, or Naples. But the details of his actual intercourse with the court and other influential circles at Rome are not available. Ancient tradition ascribes either to the whole triumvirate, or to Gallus in particular, Virgil's ultimate contact with Octavian, and represents the future emperor as personally protecting Virgil's estate from the encroachments of the soldiers. These facts, along with more circumstantial details, might easily have been derived from the text of the eclogues, and this text may easily have been strained to furnish facts that the poet did not intend to convey and that the truth of the case hardly warranted. Yet it is clear that the farm lands in the vicinity of Mantua and Cremona were threatened; that Virgil's father was at some time driven to use Siro's villa, probably in Naples, as a substitute for his northern home;

that Varus protected some estates near Mantua and Cremona; and that Octavian himself, if he did not intervene directly, was at least credited with exerting arbitrary power in Virgil's behalf. The details are not important. By the year 38, in any case, Virgil was established in the favor of Octavian and of his minister, Maecenas. In that year Horace was introduced by Virgil and his friend Lucius Varius to the coterie patronized by Maecenas, and the *Georgics,* begun in 37, was dedicated to Maecenas. All these associations mark Virgil's rapid rise to an influential position in the political and intellectual circles of Roman society.

These friends and the personal experiences of the poet do not always confuse the pastoral setting. The fifth eclogue, for example, in two long responsive songs, celebrates the death and the apotheosis of the heroic herdsman, Daphnis; the first song is a condensed form of the lament in Theocritus' first idyl, and the latter is more freely invented. Probably there is no allegorical reference to the death and apotheosis of Julius Caesar, but the shepherd's pipe which Menalcas presents to his friend, Mopsus, at the close of their competitive song is said to be the one upon which the melodies of the second and third eclogues were sung; such a passing remark easily leads the reader to think that Virgil himself is masquerading as Menalcas, although there is no further indication of the poet's intrusion. Daphnis recurs in the seventh eclogue, no longer the heroic figure, but an ordinary herdsman who, with Menalcas, listens to the competitive quatrains of Corydon and Thyrsis. The whole poem is presented as a narrative by Menalcas, one of the bystanders, approximately the technique of Theocritus' seventh idyl, but the scheme of action is drawn from the eighth Greek idyl, with constant echoes from almost all the other Greek pastorals.

Nor does the stilted eulogy of Pollio that introduces the eighth eclogue with conventional praise of his victories and

his verse lead the way to any allegorical treatment of Pollio
and his varied activities. Two plaints, one of a jealous lover,
the other of a maiden who seeks to win her sweetheart by the
art of sympathetic magic, are sung by rival soloists. The first,
based on Theocritus' third idyl, is happily interspersed with
bits of the eleventh idyl, on Polyphemus, and here Macaulay
and Voltaire, happily ignoring the imitation of Theocritus,
found their favorite passage of Latin poetry:

> Through our own garden close I guided thee,
> Thee a small maiden at thy mother's side,
> In search of dewy apples. My twelfth year
> Had scarce begun, yet standing on the ground
> I reached, and broke the bending boughs for thee.
> I saw thee and was lost, blind, mad, a slave!

Both the two complaints are set off in stanzas by recurring
refrains in the fashion of Daphnis' song in the first idyl of
Theocritus. The magic ceremony in the second song is a dull
and faded replica of the masterpiece of Hellenistic poetry,
Theocritus' second idyl, with all the intense passion and fine
psychological analysis of the Greek poem eliminated, and the
conventions of the magic ritual retained. Nor does Virgil reveal any appreciation of the conclusion of the Greek poem,
which leaves the reader in suspense as to the issue, but, as if
making a concession to a popular demand that the story shall
have an ending, and preferably a happy one, the Latin poet
lets us hear the bark of the lover's dog, marking the return of
the lover and the realization of the sweetheart's desires. So
the magic ceremony, however effective from the maiden's
standpoint, is for the reader somewhat disenchanting.

Into the midst of the maiden's magic ritual Virgil weaves
a simile which a late author, Macrobius, asserts to be a theft
from the poetry of Virgil's friend, Lucius Varius. In Varius a
dog is chasing a stag, and in the joy of pursuit, "nor streams
nor slopes retard him; by long desire outworn, he heeds not

the homeward call of lingering eve." In Virgil the maiden, as part of her imprecation, says:

> May such a love seize Daphnis as consumes
> The roving heifer when she seeks her mate
> Through copse or lofty forest wandering far,
> And wearied flings her in the sedges green
> Nigh some full stream, by long desire outworn,
> Nor heeds the homeward call of lingering eve.

The situations in the two passages are quite different, and the stag and dog in Varius are replaced by the heifer and her mate in Virgil, but one verse of Varius is appropriated without change. The phenomenon, slight as it may seem from this single occurrence, may have a wider significance. Certainly it affects considerably our estimate of his originality if, in addition to the palpable appropriations of Theocritean motives, situations, and phrases, Virgil made liberal use of the verses of his Italian friends and contemporaries.

The positive evidence bearing on this aspect of his early work is limited and may easily be distorted and abused. It consists mainly of parts of the text and ancient commentary on the sixth and tenth eclogues. After a formal dedication to Varus, the sixth eclogue narrates in the poet's own words that Silenus has been caught off guard by Chromis and Mnasylus:

> His veins, as was their wont, were swollen large
> With last night's wine and revel; from his brows
> The flowers were fallen and at a distance strewn,
> And o'er him by its handle smooth and worn
> A heavy flagon hung. On him they fell,
> For often had the old man mocked them both
> With expectation of a song.

With the help of Aegle, loveliest of the naiads, Silenus is bound with his own wreaths, and his brows smeared with mulberry juice; awakening and finding himself in their power, he consents to sing the promised song. The song lacks unity. As reported by the poet, it consists of a loose succession of themes, awkwardly linked together by prosaic formulas. An Epicurean exposition of the creation of the world, echoing Lucretian diction and phrasing, is followed by a summary statement of other themes of Silenus' song: the re-creation of the human race after the flood, the Golden Age, Prometheus' theft of fire and his punishment, the ravishing of Hylas by the water nymphs, the love of Pasiphae for the bull (the poet's summary here interrupted by a direct quotation of some length from Silenus' song), Atalanta and the apples of the Hesperides, the sisters of Phaethon and their metamorphosis into alder trees. Then the poet enlarges somewhat on the next theme, the story of one of the Muses' escorting Cornelius Gallus to Helicon, where all the choir of Phoebus rose to greet Gallus; the pastoral hero, Linus, presented him with the pipes once played upon by Hesiod, and instructed him to sing to their music of the origin of the Grynean grove, sacred to Apollo. After this expansion the poet, again more summarily, ends the array of subjects covered by Silenus' song, listing the story of Scylla, daughter of Nisus, who is described as if she were identical with the Scylla of the *Odyssey*, and her metamorphosis, the tale of Tereus and Philomela and their transformation into birds, and finally, a group of subjects comprehensively described as "every strain his blest Eurotas heard when Phoebus sang." The general setting, Silenus debauched and chained and singing under duress, is taken from Greek sources. Ancient commentators, probably too easily prompted by the Epicurean doctrine of the creation, found the philosopher, Siro, beneath the mask of Silenus, and a natural secondary inference was that the two rustics who caught Silenus off guard must be Varus, to whom the poem is dedicated, and the poet Virgil himself. Such guesses, suggested merely by the text, are open to grave suspicion. Carried to a

consistent conclusion, these ancient conjectures would issue
most naturally in an allegory, in which the implication would
be that Siro, as teacher of Virgil and Varus (in that case more
easily Quintilius Varus than Alfenus Varus), stimulated their
poetic talent by recounting a series of Greek myths, preceded,
in the style of Hesiod, by an account of the creation. Indeed,
it is a noteworthy fact that practically all the myths referred
to were covered in the *Catalogue* of Hesiod.

But any such allegory is disrupted by the manifest fact
that one of the mythical tales in Silenus' song is clearly indicated to have been the theme of a poem by Cornelius Gallus.
It is hardly to be doubted that in the passage alluding to the
story of the Grynean grove Virgil is appropriating verses
which Gallus had written in a poem on that theme, and that
the scene in which Gallus is honored by the Muses is a deft
modification of Gallus' own procemium to his poem. Furthermore, Servius' comment on the verses states that Euphorion had treated the same subject, easily leading us to the conclusion that Gallus' poem was an adaptation of some work
of Euphorion. When we add to these inferences the further
facts that several of the myths mentioned in Silenus' song were
treated in Greek by either Parthenius or Euphorion, it becomes likely that the sixth eclogue mirrors very effectually
the interrelations of Virgil and his contemporaries with Hellenistic poetry. Silenus' song becomes a catalogue of contemporary Latin poems, written either by Cornelius Gallus
or by Gallus and other friends of Virgil, in which they adapted
themes already handled by Euphorion and Parthenius, these
Greek poets, in turn, being inspired by Hesiod to no small degree. The part that Parthenius' collection of Greek plots,
dedicated to Gallus, may have played in this series of compositions is obvious. But whether Silenus' song catalogues the
content of several books of Gallus' work, or several works by

Gallus and others of Virgil's friends, is not clear from the evidence.

Such "catalogue poems," whether catalogues of mythological tales or of poems, were no novelty in classical literature. Hesiod, in his *Catalogue,* had listed many myths of legendary heroines, introducing each heroine with a prosaic formula, a practice continued by Hellenistic poets. A closer analogy to Virgil's procedure is contained in the Hellenistic poem known as the *Lament for Bion,* in which an admirer of the Hellenistic poet, Bion, represents the whole universe as mourning Bion's death, and neatly interweaves among the mourners some of the mythical characters in Bion's own poems, probably refashioning his own verses, so that the *Lament* becomes a depository of fragments of his literary remains. Such art as there may be in the appropriation of phrases from poems of one's friends, living or dead, is hidden from us so long as the poems thus appropriated are no longer extant. The dry catalogue alone remains.

By this means Virgil was provided with a special opportunity for complimenting his poet friends, and we have no sure method of estimating the range of his indulgence. In the eighth eclogue he paid tribute to Varius by the quotation of a single verse; in the sixth probably much of Silenus' song is deftly adapted from Gallus, or from Gallus and others. It may well be that the peculiarly incoherent structure of the tenth eclogue is best explained by the assumption that the poem, manifestly intended as an exclusive tribute to Cornelius Gallus, is a mere cento of passages from Gallus' own poetry.

It is somewhat difficult, without begging large questions, to state either the situation or the development of thought in the tenth poem. The singer is clearly Virgil, masquerading as a herdsman weaving a basket of mallow in the course of his song. The theme of his song is the lovesickness of Gallus.

The song itself is meant for the ears of Lycoris, who is known to us as the heroine of Gallus' sentimental elegies. Quite certainly, then, the person for love of whom Gallus is pining away is Lycoris. The scene of this anguish, however, is not Rome or Italy, but a lonely cliff in Arcadia, where Gallus lies forlorn, mourned by the neighboring mountains and by the flocks that stand about him, apparently his own flocks, of which he, albeit a divine poet, is urged not to be ashamed; and to him come other herdsmen, and divinities, such as Apollo, Silvanus, Pan, with sympathetic queries and expostulations. Apollo reproaches him for his love-madness; Lycoris has deserted him for a rival and is following the rival over the snows and through the din of war. The poet, Gallus, seems therefore to be for the time an Arcadian herdsman. This sudden metamorphosis, however, is obviously due to the fact that the singer has calmly appropriated the situation in which Theocritus put the lovesick Daphnis in his first idyl; and the sympathy of nature and of the animals, the visits of deities to comfort and strengthen the victim of unrequited love, are all transferred, with slight modifications, from the Greek poem to the case of Gallus, although the scene in Theocritus is Sicily, here Arcadia. With this merging of Daphnis with Gallus, a lovesick herdsman and poet, one might be content if the fusion were sustained and the rôle of lovesick herdsman-poet carried through the song, but to the expostulating divinities, and directly to his sympathetic fellow-herdsmen, Gallus makes this response:

> Arcadian shepherds, in these hills some day
> Ye will make verses on my love and tears.
> Who but Arcadians have a voice to sing?
>
> . . . .
>
> Would I were one of you! and of your flocks
> A keeper, or could prune your purpling vines!
> Surely had Phyllis ever been my love,
> Amyntas, or whatever flame ye will—
>
> . . . .

> In willow copses under trailing vines
> My love and I would lie, while Phyllis there
> Would weave me garlands and Amyntas sing.
> Here, O Lycoris, are cool-flowing rills,
> Here softest grass and haunts of woodland shade,
> Here in thine arms my whole life long should be.
> Now the blind passion of unpitying war
> Clothes me in steel and bids me captive be
> Mid thronging swords and foes in stern array;
> Whilst thou in exile—would it all were lies!—
> Lookest on snow-clad Alp and ice-bound Rhine
> Alone, and not with me. Oh, harmless blow
> The wintry winds; and from the sharp-edged ice
> May thy white lovely feet no wound receive!

So far, then, from being an Arcadian herdsman, Gallus wishes he were one, that he might enjoy peacefully faithful Arcadian sweethearts. In fact he is a warrior, separated from Lycoris, who in his absence follows another soldier to Northern Italy. Yet of any military campaign in Arcadia, or of any temporary stop in Arcadia in the course of a military expedition, we have no information in the historical evidence of Gallus' career.

At this point in his response to the herdsmen Gallus suddenly reasserts himself as poet and proposes "to set to the music of the Sicilian herdsman's pipe verses of Euphorion." This rather cloudy couplet seems to indicate an intention to blend the styles of Theocritus and Euphorion. The verses of the eclogue immediately preceding the couplet are said by Servius to be taken directly from Gallus' own poems, and it is probable that the couplet is also a modification of some statement made in an introduction to Gallus' poems in which Gallus similarly explained the peculiar nature of his poems. If these poems were the elegies written in honor of Lycoris, the peculiarity may have been the blending of pastoral coloring suggested by Theocritus with the elegiac form and content of poems otherwise prompted by Euphorion. And if the tenth

eclogue is largely a composite of phrases and situations adapted by Virgil from the poems of Gallus, the pastoral motives in
the tenth eclogue are not of Virgil's choosing, but simply imitations of Theocritus that had already appeared in Gallus'
elegies. Such a fusion of pastoral and elegy is well illustrated
in the elegies of Tibullus and in some poems of Propertius,
and many passages of the tenth eclogue bear a striking resemblance to bits of Tibullus and Propertius in respect to motives
and situations.

The vacillation of mood and shifting decision continue to
the end of the poem, but the thought is somewhat more coherent toward the conclusion. Gallus avers that he will go to
the lonely woods and carve his love upon the trees. While the
trees grow, his love, too, will grow. Meantime, he will be
hunting. But he checks himself in the midst of these proposals. Love cannot thus be eased or endured. No more of
nymphs, of songs, of groves! Love masters all—*omnia vincit
Amor*—"we, too, submit to Love." Even here, though less palpably, two or three situations from Gallus' love poetry may
be woven into the eclogue.

However one may mitigate the incoherence of this eclogue, it is difficult to discover any such unity of situation as
might have been provided by a conception, consistently carried through the poem, of Gallus, either as a lovesick herdsman or a lovesick warrior in Arcadia. It may not be denied
that Virgil could have allowed himself jerky flights of imagination which destroyed all unity of conception. But in view
of Servius' comments on both the sixth and the tenth eclogues
it seems perverse to explain the disconnected structure of
these two poems as due to anything, primarily, but a conscious appropriation of themes, situations, and phrases from
the poetry of Virgil's friends and contemporaries, a procedure
that finds a precedent in later Greek poetry and that probably
had considerable vogue among the Augustans. The artificial-

ity of the pastoral eclogue is appreciably increased by this method. Only in degree, however, does it depart from the pastoral masquerade of poets and musicians in Theocritus' seventh idyl, although the purpose is realized in the Greek poem without any loss of unity or poetic beauty.

Such catalogue poetry, in the most charitable estimate, reveals hardly more than a praiseworthy effort to relate the traditional literary type of the pastoral to some of the vital interests of the poet himself, his friends, and patrons. The real herdsmen of Theocritus' idyls were singers and musicians. The masquerade of Theocritus' seventh idyl introduced contemporary poets and musicians in place of actual herdsmen. Virgil has continued the Theocritean practice by transforming Gallus into an Arcadian herdsman, and his references elsewhere are more or less covert allusions to friends who are poets, or at least patrons of literature. One might easily pardon the violation of the pastoral illusion and the palpable evidences of deficient vigor and originality in weak appropriations of Theocritus' phrasing and situations if the result were an artistic whole or if the defects were redeemed by the expression of genuine and intense feeling. As it is, there is hardly more than an agreeable prettiness, devoid of vigor and spontaneity.

From these artificial products one turns with relief to the three remaining eclogues, in which there are clear indications of a growing power and intimations of Virgil's later art. In the ninth and the first eclogues personal experiences animated the subject matter, and at least in the first eclogue a truly Italian pastoral emerges with every evidence of artistic skill. The fourth, or Messianic, eclogue was written after a significant political event which inspires the poet to an elevation of thought and sublimity of diction that foreshadow the patriotic feeling and the dignity of the *Georgics* and the *Aeneid*.

Out of the ninth and the first eclogues, readers of Virgil,

as early as the time of Quintilian, derived their most substantial evidence of allegorical allusion. Probably such readers were quite correct in finding in these two poems reflections of Virgil's personal experiences, and particularly of the dangers to which his family estate near Mantua and Cremona was exposed. But this credible allegory was unwisely extended and led to an accumulation of details far beyond Virgil's intention; and once justifiably used to interpret at least the general background of these two poems, the fertile imagination of later readers exploited allegory throughout the other poems, in which the poet was often innocent of any covert meanings or of references to personal experiences or current events.

The active rôles in the ninth eclogue are carried by two herdsmen, Lycidas and Moeris. Meeting as wayfarers, they converse on topics of common interest. Moeris reports a surprising and tragic situation:

> . . . . A foreigner
> Holding our little farm, who harshly cries,
> "These lands are mine. Ye dwellers of old time,
> Away with you!" And we submit to this. . . . .

To the new possessor, "we," says Moeris, "are sending two kids as a gift." Lycidas objects that he had heard these dangers had been averted by Menalcas' songs, but Moeris dolefully observes that poets' songs are of no avail against steel-clad Mars; indeed, the very lives of himself and Menalcas have been threatened. Lycidas breaks into praise of Menalcas' virtuosity as a singer and poet, and Moeris and he quote from the songs of Menalcas. The first of the two songs quoted is only a Latin version of a passage of Theocritus' third idyl, the second is an appeal to Alfenus Varus, promising that he shall be immortalized in song if he saves Mantua and Cremona from the soldiers. Descriptive allusions to other songs of Menalcas seem to echo phrases of Virgil's fifth eclogue. At this point the general theme drifts to pastoral song in general, quite apart from the confiscation of property for the soldiers. Lycidas, like Simichidas in Theocritus' seventh idyl, modestly avows himself to be something of a poet, though inferior to Varius and Cinna, as Simichidas was surpassed by Philetas and Asclepiades. Moeris rehearses a song that is a cento of Theocritean phrases, and by request gives as encore a eulogy of the star of Caesar, doubtless an allusion to the comet which appeared after Caesar's death and was currently supposed to mark his apotheosis. Stimulated by Moeris' repertory, Lycidas is fain to stop a while and prolong the pleasure of song, or else, in fear of approaching rains, to carry Moeris' burden, that Moeris and he may sing at their ease as they walk toward the town. Moeris, however, recalls him to the business in hand and insists that Menalcas' presence is essential to inspiring song.

The poem is a fusion of the masquerade of poets in Theocritus' seventh idyl with Virgil's personal experiences at the time of the confiscations. The parade of herdsmen as poets and the general setting—the herdsmen meeting on the road and singing snatches of song composed either by them or by more notable herdsmen-poets—is Theocritean. There is no special difficulty in identifying Menalcas with Virgil; nor is there any necessity for such an identification. Ancient commentators, accepting the equation of Menalcas with Virgil, supported the reference in the poem to Menalcas' personal danger by circumstantial details, including even the name of the soldier who was supposed to have threatened Virgil's life. But the poem is easily understood without any complete correspondence between Menalcas' conditions and Virgil's; and the absence of Menalcas from the scene of action is not necessarily Virgil's absence in Rome to obtain the intervention of Octavian. It is altogether unlikely that Virgil, like Menalcas, was a tenant farmer, in partnership with Moeris or a neighbor of Moeris. Rather, with fresh recollections of his own experiences, Virgil has sketched into the framework of Theocritus' seventh idyl vivid touches of the unrest in Northern Italy after the battle of Philippi.

Similarly, but with a much higher degree of originality and artistic finish, Virgil, in the first eclogue, transfers his experiences to a herdsman, Tityrus. Virgil is not himself masquerading as Tityrus. For Tityrus in the poem is an old man and slave. The poet at this time was only about thirty years old. But without disturbing at all the pastoral illusion, he represents Tityrus as a herdsman, slave, and tenant farmer, renting his property from a rich master who lives at Rome. Tityrus takes the produce of his farm to a neighboring town, and by saving the income acquired by this disposal of his goods he might long since have bought his freedom. An extravagant sweetheart, Galatea, has prevented the realization of any such hope, and Tityrus has consequently reached old age without release from slavery. Now, in his declining years, thanks to a new and frugal sweetheart, Amaryllis, he has accumulated enough to buy his liberty when the confiscation of property to provide homes for the veterans of the Civil War endangers his farm. He goes to Rome to see his master and purchase his liberty. Once there, however, he forgets his main purpose on seeing a god, the same god whom, monthly, he has worshiped on his farm. To him, as being a god, he puts the question whether he is to lose his farm or keep it. The god, in oracular style, assures him that he shall retain his property. Such a god Tityrus must always remember.

This general situation and a profusion of details that help us to visualize the remote and immediate environment of the action are set forth in dramatic dialogue between Tityrus and another herdsman, Meliboeus. Meliboeus has already been driven from his farm by the soldiers. He is disconsolate and curious to know why and how Tityrus enjoys exemption. The action of the present scene reveals slowly and with dramatic effect the action of the past and the conditions of both the past and the present. The characters are neatly contrasted. Meliboeus is younger than Tityrus. In character he reveals the mood of the moment, but with some permanent characteristics. He sympathizes with his goats and can forget for a time his own hard luck in his curiosity to know the explanation of Tityrus' better fortune. Tityrus is the center of interest. He is more sharply individualized. We get a glimpse of his youthful frivolity in love affairs. Energy is foreign to his nature. In the background is Amaryllis, thrifty and affectionate companion.

The scene is Italian, although in details it does not closely correspond to the vicinity of Mantua and Cremona as we now know it. The time is a hot, sunny afternoon. It is a day in late autumn; the harvest is ripe and already gathered. During the conversation the sun is setting, and at the end leaves the outlines of the landscape clearly marked. Back of all the contrast of character and of fortune, good fortune made permanent, good fortune lost, content and poverty, is the tumult of confiscation, itself the issue of civil strife. But all the discord is harmonized in the perfect peace and content of the conclusion. Even Meliboeus loses his discontent in the cordial invitation of Tityrus to share his home, his fruit, chestnuts, and cheese, at least for the night.

Thus understood, the poem contains no allegory. It has no background in Theocritus, and it is surprisingly free from echoes of Theocritean diction and phrasing. It is a thoroughly Italian pastoral. The god is, of course, Octavian. But if late Greek thought had identified kings and gods, and if for over a century before Virgil the family of Octavian and Julius Caesar had traced its lineage to the goddess Venus, there is no shock for the Roman reader in the divinity of Octavian. As such a god, perhaps, Octavian had been worshiped by a Roman farmer, such as Tityrus, on his farm. But later generations refused to leave this poem free from allegory. If one turns up any early printed edition of Virgil with commentary one may easily discover the way in which Petrarch, Boccaccio, and Mantuanus understood this poem. Even in modern interpretations the older views often survive: Tityrus is Virgil, or Tityrus is a slave of Virgil, Virgil himself in that case being the rich master at Rome. And the commentator then struggles heroically with the difficulties in which he has thus involved himself. In even more extravagant allegorical interpretations of early days the two sweethearts of Tityrus are said to be Rome and Mantua, or else the two conflicting political parties of Virgil's day, and Tityrus' change of sweethearts then typifies Virgil's own abandonment of the republican cause for that of the triumvirs.

It is this allegorical interpretation of the Virgilian eclogue foisted upon the poems by post-Virgilian commentators that explains the pervasive allegory in the Latin eclogues of Italian poets in the Middle Ages and early Renaissance, and in the pastorals in the vernacular of various European countries later. For them nearly everything in Virgil contained covert allusion. So Petrarch, in one of his letters referring to his own Latin eclogues, writes: "This kind of poetry is one that cannot be understood unless a key to it is furnished by the person who constructed it. So, as I would not have you weary yourself to no purpose, I must give you a brief outline, first of what I say, then of what I mean by it." It was not merely the real Virgil, but the manufactured Virgil of intervening centuries, that determined the eclogue in these later days. This ultra-allegorical interpretation is Roman in origin. It may have begun even before Virgil's death. It found a moderate excuse for its existence in the manifest violation of the pastoral illusion in various poems. But it met with no inconsiderable resistance even among early Roman commentators on Virgil, and of these opposing forces the commentary of Servi-

us contains abundant evidence. Even on this first eclogue
Servius remarks, with commendable shrewdness, that Tityrus
is Virgil "when the sense demands it." This is only the grammarian's way of expressing what, in terms of true appreciation, becomes a transference of the poet's experience to Tityrus. And in such an appreciation the first eclogue is Virgil's
first forward step in the Romanization of late Greek poetry.

A national and patriotic interest permeates the Messianic
eclogue. The shepherd's rhyme pursues a loftier theme. Virgil becomes the mouthpiece of the Cumaean Sibyl, and with
hopeful expectancy predicts a new era. The new age is to be
introduced at the birth of a child. The ravages of civil war,
social corruption, moral decay shall give place to perfect inno-
cence and joy. The crime of the nation shall be blotted out
and the world set free from fear. At the child's birth

> The untilled earth with wandering ivies wild
> Shall mingle spikenard, and from bounteous breast
> Pour forth her lilies and Egyptian balm;
> The flock shall come unguided to the fold
> Flowing with milk; nor shall the feeding sheep
> At the huge lion tremble; fragrant flowers
> Shall from thy cradle spring; the viper's brood
> Shall perish, every baneful herb shall fail,
> And orient spices by the wayside bloom.

As the child grows to manhood and "the scriptured story
spells of glorious heroes and the mighty deeds his father
wrought," the earth shall provide food for man without human labor, and "when in after-time the strengthening years
have made thee man," trader, husbandman, artisan shall
cease to be. The child itself shall have a life divine, and the
new age shall witness once again men walking with gods.

The poem was prompted by the political compact made at
Brundisium in 40 B.C. Maecenas and Pollio acted as agents
for Octavian and Antony in putting an end, temporarily, to
civil dissension. Pollio himself became the consul of the year.

Antony married the sister of Octavian. To Octavian and Scribonia a child was born in the same year after the composition of the poem; doubtless the expectant parents hoped for a male heir, but their offspring proved to be a girl, later notorious in the *chroniques scandaleuses* of court circles.

The child of the poem is a wonder-child. It smiles upon its parents at birth. If it is called the offspring of Jove, that may be only in so far as all kings are children of Jove. In any case it is itself destined to godship. The concreteness of the expression which describes the child as reading of its father's exploits and ruling a world pacified by its father's valor points to a human wonder-child, and indubitably to the expected issue of Octavian and Scribonia. Through the apparent allusion to the royal lineage of the child, the fourth eclogue stimulated the production of court poetry in the reigns of Nero and of Charles the Great. Yet one may best realize such poetic value as the poem possesses by thinking primarily of a symbolical child, given definiteness of outline by covert allusions to the expected heir of the ruling family. Thus Virgil's friend and patron is complimented. But the Roman reader was inspired and elevated by the atmosphere of mysticism, by diction and phraseology familiar to him from the oracles of the Cumaean Sibyl in which the promise of a new age was heralded in the birth of a child, a great king, whom God was to send from the sun, and whose advent was to put an end to evil war. Those who in later years found in the child the Messiah were much nearer the spiritual value of the poem than either Virgil's contemporaries, who quarreled over the identification of the infant with various progeny of the year 40 B.C., or modern scholars, who, with vast erudition, trace the ideas of the eclogue back to oriental cosmogony and mythology. Sorrow for the sin of the first century is blended with hopeful expectancy of a regenerated people and a reinvigorated morale under the leadership of Octavian.

As a pastoral the poem has little justification or merit. It falls just short of the implication that the birth of the child is greeted with acclaim by shepherds. Its rustic detail is incidental and accidental. The spirit and the diction are the high style of oracular mystery and dignity. As a poem it marks the birth of the author of the *Georgics* and the *Aeneid*, his emancipation from the pretty trivialities of the pastoral to the higher function of spiritual earnestness and patriotic endeavor.

II. THE GEORGICS

Hail, O Saturn's land,
Mother of all good fruits and harvests fair,
Mother of men! I for thy noble sake
Attempt these old and famous themes and dare
Unseal an age-long venerated spring
And uplift Hesiod's song o'er Roman towers (ii. 173–76).

Ardent love of the motherland and mother-country prompted Virgil to write a manual of husbandry. The work was completed and read to Octavian before the middle of 29 B.C., and its composition occupied seven years, if we are to credit the biographical tradition. That Maecenas, and indirectly, Octavian, put pressure upon Virgil to write the poem is hinted in the prelude to the third book (vs. 41). Doubtless agriculture had been interrupted by the civil wars. As early as 37 B.C. Octavian may have begun his far-sighted policy of regenerating Italy, and may have included in his plans special provisions for rural improvements. Yet when such plans came to actual fruition, in the next decade, there is conspicuously little evidence of his appreciation of the economic value of rural Italy. It is idle to quote the fictitious speech put in the mouth of Maecenas by the historian Dio Cassius (lii. 27–28), in which Maecenas is represented as advocating a large standing army and urges Octavian, in 29 B.C., to sell confiscated properties, putting the land under cultivation by selling it to owners who will cultivate it themselves and acquire capital. If Maecenas ever suggested such a policy, the context of the speech in Dio Cassius clearly indicates that his main interest was in providing income to support a standing army, not in promoting the comfort of the rural population. When we find, therefore, in the poem a composite of traditional precepts, handed down by generations of pragmatic writers on husbandry, and of noble enthusiasm for Italy, we must admit that Virgil is still enslaved by the literary tradition of Hellenistic Greece, though here, at last, he has infused into it a degree of personal enthusiasm and poetic power which lift the poem far above anything that Greece produced in the field of didactic poetry. He is ambitious to become a Roman Hesiod. In fact, he vitalizes the quaint simplicity of Hesiod with the spiritual vigor of Lucretius, and the monotonous verse of Lucretius' philosophical poem is replaced by variously modulated hexameters in which the art of versification reaches its highest point of development.

The *Works and Days* of Hesiod, near the very beginning of Greek literature, was written at a time when verse, rather than prose, was the natural means of expression. It was prompted by a family quarrel. Perses, an idle and spendthrift brother of the poet, obtained the larger share of the patrimony by bribery of the overlords of Boeotia who ruled the country. The poem is a letter of remonstrance addressed to Perses. An allegory in which Discord and Honest Competition are contrasted serves to admonish Perses to relinquish wrangling in the courts and submit the case to impartial arbitrators. The myth of Pandora explains the presence of evil in mankind. The account of the five ages traces the gradual increase of this evil and the desperate state of the present. The fable of the hawk and the nightingale condemns violence and injustice. General precepts follow, emphasizing the dignity of work and the value of virtue. Then, more specifically, agriculture and trading by sea are offered as means of escaping from want and misery. Neither topic is treated systematically; technical advice and quaint maxims are curiously intermingled. More general precepts follow, touching on the smaller matters of moral and social life, and dwindling off into a rather full account of the lucky and unlucky days of the month.

To this strange cento Virgil's work on husbandry bears no

direct resemblance in form or substance. The description of the five ages in Hesiod probably suggested the Virgilian lines on the transition from the reign of Saturn to the reign of Jove; the description of the plough in Virgil's first book is manifestly abbreviated from Hesiod's fuller statement; a brief paragraph on the lucky and unlucky days is indebted for its facts, indirectly, to Democritus, but the theme may have been suggested by Hesiod; the storm in Virgil's first book is a companion piece to the Hesiodic description of winter. Such limited indebtedness makes us wonder why Virgil repeatedly declares that he "is bringing home to his native land the Muses' song from their Boeotian hill." Obviously it is because Hesiod and didactic poetry were synonymous terms, and more particularly because the Hellenistic period worshiped Hesiod as its patron divinity.

The Hesiodic tradition was continued and modified by Empedocles, the philosopher of the fifth century. Primarily interested in presenting his philosophical creed, he relieved the dryness of instruction by the saving grace of fervid personal conviction and by enthusiastic advocacy of his hobby. To him Lucretius owed in some measure the qualities that gave vigor and animation to the exposition of Epicurean philosophy. But in the Hellenistic period Greek treatises in verse on husbandry, bee culture, poisons and antidotes for poisons, astronomy, and astrology were not marked by any warmth of feeling such as gives literary value to Lucretius' *De rerum natura* and Virgil's *Georgics*. In this same late Greek period Aristotle and Theophrastus were writing in prose learned explanations of physical and biological phenomena. Contemporary poets who chose verse for the same purpose were not usually scientists or specialists in the chosen field. Their treatises are often mere compilations, sometimes mere versifications of earlier treatises in prose. The verse is a mere sugar coating, or, from a practical standpoint, assists the memory to

retain the facts. The cultivation of didactic poetry is the tribute of a scholarly age to its literary deity, Hesiod.

When the Hellenistic poet, Aratus, in the third century
B.C., came to write his didactic poem, *Phaenomena*, on the
stars, he made himself a man of one book, paraphrasing the
prose work of a scientist of the preceding century, Eudoxus.
Virgil, in his *Georgics*, was a man of many books. He was
covering in succession a variety of topics: the tillage of the
fields, the indications of stormy and fair weather that affect
the farmers' plans, the culture of trees and of the vine, the
care of various animals, and bee culture. Earlier treatises in
Latin by Cato in the second century and by Virgil's older contemporary, Varro, were directly drawn upon, and, in the parts
of the poem dealing with agriculture and the care of animals,
furnished the substantial framework. But these prose works
in Latin were often amplified from Greek sources, such as
Aristotle's *History of Animals*, Theophrastus' *History of
Plants*, and other unknown Greek authorities. Much of this
Greek material came to Virgil indirectly, perhaps, through
handbooks or encyclopedias, though when he discussed the
signs of the weather he abbreviated directly the *Diosemeia* of
Aratus, which formed an integral part of the *Phaenomena* of
that poet. It was Virgil's task to "adorn with the flowers of
poetry," as his devoted admirer, Columella, in the first century A.D., phrased it, these pragmatic accounts of the farmer's
various activities. The details of his procedure are not easily
described, apart from the Latin text, but the result is an accomplishment far greater than his relatively weak refashioning of Theocritus in many of Virgil's *Eclogues*. And obviously, the poetizing of prose is a different undertaking from his
earlier effort.

His close dependence, for matters of fact, upon these
prose sources is manifest. Sometimes over considerable paragraphs he follows the order of Cato or Varro, reproducing

even details of sentence structure. Often, however, the sequence in his Latin source is broken by amplification from Greek sources. These matters of fact are then transmuted into poetry by the substitution of poetic diction or by poetic epithets, or enhanced by similes or other imagery. In this transmutation, however, the remarkable feature is that this imagery is not always the free invention of his own fancy. More often the prose of Cato or of Aristotle calls to his mind, through associations not only of thought, but sometimes of mere sound, phrase and diction of Lucretius or of Catullus or other Latin poets, and on occasion even of his own earlier poetical expression. The source hunter delights to describe the total effect, figuratively, as a mosaic, or as melting old metal and molding it into a new form, apparently overlooking the fact that these two figures represent, each of them, an entirely different process and result. In the *Georgics,* although one topic is clearly divided from another, and frequent digressions interrupt artistically the sequence of orderly exposition, the total effect is not of a mosaic, but of a completely fused mass in which fact and fancy may be imitative rather than original, but the resultant whole is inimitable. For his *Eclogues* Virgil did not thumb his Theocritus; he had absorbed the idyls. In the *Georgics,* probably, he had not similarly absorbed agricultural manuals; more likely he turned often to his books for information, but once he had found the facts, the same retentive memory and the same quick association of sound and sense that led to the fusion of various Theocritean idyls into one eclogue, in the *Georgics* issued in the artistic blending of a vastly greater store of material into a whole that moved and inspired the reader as the weaker composition of the pastorals never could.

As a didactic poem the *Georgics* has little to offer from our present standpoint. The poet's art is revealed only through the Latin text, in diction and imagery and versification. We may briefly illustrate, however, the structural features, the descriptive power, and the spirit that animates the composition.

Virgil's exposition is well ordered and clear. It falls into four books and four sharply defined topics: agriculture, arboriculture, animal culture, and bee culture. Within these four books the treatment is not conspicuously systematic or well proportioned. The first book is better in this respect than the others, and perhaps for that reason less interesting to the general reader. It passes from an orderly treatment of tillage to the signs of the weather by a natural and easy transition. The second book illustrates the restiveness of a poet seeking relief for himself and his reader in eloquent digressions from dry subject matter. After enumerating the various natural and artificial ways of propagating trees, he enlarges upon the trees native to various countries, only to burst forth in a eulogy of Italy, in which trees and vines are quite incidental in the landscape. An abrupt transition brings him to the aptitudes of soils, in which, again, logical fitness is somewhat violated by including soils adapted to grain and pasturage. Then, in an intricate passage of considerable length, he treats of the vine as grown in the vineyard, supported by the trees, and though vines are in the foreground of the treatment, he often shifts to the culture of the trees, obtaining at least artistic variety, if at the expense of logical order. Though the olive was announced in the prologue as an important topic, it is now dismissed in five verses as a simple matter. Fruit trees and other varieties are each summarily handled in thirty verses, from which the poet emerges into the famous eulogy of country life that concludes the book.

In the third book the animals are divided into horned cattle and horses on the one hand, and smaller cattle, such as sheep and goats. The former class is more fully treated than the latter. A digression on the effect of sexual passion on all animal life interrupts and relieves the first section. In connection with breeding, the poet selects the cow and the stallion, the female of one variety and the male of the other, but subsequently merges the horned cattle and horses, with some confusion. Then, more clearly, he discusses the early training of oxen and horses in distinct paragraphs, only to fuse again the two themes, giving prominence to the bull in the description of animal passion and handling cursorily the other class. In the second portion, dealing with lesser animals, there is both more system and more digression. The pasturing of flocks leads to pictures of a shepherd's summer in Libya and a Scythian shepherd's winter. The account of the pestilence that concludes the book, in imitation of Lucretius, includes other animals than those of interest to the farmer and becomes almost an independent narrative. The fourth book starts with hives, passes on to a brief apology for omitting a treatment of gardens, then returns to the bees, their nature and diseases, and, in connection with the rearing of bees from the carcasses of cattle, concludes with an epyllium, the story of Aristaeus.

Though some of this irregularity of treatment may be due to his prose sources, much of it arises from a poet's effort to relieve the tedium of exposition. This, of course, is most apparent in the numerous digressions, but may be discerned even in the handling of dry facts, as the poet emphasizes the logically unimportant and dwells upon the picturesque, or secures variety at the expense of comprehensiveness.

In the treatment of dry fact the poetizing of prose appears mainly in diction and imagery. Varro directs that the threshing floor should be of solid earth, well rammed down, especially if it is clay, lest the heat of summer crack it and grains of corn get lost in the fissures, letting in water and discovering holes for mice and ants. To prevent this, he says, people frequently drench it with the watery juice of olives, as the latter is poison to weeds, ants, and moles. These prosy instructions become, in Virgil:

> . . . . To smooth the threshing-floor
>
> . . . .
>
> . . . . face with close-packed clay, lest weeds push through
> Or the worn surface crack; wherewith arrives
> Many a pest to plague thee: such as he
> Of subterranean house and granary,
> The small mouse; or, though prisoned by his eyes,
> The mole digs deep his bed; or lurking toad
> Peers from his hole; and many a prodigy
> The earth unnumbered breeds: the weevil tribes
> Whose legions ravage the high heap of corn,
> And ants, whose fear is age and poverty (i. 178 ff).

Translations cannot accurately reproduce the process: "Prisoned by his eyes" is a flat mistranslation and introduces a figure of which Virgil was quite innocent. But this one passage must serve to suggest the general fashion in which, as Virgil here gives poetic vigor to a prosaic enumeration of mole, ant, and weevil, so everywhere, by changing passivity to action, by suggestive adjective or other descriptive phrase, by selection and amplification of the picturesque, he raises the commonplace to the higher level of poetry.

In such passages Virgil sticks closely to the facts and deftly animates and ornaments the exposition with slight modifications of the prose sources. His descriptive power is more fully exhibited in other places, in which, still well within the limits of the immediate subject matter, he is moved by a detail in the pragmatic account and rises to flights of fancy of wider sweep and greater range. It is noteworthy that extended flights are seldom stimulated by such subjects as agriculture or the care of plants; oftener the animals of the third and fourth books stir the poet's imagination. Life and movement are already making a strong appeal to the future author of the *Aeneid*. And it may be doubted whether in the epic there are purely descriptive passages that quite equal in value these pictures of animals in action in the *Georgics*. The description of the horse in iii. 75 is hardly more than a spirited amplification of Varro, but we may suspect from it that Virgil was reluctant, in the fifth book of the *Aeneid,* to substitute a boat race for the chariot race of the *Iliad*. Mythical horses relieve the poet from the strain of poetizing Varro's prose. Again in vss. 179 ff., with slight hints from Varro, Virgil gives tremendous vigor to his account of the war horse and race horse, adorning it with a Homeric simile:

> See that thy chosen courser early learns
> To face proud warriors in arms, to bear
> The scream of trumpet and the thundering
> Of chariots as they pass; in the stall, too,
> Let him hear clanking bit and bridle chain.
> He must exult if his dear rider's voice
> Shout in his praise, and love the friendly hand
> That claps his neck so loud. These noises all
> From the first day that weans him from his dam
> Should often meet his ear. Put soft bits too
> Between his tender lips while yet his frame
> Is trembling, weak and scarcely touched of time.
> After three summers past, the fourth at hand,
> Train him to gallop circles and to prance
> With even-sounding step, to paw the air
> With freely-lifted knees. His work should show
> Strong effort; afterward the racer's speed
> Will shame the winds, as under loosened rein
> Along the open course he skims, he flies,
> Scarce printing his light hoof-tips in the sand.
> 'Tis like that wind from Hyperborean clime
> That charging down o'er Scythia's wintry plains
> Scatters the rainless clouds; the harvest fields
> Of bending corn and liquid lakes outspread
> Heave in the ceaseless blast; the forest's top
> Screams loud, and long waves pound the sandy shore,
> As onward sweeps the gale o'er flood and field.

Into his description of the vanquished bull Virgil puts a depth
of feeling that Varro suggests but hardly realizes, and again
works his way out from the prose of Varro to an epic simile
that Homer had used to mark the onset of the Greeks at Troy:

> Yonder the bulls, exchanging many a wound,
> Do battle mightily; dark streaming gore
> Their bodies bathes, as with opposèd horns
> Struggling and thrusting they make bellowings loud,
> While groves and vaulted skies the din prolong.
> No longer now the rivals in that war
> Dwell in one field; the fallen chief withdraws,
> Bound to far exile in some land unknown,
> Lamenting loud his shame, and many a wound
> The victor gave; but mourning more
> The loss of her he loved, still unavenged,
> He quits with backward glance his native fields.
> Henceforth he tests and trains his vanquished powers
> With painful care; he sullenly reclines
> On bare stones for a bed, and for his food
> Crops thorny leafage or sharp-pointed reed.
> He puts himself to proof; he disciplines
> The fury of his horns; butts at a tree;
> Would with his fierce thrusts wound the passing wind,
> And tosses up loose turf, rehearsing war.
> Soon gathering all his force, with strength renewed
> He flings his banners forth, provokes the war,
> And hurls him headlong on the slumbering foe.
> 'Tis thus some huge wave from the open sea
> Begins far off to whiten, then uplifts
> Its swelling breast and swiftly landward rolls,
> Roars monstrous through the rocks and forward falls
> Like a great mountain, while the watery deep
> Boils up in whirling, eddying surge and flings
> Aloft in air a cloud of darkening sand (iii. 220 ff.).

With only the barest hints from Aristotle and Varro, who are
describing the sending forth of a colony of bees, Virgil practices his 'prentice hand at painting a war scene in the battle of
the bees. The actual warfare of the last four books of the

Aeneid could not be relieved, as it is here, by his humorous appreciation of the miniature combatants and their quick dispersal by a cloud of dust:

> But sometimes they declare a war: for oft
> Between two kings a fatal strife begins
> Tumultuous, and one discerns from far
> The anger of the mob, whose hearts leap up
> All fury for the fight. A loud alarm
> Like hoarse-tongued blare of martial brass
> Rebukes the lingerers. A wild cry is heard
> In semblance of the trumpet's billowy sound.
> Then comes the raging charge: their little wings
> Glitter, their stings are sharp as javelins.
> They grapple limb with limb, and round each chief,
> Each king's pavilion, there is tug of war,
> As with fierce war-cry each defies the foe.
> In such wise, when some rainless day in spring
> Invites them to the open fields, they burst
> Impetuous from their portals, and the bees
> Join battle high in air; a mighty din
> Arises; they roll up confusedly
> In one great globe, then drop they headlong down;
> Not thicker is the fall of wind-blown hail
> Nor shower of acorns from storm-shaken tree.
> The chieftains in the midmost war are known
> By their far-shining wings and show abroad
> How vast a valor such small breasts contain;
> So stubbornly they hold their ground, until
> The mightier victor of this host or that
> Compels to panic flight his routed foe.
> Yet all this stir of passion and fierce fight
> If but a little dust be tossed in air,
> Will be subdued, dispersed, and die away (iv. 67 ff.).

Among the lesser animals, somewhat indirectly connected with his main theme, the gadfly (iii. 146 ff.) and the snake (iii. 416 ff.) move him to spirited digressions; the latter passage, though inspired by the Hellenistic didactic poet, Nicander, recalls the fearsome dragon of *The Gnat*.

When nature appeals to Virgil her turbulent and boister-
ous aspects, rather than her quieter moods, stir his imagination. The storm (i. 316 ff.) awakens in his mind recollections
of Lucretian phrasing and theme. The care of sheep and
goats in iii. 339 ff. leads him to portray the life of Libyan
herdsmen briefly, but a companion piece, which with rare
fidelity and fulness of detail sets in bold relief the dour experience of Scythian tribes in the far north (iii. 349 ff.), carries
him far afield into a description of winter and of local manners and customs:

> Far different is man's life where Scythia's tribes
> By the wide waters of Maeotis stray,
> Where Danube rolls its troubled, tawny waves,
> And where the ridge of Thracian Rhodope
> To southward curves. All cattle there are kept
> In well-closed barns; for in that land is seen
> No grass, no greenwood fair, but all the plain
> Lies shapeless in great banks of snow,
> Frozen deep down and drifted seven ells high.
> 'Tis winter without end, and ceaseless blows
> The frosty northern gale. Seldom the sun
> Can break the dismal gloom—nor when his team
> Bear him along th' ethereal sky, nor when
> He dips his sinking car in crimsoned seas.
> On the swift-coursing river suddenly
> Congeals a solid crust, and soon the stream
> Sustains the rolling weight of iron wheels,
> Once a ship's channel, now a wagon road.
> Brass cauldrons burst asunder, oftentimes
> The garments stiffen on one's body, casks of wine
> Are broken piecemeal with an axe, whole ponds
> Are turned to solid ice, and icicles
> Upon a man's rough beard grow stiff and strong.
> The whole wide realm of air continually
> Is thick with falling snow, the flocks and herds
> Perish, the mighty forms of oxen stand
> Frost covered, and a line of huddling deer
> Lie torpid under heavy snow, just seen

By their protruding horns. In hunting these
No hounds run forth, no net or snare is laid,
No crimson feathers cheat the trembling herd;
But while they vainly breast the drifted snows
Men slay them at close quarters with sharp steel.
They fall loud moaning, and their conquerors
With shouts of exultation bear them home.
For in large caverns, burrowed underground,
The hunters live in safety and at ease.
Oak boughs heaped high, whole logs of giant elm
They roll upon the hearth to feed the blaze.
Long nights they pass in wassail and good cheer
And imitate our vintage with full bowls
Of bitter cider and strong, yeasty brews.
Such is the tameless race of mighty men
That keep their flocks beneath the arctic star,
And by Cimmerian tempests buffeted
In tawny furs of beasts their bodies clothe.

The qualities of the Dutch *genre* picture have often been re-
marked in this portrayal, but equally striking is Virgil's ultimate diversion into the theme of the huntsmen and their joyous revels amid the gloom of winter. One may suspect that
he yearns to get away from plants and animals and nature
into the more vital experiences of human beings.

This desire finds release in the episodic conclusion of the
poem. Originally intending to celebrate Cornelius Gallus in
an epilogue to the *Georgics,* Virgil was forced, by the disgrace
and suicide of his friend in 26 B.C., to substitute the short epic
narrative of Aristaeus' mishap and the final recovery of his
bees. If Virgil was the author of *Ciris,* the pathetic epyllium
on Aristaeus marks a revival of his interest in this Hellenistic
type of poetry. Later, the tragic epyllium on Dido was more
deftly organized as part of the action of the national epic.
The story of Aristaeus remains an episode.

An ancient notion that bees were generated from the de-
caying carcasses of cattle leads Virgil to explain how this

novel method of propagation was discovered. Aristaeus, child
of a river-goddess, Cyrene, has lost his swarm of bees, and
seeks his divine mother, much as Achilles did Thetis, with
plaintive reproaches because she neglects her son and allows
the fruits of his industry to perish. The mother-goddess is in
the river bed, surrounded by water nymphs who are spinning
and listening to love stories of the gods. The poet lingers over
the scene, and in enumerating the nymphs anticipates Milton
in his fondness for musical proper names:

> Ligeia, Xantho, with Phyllodoce
> And Drymo, o'er whose snowy necks flowed down
> Their gleaming hair, Cydippe and gold-tressed
> Lycorias, the one a virgin free,
> The other to the labors lately come
> Of motherhood. There were the sisters twain
> Clio and Beroe, ocean's daughters both,
> In golden zone and gorgeous mantles clad;
> Deiopea, Opis, Ephyre
> And fleet-foot Arethusa, who at last
> Had laid her arrows by.

Through the intercession of these nymphs Cyrene is moved to
receive her son. The waters part and give him entrance to an
underworld where he sees the watery kingdom of his mother's
realm, vast rivers flowing beneath the earth, each the counterpart of the streams he has known in the world above. After
a sumptuous banquet, Cyrene instructs her son to seek out
Proteus, bind him fast as he changes into manifold forms, and
learn from him the reason for the loss of the bees. Aristaeus
finds Proteus herding his seals and resting in his cavern by
the sea. Proteus, after vain resistance, resumes his natural
form and explains to Aristaeus that Eurydice, once amorously
pursued by Aristaeus, was bitten by a snake. Her death, Orpheus' distress, his self-frustrated effort to recover Eurydice
from the lower world, Orpheus' own death at the hands of the
spiteful Thracian maidens who resented his devotion to Eury-

dice, are indirectly due to Aristaeus. The poet dwells upon the pathetic elements of the story. The picture of the other world, mainly conventional, is drawn in verses that later were useful in the broader fresco of the sixth *Aeneid:*

> The lifeless phantoms and thin shadows came,
> Loving and pitiful; like flocks they seemed
> Of birds that hide in leafy boughs, when night
> Or wintry tempest drives them from the hills.
> Mothers and husbands came, with lifeless forms
> Of high-souled heroes, boys, unwedded maids,
> And youthful manhood given to the tomb
> Before fond parents' eyes.

The fault of Orpheus in looking back at Eurydice and losing her at the threshold of the upper world is

> A fault to be forgiven, could Hell forgive.

But Ovidian epigram is rare. The emphasis is on the unending devotion of Orpheus, still crying "Eurydice" in the agony of his gruesome death. Cyrene suggests expiatory offerings to the wood nymphs, who are offended by the death of Eurydice and by Aristaeus' unconscious guilt, and from the oxen sacrificed as victims the bees are generated which replace the lost swarm of Aristaeus and restore his prosperity.

Probably there is little Virgilian art and material in this narrative. The Latin poet reveals his preoccupation with events that move to pity and compassion, but in substance and in composition he reflects a Greek model now lost to us. In form the episode recalls the structure of Catullus' epyllium on the marriage of Peleus and Thetis, into which is interwoven, or rather inset, the story of Ariadne and Theseus, equally Hellenistic in every feature of style and technique. Here, as there, story within story, framework and picture within the frame, provide a neatly interlocked form of composition. The story of Orpheus and Eurydice is the central point of interest. It is bracketed by the two interviews with Cyrene, and these in turn are framed between the two chapters of Aristaeus' personal experiences, the loss and the recovery of his bees. Yet logically, the narrative proceeds smoothly and uninterruptedly through these various chapters of action and of narrative in the chronological sequence of events. Later, in the story of Camilla's exploits and tragic fate in the eleventh book of the *Aeneid,* Virgil varied the technique of the battle scenes of the last four books of the epic by adopting the same structure, and there, probably, employed material almost entirely of his own invention.

The concern with human suffering in the episode of Aristeus is paralleled throughout the *Georgics* by constant sympathy with the pathetic experiences of animals. The vanquished bull in the passage quoted above, and the elaborate account of the pestilence at the end of the third book are typical examples of Virgil's quick sensitiveness to suffering. In spite of the prosy material, the *Georgics* is a poem of feeling as well as of action. And it is the strength of the poet's own feeling that gives it poetic value.

Modern critics emphasize Virgil's consciousness of the dignity of labor. They remark that this exaltation of work is much more prominent in Hesiod's poem, but that it is artfully insinuated in the *Georgics.* It may be so, but I think an unprejudiced reader of the poem, in one sitting, leaves that reading with an impression only of Virgil's overpowering love for Italy as motherland and mother country. If it be objected that this strong feeling finds expression only in digressions from the main subject matter, the number and extent of these digressions and the splendid eloquence of the passages only reinforce the view that Virgil is restless under the compulsion of poetizing agricultural treatises and continuing the tradition of didactic poetry, and that he finds relief, not only for his reader, but for himself, in outbursts which glorify Rome and Italy. For these his prose sources furnished no hints, and in these, unlike the descriptive passages which we have hitherto considered, he is carried entirely beyond the natural scope of his subject matter.

As motherland, producing fruits and crops, Italy may be submerged in the larger generalization of all soil as productive of sustenance for man, but it is noteworthy that when Virgil starts from the broader theme, easily suggested by the subject of his poem, he soon betrays an interest in his immediate environment. The peace of country life, for him, is in sharp contrast with the civil conflicts that have thrown the nation into turmoil and confusion. The simplicity and honesty of rural life stimulate those virtues which the exemplars of earlier Roman history possessed, and through which they made Rome supreme, and these virtues are at odds with the vices that in Virgil's time endangered the permanence of Roman power. The way of salvation lies through Octavian:

> Gods of our fathers, and protecting powers
> That watch our native land, O Romulus,
> O Vesta, sacred mother, who dost guard
> Our Tuscan Tiber and Rome's Palatine,
> Fail not to grant that our young Prince restore
> The ruined world. Too long our blood is poured
> To wash away the sinful perjury
> Of King Laomedon. Already Heaven,
> Th' Olympian dwelling, envies us for thee,
> O Caesar, and complains thou still dost choose
> Triumphs on earth; for here both right and wrong
> Lie mingled and o'erthrown. So many wars
> Vex the whole world, so many monstrous shapes
> Of wickedness appear; no honor due
> Is given the sacred plough; our fields and farms,
> Their masters taken, rankly lie untilled;
> Our pruning-hooks are beaten in hot flames
> To tempered swords. Euphrates yonder stirs,
> There wild Germania, to impious war;
> Close-neighbored cities their firm leagues forswear
> And rush to arms. The war-god pitiless
> Moves wrathful through the world (i. 498 ff.).

The oft-quoted eulogy of the farmer's life (ii. 458 ff.), incidentally interesting as a mature version of the same theme in *The Gnat* (quoted above, pp. 28–29), contrasts the simplicity and virtue of rural life and the vicious bustle of the urban rich, but the general picture is vivified with details from contemporary history—the impious strife that stirs between brothers breaking faith, the barbarous host of Dacian raiders from the rebel shores of Danube—and the conclusion recalls the rugged character of primitive Italy and her early heroes:

> . . . . The husbandman upturns the glebe
> With well-curved share, inaugurating so
> The whole year's fruitful toil, by which he feeds
> His native land, his children's children too,
> His flocks and herds, and cattle worth his care.
> Ever the flocks flow on: the liberal year
> Teems with good apples, with the flock's increase,
> And sheaves of tasselled corn; the furrowed fields
> Bestow in bursting barns their goodly store.
> When winter comes at last, the olive mills
> Receive the sacred fruit, the roving swine
> Bring home full paunch of acorns, greenwood trees
> Drop nut and berry, many autumn fruits
> Still linger, and on sun-kissed, rocky slopes
> Some sweetened clusters hang. The livelong year
> His gathered children to his kisses cling.
> His honest house lives chastely; full of milk
> Is all his herd, and on his meadows fair
> The lusty he-goats lock their butting horns.
> Such master keeps full well each festal day.
>
> . . . .
>
> Such way of life the ancient Sabines knew,
> And Remus with his twin; thus waxed the power
> Of the Etrurian cities; thus rose Rome
> The world's chief jewel, and with towering wall
> Compassed in one her hills and strongholds seven (ii. 513 ff.).

And not merely the material power of Rome and the material resources of the land, but the beauty of the landscape, are comprehended in the passionate glorification of mother-country which emerges from a general description of various trees native to various lands:

> . . . . But neither flowering groves
> Of Media's realm, nor Ganges proud,
> Nor Lydian fountains flowing thick with gold,
> Can match their glories with Italia;
> Not Bactria nor Ind, nor all the wealth
> Of wide Arabia's incense-bearing sands.
> This land by Jason's bulls with breath of flame
> Never was ploughed, nor planted with the teeth
> Of monstrous dragon, nor that harvest grew
> Of helmèd warrior-heads and myriad spears.
> But full-eared corn and goodly Massic wine
> Inhabit here, with olives and fat herds.
> The war-horse here with forehead high in air
> Strides o'er the plain; here roam thy spotless flocks,
> Clitumnus; and for noblest sacrifice,
> The snow-white bull, bathed oft in sacred stream,
> Leads Roman triumphs to the house of Jove.
> Here Spring is endless and the Summer glows
> In months not half her own. Twice in the year
> The herds drop young, and twice the orchard bears
> The labor of its fruit. But tigers fell
> And the fierce lion's brood are absent here.
> No deadly aconite deceives the hand
> That gathers herbs; nor in enormous folds
> Or lengthened twine the scaly snake upcoils.
> Behold the famous cities!—what vast toil
> Upreared them!—and the host of strongholds piled
> By hand of man on out-hewn precipice,
> While swift streams under ancient bulwarks flow.
> Why tell of two salt seas that wash her shore
> Above, below; her multitude of lakes—
> Thee, Larius, chiefest, and Benacus where
> Are swelling floods and billows like the sea?
> Why name that haven where the lofty mole
> Locks in the Lucrine lake, while with loud rage
> The baffled waters roar, and Julian waves
> Echo from far the sea's retreating tide,
> And through the channels of Avernus pours

Th' invading Tuscan main? In this rich land
Deep veins of silver show, and ores for brass,
With lavish gold. Hence sprang the warlike breed
Of Marsi, hence the proud Sabellian clans,
Ligurians to hardship seasoned well,
And Volscian spearmen; hence the Decii,
Camilli, Marii, immortal names,
The Scipios, in wars implacable,
And Caesar, thou, the last, the prince of all,
Who now victorious on far Asia's end,
Art holding back from Roman citadels
The Indian weakling. Hail O Saturn's land,
Mother of all good fruits and harvests fair,
Mother of men! (ii. 136 ff.)

Not even a highly rhetorical style can wholly conceal the warm enthusiasm and genuine feeling for his native land that Virgil here expresses. He is clearly ready to throw off the shackles of Hellenistic literature and fill a Greek mold with Italian and Roman material. The poet and patriot needs only the proper subject matter in which to realize his matured power—the story of a people and their large-souled leaders.

THE NATIONAL EPIC

I. THE SOCIAL AND POLITICAL BACKGROUND

In the Messianic eclogue and in the *Georgics* there are intimations of the national epic. Elevated thought raises the fourth eclogue far above the normal level of the pastoral. Fervid enthusiasm for the sturdy virtues of the Italian people and for the varied beauty and fertility of Italian soil and scenery relieves the rigid instruction in husbandry of the *Georgics*. Constantly, in his output during the decade from about 40 to 30 B.C., Virgil, though working in Greek molds, infuses the spirit and material of his own race and nation. Growing intimacy with Maecenas and his circle must have provided the poet with an intelligent outlook upon the dangers confronting the state and a sympathetic knowledge of the policies devised to overcome social evils. A great historical crisis in the affairs of Rome was recognized by Augustus and his prime minister, and in the decade from 30 to 20 B.C. they made organized efforts to avert imminent disaster. From this crisis the *Aeneid* issues naturally and inevitably, and it was meant to react upon the critical situation which gave it birth. Virgil intended to teach and to delight, not so much from any conscious conformity to ancient theory regarding the moral as well as aesthetic value of poetry, but simply because his environment impelled him to make poetry, in part at least, the handmaiden of the state.

Virgil's epic was begun about 29 B.C., and at the time of his death, in 19 B.C., it had not yet received his finishing touches. The first three books of Horace' odes were published in 23 B.C. These lyrical poems occupied much of Horace' time between the years 30 and 23. The general conception, therefore, of the *Aeneid,* and the elaboration of a considerable part of it, were contemporaneous with the composition of Horace' volume of short poems.

In the odes at the beginning of his third book, the so-called "Roman Odes," Horace is no longer a skilful versifier of the light themes of love and wine. He is preoccupied with the serious case of Roman social and religious life. Introducing himself as the high priest of the Muses, he addresses to the younger generation songs never heard before. The six odes that follow this solemn prelude are drawn from what Mr. Austin Dobson calls Horace' didactic tap, but seldom elsewhere does the poet indulge with such passionate intensity his pessimistic outlook upon environing social life. In the first five odes he exalts character and intelligence above wealth and brute force. In the sixth ode he mercilessly depicts the depravity of domestic life, and traces the cause of it to the neglect of the national religion. Dismantled temples and shrines, smoke-stained images of the gods, are the heritage left by civil war. Roman supremacy depends upon submission to divine control. Neglect of the gods spells ruin. The city rent by dissension has barely escaped destruction by the barbarians. This indifference to the national religion and consequent loss of divine protection, affects the family as well as the state. The age mothers crime. Home and family are the first victims. The state is a secondary sufferer. The Roman women delight in Greek dances, and even before marriage practice arts which qualify them for unfaithfulness after marriage, for shameful *liaisons* with shopkeeper and sea captain. From no such parents, says Horace, reverting to the past, sprang the men who stained the sea with Carthaginian blood, who brought low Pyrrhus and Antiochus and Hannibal. The great conquerors of earlier days were the virile offspring of a farmer-soldiery. They ploughed the field, split and brought home the firewood at the bidding of stern mothers. The present generation is the last of three, each surpassing its predecessor in vicious qualities, and the fourth generation, yet unborn, destined to be the most vicious of all.

The general trend of Horace' preachment is, clearly, that the Rome of his day needs a religious and moral regeneration which can be achieved only by a reaction to the religious and moral ideals of the early days of the Roman republic.

Several times in these odes Horace refers directly to Augustus, more or less casually, but always in a very significant context. Persistency in righteous action, he says in the third ode, opens the way to immortality. It was character, and not mere physical strength or material resources, that enabled Pollux, Hercules, Romulus, Augustus to reach the starry heights of heaven. More implicit and infinitely more suggestive is the emperor's rôle in the fourth ode. The poet is invoking the Muses; he describes them as refreshing Augustus after his military campaigns. Then, without any explicit reference to Augustus, Horace ascribes to the Muses the gift of wisdom, a wisdom that, as he elaborates the idea, includes sweetness and light, executive clemency, and the reasonableness of moderation and self-control. The conflict of this wisdom with brute force, and its superiority, he illustrates from myth, from the victory of Jove over the Titans. At the conclusion of the myth he recurs to the text in a sharp contrast between strength devoid of wisdom and strength tempered with wisdom, the dominant qualities, respectively, it should be noted in passing, of Turnus and of Aeneas in the last six books of Virgil's epic. It is quite possible to infer from such a context that Augustus is the exemplar of this virtue of efficiency and sweet reasonableness, and that the battle of Jove and the Titans symbolizes the successful conflict of Augustus with the Titanic forces of civic disorder and social corruption. Such an inference seems to be justified when the poet, after a few more mythological examples, opens the next ode of the series with the words: "in Heaven Jove is king; on earth Augustus shall be held divine after his conquests in the far West and East." In any case, the active sympathy of Augustus with the ideas expressed in these Roman odes of Horace is easily apparent from the record of the emperor's achievements.

An authentic form of this record comes from the hand of the reformer and statesman himself. Near the end of the *Monumentum Ancyranum,* in which Augustus registers his gradual rise to power and lists his benefactions, stand these words:

In my sixth and seventh consulships (28, 27 B.C.), when I had extinguished the flames of civil war, having by universal consent become possessed of the sole direction of affairs, I transferred the republic from my power to the will of the senate and people of Rome. For which good service on my part I was called, by decree of the senate, Augustus, and the doorposts of my house were covered with laurels in the name of the state, and a civic crown was set up over my door, and a golden shield was placed in the *Curia Iulia,* which declared by its inscription that the senate and people of Rome gave it to me in recognition of my valor, clemency, justice, piety. After that time I took precedence of all in rank, but of power I had no more than those who were associated with me in the several magistracies.

These simple sentences have a deep significance. In the year 27, when Virgil had already begun his epic and Horace was at least planning, if not actually composing, his Roman odes, Octavian restored in form the government under which Rome throve when it dyed the sea with Carthaginian blood, and he assumed a title, Augustus, which Ovid tells us "our fathers used in place of *sanctus,* applying it to temples that had been dedicated according to ritual by the hands of priests." Thus Octavian linked himself to the religious, his government to the political past of Rome.

His conviction that the salvation of Rome lay in a moral and religious revival marks much of Augustus' activity in

social reform. As a mere boy of fifteen he was himself dedicated to the priesthood. He joined as an active member various
priestly colleges and sacred brotherhoods and increased their
material income and spiritual influence. In the year 28, possibly just after Horace wrote the sixth of his "Roman Odes,"
the emperor repaired eighty-two temples, perhaps the very
temples that Horace describes as dismantled in the Civil War.
The Roman pantheon was reinvigorated by selecting Apollo
and Diana as special patron divinities of the imperial family,
and by granting new honors and privileges to the Vestal Virgins, whose ranks were depleted by the prevailing indifference
to religious service. He took special pains to restore the old-
est forms of worship and to re-establish ancient religious
brotherhoods. So, for example, the primitive organization of
the Arval Brothers, a rural fraternity that had passed out of
ken during the Republic, was not only reinvested with its
ancient function of praying for the success of the crops, but
was given new dignity through the special privilege of praying
for the Emperor and the imperial household and the eternal
life of the Empire.

The problem of Roman redemption, however, was not
merely religious, but broadly social. Social tradition was pre-
served largely by patrician families and by the more prominent plebeian families. Both of these had been reduced in
numbers by the civil wars. Augustus recruited patrician families from the better families of plebeians, and assisted to new
life plebeian families by generous gifts to survivors which
enhanced their social position and made desirable marriages
possible for them. That patrician and plebeian alike might
never forget their glorious past, he set up in a hall of fame the
statues of the heroes of earlier days, often magnanimously
suppressing his personal feeling and honoring with statues
the enemies of his own family.

These religious and social reforms were wisely planned;

for they affected the younger generation and promised permanent results. Augustus, as well as Horace, addressed young men and maidens. But when, in addition to these reasonable remedial policies, Augustus undertook drastic legal prohibition of social evils, he met with opposition that led to postponement and compromise, and his measures, when passed, were generally evaded and seldom accomplished the results intended. The corruption of family life which Horace lashes in the sixth of his Roman Odes was particularly fatal, now that the Roman people were decimated by civil wars. Augustus saw the necessity of providing for the perpetuation of Roman stock with all the purity and probity of republican tradition. His measures were conceived early in his principate, but actual legislation was long deferred, until after the publication of the *Aeneid*. In general he endeavored to restrain illicit relations, to regulate divorce, and to promote marriage by the imposition of penalties upon bachelors and the bestowal of privileges upon fathers of children. The disease was too widespread and too deep-seated to be cured. The very consuls who proposed his laws for enforcing marriage were bachelors, and the imperial household itself was the subject of enough scandalous stories to encourage evasion of the Emperor's ordinances.

The term "romanticism" has sometimes been attached to Augustus' dominant idea, the idea of regenerating the present by a revival of old traditions and morals. But modern labels and modern parallels are somewhat misleading. The term is used in this case in the sense prevalent in German criticism, of a sentimental reaction to a better and happier past that occurs particularly "when distressing external events deprive the individual of the sense of stability and peace, when traditions are destroyed, and the ancient landmarks are removed." Obviously the conditions of Roman society after the civil dissensions of the earlier years of the century accord with the definition, but there is nothing specially novel, and certainly nothing peculiarly modern, in the idea underlying Augustus' reforms. It was hardly more than an expression of that conservatism which was ineradicably fixed in the Roman character. The notion that Rome stands or falls according as it preserves the tradition and character of its fathers was probably far from novel when Ennius uttered it in the third century. And Cicero's echo of the same thought during the very century of corrupting influences antedates the imperial policy. Though a historian and antiquarian naturally treats of the past, Varro's interest in writing a monumental history of the human and divine aspects of Roman achievement and experience in the middle of this century, and particularly his dedication of the religious chapters to Julius Caesar, as high priest of the nation, with manifest intent to counteract the weakening of religious belief and practice, sufficiently suggest that Augustus' ideas were in consonance with the views at least of the better men of an older generation. The only novelty was in making such ideas the basis of an aggressive and consistent domestic policy. And even in this respect Augustus, perhaps, was simply elaborating a thought that Julius Caesar may have cherished, but was too preoccupied with more immediate tasks to translate into effective action.

   In one important development the unbroken continuity of Roman tradition, religious and political, had long been sanctioned by divine authority, ratified by national policy, and promoted by individual effort. The oracles of the Sibyl were lost in the fire of 82 B.C. A commission was appointed to recover them from other copies in the cities of Greece and in Greek parts of Italy. In 18 B.C. Augustus ordered this edition to be re-edited, recopied, and deposited in the temple of Apollo on the Palatine. This careful cherishing by the state of these prophetic utterances is proof of the veneration and credence which they enjoyed in the minds of the nation. In these oracles Rome was guaranteed its possession of a world-empire on the ground that Trojan ancestors of the Roman people had brought with them to Rome the sacred images of the gods from the acropolis of Troy. So the religious tradition of Troy was continued in that of Rome, and consistent divine protection assured the permanence of the kingdom which Greeks had crushed only to see it rise again from the seven hills of Rome. The legend that associated the beginnings of Rome with Troy was current long before the third century B.C., but in the year 230 B.C., two centuries before Virgil began the *Aeneid*, it was officially recognized by the Roman state in so far as the government ratified an alliance with the Acarnanians, a Greek people, on the ground that the Acarnanians, alone of all the Greeks, had not fought against Troy. By the middle of the second century B.C. the fiction of Roman descent from Trojan ancestors was being used by patrician families at Rome to add luster to their names, and genealogical tables were eagerly constructed relating such families to the heroes of Trojan history.

The most notable case of this genealogical fiction is the family of Julius Caesar and Augustus, the Julian *gens*, which, as early as the second century, had persuaded itself that the name of the *gens* could be traced back to Ilus, the mythical founder of Ilium, after whom the son of Aeneas was named. The etymology which derives Iulius from Ilus seems to us comparable to the notorious relation of Moses to Middleborough, but it was quite acceptable to some Roman authorities. For it involved, as they argued, simply the addition of a single letter: Ilus plus "u" becomes Iulus, and the difference between the initial vowel and the initial consonant did not bother them. In accord with this fiction the coinage of the Julian family about 150 B.C. shows the head of Venus, divine mother of Aeneas. The practice spread among other Roman families,

and in the next century we find Varro and Atticus, in antiquarian studies, furnishing patrician families with Trojan for-
bears.

It is apparent, therefore, that even before Julius Caesar
became supreme the fiction was generally accepted that Rome
owed its foundation indirectly to Aeneas and the Trojans;
that these Trojans were ancestors of prominent Romans; and
that Aeneas, son of Venus, through his son, Iulus, was the
progenitor of the Julian family. Early in his official life Julius
Caesar, delivering a eulogy over a kinswoman, set forth this
fiction of his descent and claimed all the sacred prerogatives
of kings and all the respect due to gods. In consonance with
this idea, after his elevation to supreme power, his statue was
placed beside that of Romulus in the temple of Quirinus, beside the effigies of the seven kings on the Capitoline, and he
assumed the dress worn by the Alban kings. Immediately
after his death a comet appeared at the games celebrated in
honor of his mother, Venus. This was naturally interpreted to
symbolize the arrival of Caesar among the gods. Augustus
himself perpetuated the fiction. He erected a bronze statue of
Caesar in the temple of Venus with a star over his head, and
he imported a famous statue of Venus from Greece and set it
up in the temple of Caesar in the forum, inscribing it as the
statue of the founder of his family. The military exploits of
Julius Caesar and the adroit statesmanship of Augustus seem
almost superfluous. Immortality was secured in advance of
any achievements by the simplest form of genealogical fiction.
We must leave to the historian the nice question how far
political chicanery, how far earnest belief and profound conviction, moved these two wise men in the exploitation of their
divine origin.

Divine prerogatives, such as Caesar and Augustus acquired by tracing their descent through Aeneas from a goddess mother, had long been the property of great monarchs in

the Greek world. At least in the second century B.C. the Romans must have become familiar with the deification of Greek kings in the fourth and third centuries. Alexander the Great enjoyed comparisons of himself with Heracles and Dionysus, the great benefactors and civilizers in Greek mythology, and Alexander's successors, particularly the Ptolemies in Egypt, were freely deified and worshiped with or without the intervention of any precise legendary account of direct descent from the gods. Thereby, perhaps, such kings gave validity and permanence to their official acts. With this practice and its advantages Caesar and Augustus were hardly unacquainted. Indeed, there is some reason for believing that the Romans, flushed with success from their conquests in Italy and the East, had come to regard themselves as carrying on the unfinished task of Alexander the Great. In that case Caesar and Augustus inherited the privileges of Alexander and his successors. Whether this be so or not, it was inevitable that in the intimate contact between Rome and Greece from the second century on, many Hellenistic ideas and institutions should be transplanted to Roman soil.

One institution established in several of the Greek kingdoms, but most effectively in Egypt in the third century, brought literary men and scholars into close relations with the court. By a large collection of books and other material for study the kings of Egypt tempted to Alexandria the intellectual men of the day. Here, relieved of worldly cares and in congenial company, they devoted themselves to the making of literature and to scientific investigation, two activities which were not so mutually contradictory as they now are. The members of this corporation of literary men and scholars were under great obligations to the court, and some of the poets, at least, were not above fulsome flattery of their royal patrons. Under these circumstances it is very easy to ascribe to the Egyptian kings a considerable amount of selfish interest in this encouragement of literary effort. The Ptolemies may have been establishing a press agency of specially reputable reporters, but the modern historian, before hastily imputing to these kings a high degree of adroit statesmanship, must reckon with two important facts: in the first place, the interpretation of literature, the making of it in a schoolroom fashion, and the public recitation of the finished product constituted the biggest part of the education of the Greek (and of the Roman) schoolboy; in the second place, these eastern kings had as tutors, from boyhood through youth, the most distinguished poets, philosophers, and scholars of the day. It is fair, therefore, to grant some measure of disinterested service in the patronage of literature and science. The recipients of these favors occasionally sacrificed their intellectual honesty, and the literature of the period, here and there, is deplorably affected.

In Greece proper and at Rome, from the third century on, literary patronage was dispensed less formally than in Egypt. Not only kings, but men of affairs, especially military heroes, attached to themselves poets and prose writers. Traces of servility and abject dependence are not wanting in some cases; a famous soldier takes an epic poet in his retinue, apparently anxious to prove to posterity that brave men lived after Agamemnon. Among the Romans, in the early period of their literature, the artists were often of low social standing, slaves or freedmen, and patronage was essential to their success. Later, when literature became a dignified profession, there was a natural drifting away, on the part of literary men, from the profane crowd to the educated and influential élite of the time. So, under Augustus, many informal circles of littérateurs gathered about Messalla, Asinius Pollio, and Maecenas. Augustus and Maecenas were themselves dabsters in literature. Their interest in Horace, Virgil, and others may well have been at the start altogether genuine and sincere.

Virgil owed something to Augustus before the poet had proved his claim to favor by any great achievement in literature and before the statesman had secured control of the government. Virgil introduced Horace into the circle when Horace was but fairly started on his career. Many of the substantial gifts made by Augustus and Maecenas to the two poets were offered before any general campaign of reform or education had matured. But once terms of intimacy were established, the projects of the new ruler may have become known to the two poets, and one need not ascribe selfish motives to Augustus or to Maecenas, or undue subservience on the part of Horace and Virgil, if one sees in the Roman Odes and in the national epic a somewhat conscious co-operation with the government in the high endeavor to regenerate the Roman people.

Similar intimacy with Augustus, apart from any literary coterie, may have influenced Livy, the historian, in the expression of his mood when he began to write in the same decade, somewhere between 27 and 25 B.C., the history of his people from the beginning of their existence. Livy describes himself as shrinking from the sight of the evils that surround him in the Rome of his own day, and seeking refuge in the splendid achievements of her glorious past. His reader, he says, shall learn to know the men and the means that won for Rome her world-power, and how she has fallen upon the present evil times when "we have not the strength to bear either our vices or the remedies that they require." In these words of the great historian there is the same earnest moral purpose that underlies the Roman Odes and Virgil's *Aeneid*.

But historian and poet, naturally, realize their purpose in very different ways. Livy dismisses the story of Aeneas and the Trojan settlements in Italy in a few sentences at the opening of his history, and proceeds in chronological sequence and with matter-of-fact fulness of detail to recount the rise of

Rome to power and her moral decay. But the poet, who is equally a historian, appreciates the symbolism, the tremendous suggestiveness of the fiction which antiquarian lore had established as the initial step in Rome's progress toward supremacy. To him the wanderings of Aeneas, his discouragement, and final emergence from despair to hope and achievement epitomized the long toil of Rome's struggle toward greatness. To him Aeneas was not merely a dignified figure serving the needs of artistic treatment and unifying the scattered incidents of the traditional narrative, but a prototype of the great leader of his own times. Kinship, the common possession of old Roman virtues, the common purpose of re-establishing the gods and their worship in a home which destiny had allotted them, link together the first and the latest of great Roman heroes, Aeneas and Augustus. Each typifies the character and the divine mission of the Roman people, the unbroken continuity of a world-power sanctioned by divine authority. Into the fabric of this significant story the poet could weave, with artistic skill and historical perspective, many threads of incident no less significant to the reader of his poem. Where Livy must tell with painful precision of the Punic Wars, the poet, in the romantic tragedy of the Carthaginian queen, may foreshadow the future conflict and supply an emotional motive for the enmity of the two peoples. If Livy ever dwelt upon the moral lessons that Catiline and his conspiracy might teach posterity, Virgil had already, less dogmatically, thrown out the essential hint in more artistic form when he portrayed the Trojan progenitor of Catiline's family as a reckless ship captain driving his ship upon the rocks. If Livy ever dwelt upon the weaknesses of contemporary society, Virgil, through his hero's vision of the criminals and their punishment in the life hereafter, brought home the lesson with more telling effect. And much as the historian may dwell upon ancient rite, ancestral custom, no historical

account could so move the Roman reader as when he found
the father of the epic hero, in a critical exigency, going
through naturally, but with absolute fidelity to all ritualistic
detail, the solemn ceremony known as the taking of the auspices. So the poet throws into a mythical past the institutions
of early Rome, and casts about them the charm and sanctity
of an even greater antiquity than they actually possessed.

A great crisis, a great leader, a national need, prompted
Virgil to exercise a high function of the poet, service to the
state. Nor had he any qualms in making poetry the handmaiden of the Emperor in his revitalizing of Roman society.
What, asks Aeschylus of Euripides in the *Frogs* of Aristophanes, a comedy of the fifth century B.C., should we admire
in a poet? Artistic skill and moral earnestness, answers the
younger poet, and there is little doubt that the Athenian audience approved the answer. Moral earnestness, however, has
probably spoiled more poems than it has ever immortalized.
The *Aeneid* is not a moral or political tract. Euripides, in his
account of the poet's qualifications, did not fail to include
artistic skill as well as a high moral purpose.

At the beginning of his third book of the *Georgics*, several
years before he began the *Aeneid*, Virgil, in an elaborate figure, indicates that he plans a military epic in honor of Augustus. "Soon," he concludes, "I will gird myself to sing the fiery
battles of Caesar." It should not have needed the suggestion
of Augustus himself to change this plan, if, indeed, the poet
ever seriously considered it. Augustus was not a military hero.
The poetic treatment of a period of civil war would revive old
enmities. The emperor himself saw the need of peace, and had
no desire to pose as a warrior. But beyond all this lay the im-
possibility of artistic treatment of such a theme.

A long line of epic poets, Greek and Roman, preceded Virgil. The conservatism of literary practice made this mass of
epic tradition a compelling force even eight centuries after

Homer. Homeric epic had fixed the verse form. It had forever established the choice of historical material as the subject matter, and of historical material from a mythical past, rather than from the more immediate past or present. In the Hellenistic period this theme had been somewhat softened and sensitized by the admixture of feeling and emotion. The substance of Virgil's poem was determined by this tradition in large measure. It was almost inevitable that he should choose his theme from the shadowy historical past, and that this theme should be presented in such a way as to portray the gentler emotions and arouse similar feelings in his audience. In these respects Virgil is residuary legatee of a long-established inheritance.

But the spirit and form of Virgil's poem are largely the expression of his own individuality and environment. To material composed of a dry legend and of rich additions from the stores of earlier literature he gave the animating soul of patriotic purpose and moral endeavor. And this traditional substance was molded into a perfection of form that no Greek or Roman predecessor had achieved. The technique of his verse, to be sure, is the issue of a long development to which his own contribution was considerable. His diction and phrasing, too, are often affected by the gravity and rude grandeur of the early epic of Ennius, and by constant echoing of other earlier poets, notably Lucretius. But in all the larger elements of structure and composition, whether in respect to the poem as a whole, or the books as separate units, or smaller chapters of action, Virgil's epic stands out as the first consistent effort to unify and dramatize a long epic narrative into an effective whole. For the first time in the history of ancient epic a high degree of somewhat conscious art went to the making of epic narrative.

II. THE LEGEND OF AENEAS

Twenty centuries after the completion of a literary masterpiece we may hardly expect to discover either the mechanical processes of the poet in the composition of his poem or the more elusive play of his fancy and the artistic fashioning of his raw material. But it is noteworthy that in the case of Virgil's *Aeneid* we can more nearly approximate the truth than in any other relic of classical literature. We are told that Virgil wrote his work in prose, distributing the material over twelve books, and then, disregarding the order of the books, recomposed his material in verse, selecting for his immediate task any chapter of the action that suited his fancy at the moment. Very likely the prose version was a mere sketch or outline. If so, it must have been in the main the legend of Aeneas and the early Trojan settlements in Latium as he had reconstructed it for his poetic purposes. The development of this legend and the condition in which Virgil found it can be determined from the literature, still extant, that antedates Virgil's poem, and our appreciation of the framework of his epic is much enhanced by a survey of this earlier material which he refashioned with due regard to the artistic needs of an epic poem.

The legend of Aeneas was not, in the main, the invention of poets or fanciful common folk, but the result of steady accretions, given currency by antiquarians and matter-of-fact historians, to a nucleus that was in itself not without some poetic content. Yet, in spite of the dryness of the facts themselves, the development of pure fiction by way of supplying dignity and grandeur to the beginnings of a nation that were in actuality of the very humblest origin is a phenomenon not uninteresting to watch. And quite apart from the connection of the legend with Rome, the observer may glean a number of valuable hints as to the human and national motives and the great social forces that propel a simple local legend forward through the ages, until, gathering volume, it not only far exceeds the intentions of its creators, but acquires a magnitude and significance which its builders from age to age were quite unable to foresee. Although we are not concerned with mythology, with religion, with the history of commerce, with national politics, with racial psychology, the observer may gain, according to his interest, no little fruitful suggestion from the constantly lengthening account of Aeneas' adventures, from the Homeric age down to Virgil's time.

Before we follow the course of the legend, however, we should have in our minds an outline of Virgil's own story. According to the *Aeneid* the hero leaves Troy only after all hope of saving it is lost. With his father, wife, and child, and the images of his gods, he starts for Mount Ida, but the wife, Creusa, miraculously disappears. Later the little company embarks from a neighboring harbor and sails to Thrace, where Aeneas founds a city, calling the inhabitants Aeneadae, sacrifices to his mother, Venus, and discovers the grave of Polydorus. From Thrace they sail south to the island of Delos; thence, farther south to Crete, and to the Strophades, where the Harpies live. From this point their course is north and west, skirting the coast of Greece and, passing the islands which the *Odyssey* had made famous as its hero's home, they land at Actium, the scene of a famous battle of Virgil's day, where Aeneas establishes a festival and dedicates a shield. Their next landing place is Buthrotum, on the coast of Epirus. Here they fall in with Andromache and her new husband, Helenus, from whom they receive directions for their journey. Thence they turn south and west and sight the coast of Italy, their destination. They land on the southeastern shore of Italy for prayer to Minerva and to Juno, but hasten on past the hostile Greek towns of Southern Italy to Sicily, reaching ultimately the harbor of Drepanum, where Anchises, the hero's father, dies. Leaving Drepanum, they are driven out of their course, by a storm, to the coast of Africa, southerly across the Mediterranean. After the Carthaginian episode the company returns to Sicily and lands again near the scene of Anchises' death, where games are celebrated on the anniversary of his burial. During the absence of the heroes at these games the Trojan women in the company set fire to the ships to end their distressing wanderings. Aeneas founds a city in which to leave the women and others who desire to stay, builds a temple to his mother, Venus, and in response to a vision sails up the southwestern coast of Italy to Cumae, to seek the Sibyl, under whose guidance he visits the other world and is encouraged by the revelation of Rome's future greatness. Thence, sailing farther north along the same coast, he reaches Latium at last, at the mouth of the Tiber. An embassy is sent to Laurentum, the abode of the native king, Latinus, whose daughter, Lavinia, has already been warned by prodigies of the approach of a foreign husband whom she must marry in place of the native prince, Turnus, a favored suitor. Aeneas, though evidently the divinely appointed husband, finds himself, in the course of subsequent events, forced to fight for his bride against both the Latins and the Rutulians, the people of the rejected suitor, Turnus. The last six books of the poem narrate the events of the war, in which Aeneas ultimately kills Turnus and wins Lavinia. This catastrophe is preceded by a divine utterance in which the founding of Rome and the complete amalgamation of Latins and Trojans is foretold:

> Let the strong master blood of Rome receive
> The manhood and the might of Italy. . . . .
> . . . . From the mingled breed
> A people shall come forth whom thou shalt see
> Surpass all mortal men and even outvie
> The faithfulness of gods.

The layman naturally believes that ancient tradition begins with Homer, but the reader of Homer may often discern, behind the artistic story of the old epic, the vague outlines of many tales that, merged in the account of the fall of Troy, lose much of their earlier significance and force. Of this fact the position which Aeneas occupies in the *Iliad* is a clear example. In the action of the poem he is a prominent and well-developed figure, but in spite of the prominence given him, only a thoughtful reader sees the much greater rôle which he must have played in local saga quite apart from the Homeric poem. Though genealogy is dry in itself, the lineage of the Trojan hero, Hector, and of Aeneas reveals a potential rivalry, which hints in the *Iliad* easily extend to active opposition, between two branches of the royal house. Only faint murmurs of this contention reach the ears of the reader, but they are echoes, undoubtedly, of a stormier conflict in the local tradition. The house of Priam was descended from Zeus. Third in descent from Zeus was Tros, who gave his name to the Trojans. Tros had three sons, the two older sons being Ilus and Assaracus. These two sons provided two rival branches of the royal house. The first branch sent forth in three generations Laomedon, Priam, Hector; the second, in the same three generations, Capys, Anchises, Aeneas. Priam and Anchises are cousins in the same generation. Similarly Hector and Aeneas, in the younger generation. The younger line, represented by Aeneas, evidently cherished a grudge against the ruling branch. So Aeneas in the *Iliad* complains that Priam does not honor him according to his merits, and Achilles taunts Aeneas in the twentieth book with the suggestion that Aeneas is confronting him in the hope of wresting from Priam's family the throne in case of a successful issue to the duel. From various incidental allusions part of the story that precedes the action of the *Iliad* may be constructed. Aeneas is the son of Anchises and the goddess Venus. Like his father a herdsman on Mount Ida, he is driven thence by Achilles in the forays preceding the final conflict before Troy and seeks refuge in a neighboring town. This town, too, Achilles sacks, and Aeneas escapes only through divine protection. He is a special favorite of the gods, though no reason is given for their interest other than his predestined greatness. In the action of the poem he is second only to Hector in bravery. Upon him Hector calls for help, and upon both Hector and Aeneas rests the heaviest burden of the war. They are the best in wisdom and prowess. By people and army, Aeneas, like Hector, is honored as a god. And the Greek foe, also, have occasion to admit his courage.

The prominence of Aeneas reaches a climax in the twentieth book of the *Iliad*. In that book Achilles is making havoc of the Trojans just before his crucial contest with Hector. Aeneas confronts him, and after a wordy debate the two fight each other with spear and sword. Aeneas is hard pressed. Poseidon, god of the sea, observes his critical danger and urges the other gods to rescue Aeneas. "For," he says, in a sentence that may have influenced the course of later legend, "it is appointed to Aeneas to escape . . . . thus shall the mighty Aeneas, and his children's children, who shall be born in aftertime, rule over the Trojans." This emphatic prophecy would hardly appear in the *Iliad* unless a considerable body of local legend already represented Aeneas as the progenitor of a race of Aeneads who were dominant in the Troad. And although the prophecy limits the realm of Aeneas to the Troad, the development of a story which ultimately carried Aeneas far beyond his home was certainly not hampered by the restriction. Not only might the Romans, centuries later, point to the founding of Rome and the Roman empire as the fulfilment of the divine utterance in the *Iliad*, but the imagination of the intervening ages might easily have been stirred by it to elaborate the fiction which we shall find slowly accumulating. During all these ages the Homeric epic was the Bible of the ancient world.

The Homeric prophecy, literally taken, restricts Aeneas and his family to the Troad. But in the course of the three centuries following the Homeric epic Aeneas became a wanderer from his native land, and his wanderings carried him, in the Greek tradition of the story, even to Italy, where the founding of Rome itself is definitely attributed to Trojans.

An early stage in the development is represented by an account in a fifth-century historian, Hellanicus. In accordance with an agreement that Aeneas and his friends shall leave the Troad in a specified time, Aeneas sails with his companions to the neighboring country of Thrace. This region seems to have been the hero's destination in early versions of the legend. So a sixth-century coin of the town of Aeneia in Macedonia pictures the hero with his father on his back and his wife and child at one side. Before the sixth century the legend had brought him to Sicily and Italy. An interesting slab, the *tabula Iliaca,* itself contemporary with Virgil, but purporting to contain illustrations of the story of Troy as told by Stesichorus, a Greek poet of the seventh century, represents Aeneas with his gods and family leaving Troy; his destination is indicated as Hesperia, that is, Italy. By the fifth century the founding of Rome is connected with Troy, but in a rather peculiar fashion. Odysseus and Aeneas are said to have traveled together from Greece to Italy; in Italy their ships were burned by certain Trojan women in the company; a city was founded and named Rome after one of the women, *Rome,* who, worn out by the journey, had urged her friends to burn her along with the ships. Much nearer to Virgil's own account is the version probably of Timaeus, a Sicilian historian of the third century B.C., according to which Aeneas, on landing in Latium, first founded the city of Lavinium and afterward built Rome itself. In any case the connection of the founding of Rome with Trojan refugees is established early and in Greek legends.

It is impossible, with our evidence, to trace in detail the development of the legend during these three centuries, but the ultimate expansion, as we find it reported in the third century B.C., conveys Aeneas past Samothrace to Delos, to Crete, to Laconia, and Arcadia on the Greek mainland; thence to Leucadia, Actium, and Epirus on the western coast of Greece; from there to the east and south coast of Italy and to Sicily; farther, if not to Carthage, at least to Campania; and finally to Latium; indeed, his wanderings do not stop in Latium, for Etruria and Sardinia claim a visit.

Doubtless much of this tradition developed in the seventh and sixth centuries, when activity in commerce and colonization brought the various peoples about the Mediterranean into closer intercourse with one another. Considerable impetus may have been given to such expansion by the existence of such myths as those of Odysseus and of Jason, in which Greek heroes "saw many towns and came to know the minds of men" after much suffering on the deep. But the story of Aeneas is conspicuously different from the tales of these Greek heroes. Their experiences are full of romantic adventure, but the stages of Aeneas' journey are marked only by comparatively prosaic occurrences. At his various stopping-places Aeneas builds a temple of his goddess-mother, Aphrodite, or performs some other simpler religious function, or founds a city, the name of which is invariably associated with his own name or that of his goddess-mother or of one of his followers. The stopping-places in his journey, if followed on the map, seem to coincide rather closely with the route that would be followed by commercial travelers of this early Greek period. The fiction, therefore, is not the creation of the poetic fancy of such a people as perpetuated the stories of the Sirens and Scylla and Charybdis and Polyphemus (though these inventors, too, may have been seafarers), but rather a pragmatic account, stimulated possibly by practical religious and commercial interests. The activity of Phoenicians in commerce in this preclassical period and their worship of a goddess closely related to Aphrodite has led to the suspicion that Phoenician traders were instrumental in propagating the expanded story at this time.

From this Greek version, as later modified by Roman hands, Virgil derived the skeleton of his action. But he also obtained some important hints from it for the filling of his structure. For it is important to observe that some of these early Greek stories supply an interesting motive for the willingness of the Greeks to let Aeneas depart from Troy uninjured. He is exempt from the cruel fate that overtakes the rest of Trojans because of the piety he has shown in saving the gods of his country and his own father at the risk of his own life. Here lies, in early Greek material, the starting-point of Virgil's elaboration of an essential trait in his hero's character, the familiar *pietas*.

The third century B.C. marks the extension of Roman influence and conquest beyond the confines of Italy. Rome was beginning to be conscious of her power, and that steadily growing power was in sharp contrast to her humble origin. Consequently, the versions of the legend of Aeneas, which had hitherto been propagated by Greek antiquarians, began to be eclipsed by a national Roman version in which the various destinations of Aeneas that had hitherto marked the end of his journey as differing according to local interest now become simply stages in a longer course of travel leading to Rome itself. This Roman version was spread by Roman poets and prose writers from the time of the epic poets, Naevius and Ennius, in the third century, down to Virgil's own day, when the great antiquarian, Varro, had doubtless given elaborate statements of variant forms of the story that were of direct service to Virgil in the construction of his narrative.

Once there was any general inclination to make use of the Greek story of Aeneas, the new Roman standpoint from which the facts were regarded necessitated important modifications and easily led to significant additions. Obviously the Romans could easily accept the general outline of the tale so far as Aeneas was concerned only with movements outside of Italy. Yet even here it was tempting, especially for a poet, to enlarge the Greek version. This temptation was most effective in the parts of the Greek story that brought Aeneas into relation with towns or countries intimately connected with Rome through political or common social interests. So, for example, Sicily was not only a near neighbor, but had commercial, religious, and political relations with Rome. The worship of Aphrodite-Venus in Rome was to some extent an offshoot from an important Aphrodite cult in Sicily. The Sicilian chapter, therefore, easily admitted amplification. Again, though the evidence is too scanty to warrant positive assertions, it is probable that the Carthaginian episode was inserted in the Greek legend, or at least developed, by the Roman poet, Naevius, about the time of the Second Punic War, obviously for political purposes, and a singular instance of the happy rôle which a poet's imagination may play in the enlargement of a prosaic legend.

But although there may be such accretions by Roman hands to the part of the legend that relates to Aeneas outside of Italy, the settlement of Aeneas in Latium is clearly the chapter of the Greek version that could not be accepted by Romans without essential changes. Any rational Roman historian must have seen that a legend which represented Aeneas, immediately after the fall of Troy, as coming to Latium and founding Rome contradicted established facts of Italian legendary history. History put the fall of Troy in the twelfth century. Italian antiquarians dated the founding of Rome in the eighth century. How could Aeneas found Rome immediately after the fall of Troy, even allowing seven years, or any other reasonable period, for his wanderings? Again, Italian legend had already accounted for the founding of Rome in a quite different fashion; what was to become of the story which made Rome an offshoot of Alba Longa and ascribed its foundation to Romulus, the son of Mars? These are considerations that occupied chronologers, historians, and antiquarians for some time, and if we chose to follow their efforts in the two centuries before Virgil's day we should find a variety of ways employed to harmonize the conflict between Italian convictions and the Greek story of Aeneas. But it is sufficient to note the final outcome in Virgil's poem. This long antiquarian struggle lies back of the curious arithmetical precision of certain verses in Virgil's first book (vss. 263 ff.); Venus, the hero's mother, is there consoled with this prophecy:

> Thy son in Italy shall wage vast war
> And quell its nations wild; his city wall
> And sacred laws shall be a mighty bond
> About his gathered people. Summers three
> Shall Latium call him king; and three times pass
> The winter o'er Rutulia's vanquished hills.
> His heir, Ascanius, now Iulus called . . . .
> Full thirty years shall reign, then move the throne
> From the Lavinian citadel, and build
> For Alba Longa its well-bastioned wall.
> Here three full centuries shall Hector's race
> Have kingly power; till a priestess queen,
> By Mars conceiving, her twin offspring bear;
> Then Romulus, wolf-nursed and proudly clad
> In tawny wolf-skin mantle, shall receive
> The sceptre of his race. He shall uprear
> The war-god's citadel and lofty wall.

In other words, the founding of Rome has been kept as Romulus' special privilege, but Romulus is introduced among the lineal descendants of Aeneas, and an interval of 333 years is provided between the arrival of Aeneas in Latium, or rather the end of the war with Turnus, and the founding of Rome itself. This neatly fills the gap of four centuries between the fall of Troy and the founding of Rome in the mythico-historical accounts, and at the same time preserves the native Italian story of Alba Longa. Nor did historians have any difficulty in supplying kings of Alba Longa to fill the three intervening centuries.

The use of Alba Longa in this connection suggests the general procedure in the adaptation and expansion of Aeneas' experiences in Italy. The Italians already had many native legends or historical accounts of events in early history, many stories explaining the settlements of old Italian towns and their political relations one with another, many traditions regarding the establishment of old cults. This native material had to be interwoven into the newly accepted tale of Aeneas' settlement in Latium. The blending of Italian elements with the Greek narrative had been thoroughly accomplished in Virgil's time, when the antiquarian, Varro, and the Greek historian, Dionysius of Halicarnassus, propagated the latest results of this long labor.

At least as early as 230 B.C. the main facts of the legend were raised from mere facts to political dogma. In that year the Roman senate used the legend to justify their action in making an alliance with the Greek people, the Acarnanians, who alone of the Greeks had not fought against Troy. Presumably such a ratification by civic authority followed, rather than preceded, a somewhat general popular acceptance of the vital facts. Fiction as it may be to us today, probably most educated Romans of Virgil's time believed that the story in its main outlines was historic fact. From this standpoint we can understand that Virgil could not, for poetic purposes, eliminate some of the dry features of the legend or change the framework of the story. The Roman reader would resent any modification of what was to him the authentic life-history of the Roman people in their infancy.

The poet, therefore, having determined to use the legend of Aeneas as the framework of his national epic, was confronted by an abundance of material which in time extended all the way from the age of the Homeric poems and the epic cycle down to his own day; some of it in Greek; some, in Latin. It is important to note two aspects of this rich tradition. In the first place, there were variant versions of details, and some variety of opinion regarding even the main outlines. In the second place, the bulk of the material was in prose, and the work of antiquarians and historians. The earliest chapter of the story, Aeneas' experiences at Troy, had been interpreted by poets. But the subsequent chapters, Aeneas' wanderings from the Troad to Italy and his experiences throughout the course of this long journey, were prosaic material without any retouching by the hands of poets except as Naevius and Ennius, in the third century, had used the legend somewhat incidentally as introductions to long epics on the Second Punic War and on the history of Rome down to the second century. These two poems, however, standing as they do at the very beginning of Latin literature, when form and style were undeveloped, could hardly have contributed much save poetic diction and epic phrasing to Virgil's generation.

Under these two conditions—variant versions of details in the legend and the almost exclusively prosaic nature of his material—the poet has one opportunity presented to him and one compelling necessity thrust upon him. He may select, and he must transmute prose into poetry. At first thought his task may seem similar to that which he undertook in the *Georgics,* when he attempted to turn agricultural treatises into verse, but the difference is more striking than the resemblance. In the *Georgics* he was adapting expository prose which did not provide for, or usually suggest, the elaboration of human character and action. In that poem poetic diction and the infusion of enthusiasm and personal feeling accomplished the desired end. But in the *Aeneid* Virgil was constructing out of narrative prose a narrative epic. The narrative prose furnished names of persons, but those persons were without substance; they were, mainly, lifeless figures mummified in the pages of the prose annalist. This same prose outlined action with the matter-of-fact precision and some of the scientific causal coherence of historic narrative. But such action seldom roused the reader's sympathy, stimulated his vision, or, by retarding effects and catastrophes at critical moments, relieved monotony and dramatized the cold facts. Nor was there in the handling, either of persons or of action, any warm personal interest, but only the cool dispassionate presentation by antiquary and historian, regardless of pathetic possibilities and scornful of decorative detail.

Virgil divided the story of Aeneas into two chapters: his adventures before reaching Latium, and his arrival in Latium and the consequent war. To each of these two chapters the poet devoted six books of the epic. In the first of the two sections history provided many stopping places for the hero, a monotonous succession of trivial experiences (trivial, at least, from an artistic standpoint), and the passage of the hero from place to place was caused only by interest in his kinsmen in some particular locality or by changes of wind and weather. Nothing unified the stages of his wanderings but the general westerly course of his travel. Virgil selects five of the stopping places in the tradition of Aeneas' visits to the Greek world, and the stop in Sicily, elaborated after Naevius the Carthaginian episode, and incorporated the stop at Cumae. By mere elimination he promoted unity, and at least in the third book he assured unity by making each stopping place an inevitable stage in the hero's quest after knowledge of his pre-

cise destination. Furthermore, Virgil uses charily the founding of cities and temples, and dignifies each stopping place
by some adventure of richer content than that furnished by
tradition. He constantly varies the experiences of his hero.
Finally, he neatly relieves the monotonous technique of the
historical narrative by abandoning chronological sequence.
The poem opens, not with the fall of Troy and the visit to
Thrace, but with the Carthaginian episode. Into this episode
he weaves the hero's own account, in the first person, of the
preceding stages of the journey, and after the conclusion of
the episode, in the fourth book, brings the hero back to Sicily
and to Cumae.

In the second chapter, events in Latium, the poet obtains
the same results by somewhat different means. His principle
is not so much elimination as condensation. History provided
a series of wars, in each of which a prominent chieftain fell:
Latinus, Turnus, Mezentius, and in that order. Virgil concentrates by condensing these wars into a single campaign with
several decisive conflicts. This condensed form of the contest
in Latium is then given effective unity by making Lavinia the
prize of victory, and by concentrating attention upon the two
suitors for her hand, Aeneas and Turnus, instead of dispersing
it over the various heroes of the historical account. The duel
between Aeneas and Turnus becomes the natural conclusion
of the poem, and the death of Mezentius precedes the death of
Turnus, as one of the many events that lead to, and retard,
the final issue.

Any such processes of selection and condensation provided hardly more than a skeleton of the action. Distinctive
and varying adventures must mark the stopping places in the
first chapter. Here history offered nothing but foundings of
cities and temples and a few oracles and prodigies. Again, the
successive battles of the second chapter must be filled with
appropriate detail. History, so far as we know, provided only

a summary account of the main incidents. The modern reader might suppose that at this point in his composition Virgil would employ his fancy, but no such thought occurred to him. He was thoroughly imbued with the spirit of the later Greek age. The practice of Hellenistic poets, when they undertook a long epic, was thoroughly established. They must write in the verse of Homer; they must employ his diction and his similes; the world of their epics must be the Homeric world. Virgil was only true to the conviction of his age when he turned mainly to Homer for his enrichment of the legend of Aeneas. So far from feeling ashamed of any lack of originality, he gloried in being a Roman Homer. There is no attempt at concealment, no subterfuge. Other poets of his time delighted to record their indebtedness to older Greek literature. Horace regarded it as creditable that his epodes echoed Archilochus, that his odes continued the tradition of Alcaeus and Sappho. In this dependence upon early Greek literature the Augustan poets were still completely Hellenistic. But they had the great satisfaction of outdoing their Hellenistic rivals. The Hellenistic poet perpetuated the style and content of Homer in Homer's own language. The Latin poets, as they take pains to tell us, performed the greater task of continuing the old Greek tradition in a new tongue. Imitation was a patriotic achievement.

Within this thoroughly approved process of imitation individual poets may, paradoxically speaking, show different degrees of originality. We shall presently be illustrating the special nature and extent of Virgil's originality in transforming Homeric material. For the moment we may emphasize his dependence upon Homer for the expansion and enrichment of the legend of Aeneas.

The Sicilian episode and the stop at Cumae, comprising the fifth and sixth books of the poem, are dignified by action which in its main outlines is taken directly from the *Iliad* and

Odyssey. As Achilles celebrates funeral games over his friend, Patroclus, so does Aeneas, at the anniversary of his father's death. Odysseus sees the inhabitants of the other world as does Aeneas in the sixth book. The battles in the concluding books of the *Aeneid* in general situation and construction are frankly modeled after definite contests in the *Iliad.* But this correspondence in main outlines is a small matter. It is more important that the details of the games in the fifth book correspond to the details of the various competitions in the twenty-third book of the *Iliad;* that Aeneas in the other world, like Odysseus, meets a companion who was recently killed in an accident, a personal enemy who is still unreconciled and refuses to recognize him, and an old comrade-in-arms; that in the last books of the poem, Turnus, like Achilles, is diverted by a phantom from following his foe; and that the duel between Aeneas and Turnus is fought in the same three phases as the duel between Achilles and Hector. It is evident that Virgil did not enrich his treatment by visualizing action, but that he sought analogous situations in Homeric epic and transformed them to suit the needs of the new environment. Obviously, therefore, neither the poet's dependence nor his power in refashioning the substance which he took over into his own epic narrative can be appreciated without some knowledge of the Greek epics, particularly of those portions which Virgil found best adapted to the need of giving substantial body to the dry skeleton of the legend of Aeneas.

III. EPIC TRADITION

The point of view from which we purpose to regard the Homeric poems has at least the charm of novelty. To us today the name of Homer suggests a variety of pleasant associations; the qualities of a noble style as Matthew Arnold defined them in a notable essay, the romance of archaeological finds in the disinterred Mycenae, Tiryns, Troy, not to speak of the long vistas that open up of earlier ages before the time of Homer or the Trojan War, the speculations of great scholars as to the evolution of early epic, by which they attempt to explain the linguistic mixture, apparent or real stratification of custom and myth, inconsistencies of fact, irregularities of form. It is much to our advantage that in our discussion of the *Iliad* and *Odyssey* we do not care whether the Trojan War was real or fanciful, whether Homer ever lived or wrote, whether the Homeric epic is expurgated or not, whether, to appropriate the words of a reviewer, "Odysseus was a human ruler with a human wife" or "he . . . . a divine wolf howling along the snows of Parnassus and she a divine duck quacking along the waters of Arne," whether one poet or many hands fashioned our present text. We stand comfortably on the shore and observe with indifference the storm-tossed Unitarian and Separatist on the seas of Homeric controversy. The text of Homer that Virgil read was essentially the text of Homer today, as made by Hellenistic scholars from the tradition of earlier centuries; but Virgil was happily free from all the rubbish of modern speculation; nor did he need the bright light of modern archaeology, anthropology, philology, to illumine the pages of the *Iliad* and *Odyssey*. They were to him two poems from one hand, the hand of a poet whom he called Homer.

A. THE ODYSSEY

The Greek world, including Greece proper, the coast of Asia Minor, and the "dissociable" ocean, was a world largely of islands and almost-islands; the centers of Greek life were on the sea or near the sea; many of them were placed with hills behind or about them, but in the foreground lay the illimitable blue of ocean. Inhospitable and terrifying as this ocean often was, there could hardly ever have been a time, even before the days of more active commerce and colonization, when fisherman, pirate, and peaceful trader did not move freely over it. Possibly there were few who engaged in venturesome long sea journeys; if so, their occasional stops at convenient harbors and coast towns must have been events in the lives of the stay-at-homes. For they brought with them, not only wares from other centers and sea food, but more precious merchandise, sailors' yarns. They had themselves gone far beyond the easily known Greek world, and at the uttermost edge of their own travels they had met others who had pierced farther into the unknown or who had heard tales of a great beyond. In such a case a slight nucleus of fact grows easily to entrancing fiction. The vague and unexplored beyond stimulates the imagination; the native of a more remote region consciously imposes upon the new arrival, curious and guileless; or the sailor himself, by his own fertile fancy, expands concrete and natural experience to romantic adventure. By any or all means a distant island, where inhospitable savages tend their flocks by day and house themselves and their animals by night in caves, is peopled with one-eyed giants; or some dangerous coast against which the waters dash with weird melodious sounds becomes the abode of siren-voiced maidens; or the misty unknown, off toward the sunset, is identified with a land of sleep and death, whose inhabitants, noble-spirited but shy mariners with magic powers, sail the seas in barques that need no rudders or pilots, for the barques themselves understand the thoughts and intents of men. Precious cargoes of such sea tales would land with special frequency at halfway points in the traders' journey. So, after a long jaunt from the lower Mediterranean or across the Aegean, trader or traveler might choose to stop on the northwest coast of Asia Minor in the Troad before starting on his northeast passage through the Hellespont and over the Black Sea, or, homeward bound, here he might rest, and regale the natives with his yarns. Such tales of the sea became domesticated in Asia Minor, and slowly attached themselves to other Greek stories of seafarers, of a Greek chieftain, Odysseus, one of many who, after the fall of Troy, reached their Greek homes only after perilous adventure. A poet unified this blend of local legend and pure romance, and the *Odyssey* was made.

This explanation of the *Odyssey*, too, is pure romance, and may not square with any of the various theories which modern scholars offer, but it will serve to indicate how different the atmosphere of this epic is from that of the *Iliad*, and how remote from the pragmatic account of Aeneas' wanderings is the fanciful journey of the Greek hero, impatiently awaited by a faithful wife and eager son, while lordly wooers for Penelope's hand mind them of meat and drink, song and dance in the palace of Odysseus. Though Odysseus may have left a real Troy and perhaps reached a real Ithaca or Leucas, in between he traveled in the land of Nowhere, however precisely Homer in his own mind, or pedants after Homer, may have located his stopping places.

But before Virgil wrote his *Aeneid*, the places in the voyage of Odysseus had been rudely brought down to earth and somewhat definitely fixed. Nobody doubted where Scylla and Charybdis were, the island of Circe, or of Calypso; the island of the sun god, the lands of the Phaeacians and of the lotus-eaters could be found on the map; Polyphemus was forever at home in or near the island of Sicily. As early as the third century Apollonius, a Greek epic poet, in narrating the journey of Jason and his Argonauts in search of the Golden Fleece, had felt obliged to direct the homeward course of his hero in such a way that he should visit the stopping places of Odysseus; nor was Apollonius original in so doing. The fourth book of Apollonius' poem becomes at times almost a Baedeker for one who wishes to retraverse the route of Odysseus as the geography of the time had defined it. Such a practice was firmly established by this later Greek poet, and no doubt others before Virgil had helped to confirm, as part of the literary convention of epic treatment, this curious blending of Odysseus' adventures with the wanderings of other seafaring heroes. Virgil could hardly resist the prevailing tendency without inviting hostile criticism.

Strongly as epic convention may have drawn him to merge the wanderings of Odysseus with the journey of his own hero, there were also opposing forces which limited the extent of any such fusion. Primarily, there was, as we have seen, a flat contradiction between the romance of Odysseus' adventures and the pragmatic prose of the Aeneas legend; though supernatural elements such as the intervention of gods and oracles and prodigies were legitimate enough in the fundamentally religious atmosphere of the story of Aeneas' safe transportation of the gods of Troy to Italy, it would be difficult for Virgil to justify, in his day and generation, the meeting of Aeneas, a very real person in the mind of the Roman reader and the hero of an authentic account of Rome's founding, with such wildly fanciful creatures as the Sirens, the lotus-eaters, or such uncanny monsters as Scylla and Charybdis, though Virgil does allow for special purposes a chance adventure with the Harpies. The realities of Aeneas' sentimental affairs with Dido and Lavinia hardly harmonized with tales of elfish mistresses such as Circe and Calypso. In the second place, even if such a blend could be justified, the very nature of Odysseus' adventures made it impossible to organize them with the story of Aeneas; Virgil could easily adapt the battles of the *Iliad* and the funeral games, but if he attempted to bring over any of the fairy tales of the *Odyssey* they had to remain mere decorative episodes, and Virgil abhors the episode. In using them as episodes, the Roman poet would invite dangerous comparisons with Homeric masterpieces. These considerations explain why the only extensive obligation of Virgil to the *Odyssey* is in the visit to the other world in the sixth book; this theme, though of course fanciful, had been thoroughly established in many types of literature outside of the Homeric epic, and had lost thereby exclusive association with such creations of popular fancy as the tale of the Sirens, or Scylla and Charybdis.

In the main, therefore, Virgil pays only the polite consideration of passing allusion to the landmarks in the wanderings of Odysseus. His own hero, in the developed prose legend, was brought into the same general region where current opinion often located the land of the Phaeacians, Scylla and Charybdis, the island of Circe, and the island of the Sirens; this made it hard to leave them entirely out of Aeneas' itinerary. So Virgil uses them here and there to adorn his poetic geography: "Soon sank Phaeacia's wind-swept citadels out of our view," says Aeneas in recounting to Dido his journey along the coast of Epirus. And as they sail away from Sicily, "in swift course across the level sea the fleet sped safe, protected from all fear by Neptune's vow. Yet were they drawing nigh the Sirens' island-steep, where oft are seen white, bleaching bones, and to the distant ear the rocks roar harshly in perpetual foam." Thus deftly the poet calls up in the reader's mind associations with the Homeric epic, but refrains from elaborate digression. This guidebook comment is enlarged, however, in the case of Scylla and Charybdis; the prophet Helenus in the third book gives the hero some general directions for his journey, and here, in the midst of warnings against peculiar perils, the poet allows Helenus to speak of "pitiless Charybdis, who draws down to the wild whirling of her steep abyss the monster waves, and ever and anon flings them at heaven, to lash the tranquil stars," and of Scylla "prisoned in her eyeless cave . . . . where grim rocks echo her dark seadogs' roar." But this greater detail is justified as a means of giving impressiveness to the prophet's warning. In the journey itself, however, there is somewhat more than passing mention of the island of Circe, the uncanny daughter of the sun, who transformed men into beasts; her land was located off the coast of Italy, and the story of her had become a part of Italian legend; of this the modern name, Monte Circello, is still a faint echo. Such dangers as the region had for the Trojan travelers were the last perils they had to face before reaching Latium; accordingly the poet, in letting them pass safely by, suggests the moonlit weirdness of the spot:

> Freshly the night-winds breathe; the cloudless moon
> Outpours upon his path unstinted beam,
> And with far-trembling glory smites the sea.
> Close to the land of Circe soon they fare,
> Where the Sun's golden daughter in far groves
> Sounds forth her ceaseless song; her lofty hall
> Is fragrant every night with flaring brands
> Of cedar, giving light the while she weaves
> With shrill-voiced shuttle at her linens fine.
> From hence are heard the loud lament and wrath
> Of lions, rebels to their linkèd chains
> And roaring all night long; great bristly boars
> And herded bears, in penfold closely kept,
> Rage horribly, and monster wolves make moan;
> Whom the dread goddess with foul juices strong
> From the forms of men drove forth, and bade to wear
> The mouths and maws of beasts in Circe's thrall.

But kind Neptune "sped them on in safety past the perils of that sea."

THE STORY OF POLYPHEMUS

One exception Virgil makes to his general practice of brief and casual allusion to the stopping places of Odysseus. The Greek hero's adventure on the island of the Cyclopes and his shrewd outwitting of the one-eyed giant, Polyphemus, seem to have eclipsed all the other exploits of Odysseus in the minds of later generations. The satyr-play of the tragic poet, Euripides, the sentimentalizing of the story in Theocritus are merely suggestive hints in the scanty tradition between Homer and Virgil of the popularity of this folk-tale. Virgil seems to have felt that he could not let his hero pass the region of the Cyclopes, coming as it did directly in the path of Aeneas' journey from Sicily to Italy, without more than a guidebook reference to it. Furthermore, in the Aeneas legend, as it had developed by Virgil's time, the hero was reported to have fallen in with Odysseus himself while both were journeying about the coasts of Italy and Sicily after the fall of Troy. The Roman poet could hardly afford to use this feature of the story in his poem; there was danger in bringing together these two great heroes; the artistic problem of giving Odysseus the prominence he deserved without dwarfing the hero of his own epic was, possibly, too difficult for Virgil to solve. It may be, therefore, although proof is not attainable, that the poet's greater elaboration of the Polyphemus story is not only a tribute to the fame of the episode, but a compensation for the omission of a striking feature of the Aeneas legend, the meeting with Odysseus; for in Virgil's treatment Aeneas meets, not Odysseus, but a survivor of Odysseus' grim experience on the island of the Cyclopes. The poet's handling of the scene illustrates the dangers that he wisely avoided elsewhere by refusing to employ material that the *Odyssey* temptingly offered. For he does not succeed in making the incident anything but an episode, and in spite of his characteristic modification of the theme he cannot escape a comparison with the

Homeric original, which is fatal to his own slighter achievement.

Yet it is not uninteresting to see the Virgilian qualities of the remodeled theme. In Homer Odysseus tells in the first person of his visit to the inhospitable Cyclopes, of their occupation as herdsmen, their impiety, their repulsive physical appearance; one of them, Polyphemus, a cruel one-eyed monster, confines Odysseus and his comrades in the cave where he lives with his flocks; he devours with cannibal-like ferocity some of Odysseus' companions, and the lives of all are saved only by the cunning strategy of the Greek hero. Similarly, Aeneas tells Dido at the end of the third book how, as they were passing the volcanic fires of Aetna, a man suddenly appeared from the woods on the shore and stretched out supplicating hands to the Trojan ships: "A startling shape of hunger-wasted misery; a man in wretched guise . . . . all grime and foulness he, with long and tangled beard, his savage garb fastened with thorns." The Trojans recognize him as a Greek and consequently an enemy; he, too, is amazed to see Trojans, and momentarily despairs of winning their help and sympathy, but in his desperation hysterically begs them to take him aboard and save him from the Cyclopes. In response to cheering words from Anchises he tells his story; he came with Odysseus and lived through all the horrible experiences within the Cyclops' cave, but was accidentally left behind in the hurried departure of Odysseus from the island. In his story it is noteworthy that he retells the narrative of the *Odyssey* only up to the point where the Greeks were devoured by Polyphemus, and Odysseus, befuddling the giant with wine, bored out his one eye with the sharpened stake; the intellectual skill of Odysseus in afterward devising a safe issue from their confinement in the cave he leaves unmentioned. In other words, his narrative emphasizes only the pathetic and gruesome features of the Homeric episode. And he concludes his narrative with a stirring account of his own hardship in the three months since Odysseus' departure and warns the Trojans of the dangers they may have to face if the Cyclopes discover them. Hardly is his story finished when the giant shape of Polyphemus appears on the crest of a hill, "huge, shapeless, horrible, with blinded eye," . . . . making his footing sure with the aid of a pine tree, "while the white, fleecy sheep, sole pleasure now, and solace of his woes, ran huddling at his side." The Trojans hastily pick up the Greek survivor and pull away from shore clean out to sea, and then, from a safe distance, halloo to the giant; Polyphemus

> Whirled sudden round. . . . .
> He raised a cry incredible; the sea
> With all its billows trembled; the wide shore
> Of Italy from glens and gorges moaned,
> And Aetna roared from every vaulted cave.
> Then rallied from the grove-clad, lofty isle
> The Cyclops' clan, and lined the beach and bay.
> We saw each lonely eyeball glare in vain,
> As side by side those brothers Aetna-born
> Stood towering high, a conclave dark and dire:
> As when far up some mountain's famous crest,
> Wind-fronting oaks or cone-clad cypresses
> Have made assembling in the solemn hills, ...

Thus Virgil, with a wealth of new detail, realizes all the pathetic and picturesque possibilities, not only of the old story, but of the additions which his own fancy made to the Homeric narrative; and loose as the external connection of this episode may be with the environing action, the poet has made it count for something by using it to enrich the inner content of his own narrative. For the refashioned incidents of the *Odyssey* are made to illustrate the generous sympathy and helpfulness of the Trojans toward a natural enemy, a Greek, and this quality is magnified when the reader, who has just left the narrative of the second book of the *Aeneid,* recalls, as he naturally does, that in the second book this same generous sympathy extended to a similarly pathetic Greek refugee, Sinon, advanced the treacherous plans of the Greeks, and brought about the fall of Troy; even after that ominous experience the Trojans exercise the same clemency, a clemency which the Romans of Virgil's own day claimed, if they did not always justify the claim, in their attitude toward their conquered enemies.

THE VISIT TO THE OTHER WORLD

Visions of the other world, descents to Hades, were from the Homeric period to Virgil's time a favorite theme of poet and philosopher; popular fancy and speculative thought had invested the theme with a rich variety of incident. In his sixth book Virgil inherited from past ages an abundance of material, and by his organizing power and poetic inspiration gave to the rich stores of tradition a significance which they had never before suggested. The eleventh *Odyssey* is only one of many ancient masterpieces in which elevation of thought and the pathos of situation mitigate, for the modern reader, the somewhat gruesome concreteness of these visits of living men to the world of the dead. From this epic treatment the Roman poet derived to some extent the framework of action in Aeneas' descent, but as usual his modifications are more important than the apparent dependence upon Homer.

At the end of the tenth book of the *Odyssey*, Circe, the enchantress, sends the hero from her island, bidding him seek the spirit of the blind soothsayer, Teiresias, in the other world, who shall give him directions touching his homeward journey. Circe instructs Odysseus how to reach the world of the dead: it lies across the stream of ocean. She also tells him the ritual of evoking the spirits of the dead: he is to dig a trench, pour drink offerings to the dead, entreat them with prayers and sacrifice; then, when the spirits come, he is to let those with whom he wishes to converse drink of the blood of the sacrificial victim; the others he is to keep away with his sword. Just before Odysseus leaves Circe an accident overtakes one of his companions named Elpenor: the youngest of the company, he was sleeping on the roof of Circe's house, heavy with wine; hearing the noise of his comrades moving below, he awoke suddenly, and leaping up, fell off the roof and was killed. Odysseus and the rest sail away to the limits of the world, reach the land of the dead, and carry out Circe's instructions. The first soul that comes in response to the blood-offering at the trench is that of Elpenor, whose corpse, in the hurry of departure, had been left unburied; he implores Odysseus, after his visit to the other world, to return to the island of Circe and bury the corpse; this Odysseus agrees to do. The next to appear is the mother of Odysseus, Anticleia, with whom, for the time being, the hero does not converse, though she moves him to tears and compassion. Then comes the soul of Teiresias, who drinks of the blood and assures Odysseus of a safe return home if he will do no violence to the cattle of Helios, the sun god, on the island of Thrinacia; Teiresias warns him of the wrath of the god, Poseidon, and instructs him regarding the punishment of the suitors in his home and his subsequent action. After this encouragement and direction, which, we infer from Circe's commands in the previous book, were the main object of Odysseus' visit to the other world, the hero inquires how he may talk with the ghost of his mother, and Teiresias tells him that he may have converse with any of the spirits whom he allows to draw near the blood and drink of it. In the action that follows, Odysseus, accepting the prophet's suggestion, converses first with his mother, Anticleia. Then a company of heroines, the fair women of Greek mythology, appears, each of whom—Tyro, Antiope, Alcmene, Leda, Phaedra, Procris, Ariadne, and others— is formally introduced; these interviews with the mythological

heroines are not reported in dramatic dialogue, but Odysseus
in his narrative simply states the lineage of each and special
items of interest in her history. After these interviews there
is a break in the narrative. It will be remembered that Odysseus is telling to Alcinous and Arete, king and queen of the
Phaeacians, this narrative of his visit to the other world, along
with his other adventures. After he has described the heroines the Phaeacian audience express to one another their admiration of Odysseus, but King Alcinous, interested in his
narrative, inquires if Odysseus saw in the other world any of
the Greek captains who fought at Troy. This interruption of
the narrative not only serves to justify the hero's additional
account of other interviews, but gives a special prominence to
the interviews with Agamemnon and Achilles and Ajax, which
are, from an artistic standpoint, like that of Virgil, the best in
the book. In recounting these Odysseus resumes the dramatic
form, the reproduction of the actual dialogue instead of mere
description. The quality that gives distinction to these conversations between Odysseus and his former comrades-in-
arms before Troy is the poet's careful adaptation of speech to
character; the hero, Agamemnon, tells with bitterness and
pathos of the fate that overtook him at the hands of his wife,
Clytaemnestra, and her paramour, Aegisthus, when he reached
home, and as the result of his own experience he tries to inspire distrust even of the faithful Penelope in the mind of
Odysseus, at the same time revealing his pathetic consciousness of the happier state of Odysseus in having a son to greet
him on his homecoming, and inquiring vainly if Odysseus
knows whether the goodly Orestes, Agamemnon's own son, is
still living. Similarly, the speech of Achilles is occupied entirely with inquiries for his father and son; of the latter Odysseus is able to give a good account, and after his report the
poet says, "the spirit of Achilles . . . . passed with great
strides along the mead of asphodel, rejoicing in that I had

told him of his son's renown." Nor anywhere else does Homer's art appear to better advantage than in the happy contrast between the cordiality and sympathy among these three great heroes of the *Iliad* and the equally characteristic sulkiness of Ajax, whom Odysseus now attempts to conciliate; after the death of Achilles, according to a story that lies beyond the time covered by the *Iliad,* a quarrel had arisen among the surviving Greek chieftains as to who should come into possession of the armor of Achilles; it was awarded by Athena and the Trojans to Odysseus, and this decision stirred in the soul of Ajax a resentment from which he never recovered. Odysseus, seeing the shade of Ajax standing apart, still angry, attempts with gracious compliment to turn away the wrath of the sulky hero, but Ajax "uttered not a word, and passed on to Erebus." So here, as in the interviews with Agamemnon and Achilles, the emphasis lies, as it so rarely does in Homer, on the portrayal of feeling rather than of action—an anticipation of one of Virgil's dominant interests. But the Greek poet immediately changes his emphasis; rather awkwardly he makes a transition to a new group of characters by letting Odysseus say that even then he would have spoken to Ajax, but he was minded to see the spirits of those others that were departed. Thereupon, abandoning dramatic dialogue and falling again into description, Odysseus catalogues with conventional detail the stock figures with whom popular fancy had peopled Hades: Minos, Orion, Tityus, Tantalus, and Sisyphus. Heracles concludes the list, and here the poet recurs to speech in place of description, but without thereby giving any special distinction to the end of this chapter of Odysseus' narrative.

In brief, the eleventh *Odyssey* presents grandly conceived individual scenes, but without coherent and progressive action. The Greek poet, by the mere choice of situation from which the action issues, has made impossible any well-knit or dramatic narrative. Odysseus remains in his position by the trench, about which gather various spirits; simply because he is merely evoking the shades of the dead it is impossible to make the appearance of any particular ghost inevitable; any order in the appearances becomes an arbitrary order; and the hero himself, directed to call up the dead, becomes almost a passive spectator of the scene. The previous directions from Circe make the appearance of the prophet Teiresias the climax; for the interview with him is the main purpose of the visit. But the poet, not caring for the dramatic effect of a climax, makes Teiresias appear immediately after the apparition of Elpenor, so that the other appearances, of heroines and warriors and stock figures of mythology, seem like purely arbitrary additions after the natural climax; the only inevitable figure, Teiresias, appears at the very beginning. And in the choice of the persons with whom Odysseus converses, after receiving the prophecy from Teiresias, the poet does not always redeem the anticlimax by selecting characters who are closely bound to Odysseus by strong ties of kinship or community of interest; thus the heroines and the stock figures, such as Tantalus, Sisyphus, and Tityus, become purely ornamental additions; on the other hand, the mother of the hero, and the three warriors, Agamemnon, Achilles, and Ajax, are very happily chosen, for not only the definite request of King Alcinous for information about the Greek chieftains, but the personal interest of Odysseus himself make the conversations with his mother and former comrades-in-arms natural and impressive. The description of the heroines and stock figures, on the other hand, is a mere conventional addition to meet the demands of an audience who felt that any account of Hades was incomplete without these decorative elements. But such defects as there may be from an artistic standpoint in the structure of the action and choice of characters are easily condoned in view of the rich emotional content of the meetings with Anticleia and with the triad of Greek captains; seldom did Homer so nobly conceive, and so ably realize, scenes in which character and feeling are expressed with vividness and truth.

The same activity which had definitely located, by Virgil's time, the other stopping places of Odysseus had settled upon Lake Avernus, near Cumae, in Italy, as the scene of the eleventh book of the *Odyssey*. Various artistic possibilities which we must not stop to consider at present led the Roman poet to make Cumae a stopping place in his hero's wanderings and to enlarge from the *Odyssey* and other sources the action of Aeneas in this chapter of his story. The material available for the poet's purpose outside of the *Odyssey* was considerable, and the sixth book of the *Aeneid* is a fusion of various ingredient elements in which the poet's imagination and constructive skill combined to make, as usual, a new whole organically connected with the main action. For the moment we must limit ourselves to a brief sketch of the more obvious points of contact with the Homeric narrative.

The function of Circe in providing directions is transferred to the Sibyl; but a part of Circe's general instruction is given to the hero's father, Anchises, who, in a dream at the end of the fifth book, admonishes his son to seek him out in the Elysian fields and "visions I will show of cities proud and nations sprung from thee." This statement of Anchises settles the climax of the action in the sixth book. The meeting with Anchises corresponds to the meeting with Teiresias in the *Odyssey;* but Virgil has put the climax at the end of the action, not at the beginning, as Homer did. The possibility of a climax properly placed at the end of the action was easily realized by Virgil because he had abandoned the *Odyssey* in choosing the situation from which the action of the sixth book issues; in the Homeric poem Odysseus sat by a trench and called up the spirits of the dead; in the *Aeneid* the hero descends to an underworld, passes from place to place in it, and only after a natural progress reaches at last the Elysian fields and receives from Anchises the revelation of Rome's future greatness. The interviews which Aeneas holds along the way become, consequently, so many stages of a journey which the reader follows with suspense and growing interest as retarding elements that postpone the inevitable conclusion, the meeting of Aeneas with his father. So movement, action, dramatic progress take the place of mere situation, passive observation of apparitions, and anticlimax. But this change, so desirable for artistic purposes, we may not ascribe entirely to Virgil's originality; he had the pattern of it before him in innumerable accounts of descents to the underworld of Heracles, Theseus, and others in the literature between Homer's day and his own; he simply shows in his selection his usual regard for dramatic structure, and very likely a higher constructive ability than his Greek models.

In the interviews with ghosts in the other world Virgil has in general followed suggestions in the *Odyssey*, but the result is a consistent emphasis upon character and feeling, which in the *Odyssey* was limited to several among the many interviews.

Elpenor, who had fallen off the roof in suddenly awakening from his drunken slumber, is the first to greet Odysseus, and asks for the proper burial of his body. The manner of his death does not suit Virgil's ideas of propriety; he substitutes, taking the person probably from the developed legend of Aeneas, Palinurus, whom at the end of the fifth book he describes as having fallen asleep at the rudder and as being flung forth into the ocean at night when his comrades could not hear his despairing cries; Palinurus, like Elpenor, is the first to meet the hero in the other world and asks for burial rites.

In the meetings with Dido, Deiphobus, and Anchises the

poet is clearly influenced by the interviews, respectively, with Ajax, Agamemnon, and the mother, Anticleia, in the *Odyssey*. Dido "glared with fierce relentless gaze," while Aeneas "with fond words and tearful plea, would soothe her angry soul." But the reminiscence of the tragedy of the fourth book, the closer bond which binds Aeneas to Dido, give much deeper pathos to this brief scene than Homer could convey in his picture of the sulking Ajax. Virgil, in all the interviews that are dramatically presented, selects as the persons *only* those who are attached to Aeneas by close ties of sentiment or kinship; Deiphobus is not only a comrade-in-arms, like Agamemnon, but son of Priam and cousin of Aeneas. The account of Helen's treachery and the murder of Deiphobus through her co-operation with the Greeks corresponds to Agamemnon's report of his faithless wife and his own death at the hands of a paramour. But here Virgil, though bringing out the pathetic features of the narrative, perceptibly diminishes the grandeur of the scene in the *Odyssey,* which is inseparable from the more prominent and dignified figure of the great captain of the Greek hosts. The final interview with Anchises is perhaps suggested by Odysseus' meeting with his mother, Anticleia, but Virgil has so changed and enriched the special situation that the resemblance is superficial. The heroines and the stock figures of mythology Virgil does not deny himself; his audience, like Homer's, still demands them. But the heroines he limits to lovestricken women residing in the Fields of Sorrow, and from the brief list of mythical women Dido emerges into the dramatic action in such a way that the catalogue of heroines seems a mere prelude to the scene with Dido; similarly, Deiphobus emerges from a mass of brave warriors briefly listed. The figures who never fail to adorn descriptions of Tartarus—Tityus, Ixion, and the like—are brought in as part of the Sibyl's account of what she has seen in previous visits to Tartarus; Aeneas is not supposed to see them; and the description in the Sibyl's mouth gains a special force in that she adds to the conventional list certain unnamed criminals who are tortured in Tartarus and whose crimes are evidently representative of the sins of Virgil's own age. So the conventional list is given a suggestive force by the immediate relation of the general theme to Virgil's own environment.

In general, however, the Roman poet's success in the sixth book lies quite apart from his reconstruction of the action in the *Odyssey*. And such individualizing of character and portrayal of feeling as Virgil attempted had already been accomplished under much more favorable conditions in the Greek poem.

But here, as in his use of the battles of the *Iliad*, his organizing power is manifest, and the intimate relation of cause and effect which he emphasizes binds the inner to the outer action. This coherence, in contrast to the looseness of Homeric structure, is well illustrated in a comparison of the general situation in the opening books of the *Aeneid* with the analogous scenes in the *Odyssey*.

THE SHIPWRECKED TRAVELER

Near the end of the fifth book of the Greek epic, Odysseus is shipwrecked off the coast of Phaeacia, the land of Alcinous and Arete; the disaster is directly caused by the wrath of the sea god, Poseidon. The hero, making his way to shore with difficulty, falls in with the daughter of the king and queen of the land, Nausicaa. The poet takes no little pains to interest us in the princess, both in detailed narrative of events that lead to her presence at the spot where Odysseus reaches the shore and in the description of her maidenly modesty and gracious courtesy after the hero has been discovered. Odysseus himself, thanks to the goddess Athena, is made attractive to the maiden; the goddess sheds a grace about his head and shoulders which moves the young princess to express the wish that such a one might be called her husband. Nausicaa escorts him to the walls of the city and there leaves him, fearing to excite the criticism of the Phaeacians if she be found in company with a stranger; for her countrymen will mistake him for a husband, and will charge her with overlooking the merits of her Phaeacian wooers. Under the guidance of his patron goddess, Athena, the hero moves through the city, and she acquaints him with the history of the royal house and the honor and influence of the queen, Arete; as he passes through the town he has occasion to see and admire the harbors and gallant ships, the place of assembly of the people, the long high walls crowned with palisades, and when he reaches the palace the poet detains us with a detailed description of the splendor of the house and grounds. Odysseus is well received by the king and queen, and when they learn that he has met their daughter, they blame her for not having brought him to the house, but Odysseus chivalrously tells an untruth, declaring that the princess had urged him to accompany her, but he had declined for fear of her father's anger. Alcinous, however, denies that he is so easily wroth, and wishes that so goodly a man as Odysseus, and like-minded with himself, would wed his daughter and be called his son, there abiding in Phaeacia. In the course of the entertainment that follows on the subsequent day, Alcinous inquires of Odysseus his adventures, and in response to this question we get the long episodic story of the hero's romantic experiences which covers Books ix–xii of the *Odyssey;* even before Odysseus tells his story the Phaeacians promise him safe escort from the land, and after the narrative is finished this promise is kept, rich gifts being added to the equipment of the ship.

It is, perhaps, significant of Homer's power that the modern, like the ancient, reader is too absorbed in the story of Odysseus from the time he reaches the Phaeacians until he leaves them ever to notice, or, having noticed, to care, that this part of the poem is absolutely unorganized, that no two events in the action in Phaeacia itself, no two episodes in the hero's narrative of adventures, are indispensable to each other or bound each to each by any indissoluble bond. What does it matter if the elaborate introduction of Nausicaa, the detailed suggestion of her maidenly charm, lead to nothing but our own delight in her personality, or if the mutual liking of the princess and the hero, and the king's cordial appreciation of Odysseus as an ideal son-in-law, lead to no sentimental issue, but only reinforce our admiring interest in daughter, father, and hero? Odysseus listens to Athena's account of the people and their history, sees with approving eye the city and its furnishings, the royal palace, but his knowledge and approval have no issue in the subsequent events; he tells a long story of his romantic exploits to the king and the queen, but *that story* does not win him safe escort from the country; such a deliverance is already promised him before the story begins. It is quite clear that the countless generations who have enjoyed the Phaeacian episode of the *Odyssey* have not needed the devices of a sophisticated art to enhance their enjoyment.

Yet it will not mar our pleasure in the *Odyssey* or exaggerate the lesser excellence of the story of Books i–iv of the *Aeneid* if we stop to observe the sureness with which the Roman poet takes this loosely dovetailed framework of the Greek poem and makes of it a close-built structure from which no part can be removed without demolishing the whole. Aeneas, shipwrecked on the coast of Africa, finds his way, under the guidance of his mother, Venus, to the city in process of building under a woman's supervision; his goddess-mother tells him the story of this wonderful queen, her tragic history, and her energetic self-deliverance from the pressing dangers that surround her until now she is accomplishing a man's task, the building of the city of Carthage and the administration of a kingdom; he approaches the city, sees the result of her work, and discovers the queen herself dispensing justice to her people; Dido, not unfamiliar with his own exploits, receives him hospitably, entertains him, calls for the story of his adventures, and, that story finished, the love which was incipient at the end of Book i becomes a consuming fever at the beginning of Book iv, and issues in a tragic catastrophe. Here all the detail of Venus' narrative, the approving observation of Dido's work, lead to the hero's interest in the heroine; the queen's interest has been already aroused, and the story of his achievements and suffering advance admiring interest to love:

> Now felt the queen the sharp, slow-gathering pangs
> Of love; and out of every pulsing vein
> Nourished the wound and fed its viewless fire.
> Her hero's virtues and his lordly line
> Keep calling to her soul; his words, his glance
> Cling to her heart like lingering, barbèd steel. . . . .

So every detail becomes a link in the firm chain that binds indissolubly the first four books of the poem.

B. THE ILIAD

To Virgil the story of the *Iliad* was historic fact retouched by a poet's hand. Eight or more centuries had passed since the poem was composed; the ancient world had grown from childhood to maturity and was even approaching its decline. The Roman poet, like the modern reader, had inherited a wealth of experience from the intervening ages; he could enjoy the noble dignity of expression, the simple directness of narration, the vivid portrayal of physical struggle between heroic figures over whom even more majestic gods—their personal interests sometimes balancing, sometimes outweighed by the scale of destiny—stand watchful guard, often themselves joining in the struggle. Nor did Virgil, in spite of the Greek poet's obvious absorption in purely external action, miss the occasional glimpses of an inner conflict, such as, in the pride and easily excitable temper of Achilles and the arrogance of Agamemnon, served to link together the chapters of external action in a unity that even today establishes for many of us the indivisible entity of the *Iliad*. Virgil's delight was not qualified by contradictions of fact or any other irreconcilable oppositions in the subject matter of the story; Virgil himself reveled in such perverse contradictions in his own epic, many of which not even the finishing touch of the poet himself, stayed by a premature death, would have removed from the *Aeneid*. Only the modern scholar, his judgment prejudiced by his favorite hypothesis, sees and exalts the importance of many trivial discordances in the facts of the Homeric story. The wrath of Achilles at being unjustly deprived of a slave woman whom he has won by right of conquest produces the conflict with Agamemnon and Achilles' withdrawal from the action of the war; that wrath subsides only when Patroclus, the dearest friend of the hero, has been killed by Hector; the love of Achilles for his friend draws Achilles back to the contest, and leads to the final catastrophe, the duel between Hector and Achilles and the supremacy of the Greeks; the games at the funeral of Patroclus conclude with visible recognition of the renewal of amity between Achilles and Agamemnon, and the last book reveals the essential nobility of the hero in that, reminded of his own gray-headed father, he delivers to aged Priam the body of Hector, bruised and torn by his own vindictive hands; so both the inner and outer action are substantially unified. In between the withdrawal and the return of Achilles the action comes back to him sufficiently to preserve in the reader's mind a consciousness that Achilles is the center of interest; in Book ix Agamemnon sends a plea for help to Achilles, which he indignantly rejects; in Book xvi, still unreconciled, Achilles reluctantly allows his friend Patroclus to don his (Achilles') armor and represent him on the field of battle; these are the important stages in the rising and falling action between his withdrawal in the first book and his reconciliation with Agamemnon in the nineteenth. So not only are the end and the beginning knit together, but the thread of action is unbroken from start to finish. Yet, unbroken as it may be, Virgil would have felt that it was a mere thread, too fragile to establish any real coherence, from his standpoint. Though there are in the first eighteen books of the *Iliad* some parts that are better organized than others, the general impression made upon the reader is of a series of fights, mainly duels, of which some may be more important than others, but most can be eliminated without any serious loss to the action; in brief, there is nothing inevitable in the inclusion of any member of the series, and no bond of cause and effect to bind the members of the series. The poet is evidently composing for an audience whose joy is mainly in the realities of war, and a war in which individuals, not masses of men, are the controlling forces. For two-thirds of the poem, then, the reader's attention is dispersed over no small number of lesser heroes—Diomed, Ajax, Aeneas, Hector—and these heroes are in prowess quite equal, and in character only seldom and slightly differentiated.

THE BATTLE AT THE SHIPS

The seventh book of the *Aeneid* concludes with the muster-roll of Latin forces; the eighth book records Aeneas' visit to Evander and to the Etrurians to obtain recruits for the Trojan side; in Aeneas' absence the war begins; Turnus seizes the opportunity to attack the Trojan camp while the Trojans are without a leader. Four books, the ninth to twelfth, inclusive, a third of the entire poem, are devoted to descriptions of battles. The economy of the poem required that considerable space should be allotted them; Aeneas must be given a chance to display his heroism, and especially to recover the prestige lost at Troy. Battles and sieges filled the later history of Rome; its early history should record similar sublime achievements. The type of heroic battles was furnished by the *Iliad;* Virgil could not think of changing this type or substituting a new one; the *Iliad* had exhausted almost all conceivable phases of the type, and any attempt to evolve new forms would have resulted simply in eccentricities. Accordingly, Virgil is here dependent upon Homer as he is nowhere else except in the funeral games of the fifth book; yet the descriptions are thoroughly Virgilian.

The difficulties were not slight. Tradition furnished Virgil with very few suggestions for the characterization of minor heroes such as were necessary to the detail of general conflicts; he was forced to create characters, and his success in that respect we shall consider later. At present we are concerned with the action, the scenes, the motives, the structure. Here it was easy to draw upon Homer, but Virgil could not count upon such an excessive interest in fights between individual heroes as Homer found in his audience; it is true that in Virgil's day, as in Homer's, the valor of the individual rather than of the mass settled the issue, but few of Virgil's audience had an active interest in military achievement based on personal experience; Virgil could count only upon general human sympathy. The working rule which he evolved from these circumstances was to concentrate interest upon as few persons as possible, to make the descriptions appeal to his readers by the cautious use of Roman and national features, to emphasize the universally human, that is, the psychological content of action, and in the general composition to keep the reader in suspense by the varied and energetic dramatic movement of his narrative.

At the opening of the ninth book Juno sends Iris to stimulate Turnus to attack the Trojans. The Trojans have been bidden by Aeneas not to leave their fortifications during his absence. The Latins consequently find no immediate outlet to their impulse save in the ships, which, left by the river bank, are exposed to direct attack; these ships they burn, but by a miraculous intervention, which the poet explains as due to the immortal nature of the trees out of which the boats are constructed, the ships are saved; they change into water nymphs, who swim proudly down the Tiber to the sea; none the less, the Trojans are deprived of a means of escape from Latium, and the Latins are thereby encouraged. The Latins encamp for the night, and the Trojans begin to consider plans for the next day's action. Two sentries in the Trojan intrenchments plan a sally through the Latin camp as an effort to convey to Aeneas the tidings of impending disaster; this episodic exploit of Nisus and Euryalus fills the interval between the burning of the ships and the next day's general engagement. It is the engagement of the next day which constitutes the first battle of the campaign.

This battle (vss. 503 ff.) is conspicuously different from the three subsequent engagements in so far as it becomes primarily an account of the prowess of the chief antagonist, Turnus. He is the central figure, and the poet's art consists mainly in keeping him before our eyes without our losing sight of the large masses of combatants. It will be observed in our sketch of the action how consistently the events lead up to and away from him; Turnus is the unifying element of the description. The fight is directed against the fortified camp of the Trojans. The poet gives us first a description of the masses, the Volscians, Trojans, Rutulians, as such; then, of other large bodies of troops indicated by the names of their leaders, Mezentius and Messapus. The last two form a transition to Turnus, who is brought prominently into the foreground in an invocation of the Muses. The account of his achievements begins with the destruction of one of two towers in the Trojan fortifications, which Turnus burns with his firebrand; he catches one of the two Trojans who escape from the collapse of the tower, and then demolishes part of the wall. This encourages the Latins to renewed attack, and a scene of general massacre is described which momentarily diverts our attention from Turnus as the poet lists with some particularity, though with a redeeming artistic symmetry, the names of the warriors who fall on both sides; this list, however, culminates in Turnus' achievements, but only again to lead away from him to a rather lengthy episode in which young Ascanius is given a chance to show himself worthy of his sire. The success of Ascanius marks a temporary shift in favor of the Trojans; they not only hold their ground, but two among them, Pandarus and Bitias, stalwart giants, open the gates of the camp, of which they are the sentries, and kill the Latins who press in through the opening; the Trojans, thus encouraged, sally forth from the gates, disobeying Aeneas' express command; this marks the high tide of Trojan success. At this climax the opposing force, led by Turnus, turns the scale; rushing upon the Trojans, he kills those who are farthest out; then Bitias, right at the gates; the Trojans flee before him; Turnus rushes through the gate into the Trojan camp; Pandarus imprudently shuts the gate; a duel between Turnus and Pandarus, set off by speeches, marks the climax of Turnus' achievements; Pandarus is slain; the Trojans are terrified. But Turnus, in a blind and bloodthirsty rage, neglects a great opportunity; instead of opening the gates so that his Latin forces may enter and co-operate, he endeavors single-handed to destroy the enemy; though he kills the fugitives in crowds, he cannot hold out for any length of time; as soon as the Trojans are brought to their senses by the speech of Mnestheus, they mass themselves against him. In spite of his renewed efforts Turnus is forced to give way; Juno's help, which protected him in the crisis of the duel with Pandarus, now fails him; but by leap-

ing into the Tiber fully armed and swimming safely back to
his men he performs a great feat even in the act of retreating.

This narrative has all the marks of Virgil's art. It leads
up gradually to Turnus, brings him into the action with an
important achievement, leaves him temporarily in what follows, but only, always and inevitably, to return to him again,
and ultimately to stay with him entirely. He is the center of
the action, and yet not he alone, but the fight as a whole, is
described. So far as possible the narrative is coherent; this
coherence is attained by bringing out the effect of individual
feats upon the masses; then the effect upon the masses issues
again in individual achievement. The movement of the narrative is not in a straight line; neither Turnus nor the Trojans
win one success after another; but an advantage on one side
is followed by counteraction; this is overcome, in turn, by
further counteraction. Nor is this broken line of action
marked by regular rise and fall with monotonous effect, but
there is a carefully planned rising movement such that the reversal of fortune sets in when a high point is reached. The
action in this battle cannot end at a climax, at the highest
point, for the chief antagonist, though entitled to an opportunity to display his prowess, must not achieve success in
storming the camp at this stage of the narrative. Consequently the poet can mark the conclusion only by a distinctive exploit, Turnus' safe escape, not by the strongest effect of a
genuine climax; interest, however, is increased at the end.
Throughout the story there is no repetition of motives and
situations, and only one episode, the exploit of Ascanius; and
that is closely organized with the environing action.

The unity and concentration in Virgil's narrative are even
more patent when we compare the Homeric story of the fight
at the ships in the twelfth *Iliad* which was Virgil's model.
Here there is a walled camp with a dike in front of it. The
attacking party plans to attack in chariots, but is dissuaded.

Five divisions march on foot against the wall. One leader, apart from the rest, insists on approaching in his chariot; not, however, across the dike, but against an open gate; there he finds two giants confronting him (corresponding to Bitias and Pandarus in Virgil); what happens to him we never learn, though Homer indicates an unsuccessful issue. Meantime the five divisions on foot make some headway, largely through the efforts of a second hero who demolishes part of the wall, but vainly tries to climb over it. Homer informs us that without this second hero the attacking party would never have got within the walls, but instead of making this clear in the action, the Greek poet transfers our attention to a third hero, Sarpedon, who breaks down an entirely different part of the wall with a rock. So in Homer we follow three distinct chapters of action, each entirely unrelated to the other, with consequent incoherence and absolute lack of unity. Virgil made all three chapters one, and made a single hero, Turnus, the controlling force in every chapter.

THE COMPACT AND THE DUEL

The fights in the *Iliad*, as we have seen, are mainly duels; the action of the *Aeneid* concludes with a duel between the hero and his chief antagonist, Turnus; the prize of victory is the hand of the princess Lavinia; in so far as a duel between the two prominent characters of the poem concludes the main action, the fight between Hector and Achilles in the *Iliad* is an obvious parallel, and without doubt suggested to Virgil the dramatic end of his epic. But so far as this duel is fought to win a woman, the parallel situation is not the duel between Achilles and Hector, but the earlier scene of the third book of the *Iliad*, in which Paris and Menelaus, the paramour and the husband of Helen, agree to fight together, letting the issue of the duel determine the issue of the entire war. Virgil, characteristically, combines both these scenes of the *Iliad* into a new whole.

At the beginning of the first general contest in the *Iliad*
the Greek Menelaus, husband of Helen, catches sight of Paris,
who has stolen his wife from him; Menelaus rushes fiercely
upon the Trojan, and Paris cowers before him; Hector, Paris'
brother, taunts Paris with his cowardice, and in response to
his chiding words Paris offers to fight in single combat with
Menelaus, the winner to carry off Helen and the war to be decided accordingly. Preparations are made for sacrifice and
the solemn swearing of oaths preliminary to the duel. The
poet, meantime, draws our attention away from the scene of
the duel to the chamber of Helen, who is urged by a goddess
to go to the walls of Troy and witness the combat between
her husband and her paramour. There follows one of the
most famous and effective scenes of the *Iliad*, in which Helen
introduces to Priam the various Greek chieftains whom she
knows but whom the aged Trojan king is supposed to be seeing for the first time. The two chapters of the action, the
preparation for the duel and the scene on the wall, are neatly
joined by the approach of a messenger who summons Priam
from the wall to take part in the ceremony preliminary to the
duel. Up to this point Virgil had no occasion in his scene to
draw from the *Iliad*, and the famous scene on the walls of
Troy he might well have hesitated to emulate. The duel now
begins; Menelaus is successful, but as he is about to kill
Paris, the goddess Aphrodite snatches up Paris, "very easily,
as a goddess may," and sets him down in his perfumed chamber at home, to which she now calls Helen from the walls of
Troy. The poet concludes the third book by representing
Menelaus as looking vainly for Paris. The Trojans and their
allies, he says, did in no wise hide Paris from Menelaus out of
kindly feeling for Paris; they would have discovered him to
Menelaus, had they known where he was, for they hated Paris
like black death. Agamemnon then formally declares that the
duel has been won by Menelaus and formally demands the

surrender of Helen. At the beginning of Book iv the poet
again shifts our attention, this time to the assembly of the
gods, met to decide the issue; shall they allow things to take
their course and award victory to the Greeks, or intervene and
promote the continuance of the war? The second alternative
is adopted after a vigorous dispute among the gods, which the
poet describes in detail. Athena, a goddess, goes down from
Olympus to the battlefield and persuades one of the Trojan
allies, Pandarus, to shoot an arrow at Menelaus; she tells
Pandarus that thus he shall win favor and glory before all the
Trojans, and before Paris most of all. Pandarus, as the poet
suggests, is foolishly won over, shoots the arrow, and wounds
Menelaus. The poet describes in detail the bow of Pandarus,
the preparations for the shot; we hear the bow ring, the string
twang, we see the arrow leap into the air; we see it strike; we
see the bloodstains on Menelaus' body. There follows a long
speech of Agamemnon to Menelaus in which the former comforts his brother. Menelaus assures him there is no danger,
but a surgeon is sent for, whose skilful handling of the wound
is described. Meantime the Trojan army advances to join battle. Agamemnon, on the Greek side, in two hundred verses
moves about from one Greek hero to another, stirring him up
to war. Then the battle begins.

The striking characteristic of this Homeric scene, from
Virgil's standpoint, was the vivid and detailed description of
all the external features: the reader, by following Homer's
account, can make the garments that Menelaus wore, construct the bow that Pandarus used for his shot, and the shot,
the wound, the healing process, all are photographed for our
benefit. On the other hand, Homer neglects entirely to relate
the external action to any inner forces; he expressly says that
the Trojans and their allies hated Paris, but immediately Pandarus, one of these allies, is persuaded to advance the interests
of Paris by shooting at Menelaus. In other respects he omits

inner motivation entirely; the connection between the duel and the breaking of the compact is so loose that modern critics resort to their usual device: Homer could not have done this; some later poet joined scenes originally separate and distinct and botched it. Virgil saw the defect, but probably condoned it; his art, however, was matured; he could not himself so childishly place one chapter of the action alongside another without any organic connection. We may imagine him raising the question: Why should the Trojans, after Pandarus' shot, move at once against the Greeks; why don't the Trojans stone Pandarus to death for breaking the terms of the compact? Why does Agamemnon marshal the Greek forces; why does he not restrain them, and appeal to their sense of honor? These questions, however, be it understood, do not express harsh criticism of Homer; they only suggest what had happened in the development of epic art in the eight centuries that intervene between Homer and Virgil. Finally, Virgil would have noted that this narrative, vigorous as it may be in individual chapters, as a whole moves with great slowness and halts all along the way. The council of the gods on Olympus, the long dialogue between Agamemnon and Menelaus after the latter is wounded, the activity of the surgeon, the two hundred verses of Agamemnon in which he stirs the Greeks to action—these even the modern reader admits as genuine epic episodes, to be expected in the early stages of the artistic epic, but to Virgil they disturb the main action.

The twelfth book of the *Aeneid* opens with Turnus, the chief antagonist of Aeneas and the rival suitor for the hand of the princess Lavinia, furiously eager to meet Aeneas. The father and the mother of the princess endeavor to restrain him, but he wins them over; a duel is arranged between the two heroes. The people gather to exchange oaths and swear agreement to the terms of the duel, which is to decide the issue of the war. But while they are gathering, the goddess

Juno confers with the divine sister of Turnus, expresses her anxiety and distrust, and urges the sister of Turnus to use her discretion in nullifying the compact and renewing the general engagement. This corresponds to the council of gods in Homer, but Virgil has changed the position of the scene; it comes before the duel, not after the critical moment of the duel. The oaths are taken. But before the duel begins, says the poet, the followers of Turnus begin to feel that the match is unequal, that their leader is at a disadvantage. Turnus himself stands silent, dejected. His divine sister notes the growing murmurs and takes advantage of them; she goes from one soldier to another and inquires if it is fair to let one life be staked for many heroes. The doubts and distrust increase. The enemies of Aeneas are already clamoring to annul the compact. The divine sister seizes the psychological moment. She sends a deceptive augury. An augur among the followers of Turnus interprets it to mean the forced departure of Aeneas from the shores of Latium. So saying, he hurls his javelin and strikes a follower of Aeneas; the wounded man is one of nine brothers; his eight kinsmen are naturally eager to avenge him; the followers of Turnus are only too willing to oppose them. So the desire for a general conflict spreads through both forces; there is a tumult round the altar where the oaths are sworn; but Aeneas checks the uprising: "The pledge is given and all its terms agreed. 'Tis only I do lawful battle here." An arrow from an unknown source wounds him; he retires from the scene to attend to his wound; the battle begins.

It is easy to see what Virgil has gained by his rearrangement; the emphasis is entirely on dramatic movement and on the motivation of action from within; all the external descriptions of Homer, which cover hundreds of verses, Virgil omits, except for two verses in which is mentioned the part of the body struck by the augur's javelin; the conference between the two divinities is put first, the wounding of Aeneas is the final act. The breaking of the compact is motivated with particular skill and care; the opposition develops gradually and reaches its climax only when the augur, misled by the omen, hurls his spear; the general fight breaks out only after Aeneas has appealed to the sense of honor of his followers; once Aeneas is removed, Turnus' courage is revived, and the engagement begins. Virgil's dependence upon Homer for the general situation—the compact; the shot, which he divides into two shots; the breaking of the compact—need not blind us to his originality in the dramatic organization of the material and in the psychological explanation of the action.

This scene, at the beginning of the last book of the *Aeneid*, by withdrawing Aeneas from the fight, postpones to the end of the book the actual duel, and thus postponed it finds its analogue in the duel between Hector and Achilles instead of that between Menelaus and Paris. In the twenty-second book Homer has knit together much better than in the third book the chapters of the action. The duel is fought in three scenes; Hector, in the first scene, though doubting his wisdom, decides to confront Achilles, but is so dazzled by his resplendent armor that he turns and flees; Achilles pursues him three times around the walls of Troy. At this point the gods convene, and in a brief scene Athena is encouraged by Zeus to assist her favorite, Achilles; as a result the two heroes now face each other and fight ineffectively, before which, however, Zeus has balanced the fates of the two heroes and indicated the ultimate doom of Hector; this balancing of the fates, briefly dismissed, seems to be at odds with the short dialogue between Zeus and Athena that precedes it. The third scene is a hand-to-hand fight, in which Hector swoops down with his sword, and Achilles, with fatal effect, hurls his spear.

Virgil uses three scenes, but in rearranged order and with other changes. The heroes are brought together, hurl their

spears, and then engage in a long indecisive sword fight; the
contest is an even one when Jupiter balances their fates and
dooms one of them to die. At this point Turnus' sword breaks;
there is no recourse but flight; Aeneas' wound prevents him
from a close pursuit; he hurls his spear, but it sticks in a tree,
from which he cannot remove it; then Turnus' divine sister
provides Turnus with a sword, and Venus, incensed at this,
helps Aeneas pull his spear from the tree. In the third scene,
therefore, the heroes again face each other. At this critical
moment the gods assemble in council, and in a much longer
passage than that in the *Iliad*, Juno is persuaded to renounce
her wrath and the gods formally agree to the supremacy of
Aeneas and the union of Latins and Trojans in an empire destined to greatness. The final issue of the duel carries out the
divine decision.

Here Virgil has accomplished less. He has increased the
complexity of the action and improved the dramatic effect,
but with slighter changes. The flight he has transferred to the
second scene, and he has increased the number of obstacles
confronting successively each hero, so that rising and falling
action is more marked than in the *Iliad*. But he has violated
one of his own principles in allowing a long episode, the assembly of the gods, to interrupt the main action just before
the issue; he puts it later in the action than Homer put the
conversation between Zeus and Athena, and to advantage. He
allows himself the episode at this critical point because the
beginning of the entire poem, in which Juno's wrath is elaborately set forth as the divine force that sets in motion all the
troubles of Aeneas, must find a counterpart at the end, where
the goddess, reconciled, consents to a compromise, the supremacy of Aeneas, but the recognition of her favored people, the
Latins, as co-workers with the Trojans in the establishment
of the Roman empire.

The dramatic sense and the human sympathy of Virgil

are admirably illustrated in a comparison of the closing scenes of these two duels; in the *Iliad*, Hector, struck down by Achilles, in his last words simply considers the disposal of his corpse, and Achilles brutally refuses his request. In the *Aeneid*, the hero, in the act of slaying Turnus, though Turnus does not ask for mercy, is moved to pity and hesitates, but his hesitation is removed when he sees Turnus wearing the belt which he took from the body of Aeneas' young friend, Pallas, after he had slain him. So the dramatic suspense and the appeal to the emotions are maintained to the end.

THE NIGHT SALLY OF TWO SPIES

In the tenth *Iliad* the Greeks have been hard pressed in a long battle that threatens their ships; it is night; both camps are asleep; all in the Greek camp save Agamemnon, who, worn out by anxiety, seeks counsel; the poet expends two hundred verses in getting together the Greek chieftains for the conference. At the meeting Nestor suggests that they send a spy to the Trojan camp to discover the plans of the enemy and take such spoils as may be available. Diomed volunteers, but asks for a companion; many offer their services; Diomed chooses Odysseus; so wisdom and prowess are combined. The two start forth after somewhat elaborate preparations. The poet now carries us to the Trojan camp. Here, too, Hector is wakeful. He calls the Trojan heroes together (the poet uses fewer verses for this assembling) and proposes to send a spy to the Greek camp to find out whether the Greeks are preparing to sail away discouraged or are still watchfully guarding the ships. Dolon is attracted by a large prize to undertake the task. He starts off. We now return to the Greeks, Diomed and Odysseus, who, catching sight of Dolon, let him get past in the dark, and then scurry after him and frighten out of him the information they require about the Trojans, with the further news that there is rich spoil available at the edge of the

Trojan camp in the horses and rich trappings of Rhesus; Diomed and Odysseus then kill Dolon and hasten to the Trojan camp, where Odysseus steals the horses of Rhesus and Diomed kills Rhesus and his companions; Athena reminds them to return before they are caught by the Trojans. Accordingly, they drive the horses back to the Greek camp, stopping only to gather up the corpse of Dolon, and reach camp safely without further adventure. It will be observed that there is not a single obstacle to the success of the two Greek heroes, and that the reader's interest is supposed to be solely in the mere exploit of their venturesome journey.

In the ninth *Aeneid* Turnus takes advantage of the absence of Aeneas to make a furious attack upon the Trojan camp; he espies the Trojan ships, sets fire to them, but they are miraculously saved. Night falls, and the two camps prepare for the next day's conflict, Turnus and his comrades encouraged, the Trojans anxious, for their Aeneas is separated from them by the camp of the enemy. Among the Trojan sentries are two young men, Nisus, "a youth of eager heart for noble deeds," and Euryalus, his friend, "upon his cheek unshorn the tender bloom of boyhood lingered still. Their loving hearts were one, and oft in war they battled side by side, as in that hour a common sentry at the gate they shared." Nisus suggests that he might, all by himself, take advantage of the sleep and drunkenness of their foes and seek a way through the enemies' camp to Aeneas. "The amazed Euryalus, flushed warm with eager love for deeds of glory," assents, and demands that he be allowed to accompany his friend. But Nisus objects to taking a mere lad on such an enterprise: "thy years," he says, "suit better with more life." Euryalus insists, and both of them post off to the Trojan chieftains who are already assembled to discuss plans of action. The proposal is accepted, and the young Ascanius, son of Aeneas, promises the two young men all sorts of prizes if they will restore his father to him. The lad Euryalus asks only that Ascanius, in case of a fatal issue, care for his mother, whom Euryalus leaves without farewell, and Ascanius promises "thy mother shall be mine." Coming to the enemies' camp they find the Rutulians in drunken slumber. Nisus, forgetting his main purpose, urges Euryalus to join him in murdering the helpless foe; they deal havoc far and wide, and take valuable plunder. Nisus reminds Euryalus that dawn is coming, but Euryalus, with an eye to bright colors, stops to seize the blazonry of Rhamnes, his golden belt, and even puts on his head the "gorgeous, crested helm" of Messapus. But as the young fellows hasten on through the camp after this success they fall in with cavalry who are coming to reinforce Turnus; it is dark, and they might still have escaped notice, but the bright helmet on Euryalus' head discovers them to the horsemen. In attempting to escape, Euryalus is separated from Nisus; Nisus turns back to look for him. He hears the tramp of horses, an anguished cry; Euryalus is "facing the whole onset overwhelmed by a loud mob of foes." Nisus bravely attacks and wounds the leader; the leader, maddened, wreaks vengeance by killing Euryalus, in spite of Nisus' loud cries that it is he who dealt the wound; "Euryalus sank prone in death; upon his goodly limbs the life-blood ran unstopped, and low inclined the drooping head; as when some purpled flower, cut by the ploughshare, dies, or poppies proud with stem forlorn their ruined beauty bow before the pelting storm." Nisus flies straight at his foes to kill the man who slew his young comrade, but is surrounded by the enemy; with his last blow he kills the murderer of Euryalus, and himself upon his comrade's breast "found tranquil death and sure repose."

Virgil concentrates: the story starts with Nisus and Euryalus and never leaves them. The action moves with dramatic rise and fall; at the climax of their achievement their fortune is suddenly reversed; and from that point it rises to the close, the revenge and death of Nisus. The poet loses no opportunity to bring out the pathos of his story and the inner impulses that determine the outer action. It is the ambition of Nisus that suggests the venture; the ambition of Euryalus overcomes Nisus' gentle consideration of him; the same ambition brings disaster; they are hardly started before they are eager to return with spoils. Nisus can admonish his friend and caution him that dawn is coming, but he cannot deny him the joy of decking himself in bright colors; it is the bright helmet that invites ruin; once they are caught, Nisus' sole thought is for his friend. Obvious duty was neglected for other considerations, but noble motives underly all their actions. The poet is no moralist; he is content to stir our admiration and regret; but Homer's narrative led to mere interest in the adventure and its issue; Virgil's contains universal truths.

THE FUNERAL GAMES

Religious ceremony is to us something essentially solemn; to the Greek or Roman it might be altogether hilarious, or a happy mingling of the gay and the severe. Even the ritual of death and burial was not devoid of festal elements. From the early republican period to Virgil's own day the funerals of distinguished men on occasion were celebrated in the form of a festival, and such a festival might include the performances of tragedies and comedies and gymnastic contests. In marking the anniversary of Anchises' death by funeral games Virgil was not merely reproducing the custom of the Homeric Age, or earlier; he was reflecting his own environment, and the Roman reader found in the fifth book events with which he was perfectly familiar in his own experience. But the relation to contemporary life is largely accidental; in the main it was the constraint of epic convention that bound Virgil to include funeral games in his poem. The twenty-third book of the *Iliad* represented Achilles as celebrating funeral games over the death of his devoted friend, Patroclus; the theme, once established in epic by Homer, became the vogue, and Greek epics as late as the fifth century after Christ still perpetuate the subject as essential to the completeness of epic.

Such a subject, elaborately treated, is inevitably an episode; the poet may succeed in organizing the whole event as an integral part of his poem, but the fulness of the description always strikes the modern reader as retarding the main action unjustifiably. The ancient reader, however, as the popularity of the Olympic games and of the Roman imitations attests, was easily carried through the detail of description by his consuming interest in athletic sports; the battlefield and the friendly conflict of competitive games never failed to draw the crowd and to move the reader; if there is any difference today, it is only that the crowd is not so much interested in a literary treatment of games as in the games themselves. Virgil managed much better than Homer the perfect organization of these games as part of the action of his poem. In Homer the celebration has little close connection with the main action; the only trace of such connection lies in the fact that Achilles, the giver of the games, shows special favor to Agamemnon; inasmuch as the main theme of the *Iliad* is the quarrel between these two heroes, the celebration to that extent contributes to the development of the main action; but even this is so casually treated that one may well doubt if Homer was conscious of any imperative necessity of relating the games to the theme of the poem as a whole. In Virgil, on the other hand, the games lead to the preoccupation of the men in the Trojan company; in the absence of the men, the women, who are tired by their long wanderings, have an opportunity at last to realize a mischievous intention and end their tedious travels. While the men are busy with the contests, the women plot and achieve the burning of the ships. So the games are closely knit to the following chapters of action. The connection with what precedes is not so close, but satisfies all reasonable demands; here Homer had the advantage of being able to introduce his games immediately after the death of Patroclus; the festival in Homer issues directly in point of time from the circumstances of Patroclus' death. Virgil could not so arrange the event. He had to choose a person of distinction in whose honor the festival should be given; he wisely chose Anchises, the father of the hero; so the games become a further illustration of the hero's devotion to his father. But as we have seen, Anchises had to be removed from the action before the love affair with Dido, which the presence of the hero's father would have made impossible; and once the death of Anchises is put before the Carthaginian episode, the poet cannot easily put the games immediately after Anchises' death; for in that case Aeneas must include the festival in his narrative to Dido at Carthage, and a description by him of peaceful and happy events such as the games would be out of harmony with the trials and tribulations which his story to Dido emphasizes. The games, therefore, must be an anniversary celebration, and to that extent they are somewhat less inevitable than the Homeric contests. If they are to be natural anniversary games, Aeneas must somewhat accidentally return to the place where Anchises is buried; so, after he has torn himself away from Dido, the fleet happens to approach Sicily again just where the Trojans left it prior to the storm that drove them to Carthage. This place in Sicily, it should be noted, was one that deserved to be dignified by an elaborate event; it was well within the ken of the Roman reader, unlike the places in the Greek world which Aeneas had touched in the story of the third book; it was near Mount Eryx, and the town which Aeneas ultimately establishes here is the later Segesta, which in the first Punic War was the one Sicilian town that immediately took sides with Rome against Carthage; here at Mount Eryx was the

great cult of the goddess Venus which the Romans knew as
the mother of their cult of Venus at Rome. Virgil, then, could
not have selected a better place for an important chapter of
the action of his poem; this region was full of notable associations in the mind of every Roman reader of the poem.

The material with which the poet enriched the action was
suggested by the twenty-third *Iliad;* the Aeneas legend contained no such incidents as funeral games; it did include the
burning of the ships, though not necessarily at this place.
Virgil, then, has at the same time prepared for the burning
of the ships by the celebration of the games and dignified the
stopping place by significant action His indebtedness to
Homer is so exclusive and manifest that we have clearer evidence in the fifth book of his artistic purpose than anywhere
else in the *Aeneid*.

The games in Homer are numerous, eight in number, and
arranged so that the reader's interest decreases from beginning to end; more might be added, or some subtracted, without disturbing the effect; of artistic unity the Greek poet has
no conception. Virgil strives both for symmetry and unity, at
least such unity as the subject matter admits; the descriptions
of the first and third contests are much longer than those of
the second and fourth, and the limitation to four games makes
unity easier to attain. This unity is secured simply by giving
special significance to the last contest, in archery. It is distinguished from the others by a miraculous sign from heaven;
this sign stimulates the reader's feeling to the highest point,
and so serves as a sort of climax toward which the action in
the three preceding contests moves. After this fourth contest
there comes, not a fifth competition, but the so-called "Trojan
game," a cavalry maneuver by the young Trojan lads, a
peaceful sport, serving as a restful fourth act after the climax; and immediately there follows the tragic issue of the
play, the burning of the ships. Of course the generally happy

features of the games make the comparison with a tragedy far from perfectly appropriate, but the point is that Virgil has definitely striven to organize the chapters of the action into a series of well-knit parts, into a unity marked by increased tension at a critical point, and by progressive action toward a final issue.

Not only symmetry and unity, but variety, are essential to Virgil's realization of his ideals. The eight games in Homer are marred by tedious repetition. The Greek poet has a number of mechanical details, such as the announcement of the contest, the description of the prizes, the names of the contestants, which he allows himself to bring in without any variation of formulas; Virgil, though compelled to include these same details, takes pains to vary from contest to contest the manner in which these prosaic facts are stated. In respect to the number and the nature of the contestants Homer was content to repeat himself constantly; Virgil has only one contest in which two competitors appear; only one in which a large number of contestants take part; four heroes struggle for the prize in the boat race and in archery, but even here the first contest is differentiated from the fourth by the fact that the crews of the four captains are among the competitors, while in archery four individuals compete. Again, Virgil introduces a variety of persons in his four contests. In the boat race the competitors are mature men, ancestors of famous Roman family, the patricians who rank next to the hero Aeneas himself; in the foot race the young men still without reputation are the runners, and the youngest wins the race; in the boxing match it is the aged Entellus who wins, and the two contestants are half-mythical persons, for reasons which we shall presently consider; in the archery contest, though the match otherwise corresponds to the boat race, the fact that their Sicilian host, Acestes, takes part and wins gives the match special distinction. Finally, as regards the issue of the dif-

ferent contests, although all the issues in Virgil were anticipated by Homer, Virgil has used each type of conclusion once,
while Homer, forced thereto by the greater number of contests in his poem, has repeated the different types; so in Virgil the boat race is the only one in which the conclusion is perfectly normal; in the foot race Nisus' dubious trick of trip-
ping up a runner makes the issue questionable; in the boxing
match the fighters have to be separated before the end; and in
archery the victory is attended by a sign from heaven.

Virgil's choice of contests and scheme of characters were
affected by many different considerations; so far as possible
he followed in these matters his model, Homer; but his own
environment and special artistic considerations sometimes led
to modifications. It should be remembered that such a theme
as these athletic sports could not fail to be affected by contemporary conventions. Augustus had done a great deal to
encourage interest in competitive games, not only because he
was himself capable of enjoying them and because the people
found them entertaining, but also, probably, because he found
in them a means of improving the physical vigor of a people
whose strength had been sapped by the civil wars. He had
founded on Greek soil a new contest, the games sacred to
Apollo, at Actium, which Virgil had in mind when he represented Aeneas as stopping there, in the narrative of the third
book, and celebrating games; as in the Greek games of the
earlier classical period, so in these Roman imitations it was
proper enough for Romans of noble family to appear as contestants in most of the competitions, but with some limitations; for Roman patricians, though they might drive in a
chariot race or run in a foot race, would hardly think of strip-
ping themselves and cudgeling one another in public. These
conditions are reflected in Virgil's account. Patricians take
part in the boat race, as they might in a chariot race in Virgil's day; and the young nobles run in the foot race; nor is the

archery contest undignified. But when we reach the boxing match we find a very different situation; here it would be impossible for a respectable Trojan or Roman to participate; Virgil carefully excludes any possible connection with his immediate environment; he emphasizes the mythical past from which the boxers come; Dares has already vanquished the Berysthian Butes at the funeral games of Hector; Entellus was taught his art by the deified Eryx, who fought with Hercules on the shore of Sicily; the gloves are made of seven thicknesses of bull's hide, as mythical as the contestants themselves; so we are conscious that a semi-mythical past, rather than Virgil's own time, is reflected in this contest.

In choosing the contests the poet followed Homer in selecting the foot race, the boxing match, and the archery contest; except in the last case these games were common in his own time; archery was hardly a real pursuit of the Romans; it comes from the mythical past of the Homeric age, and for that reason the king, Acestes, son of a god, more easily takes part in it, and the supernatural sign is in harmony with the unreal character of the competition. As the first contest Virgil undoubtedly would have taken the chariot race from Homer if he could have done so; but the Trojans, having traveled over the sea in ships for more than seven years, had little occasion to make use of chariots or horses; here then, the conditions of his own story led Virgil to substitute a boat race, which, however, he modeled after Homer's chariot race. For all four matches, therefore, there was a scheme of action supplied by Homer; and even traits of character were more richly provided in the Homeric narrative of the action than was usually the case in the Greek poet, who generally is too absorbed in the mere events to individualize the actors themselves. From a comparative study of the action and of the characterization in the separate contests we gather the clearest evidence of Virgil's ideals and of his ability in realizing them.

The chariot race in Homer brings five heroes into competition; one of the five Homer practically eliminates from his narrative; we learn that his horses are slow, and that he himself is the least competent of the drivers; but he plays no part in the narrative of the race. It will be observed that this is realistic; any race may have such an unskilful team and driver; but in the artistic treatment of a race this realistic feature offends the sophisticated taste which requires a poet to keep the movements of all the contestants within our view; this fifth driver is lost sight of as soon as he is mentioned; the race of the remaining four is then treated in two distinct chapters; we learn what happens to 1 and 2, then of the experiences of 3 and 4, but Homer never brings together these two pairs—again thoroughly realistic. So an actual race might have turned out; but the artistic effect is better if the poet manages to keep all four before our eyes. Nor does Homer attempt, except in one case, to emphasize the character of the drivers; and in that one case the effort is incomplete; the poet represents the aged Nestor as giving elaborate advice, the fruit of his own matured experience, to his son, Antilochus, before the race; paternal interest and filial respect are happily suggested, but when the race comes off, Nestor's advice has no practical issue, and the preliminary scene becomes an episode, effective in itself, but isolated. It is, however, to an inner quality, his sagacious driving, that Antilochus owes his victory over Menelaus. In the course of the action the poet distracts our attention from the race to the grandstand, again a bit of realism; in the grandstand two heroes are disputing who's ahead in the race, and betting on their own keenness of vision; it is in itself, or might be, a pleasant relief from the tension of the race, but the reader is conscious of being abruptly diverted.

Virgil's problem and his accomplishment in the boat race were very different. Here, and in all the other contests, the Roman poet was handicapped; Homer could use as competitors famous heroes whom every reader of Greek epic knew from his reading of earlier chapters of the *Iliad;* these were the same heroes who had interested him on the battlefield in other books of the poem. It is surprising that Homer took any pains to characterize, for he could count on the reader's interest without any individualizing of the participants. But Virgil, up to this point in his story, had not had occasion to introduce any less important characters than Aeneas, Anchises, and Ascanius; the faithful Achates and one or two others had appeared incidentally, but the reader was as yet quite unacquainted with the minor heroes who accompanied Aeneas on his journey; nor were they, in any case, men of such paramount importance as Odysseus, Ajax, Agamemnon, and other contestants in the *Iliad.* Virgil had practically to create new characters for the action of the fifth book and interest us in them immediately. His efforts are only partially successful. The captains of the ships in the boat race are made as prominent as possible by representing at least three of them to be progenitors of Roman families; but the choice of Roman families seems to us rather unsatisfactory; the Memmian and Cluentian families which Mnestheus and Cloanthus represent were hardly famous enough in Roman history to suggest at once distinguishing characteristics to the Roman reader; the Sergian family descended from Sergestus is better chosen; the Roman reader probably recalled Sergius Catilina, the great conspirator of the first century, and such a reader may easily have seen in Sergestus' rash action in the race—he is shipwrecked in trying to find a short cut round the rocks— the prototype of Catiline's experience and the explanation of his reckless nature. It is the pre-eminence of the inner qualities of the captains, rather than the excellence or inferiority of their ships, as determining the issue of the race, that sharply differentiates Virgil from Homer. Sergestus acts as he does in a moment of frenzy; Gyas would have won but for a foolish fit of temper in which he throws overboard his pilot; Mnestheus, swept on by a consuming ambition, stimulates his men to extreme exertion, and would almost have snatched victory from Cloanthus, who, by skilful steering in spite of a crippled ship, has overtaken them all, but Cloanthus at the last moment shrewdly secures the help of divinities, and through his opportune piety speeds in ahead. So character, supernatural assistance, excellence of tools combine to decide the issue, and in that order of importance; in Homer the same three factors appear, but in reverse order: the best horse wins in Homer, the best man, in Virgil. In the structure of the action, too, Virgil illustrates the development of conscious art in the centuries intervening between Homer's time and his; the episodic scene in which Nestor gives advice to Antilochus, the abrupt distraction of the reader's attention from the race to the grandstand, find no place in Virgil, and the two distinct and separate chapters of the account of the race become a closely knit unit, in two parts to be sure, but both parts organized in such a way that we never lose sight of the contestants from start to finish. The decisive moment in the race is made the turning midway in the contest; we learn first how the contestants stand as they approach this turning-point; first Gyas, then Cloanthus, then, changing in position or side by side, Mnestheus and Sergestus: The order, then, is 1, 2, 3, 4; then 2 gets ahead of 1 by a skilful maneuver; 1 loses his pilot; 3 and 4 hope to overtake 1; 3 is less than a ship's length ahead of 4; 4 urges on his oarsmen; but before 3 and 4 can overtake 1, 3 runs on the rocks; 4 then catches up with 1, and creeps up close to 2. Here the second part begins, with two ships outdistanced and the issue lying between 4 and 2; the zeal of the rowers and the interest of the spectators increase; the suspense continues to the end; only just before the harbor is reached does 2 appeal to the gods and win the victory. Nor does Virgil lose sight of the grandstand in describing the race; at the start the various sympathizers in the audience applaud their favorites; when the pilot is thrown overboard there are shouts of laughter from the grandstand; when Mnestheus makes his final spurt, the spectators cheer him on; and when Sergestus, who, through his rash impetuosity, was wrecked in the course of the race, comes pulling in his boat with broken oars after the race is over, the grandstand greets with jeers his belated appearance. And his disgrace is happily emphasized by the fact that he arrives after the prizes have been awarded, the victors crowned, and the victorious crews decked with fillets; Homer, less effectively, had Eumelus, who met with a similar accident in the chariot race, come slowly in before the award of prizes; so the action drags in the interval of waiting for Eumelus before the award is made. Homer, however, may be credited with taking less pleasure in the misery of the unsuccessful contestant.

The foot race in Homer is run by Ajax, Odysseus, and Antilochus; Antilochus falls behind; the final issue rests with the two others; they are evenly matched; Odysseus is close on the heels of Ajax when the goddess Athena intervenes; Ajax slips, and Odysseus wins. Divine intervention, accident, settle the race. We might perhaps expect Antilochus to reappear in the action and creep up on Odysseus, but the poet eliminates him almost at the start. Virgil takes over this plan of action, but with characteristic changes. There is a large number of competitors, but Virgil, after mentioning seven by name, along with a number whom fame forgets to tell, follows the action of five. His introduction lingers affectionately over Nisus and Euryalus, whom, later in the poem, he makes the heroes of a pathetic episode; Euryalus is "for beauty's bloom

renowned, Nisus for loyal love"; otherwise the competitors
are vaguely described. Nisus at the start gets a good lead;
second, but at a long interval, comes Salius; as third, Euryalus, and close at hand, two other contestants. Nisus' victory
seems assured, but he slips and falls; this, of course, corresponds to Ajax' slip in the *Iliad;* but Virgil is not content with
this single reversal of fortune; he has already celebrated
Nisus' friendship for Euryalus; Nisus, accordingly, in falling
thrusts out his foot, trips up the second man, Salius, and so
brings in his own young friend, Euryalus, a winner; the trick
is not sportsmanlike, and Salius claims the prize as cheated of
the victory; but "general favor smiles upon Euryalus, whose
beauteous tears commend him much, and nobler seems the
worth of valor clothed in youthful shape so fair." Aeneas consoles Salius with a special reward. This is true Virgilian handiwork. Virgil is not content with the simple action of the
Iliad; he must make it more dramatic; the one fall leads to
another, and the action is complicated; nor does the Roman
poet fail to justify the second bit of action psychologically:
he repeats the first accidental fall, but the second slip is due
to Nisus' devotion to his young friend; for his sake Nisus, in
his affectionate zeal, forgets how dubious his manœuver is from
a sportsman's standpoint. Nor is Virgil, in dwelling upon this
incident, unconscious that the reader of the tragedy which
overtook these two devoted young friends in the battle scenes
later in the poem will be more deeply impressed by that catastrophe in recalling this manifestation of the loyalty of the
young fellows in peaceful competition.

The grim, huge-bodied giants in the boxing match are in
contrast to the supple young fellows in the foot race. The
scheme of characters is taken from the *Iliad;* one competitor
is a recognized champion, confidently claiming the prize; the
other confronts him reluctantly. But the self-assertive champion in Virgil is not so rough as Epeius in Homer; Epeius

loudly boasts: "Thus I declare and thus shall it come to pass;
I will bruise his skin and break his bones." Dares, in Virgil, is a much-softened Epeius, and in the softening has lost
some of the clearness of characterization which the Homeric
boxer possesses. But the reluctant opponent is enriched and
strengthened by Virgil; in Homer ambition and desire for the
prize stimulate Euryalus to combat on unequal terms; Diomed encourages him to fight, as Acestes does Entellus in the
Aeneid; but Entellus is more seriously affected in the course
of the match by his own feelings; he is stirred to take part by
the words of Acestes, but also by his own consciousness that
as pupil of the divine Eryx he must justify his fame; he is a
champion of Sicily against Troy. Entellus aims a heavy blow
at Dares; Dares dodges, and Entellus falls heavily to the
ground, his blow wasted; but this mishap stimulates him to a
furious attack; the disgrace, the consciousness of what he
once was and still is, redouble his strength and bring him a
glorious victory. All this elaboration of the effect upon his
feelings is Virgilian. Homer realistically lets the best fighter
win; one may doubt whether so competent a man as Dares
would actually give way before the sudden fury of Entellus
as Virgil represents the action. But Virgil is indifferent to the
muscular strength or technical skill of the fighters; he attrib-
utes the outcome, not to Entellus' physical strength, but to
his inner qualities.

Similarly in the action itself Virgil has modified the structure. The different possibilities in the handling of a boxing
match are illustrated by four ancient poets: Homer; Apollonius in his account of the boxing match between Polydeuces
and the barbaric Amycus in the second book of *The Argonauts;* Theocritus, in his twenty-second idyl on the same general situation as Apollonius; and Virgil, in his modification
of Homer's scheme of action. In Homer the action is very
simple and brief; Epeius, who challenges the field, wins as a

matter of course over Euryalus, who has to be forced into the fight by Diomed; the fight itself is briefly described; a quick thrust by which Epeius gets the better of his opponent ends the contest almost as soon as it begins. Apollonius gives much more detail, but it does not bear upon the fight itself; the Hellenistic poet devotes most space to the preliminaries, and on reaching the fight prefers to give us pretty similes rather than facts; still, he has made over the scheme of action; Polydeuces dodges a heavy blow and hits his opponent, now off his guard, with such force that Amycus collapses. Theocritus thought he was improving the description; if a fight is to be described, it must be a real fight, such as one actually sees in the stadium; so all the different thrusts and feints, spitting of blood, and bruises are described with the fulness of expert knowledge, and the final bout, which runs much the same as in Apollonius, is faithfully reported for the benefit of the sporting world. Virgil refuses to indulge in any such realistic detail; he draws a comprehensive sketch in the manner of Apollonius, and differentiates the two contestants by peculiar traits of character; but in the scheme of action he follows none of his three predecessors; the simple line of action in the earlier poets he complicates by introducing an unexpected reversal of fortune; Entellus, who, conscious of his stiffness, has hitherto stood in one spot and kept on the defensive, suddenly becomes a different man as the result of his own ineffective blow which lands him on the ground: his strength intensified by shame and anger, he drives his opponent before him with a hailstorm of blows, and but for Aeneas' intervention would have done Dares serious injury.

Such psychological factors are missing from the fourth contest in archery. The poet does not attempt to characterize the participants. The appearance of Acestes, who is a Sicilian, though of Trojan descent, and their host, gives the match special distinction; and from Acestes we may expect something startling. In the action Virgil follows Homer's account of the same competition very closely, but the slight changes are productive of striking results. The target is the same in Homer and in Virgil: a dove tied by a cord to a mast. In Homer there are only two shots; the first shot misses the dove, but cuts the cord, and the dove flies off; the second competitor, however, with quick but sure aim, hits the dove on the wing. This is neatly devised, but Homer has spoiled the effect by making, as part of the conditions of the match, the very unlikely hitting of the cord a condition for obtaining the second prize. Virgil omits this, properly enough; such a hitting of the string should be an accident. But he has also increased the number of shots. The first shot hits the mast; the second cuts the cord; the third hits the dove in flight; Acestes, left without a target, shoots his shaft into the air, and quite unexpectedly brings a sign from heaven—his shaft "takes fire, tracing its bright path in flame, then vanished on the wind." By this miracle the feeling of the spectators is wrought to the highest pitch just at the close of the games; no other contest can follow; it would have the effect of anticlimax.

The significance of this miracle has been variously understood by modern readers. The conventional view is this: in the games celebrated in the year 43 in honor of Venus just after the death of Julius Caesar a comet appeared which the people interpreted to indicate the deification of Julius Caesar; Virgil introduced this miraculous sign at these games to suggest to the Roman reader this event of the year 43, and as a compliment to the Julian family. In this case, it will be noted, this sign has no inevitable relation to the action of the fifth book, and becomes a mere spectacular detail introduced, or rather lugged in, for special temporary purposes. Such an interpretation runs counter to all that we have seen of Virgil's artistic ideals; Virgil has everywhere shown his aversion to the purely episodic and ornamental. Nor does a study of the

context justify us at all in accepting this view and supposing
that Virgil here for once neglected to organize this detail as
an inevitable part of the environing action. At the outset we
may note that a meteor such as is suggested in the *Aeneid* has
little correspondence to a comet which appeared for seven
days in succession after Caesar's death. But it is more significant that the subsequent action in the *Aeneid* does not reveal
the slightest reference to Caesar. Aeneas immediately interprets the sign as referring to Acestes; it suggests that Jove
intends Acestes to receive peculiar honor; Aeneas, therefore,
presents him with a special prize; but the significance of the
omen bears not only upon the immediate, but upon the distant, future of Acestes; this is made clear in the parenthetical
comment of the poet in his description of the sign: "Then
suddenly all eyes beheld such wonder as portends events
to be; a great issue in later days made clear the meaning,
and awe-inspiring prophets foretold ominous events long-deferred." This mysterious sentence modern commentators explain as meaning that the omen of the meteor in Virgil fore-
bodes the second omen of the comet at the games of Venus;
but this is a singular proceeding; one omen does not foretell
another omen in ancient religious practice and belief. This
omen we should expect to refer only to Acestes, and the
mystical sentence is clear when we consider what happens to
Acestes in the less immediate future of the action. After the
games are over it is discovered that the Trojan ships have
been burned by the women; it becomes necessary to establish a town here to accommodate the Trojans who cannot
travel on to Italy now that the ships are burned; Acestes is
made the king of this new settlement; the new settlement becomes in historic times the important city of Segesta, which
every Roman reader remembered as the one Sicilian city
which in the first Punic War sided with Rome against Carthage. These are the long-deferred events which the awe-in-

spiring prophets foretell as indicated by the miraculous sign:
Acestes receives immediately a special prize; less immediately, a peculiar honor in being made king of the new settlement;
later still that settlement is involved in the terrible struggle
between Carthage and Rome. So the sign is inevitably related to the action of this book, not an ornamental addition
complimentary to the family of Caesar.

After the suspense occasioned by this miracle comes the
relief of the Trojan game, not a contest, but a picturesque and
peaceful maneuver which proceeds without interruption. Once
the feelings of the audience are quieted by this spectacle, the
tragic news of the burning of the Trojan ships may produce
its full effect.

For the Trojan game Virgil of course had no model scene
in the twenty-third *Iliad*. Both characters and action are his
own invention. He represents the young lads in the Trojan
company as engaging in a childish make-believe of the real
fighting for which this maneuver serves to prepare them. In
so doing he was primarily paying Augustus a compliment;
for among the various physical exercises which the emperor
cherished and encouraged his people to practice, none was a
greater favorite with him than this Trojan game. In the Rome
of Virgil's day it was as popular as football with us, and not
without some of the perils of the American game; for, later,
serious accidents to the young aristocrats who participated in
it spoiled the Emperor's pleasure and diminished its general
popularity. In Virgil's account, however, it is an innocent
pastime. The poet evidently enjoys the picture of these young
fellows; he represents their Trojan fathers as receiving the
shy-faced boys with loud acclaim, and joyfully tracing in the
features of the sons their sires; he interests the Roman reader
by making the young leaders of the cavalry company ancestors of noted Roman families, and somewhat obtrusively connects this particular occasion with the sport of contemporary

Rome by telling us that Ascanius introduced the game into Alba Longa, whence it was transmitted to Virgil's own day and generation. But Virgil is not mechanically explaining contemporary custom; nor is the prominence which he gives to young Ascanius and the other progenitors of Roman houses merely an attempt to dignify officially the genealogical fiction of his own time. The poet loves these young men; he rejoices here, as elsewhere in the *Aeneid*, to dwell upon the distinguishing traits of youth; and in such scenes Virgil is original, as he seldom is in his characterization of older men. In the first book he lets Cupid assume the form of Ascanius; in the fourth book Ascanius gives vent to a childish eagerness, in the African hunt, to fight with some real wild beasts instead of the tame varieties that the occasion afforded; and earlier in these games we have seen the poet's delight in bringing out the youthful beauty of Euryalus and the loyal friendship of Nisus. The same Nisus and Euryalus, endowed with the splendid beauty of youth, young Marcellus, Pallas, and Lausus—all these in later books are doomed to an early death, and in these tragedies of premature death the poet reveals his own personality in the genuine feeling and tender compassion with which he relates their tragic fate. Though such peculiar interest in young men is a characteristic trait of the poet, it is quite in accord with the sympathies and active efforts of the emperor, Augustus; he too was much concerned with the moral and physical welfare of the growing generation, and hoped to see his people reinvigorated by the new blood of young Rome.

Somewhat obscured by the numerous participants in the various games stands the giver of the games, the hero Aeneas. In the *Iliad* Homer succeeded splendidly in giving Achilles slight but distinguishing traits which prevented the giver of the games from being overshadowed by the contestants. Achilles frankly praises his own horse, naïvely rejoices in

Antilochus' praise of him, is amusingly complacent when his prizes are approved by the competitors; Achilles settles the quarrel in the grandstand during the chariot race; he is magnanimous to his former enemy, Agamemnon, and takes kindly notice of aged Nestor. Virgil is not able to accomplish so much for Aeneas. And in what little he has accomplished, he has merely sifted out available themes from the Homeric material. Aeneas shows a princely generosity toward his host, Acestes; his sense of justice moves him to compensate the contestants for accidents that are not their fault, as does Achilles; he interferes in the boxing match and saves Dares from serious danger, as does Achilles similarly in the wrestling match in Homer. But in general Aeneas is far weaker than Achilles.

If, however, Virgil has failed here, he has succeeded in giving an atmosphere, a dominant tone, to the whole celebration which is entirely wanting in Homer. The Roman poet has completely transposed himself into the situation of his active characters, and communicates to the reader the feeling of the participants. This dominant feeling is joy. The key note is struck at the beginning of the book in the joy which Acestes feels in the unexpected return of the Trojans; in joyful mood the participants gather in the bright morning of the festal day, and this mood, never darkened save for a moment in the boxing match, reaches its highest point in the last spectacle, the brilliant procession of joyous young men. As the poet lingers affectionately over the cheerful splendor of the beginning and of the conclusion of the games, so all the way through he seizes every opportunity to adorn his picture with bright cheerful colors: the green of the branches and of the wreaths, of the grass-grown natural amphitheater and stadium, the purple of the victors' fillets, the gold-bordered mantles of the princes and of the garments offered as prizes, the glitter of weapons and costly ornaments—all this is the outer complement of the joyous inner mood of the spectators, of their tense moments of joyous suspense, and of the happy mood of the proud victors in the games, of Aeneas, and of Acestes, to whom so unexpectedly comes the highest prize in the contests. Nor need any reader be reminded how much this atmosphere of joy contributes to the artistic effect of the environing action. The fourth book ended the tragedy of Dido, and in that drama came the discouraging chapters of the hero's adventures, his trials and tribulations, his inevitable abandonment of Troy, his unwearied but wearying efforts to find the new home that fate and the gods promised him; after the games comes the calamity of the burning of the ships, and in the sixth book the hero leaves the world of light for his journey into the realms of the dead. In the midst of this tragedy and gloom, of exposure to perils at Troy, hardship at sea, and the loss of their ships, is a brief chapter of action in which joy and peace are supreme; so the poet, consciously or unconsciously, varies restfully the dominant tones of his narrative.

Such an extended comparison of Virgil's poem with the Greek epics leads to the discovery of touchstones by which we may recognize the Roman poet's originality and his principles of art. In the organization of action into well defined and coherent wholes, in the progressive development of action by alternating rise and fall toward climax and catastrophe, in the careful interrelation of outer action and inner forces, in emphasis upon character, in the elaboration of pathetic effects, we are likely to find Virgil himself, his ideals, his mint mark upon the gold drawn from the rich mines of earlier epic.

In this comparison it has often been convenient to imply that Virgil improved upon Homer and that his remodeling was better than the original. But such implications must not be seriously considered. It is not a matter of better or worse, but only of difference. The poems must be valued with reference to the time of composition and to the environing conditions which produced them. Some modern readers may be so sophisticated as to prefer the dramatic refashioning and the psychological explanation of action for which Virgil stands. We are emphasizing the fact that in these principles and their application lies Virgil's distinctive accomplishment. There is no trace, in our remains of epic narrative between Homer and Virgil, of such preoccupation with the dramatizing of epic story in an epic poem, no indication in the long epic of such consistent and artistic emphasis upon the inner life. But there are always losses and compensations. The inward-turned eye must often see spiritual torment and distress. The serious drama must be tragedy rather than comedy. The *Aeneid*, says a stimulating critic, is one long *Miserere*. In spite of Virgil's achievement we shall always seek new vigor and rejuvenating force in the noble directness of Homeric narrative. Perhaps because the tired world today is more closely akin to Virgil's world than Homer's it may need the refreshing artlessness of the Homeric story.

C. HELLENISTIC EPIC

Although the *Iliad* and *Odyssey* were pre-eminent in Greek tradition, epic poems, less significant from an artistic standpoint but hardly less potent in their effect upon epic tradition, were written, both contemporaneously and somewhat later, upon the usual mythological themes. These poems have come to us only in fragments, and those few in number, but the Greek tragedians of the fifth century derived the material of their plays largely from these minor epics of the so-called "epic cycle" as well as from the Homeric poems; and the lyric treatment of myth in the preclassical period of Greek literature is also probably much indebted to the epic cycle for its subject matter. After the age of Homer and the epic cycle, however, the composition of epic poems becomes a rare form of literary expression, although the older Greek epics continue to be recited in public and in that way, as well as through use in the schoolroom, are kept very much alive in Greece through the classical period; but the treatment of myth in the fifth century is usually dramatic, and the great triad of Greek tragedians in the classical period occupy the foreground of literary history. Narrative epic is limited at this time to occasional versions of the myths of Heracles and Theseus; one isolated case of a novel departure from conventional subject matter is the attempt of Panyassis, a kinsman of the historian Herodotus, to write an epic on the Persian Wars; but this resort to contemporary history is seldom repeated in the subsequent centuries. Toward the end of the fifth century Antimachus of Colophon, in an epic on the story of The Seven against Thebes, marks the transition from the older epic to the revived form of Greek epic narrative which was cultivated from the fourth century on in the Hellenistic period. Antimachus' poem, so far as we may judge from ancient criticism of it—for it is not extant—was grounded upon a faithful, scholarly study of the verse and language of the Homeric epics. The poem won the admiration of Plato, and in later times Antimachus was regarded as second only to Homer, but hardly a close second; Quintilian, the Roman critic, notes the absence of certain artistic qualities.

The activity of scholars in the Hellenistic period was to a considerable extent devoted to the establishment of standard texts of the works of authors who, in the earlier centuries, had come to be recognized as master-workmen. Such scholars not only decided questions of text—variant readings, interpolations, and what not—but provided comments on forms, syntax, and the whole range of antiquities as suggested by the poem which they were editing; this thorough study of the masterpieces of the Homeric and classical periods naturally led them to speculation, to more or less academic theorizing, about the canons of literary art, and they evolved certain general principles from their observation of various literary types; an early example of this speculation is Aristotle's *Art of Poetry*. These same scholars were not only the editors of the older literature, but themselves often produced the poetry of the Hellenistic period.

About the beginning of the third century academic theorizing had led to a controversy over the fitness of the long Homeric epic in the new conditions of the later period. Some contended that such long poems were no longer feasible; an epic poem should be brought within the compass of a single recitation, or, as we should say, should be short enough to be read at one sitting. The evidence for this controversy is slight, and the underlying thoughts of the disputants are not easily discoverable. But we may suspect that the argument was the result of a somewhat sophisticated taste that demanded a more essential unity of composition than the older epic exhibited. In recitation of the *Iliad* and *Odyssey* chapters of the older epic were selected for public reading, and such chapters of Homer were often very loosely constructed; the intensive cultivation of such short units quite independent of the long epic would promote concentration and coherence. But whatever the arguments in the controversy, the practical result was the development, in the Hellenistic period, of short epic poems alongside of the continuation of the long Homeric epic. Virgil, of course, in choosing the long form, was not so much taking sides in any such controversy as consulting the needs of his subject matter; it would hardly do to confine within the narrow limits of a short epic the national legend of Rome's nascent greatness. In his youth, perhaps, he had followed the opposite Hellenistic tendency in his short epics on the gnat and the sentimental story of Scylla, if he wrote those poems.

Only one example of the perpetuation of the long Homeric epic has come down to us from the Hellenistic period: the story of the Argonauts as told by Apollonius of Rhodes in the third century. The value of this poem lies not so much, from our present standpoint as students of the *Aeneid,* in Virgil's occasional dependence upon it, but rather in its general significance as an illustration of Hellenistic methods in the continuation of Homeric epic. Virgil, in taking over the language and verse of Homer, the machinery of Homeric epic, the Homeric world, was still under the influence of those Hellenistic models whose work had determined the course of Latin poetry in his youth and seriously affected Virgil himself in his juvenile verse and in his *Eclogues* and *Georgics.* The Roman poet in his maturer years is still following the current, but maturity has brought no little independence; we can hardly estimate either his subservience to Hellenistic methods and ideals or his own reservations and modifications without considering, not merely the parts of Apollonius' poems which Virgil happened to use, but the broader aspects of the Greek epic which illustrate the later Greek ways of handling epic narrative.

Apollonius was a scholar-poet. He held the position of librarian at Alexandria, to which only eminent scholars were appointed. His epic poem, when the modern scholar studies its diction, its choice and extension of Homeric forms of speech, at once reveals Apollonius as taking sides on questions of grammar that were disputed by him and his scholarly contemporaries. Even the layman as he reads will easily find traces of bookishness; the poem on its face suggests the study of many volumes of mythology, religious rites, customs in general, topography; it carries the heroes through a vast extent of territory, at every step revealing full knowledge of the most remote peoples, their lands, their superstitions, and customs. Nothing that we know or can guess of Apollonius' actual experience discovers any first-hand acquaintance with so much of the ancient world. It all points to faithful grubbing in various books. Such grubbing is to a large degree a Hellenistic feature; so Virgil devoured his Cato and Varro and Greek handbooks on agriculture in writing his *Georgics,* and even thumbed the volumes of earlier historians and antiquarians in writing his *Aeneid;* but the important point is not the bookish interest preliminary to the poet's own composition, but the extent to which he allows his bookishness to appear in his own finished poem. Apollonius opens the door of his workroom; Virgil, with some striking exceptions, conceals in the *Aeneid* his diligent study of myth and history.

The Greek poet reveals his bookishness to the largest degree in the accumulation of stopping places which serve to show his purely literary acquaintance with remote parts of the world without being made significant by any important adventures. Next to this interest in localities from a purely cartographical standpoint comes an exaggerated emphasis upon the real or imagined connection between the present and the remote past; an adventure, admirably portrayed, often with deep pathetic effect, is concluded by the reminder that the incident gave rise to a custom perpetuated in his own time, or to the name attached to that locality. This interest in the cause, in what we call aetiological myth or legend, is a singular characteristic of the less realistic types of Hellenistic poetry; in a measure it is only a phase of that conservatism which delights to link the present and the remote past, but in the Hellenistic period, as offering an explanation of contemporary institutions, it probably reflects an antiquarian interest stimulated by the new conditions of the new era. From this Hellenistic trait Virgil does not entirely free himself; so, for example, he concludes the pathetic story of Misenus by telling us that the promontory was ever afterward called by his name. But in general it is noteworthy that Virgil leaves to the

reader such obvious relations between the past and present;
so he has Aeneas establish games at Actium without the
slightest explicit relation to the festival which Octavian had
founded; and in the second book Anchises goes through all
the precise ritual of taking the auspices, but Virgil leaves the
reader to discover that he means the incident to be the prototype of the familiar procedure of his own day. In all such
matters the Roman poet artistically trusts the national feeling
to interpret the significance of the event.

The story of the Argonautic expedition starts with Jason;
his uncle, Pelias, has stolen the kingdom of Jason's father.
Jason's claim to the kingdom of his father is indisputable, but
his uncle imposes upon him the labor of obtaining the Golden
Fleece, which is guarded by a dragon in the kingdom of
Aeetes, in the land of the Colchians, at the eastern end of the
Black Sea. Jason gathers about him the great heroes of the
Greek world—most of them men of greater renown than he—
and the company sails from Thessaly, on the northeast coast
of Greece, under his leadership in the good ship Argo. The
action of the poem carries them directly across the Aegean,
through the Hellespont, Propontis, and Black Sea; but on
reaching Colchis the preliminary labors imposed by Aeetes
and the final theft of the Golden Fleece are made possible
only by the magic power of the king's daughter, Medea, who
has fallen in love with Jason and elopes with him. The enmity of the Colchians thus aroused necessitates a different
homeward route, which takes the heroes through Southern
Europe, north of Greece and Italy, thence south, east, and
north to their starting-point in Thessaly, an almost complete
circle. The journey both to and from Colchis is replete with
adventure, but the chief unifying element is the destination,
Colchis, in the first half of the poem, and the winning of the
fleece, and their safe return to Thessaly in the second half.
The adventures, therefore, constitute a mere string of epi-

sodes. The action is symmetrically divided; the journey to Colchis is covered in the first two books; the adventures in Colchis, in the third book; the homeward journey, in the fourth book.

Any poet who attempts an epic narrative on such a theme at the outset renounces organic unity of action and confronts an almost hopeless task in the treatment of character. Individual chapters of the action may be successful, but they must remain episodes; individual characters may be well drawn, but concentration on any one character or small group, and the proper subordination of others to the smaller group, are impossible.

It may safely be said that Apollonius handles character better than action, but he cannot surmount insuperable obstacles. It is no easy matter to give Jason a strong individuality and at the same time allow Heracles and Peleus and Polydeuces the prominence their importance warrants without dimming the luster of Jason's achievement. Aeneas, in the Roman epic, is attended by no such large and distinguished company; in the *Aeneid* it is easier to throw into sharp relief the hero, and to give distinguishing traits to minor characters without lessening the prominence of Aeneas. So it happens inevitably that Jason does not dominate the action as does Aeneas or Odysseus in other epics; in this respect Apollonius' problem is like that in the *Iliad*, but in the *Iliad* the author was relatively indifferent to character treatment. In the succession of episodes in the story of the Argonauts various heroes are brought into such prominence as their reputation merits and requires; the boxing match in the second book exhibits the excellence of Polydeuces; Heracles is the hero of the conflict with the earth-born giants in the first book, and of the Hylas episode; the sons of Boreas are prominent in the adventure with Phineus and the Harpies; and so on. Jason is the center of interest in the labors of the third book, which consequently has more unity than any other part of the poem, and in episodes here and there. But in general the action of the poem does not find its central point in Jason exclusively, and does not consistently issue from him or any other hero.

Under these conditions the character of Jason, so far as it is revealed, is likely to prove weak. The poet has little interest in establishing strong motives for Jason's activity. There is some consciousness of a sacred mission implied here and there, but nothing that compares with Aeneas' insistent effort to establish the gods of Troy in a new home in Italy. We might suppose the Greek poet would strongly define Jason's obligation to his own father, who has been robbed of his kingdom by his brother, Pelias; but what little consciousness Jason may have of the necessity of laying the ghost of Phrixus or of proving his own claim to the throne of Pelias is dispelled in the island of Lemnos by a queen, Hypsipyle, whom the poet does not equip with any such charms or strength of character as Aeneas might find in Dido to justify his own temporary neglect of a sacred mission. The best indications of a forceful personality appear in the Jason of the third book. There the action is dominated by him, and even in the fourth book his leadership is better justified than in the first two books. But in the last two books there is a vagueness, or, less charitably expressed, a positive inconsistency, in the portrayal of Jason: if one grants that in the third book the hero is genuinely in love and sincere in his protestations of loyal devotion to Medea, the action of the fourth book puts him in a bad light. It is true that the poet does not make it possible to establish any charge against Jason of faithlessness toward Medea, but the two occasions in the fourth book on which the heroine's escape to Greece is jeopardized are not marked by any positive activity in her behalf on Jason's part. The elopers are pursued by the Colchians under the leadership of

Medea's brother, Absyrtus, and the danger of her being recovered by the Colchians is imminent; it is Medea's own strenuous interference that insures her safety. Later, when they reach the land of Alcinous and Arete, with the Colchians still at their heels, the question whether Medea shall be surrendered to her own people or be allowed to remain with Jason is referred to King Alcinous for arbitration; it is Medea's intercession with the queen, Arete, that leads to the anticipation of the king's decision. He confides to his wife that he shall decide in favor of Jason if the pair have been married; Medea, learning this from the queen, takes pains to have the marriage consummated before the king renders his decision. In all this action Jason is passive; policy, rather than sentiment, seems to be the controlling factor in his mind, and Medea becomes the Lavinia rather than the Dido of the Greek poem. It is true that these episodes serve to individualize the heroine, but the poet should succeed in this without making the hero absolutely unheroic. The passive attitude of Jason in several episodes of the last two books harmonizes with the dejection of the hero in the midst of the trials and tribulations of the first two books; here Jason has to be stimulated to action by the more vigorous Argonauts; again he falls far short of the heroic.

The essential weakness of Jason I have elaborated because it seems to me to suggest an explanation of the peculiar treatment of his own hero, Aeneas, by Virgil. Modern criticism has often noted that the Aeneas of the last six books is a strenuous, forceful Achilles, but in the first six books at best only a patient hero, and at the worst, dispirited and wholly wanting in heroic energy and resourcefulness. Out of this discord between the Aeneas of the first half and the second half of the poem recent criticism has endeavored to evolve an artistic development of character within the action of the poem; Aeneas, patient and even dejected in the first five books, is encouraged by the revelation of Rome's future in the sixth book, and appears in the last six books with his latent courage and energy revived. Such development of character would be almost unique in ancient literature; it is peculiarly modern. I think it more likely that the patient Aeneas of the first six books is a lineal descendant of the dejected wanderer whom Homer had not infrequently depicted in his Odysseus, and whom Apollonius, with considerable injury to our modern requirements, had elaborated in the case of Jason. The Hellenistic elaboration of the figure is due to special conditions of the thought and literary ideals of the period; such a character makes possible an appeal to the pity and sympathy of the reader, and a revelation of the distress and torment of the soul which Hellenistic poetry delights to portray; in the second place, at least in the case of Aeneas, philosophical theory emphasized patience, submissiveness, as characteristic of the wise man in his attitude toward the perils to which his destiny exposes him.

The heroine of Apollonius' poem is a better creation. The myth provided a barbaric and uncanny princess; Medea is descended from the sun god; Circe, the cruel magician of the Odyssey, is her aunt; Medea inherits supernatural power and unfeeling exercise of that power. Poetic treatment of myth often humanizes such a character; Euripides, the tragic poet of the fifth century, had made a dramatic conflict between the barbaric cruelty of Medea in planning to kill her children and the human weakness of motherly love. Apollonius, largely because of the strong sentimentalizing tendency of Hellenistic poetry, makes Medea strong and weak by turns; in the fourth book she reveals the qualities which the barbaric princess of the myth leads us to expect; she rends in pieces her brother, Absyrtus; and her forceful action in various emergencies is in accord with the heroine of the old story. In the third book she is introduced as priestess of Hecate, and her uncanny power is manifested in the drugs which she gives to Jason to enable him to perform his tasks. But the love story of the third book presents her as an ordinary human being, quite in contrast with the glimpses we get in the fourth book of the barbaric princess, priestess of Hecate, grandchild of the sun god. She is the conventional woman in the distress of love; psychologically true as her vacillation may be, realistic as the emotional disturbance is, she is thoroughly humanized and weakened beyond the needs of the situation. Like a conventional woman, she hesitates to elope with a stranger; it is a matter merely of maidenly modesty, an obstacle easily overcome. Apollonius could not provide any such dramatic conflict as Virgil employs in the story of his barbaric queen, Dido, whose loyalty to her first husband makes any yielding to a new love a genuine difficulty.

Nor are the minor characters of the poem sharply or consistently individualized. Orpheus is perhaps the most winning of them all, but not through any peculiar trait revealed in action; he is picturesque; as a hero interested in music, he stands apart, in sharp contrast with his strenuous peers; there is a beautiful sweetness amid the risk of adventure in his song of creation in the first book, in his drowning of the siren voices with his own melodies. Heracles is well portrayed as long as he remains in the action of the poem; his magnanimity at the outset in declining the leadership of the expedition, his prowess in the fight with the giants, his unwearied rowing after all the others have lost their strength, his amusing wrath when his oar snaps, his devotion to his young favorite, Hylas, his scorn of Jason when the hero forgets the purpose of the expedition in the company of women who have lured them to the island of Lemnos—these are abundant and consistent traits, but the easy characterization of Heracles illustrates the poet's difficulties. The same poem cannot contain Jason and so strong a character as Heracles; hence, per-

haps, Apollonius removes Heracles entirely from the action at
the end of the first book. One of Virgil's best characterizations, that of the Etruscan tyrant, Mezentius, is curiously anticipated by the Greek poet; Idas, in Apollonius' epic, is a
Mezentius in embryo; his only god is his spear; but Apollonius declined to develop Idas as Virgil has developed Mezentius; he remains a mere suggestion of unrealized possibilities.
Polydeuces, who comes to the foreground in a boxing match
at the beginning of the second book, is a gentlemanly athlete,
in pleasing contrast with the brutal giant with whom he
fights. Pathetic elements are emphasized in the figure of the
blind prophet, Phineus, whose food is stolen from him by the
Harpies.

As consistency is often wanting in the treatment of character, so in the structure of action there is little organic unity.
The episodes are loosely strung together; the winds and the
coming of darkness or of dawn are alone responsible for the
landings of the heroes at particular places, or their departure.
The romantic story of Jason and Medea, of course, rises to a
distinct climax, and the vacillation of Medea in making up her
mind provides a retarding element; but there is no real dramatic conflict, or any such dramatic progress as Virgil develops in the story of Dido. In the fourth book the pursuit of
the Colchians, the murder of Absyrtus, and their imminent
danger from the remaining pursuers until Alcinous arbitrates
the case, supply some dramatic elements, but the dramatic
effect is lost in the guidebook enumeration of stopping places
and in pedantic digression. Individual episodes in the first
two books are sometimes vigorous, but Apollonius enjoys the
stationary and picturesque scene; action, and character issuing in action, do not interest him so much as sight and sound;
he appeals to the eye and ear, and above all, to the emotions,
of his reader. The nearest approach that he makes to the
combination of dramatic structure with pathetic effects is in

the Dolian episode in the first book; the young king of the
Dolians, newly wed, leaves his bride to welcome the Argonauts and generously entertains them; on leaving him they
are confronted by the giants, who block their way out; forcing
their way through the giants, the Argonauts, without knowing
it, are driven back by contrary winds to the land of the Dolians, whence they started; the young king, now mistaking
them for hostile neighbors, sallies forth to attack them, and in
the conflict that follows is killed by those whom he has just
entertained with generous hospitality.

But Apollonius, in the constant appeal to the feelings of
his readers, is usually not content with stirring pity and sympathy; he runs to gruesome adventure and stimulates horror
and awe. The realistic description of the shriveled skeleton of
the prophet, Phineus, and the loathsome details of the Harpies' vicious attacks upon him, illustrate the less attractive
expression of the poet's effort to move the reader. The dragon
and the tasks preliminary to the acquisition of the Golden
Fleece, the whole environment of Medea in her Colchian home,
are grim and awe-inspiring. It is interesting to note that Virgil, who is entirely in the current of this Hellenistic emotional
appeal, excites the gentler emotions of pity and sympathy and
avoids or mitigates the grim and gruesome. Even in the content of his similes and incidental features of description Apollonius, like Virgil, reveals a pervasive human sympathy, a
keen sense, for example, of the pathetic possibilities of the
relation of mother to babe and of the other domestic ties
which the Roman poet so frequently emphasizes; but the
Greek poet loses all restraint, and often betrays a distinct
straining for effect, a conscious effort to attract attention. So,
in a conventional epic description of night, endeavoring to
describe the universal sleep of nature and of humanity, he is
not content to tell us that the dogs had stopped barking, that
wayfarer and sentry were intent on sleep, but has to add that

deep sleep overcame many a mother of dead children; Virgil would have omitted the gruesomely tragic adjective and suggested that even the tired mother found rest, but Apollonius is tempted to make the picture sensational.

In the love story, emotion is regnant. As the earliest extant treatment in any full form, and from a modern standpoint, of the sentimental situation, it is desirable to observe the poet's manner of handling this theme in comparison with Virgil's management of Dido's love story. Apollonius represents, in the main, Hellenistic methods with which Virgil was certainly familiar.

The love of Medea is not the result of natural causes; it is inspired by supernatural agents. Hera and Athena, fearing the dangers to which their favorite Jason is exposed in obtaining the Golden Fleece, attempt to win the aid of the enchantress, Medea, in his behalf by causing her to fall in love with the hero. The two goddesses seek Aphrodite and persuade her to urge her son, the boy Eros (Cupid), to shoot his fatal dart. The poet devotes much space to this preliminary action, and introduces into it an elaborate picture of Cupid as the Hellenistic period conceived him, a saucy mischievous boy; his mother finds him cheating Ganymede at a game of dice, and has to bribe him with the offer of a ball to do the service desired. The boy betakes himself to the palace of Aeetes, which the poet describes at length, and shoots his dart at Medea while the king is giving audience to Jason and his followers: "Deep down in the maiden's bosom burned his arrow like unto flame; and at Aeetes' son (Jason) she cast side-glances of love evermore, and panted hard and fast 'neath its burden her heart in her breast, nor did any remembrance remain of aught beside, but her soul was melted with rapturous pain." A long quarrel ensues between King Aeetes and Jason, the latter leaving the interview much depressed by the prospect of labors to be accomplished before he shall win the fleece. And as Jason leaves the hall, "ever wandered the maiden's eyes askance unto him, as she stealthily parted her veil's soft gleam. And her heart was a smouldering fire of pain; and her soul, as a dream, stole after her love, flitting still in his track as his feet fared on." Medea herself now leaves the royal presence, and the poet continues: "Surged like a rushing river the thoughts through her breast—the thoughts that Love awakeneth ever. And before her eyes the vision of all evermore she had—himself, even like as he was, and the vesture wherein he was clad; how he spake, how he sat on his seat, how forth of the doors he strode, and she dreamed as she mused that all the world beside had showed none other such man. In her ears evermore the music rang of his voice, and the words that in sweetness of honey had dropped from his tongue." Once she reaches her chamber she is filled with pity and anxiety for him, to which she gives expression in a soliloquy. The poet then returns to the external action. At the suggestion of Medea's nephew, Jason and the others decide to obtain the help of Medea in accomplishing the tasks; for her power as an enchantress may be valuable; the nephew hopes to win the aid of Medea through the intervention of his mother, Medea's sister, Chalciope. The nephew goes to seek his mother. Meantime the poet returns to Medea; she is having dark and deceitful visions in which she seems to herself driven to choose between her parents and Jason, and chooses Jason. Waking from the dream, again in soliloquy, she rejects the thought of helping Jason—unless her sister asks her to help the hero; she gets out of bed yearning to go to her sister, but lingers, held back by shame, and finally rushes back into her chamber and throws herself in panic and writhing upon the bed. A maidservant, observing her strange actions, reports them to her sister, who hastens to Medea inquiring her trouble; Medea craftily says that Chalciope's sons are in danger in the event of Jason's failure; in the conversation that follows Chalciope persuades her to help Jason. But no sooner has the sister left than Medea is filled with shame and fear, and after the poet has described her irresolution, Medea, again in soliloquy, wavers this way and that, weighing the infatuate folly of loving a stranger over against the strength of that love; but at last the decision is made, and she draws forth the casket containing the magic drugs and goes to meet Jason, with whom her nephew has now arranged an interview for her. The meeting place is the temple of Hecate, and here Medea waits with her handmaidens; the maidens sing and dance, but Medea has no thought for song and dance: "Her eyes ever wandered askance . . . . and over the ways, turning aside her cheeks, far off ever strained she her gaze. . . . . The heart in her breast oft fainted, whenever in fancy she heard fleet past her the sound of a footfall, the breath of a breeze as it stirred." The hero comes at last: "Then it seemed as her heart dropped out of her bosom; a dark mist came over her eyes, and hot in her cheeks did the blushes flame, nor backward nor forward a step could she stir; all strength was gone from her knees, and her feet to the earth seemed rooted. . . . ." Once the two confront each other, they "all stirless and wordless stood face to face; as oaks they seemed, or as pines upsoaring in stately grace, which side by side all still mid the mountains rooted stand when winds are hushed; but by breath of the breeze when at last they are fanned, stir they with multitudinous murmur and sigh—so they by love's breath stirred were to pour out all in their hearts that lay." Jason begs the favor of her help, reminding her how Ariadne helped Theseus and Theseus eloped with Ariadne, and praising Medea's beauty. Medea's "eyelids drooped, while played a nectar smile on her lips; and the heart of the maid by his praising uplifted melted; her eyes are a moment upraised to his eyes, and all speech faileth; no word at the first of her lips may rise; but in one breath yearned she to speak forth all her joy and pain." She draws forth the drug from her girdle, and the poet says: "Now would she even have drawn forth all her soul from her breast and had laid it with joy in his hands for her gift, had he made request. . . . ." In the conversation that follows Medea gives him directions for the use of the drug in his labors, and coyly seeks to learn more about that Greek maiden, Ariadne, who helped Theseus and ran away with him. Only at this late point in the story does the poet allow Jason's love for Medea to be manifested; and after some toying with the suggestive theme of Ariadne, the hero's proposal of elopement is made and accepted, all with tender caressing words from Jason and much shedding of tears by Medea. From this stage on the narrative centers about Jason, who successfully accomplishes his labors and wins the Golden Fleece; nor does Medea henceforth show any of the weaknesses of a love-stricken heroine; she exhibits, on the contrary, infinite resources in energetic initiation and forceful execution of plans to save herself and Jason in their perilous journey to Thessaly.

No modern reader, on considering the poet's elaboration of Medea's suffering in the torment of love, can fail to note the contradiction between current notions of classicism, as literary critics use the term, and this presentation, full and frank and realistic, of Medea's unregulated emotions. Here is none of the restraint, dignity, taste, sense of proportion that we attribute to classical, as distinguished from modern, art; on the contrary, the portrayal of Medea's frenzy is thoroughly modern, though nowadays most of such detail is relegated to rather cheap grades of fiction. It was this frankly realistic handling of love, with emphasis upon the physical effects of the disease—for so the Greeks regarded it—that Virgil found established in literary tradition when he came to write the story of Dido. His story bears no relation in theme to the

third book of Apollonius; Dido's story is that of an abandoned sweetheart, not of a successfully accomplished elopement; in that respect the analogous situation in Apollonius is
the story, earlier in the poem, of Hypsipyle, the queen of
Lemnos, who, having with the other women ejected from their
island all their own men, invite the Argonauts to abide with
them; in this case Jason, like Aeneas, is temporarily diverted
from the purpose of his journey; but in the story of Hypsipyle
Apollonius, instead of handling the situation in the fashion of
his own age, resorts to the methods of Homeric epic; Jason,
after enjoying for a space the intimate friendship of Hypsipyle, leaves her without any great upheaval, much as Odysseus, in the *Odyssey*, finally parts from his elfish mistresses,
Calypso and Circe. But though Virgil's story finds no precise
analogy in Medea's situation, all the details of Medea's
physical suffering and torture of soul recur in Dido's experience; not that Virgil was imitating Apollonius, but simply
that the Roman poet was conforming to Hellenistic methods.
Yet he does not slavishly conform; the realistic frenzy and
vacillation, the unregulated emotions of Medea become, in the
case of Dido, carefully developed emotional stages in the
heroine's love tragedy, each stage marking a distinct advance
over the preceding stage; furthermore, every period in Dido's
inner disturbance is made to issue directly in some corresponding change in the external action; the result is a progressive development to climax and tragic catastrophe, with
the inner experience and outer action closely related; in brief,
Virgil, though accepting all the conventional details of the
Hellenistic love story, artistically regulates the emotional experience of his heroine.

And there are other illuminating points of difference and
resemblance. Apollonius provides Medea with a sister who is
employed by the poet to connect the outer action of Jason
and his friends with Medea's wavering resolution to love and

help Jason; but this sister has no organic connection with
Medea's emotional distress; she is not on confidential terms
with the heroine. Virgil, too, provides Dido with a sister; but
Anna is Dido's soul mate; to her Dido confides her distress;
the Greek poet, by isolating Medea, has no way of portraying
her experience except through description and soliloquy; the
confidante, Anna, in the *Aeneid* makes it possible for Virgil to
dispense almost entirely with soliloquy and reveal his heroine's suffering in dramatic dialogue between Dido and her
sister.

Although the epic of Apollonius is of interest to us, mainly, simply as representing Hellenistic methods in epic narrative, in one or two relatively small matters Virgil drew directly upon the Greek poet. Aside from a few descriptions and
similes, his indebtedness lies in two incidental themes. In
the third book of the *Aeneid* the adventure with the Harpies is
a curious blending, with some awkward results, of the adventure with the cattle of the sun god in the *Odyssey* and the
story of the Harpies in Apollonius' second book. The other
contribution made by Apollonius is in the cave scene of the
Dido story. Here the Roman poet has transferred simply the
scene setting; in Apollonius' fourth book, as we saw earlier,
Alcinous has decided that Jason shall be allowed to keep
Medea if he has married her; Medea, learning Alcinous' decision, takes pains to have the marriage take place before
Alcinous announces publicly his judgment. The wedding is
celebrated in a "hallowed cave," and Hera sends the nymphs
with offerings of flowers to the scene of the ceremony; similarly, Virgil, though arranging very differently the details and
carefully explaining the resort to the cave by means of the
storm that interrupts their hunting expedition, takes over the
scene and the nymphs and makes Juno herself participate in
the ceremony; but Virgil's elaboration of the material gives

an impressive significance to the borrowed situation which Apollonius fails to convey.

Virgil's dependence upon Homer only brings out clearly his own artistic principles and ideals. Apollonius does not suggest that Hellenistic epic had anticipated the Roman poet in the careful structure of dramatic action, but the poem on the Argonauts does certainly limit the extent of Virgil's originality in his constant appeal to, and portrayal of, the emotions; this is clearly a field already cultivated as part of the introspective activity of later Greek literature. No phase of Virgil's art is nowadays more promptly recognized than his human sympathy, his emphasis upon domestic ties, his emotional appeal in general; yet this is not exclusively a Virgilian characteristic. There is, however, in Virgil's use of the emotional possibilities of his narrative, an individual trait. The Hellenistic poets had opened the floodgates to every variety and to the full tide of emotion; Virgil reveals in his epic a sense of propriety which is not unlike the restraint of fifth-century Greek art; like the Hellenistic poet, he is sensitive to every opportunity to reveal the inner feelings of his characters and to stir the emotions of his readers, but he eschews the grim and gruesome and prefers to excite pity and sympathy rather than horror and awe. And even in the stimulation of these gentler emotions and in the portrayal of conditions that produce them he seldom allows a realistic hysteria, but artistically regulates the emotional disturbance, and in the portrayal carefully relates it to external action.

The tragedy of Dido illustrates both Virgil's sympathy with the prevailing tendencies of his day and his individual aversion to the prevailing neglect of action in favor of feeling; in this part of his story, therefore, he happily harmonizes the emotional interests of the newer Hellenistic Greek literature with the dominant emphasis of Homeric epic upon action quite apart from any inner impulses.

IV. THE STORY OF DIDO

Immediately after Virgil's death and the publication of the *Aeneid,* contrary to the poet's desire, by his literary executors, the poem won approval and excited hostile criticism; and in the ensuing centuries this mingled chorus of praise and blame seldom failed to concentrate attention upon the *Aeneid* as the literary work most representative of Roman artistic achievement. Scholarly activity was lavished upon it in the centuries after Christ, and has reached us mainly in the Latin commentary of Servius, which, in its present form, is a composite of an earlier nucleus, made about the fourth century after Christ, and later additions; in this and in smaller Latin commentaries are embodied the opinions of the later Romans upon many phases of the poem. The interpretation of scholars in the centuries all the way down through the Middle Ages to the Renaissance was marked by constant emphasis upon the supposedly mystical and allegorical features of Virgil's work, and this understanding of the poem reached a culmination in Dante's *Divine Comedy.* From the early Renaissance on, this mysticism gave way before a constantly increasing admiration for the beauty of Virgil's verse and the grandeur of his epic diction. Such aesthetic considerations lost their vogue near the end of the eighteenth century, when the coldly critical eye of a rational age began to study the language and style and ideas of Virgil, and qualified, or even obliterated, the unreserved praise which the Humanists of the Renaissance had lavished on the Roman epic. It is gratifying to find, in the last half of the nineteenth century, a wise blending of the aesthetic and the historical study of the *Aeneid:* without renouncing at all the dispassionate scientific attitude toward the poem, recent criticism is recognizing that one may admit and appreciate obvious defects without over-looking the conspicuous contribution that Virgil made to the development of literary art.

Epic convention demands a prelude. The Muse must be invoked; the poet is her spokesman; his inspiration is divine. And prelude may be prologue, for epic poet, as readily as dramatic poet, divulges the plot; epic and tragedy deal with myth, and the particular myth is already known to the audience; Virgil, like Euripides, without sacrificing any essential dramatic possibilities may assure the reader—what the Roman reader already knew—that Acneas, after suffering the effects of divine wrath, brought his Trojan gods safely to Latium, established for them a home in Lavinium, whence Alba Longa, whence imperial Rome. So Homer, again and again through the *Iliad,* anticipates the conclusion.

But Virgil's brief compact prelude emphasizes valid truths that the reader must know at the outset and carry with him through his reading: the main chapters of the hero's experience are controlled by Fate; the personal enmity of Juno, a divine being whom Acneas cannot hope to overcome, is responsible for his wanderings; that divinity only temporarily thwarts higher decrees of destiny which promise the continuity of Trojan and Roman history, and guarantee the sanctity of Roman religion as a tradition divinely protected in its transmission from Troy to Rome. So the national feeling of the Roman reader is awakened at the beginning of the poem by the thought that destiny and a divine providence have watched over his progenitor, Acneas, and the religion of the state.

The Muse is invoked to tell the causes of Juno's wrath: why should Juno attack a man "whose largest honor in men's eyes was serving heaven. Can gods such anger feel?"

The explanation of Juno's anger is found in the goddess' hope, thwarted again by destiny, to establish at Carthage "a throne of power o'er nations near and far"; destiny decrees that a breed of the Trojan blood shall overwhelm Carthage. This knowledge of Trojan-Roman superiority recalls to the goddess her ancient quarrel with the Trojans in the war at Troy; this, in turn, found its beginning in the judgment of Paris, who offended Juno in awarding the prize of beauty to Venus. So the poet elaborates the age-long grudge of the goddess and justifies, by an accumulation of causes, divine wrath against even the pious Aeneas.

The poet's description passes to soliloquy in the goddess' own words in which she questions whether Fate can oppose her wish. Why should Athena have power to punish the Greeks, but Juno herself, Jove's sister and his spouse, avail not to overcome the Trojans? So she resorts to Aeolus, the god of the winds, persuades him to rouse a storm against the Trojans. Aeneas finds himself engulfed, his ships shattered, his comrades lost. Neptune, the sea god, angered to find his authority invaded by the god of the winds, "calms the whole wide sea." Aeneas reaches the coast of Africa in safety.

Thus the poet introduces us, not to the beginning of his story, but to the very center of it, and in a turbulent scene in which his hero is buffeted about, not only by the natural elements, but by the clashing wills of supernatural forces—Juno and the wind god against Neptune, Juno herself against irrevocable decrees of Fate. How can a hero ever be heroic if, despite all his service to heaven, he is subject both to capricious gods and goddesses apparently endowed with human weaknesses, and to a still higher Fate which even gods and goddesses at times vainly endeavor to thwart? What is Virgil's attitude toward the great questions of predestination and free will? toward the religious belief and philosophical theory of his day? What artistic use of supernatural forces does he make in his poem? Why should he use them at all? These are large questions which confront the modern reader at the outset. If we attempt a brief answer to them, be it understood that such large problems are difficult to solve, that students of the poem may well disagree, and that we ourselves wish only to offer suggestions to help the modern reader to understand this strange aspect of ancient epic, without forcing upon him dogmatic assertions.

The natural inquiry why Virgil does not allow the storm which shipwrecks his hero to occur as a mere accident of the weather finds its answer in the *Odyssey* of Homer; the whole situation here is borrowed from the shipwreck of the Greek hero just before his arrival in Phaeacia. In the *Odyssey* the storm that wrecks Odysseus is stirred up by Poseidon, the sea god, who is angry with Odysseus for having blinded Polyphemus. Virgil, in accord with his selection of the hostile and favoring divinities for his own hero, simply transfers the function to Juno. In general the intervention of divine beings in the *Aeneid* is part of that Homeric world which the Roman poet took over under the influence of an irresistible epic tradition. But in appropriating these supernatural agencies Virgil had to accommodate them to their new environment. The religious beliefs of Homer's age, or whatever other earlier age may contribute the religious atmosphere of Homeric epic, were far different from those of Virgil's own time. Nor was an educated man such as Virgil in the Augustan period necessarily a devout believer in the state religion of his own day; philosophical theory was seriously affecting the religious notions of the poet and his circle. The treatment of the gods and of the whole supernatural machinery of Homeric epic, therefore, has to undergo a change in which it becomes adapted in some respects to the orthodoxy of the Roman state, in some respects to the heterodoxy of Virgil and other educated men of his time. Nor must we forget that Virgil, as an artist, may sometimes have allowed artistic considerations, as well as religious convictions, to affect his handling of the supernatural.

In Homer the gods participate in the action; they fight on the battlefield; they are plentifully equipped with every variety of human weakness; they obey the same psychological laws as men. Fate stands, a mere shadow, in the background, seldom affecting the action. Man is in Homer largely master of his fate; his own wish and will control him; the divinities help or hinder him according as he has won their favor or their enmity; even Achilles has at least the choice between a long life without fame and a premature death after glorious achievement. The gods and goddesses appear usually as advisers, sometimes as malicious advisers, and mortal men follow the advice, not because of any moral obligation, but because the advice seems good.

In Virgil, on the other hand, it is Fate or the will of Jove— the two are identical—which directs the action, though it stands completely outside the action; such a fate is not explained; we are not supposed to ask why it so decrees; Aeneas is a mere tool that Fate employs in its intention to lay the foundations of the Roman empire. Aeneas is under the strongest moral obligation to submit to that fate; in such submission is piety; he may be temporarily weak or stubborn, but as a true hero he overcomes such weakness and follows the god, and that god is Fate.

As Virgil reveals contemporary belief in this attitude toward Fate, so, in his treatment of the gods, he makes them not merely decorative, but an effective means of expressing his religious-philosophical views. The gods in Homer are independent personal agents: Zeus is first, but first among his peers; Fate is vague and shadowy. But Virgil leaves no doubt that his Jove is almighty, that eternal power resides in him alone, and that to his power gods and men are subject; Fate is identical with the will of Jove. The other divinities, and Jove himself, are presented as persons, but Virgil limits so far as possible their human qualities; the other divinities are hardly

more than manifestations of the varied powers of the godhead, Jove. Such pantheism does not find explicit expression;
the poet could not express it without destroying the reality of
his gods and goddesses; nor could he afford so to contradict
the religion of the state; but the reader will find the hints both
in Virgil's conception of Fate, which leaves no room for individual gods as active independent personal agents, and in the
suggestive treatment of the gods themselves.

Such an all-powerful deity, though intelligible enough to
philosophers of Virgil's day, was not available in an epic poem
without some modifications. The hero of such a poem must be
left a certain amount of freedom. The poet, therefore, concedes to Fate control over the larger main facts of the action,
but leaves minor matters undetermined, so that Jove may be
moved by prayers from men and entreaties from the other
gods. Thus, for example, the prayer of King Iarbas that Jove
shall send Aeneas away from Carthage is granted; and at the
end of the poem Jove is willing to grant Juno what no decree
of Fate forbids.

Further concessions Virgil makes in the treatment of the
divinities subordinate to Jove. Of his own conviction that
such divinities had no existence except as manifestations of
the various powers of the supreme deity he gives plentiful
hints, but he submits with some modifications to the practice
of Homeric epic in giving these divinities independent person-
alities. They are on a higher plane than Homer's gods; their
human weaknesses are limited; Juno may be angry like any
human being, but the poet expresses perhaps his own conviction in his query to the muse: "Can gods such anger feel?"
These gods must conform to orthodox Roman, not to Homeric,
notions, which allow them the very lowest grades of human
weakness. Furthermore, in the main, the activity of the gods
is directed primarily to help their favorites, not to injure others; so even Juno's anger in our scene is motivated more by

her desire to advance Carthage than to injure Aeneas. Finally, although the divinities are often presented as persons, concretely, they are quite as often poetic fiction; Virgil's readers might perhaps not appreciate the fiction; it is quite conceivable that the poet, for example, may intend a symbol, but the orthodox reader may find a hard fact. The activity of Fama in the fourth book, and of Allecto, the fury, in the seventh, could hardly have been intended to present anything but allegorical figures; but just how far we are to extend such symbolism in our interpretation is a matter on which individual opinion may well differ. No such symbolism is possible in the scene in which Venus appears to the hero and tells him in full the history of Dido; here Venus appears as Athena did to Odysseus when he reached the city of the Phaeacians, informing him of the history of the Phaeacian people. In general, it is helpful to watch the differences between Homeric treatment of the supernatural and Virgil's, and to consider in each case the cause of the difference. So, in our own scene it is noteworthy that Neptune is not like Poseidon in the *Odyssey;* Poseidon in the Greek poem has the sea for his domain, but lives on Olympus, takes part in the war, and is active outside his domain; but in Virgil Neptune is inseparable from the sea.

Such then is, in brief, one answer to this much-disputed question of Virgil's treatment of the supernatural. The answer is that Virgil is at bottom an adherent of a philosophical school which emphasizes Fate, the necessity of submission to Fate, and interprets the gods in terms of a physical theory, but explicit statement of his convictions must not be expected; his general attitude is a compromise between his own personal convictions, which appear only beneath the surface, and the Homeric conventional treatment of the gods as part of epic machinery on the one hand, and orthodox Roman notions of the gods on the other hand. The significance of the situation is that he does not use such material mechanically, under the in-

fluence of epic tradition or purely for decorative effect, but
finds in it a means of expressing vital ideas current in his
own day.

Returning, then, to Juno's cherished plan of advancing
the power of Carthage, we find her hopes qualified by the
thought "if Fate opposed not"; she understands that Fate is
invincible. And in the following soliloquy she questions whether Fate can oppose her in keeping the Trojans from Italy only
because of her anger at the apparent success of Jove's daughter, Minerva, in destroying the Greeks as contrasted with
Juno's own failure in her efforts against the Trojans. Her resort to Aeolus and rousing of the storm winds is not an attempt
to cross the will of Jove, but at most to influence his will and
change it; if we follow her activity through the poem, she acts
much like the human being struggling against destiny. In this
book she imagines she may influence Fate by her exercise of
divine power; in Book vii she has given in, but nourishes a
vengeful spirit; in Book x, at the beginning of the book, she
tries to explain her action as not opposing Fate, but at the end
of the same book gives up all opposition, only hoping to
change Jove's purpose; in Book xii she finally renounces even
that effort and contents herself with asking only for what no
law of Fate forbids.

Juno's visit to Aeolus leads the poet to describe the wind
god and his function. Homer had already drawn a picture of
Aeolus at the beginning of the tenth Odyssey. There he is residing on a floating island, dearly loved of the gods, and surrounded by his wife and twelve children; Zeus has made him
keeper of the winds, either to lull or rouse what blasts he will;
the island is fortified by walls of bronze and by a sheer preci-
pice rising from the sea. When Odysseus leaves, Aeolus gives
the hero the winds tied in a wallet. Virgil, under the influence,
probably, of later accounts, has dignified Aeolus and the details of the situation; he emphasizes the power of the winds

themselves, represents them as persons, describes them as prisoners that must be kept confined unless the world is to be destroyed by their force. Aeolus is no longer mere friend of the gods and keeper of the winds, but a jailor appointed to a responsible office by Jove, who has the forces of nature under his own immediate control. Aeolus, in Virgil, is not a family man living in a house and surrounded by wife and children, but an old bachelor and proud king, sitting in state, scepter in hand, on the top of huge mountains which are piled upon the roaring winds, chafing in their bonds. To this bachelor-king Juno offers a bride as reward for his service in her behalf. The artistic value of the modifications of the Homeric situation is apparent in the action that follows. The winds tied up in a wallet do not accord with Virgil's idea of epic dignity; by representing them as turbulent prisoners he prepares for the picturesque action of Aeolus in smiting "with spear reversed the hollow mountain's wall; then rush the winds through the wide breach in long embattled line, and sweep tumultuous from land to land"; and the personal nature of the winds gives vigor to the subsequent scene in which Neptune "with indignant mien uplifted o'er the sea his sovereign brow" and calls loudly on the audacious winds to hasten home and remind Aeolus that his function is limited: "In his barbarous mansion there let Aeolus look proud and play the king in yon close-bounded prison-house of storms."

In the description of the storm itself Virgil was dealing with a well-worn theme; not only the storm in the fifth *Odyssey*, but innumerable other descriptions in the Homeric poems and in later poetry provided him with details. But the descriptions in Homeric epic are marked by a simple directness; those in Hellenistic poetry, by a wealth of stationary picturesque detail. Virgil here recurs to the style of older epic in the energetic brevity of his description; and, as often in Virgil, the description is made to approximate narration. The poet,

instead of putting stationary details side by side, aims to
bring out consecutive events in the order of their happening;
so we get first the rush of the storm winds, then the shouts of
the terrified sailors, the coming of night, and the rolling of
thunder and glare of lightning; then the effect upon the mass
of sailors, and upon the hero, Aeneas; this leads to Aeneas'
appeal to heaven in eight verses; then the action of the elements subsequent to his appeal; only at this point are there
two purely descriptive verses; and thereafter narrative of the
action of individual sailors in the midst of the wreckage. Nor
is the usual dramatic effect wanting. The storm breaks loose;
the Trojans approach nearer and nearer death and destruction; one ship is sunk; four others are in imminent danger;
at this critical moment Neptune lifts his head from ocean, the
winds withdraw, the sea subsides, the ships, though separated,
reach the African coast.

The action of these three introductory scenes is carefully
organized and unified; the soliloquy of Juno, the storm, the
calming of the storm, are not isolated chapters, as they would
be in Homer. The poet's description and Juno's monologue, to
be sure, do provide rather broad exposition; but the impending danger is mentioned early in Juno's speech, and the poet
moves rapidly toward it. In the first scene Juno is the center
of interest; in the third, Neptune; and the middle scene is a
connecting link—Juno appeals to Aeolus, the winds are portrayed as rebellious persons welcoming release from captivity,
Neptune quells the rebellion. The hero himself is introduced
in the midst of critical danger; of the preceding action, of
necessary presuppositions, we hear nothing except that the
Trojan fleet was just losing sight of Sicily when the storm
broke; the Roman reader did not stop to ask how the Trojans
happened to be there, or what happened to them before they
reached that spot; in a general way he was familiar with the
wanderings of Aeneas. Nor does the modern reader, inter-

ested in the peril of the hero, care to learn immediately the presuppositions; he follows the action with interest and receives the necessary information in Books ii and iii, when Aeneas tells the prior events to Dido.

The hero himself, upon whom the poet centers our thought in the midst of the storm, becomes henceforth our main interest. In the storm he appeals to heaven; and in this appeal Virgil reveals a striking feature of his methods. From our modern standpoint we should suppose that the poet would put himself in the hero's place and reproduce the feelings and expression natural in that situation. Instead of which Virgil turns to the fifth book of the *Odyssey*, where Odysseus similarly is shipwrecked and prays to the gods, and simply appropriates, with hardly any essential change, the speech that Odysseus in Homer's poem makes. Such absolute dependence, it should be observed, appears specially in the case of stationary scenes or descriptions; chapters of action Virgil seldom transfers without essential modification. "Thrice blessed those Danaans," cries Odysseus, "yea, four times blessed who perished on a time in wide Troyland, doing a pleasure to the sons of Atreus. Would to God that I, too, had died and met my fate on that day when the press of Trojans cast their bronze-shod spears upon me, fighting for the body of the son of Peleus." And so Aeneas: "O thrice and four times blest, ye whom your sires and whom the walls of Troy looked on in your last hour. O bravest son Greece ever bore, Tydides! O that I had fallen on Ilian fields, and given this life struck down by thy strong hand, where by the spear of great Achilles fiery Hector fell, and huge Sarpedon. . . . ." But in this appropriation of Odysseus' wish that he might have perished in the fight before Troy instead of in a storm at sea, Virgil, by his transference to Aeneas of these words, has conveyed one idea that Odysseus could not express and that the Roman reader no doubt appreciated: Aeneas, in giving utterance to this thought, is expressing the patriotic desire to die for his country; Odysseus' service to the sons of Atreus is a less noble motive.

This Greek insertion is offset in the Roman simile with which the poet decorates the account of Neptune's calming of the storm (vss. 148 ff.):

> As when with not unwonted tumult, roars
> In some vast city a rebellious mob,
> And base-born passions in its bosom burn,
> Till rocks and blazing torches fill the air
> (Rage never lacks for arms)—if haply then
> Some wise man comes, whose reverend looks attest
> A life to duty given, swift silence falls;
> All ears are turned attentive; and he sways
> With clear and soothing speech the people's will.
> So ceased the sea's uproar, when its grave Sire
> Looked o'er the expanse, and riding on in light,
> Flung free rein to his winged obedient car.

Here is a Roman street scene from Virgil's own troublous times. So Cicero, in his speech for Cluentius, refers to the common saying, as he calls it, that like the sea which, though naturally tranquil, is upheaved by the force of the winds, so the Roman people, though naturally calm, are agitated by the words of seditious men and their violent storms of passion.

Virgil returns to the *Odyssey* (xiii. 97 ff., the harbor of Phorcys) in his description of the African harbor which welcomes the storm-tossed sailors, but he appropriates only a small detail and himself elaborates the description with a view to contrasting the peace and quiet shelter of the spot with the turbulence of the scene which he has just described. There follows transitional action, relatively quiet, which binds together the storm scene of the introduction and the main theme of the first four books, the story of Dido. This transitional action is natural enough, though conventionalized in some respects. Aeneas reaches the harbor with seven ships; the Trojans disembark, make a fire, prepare their food; these details are conventional in epic narrative; nor does the epic poet scruple to repeat them many times in his poem. Aeneas climbs a cliff to look for his lost companions, sees some deer, and kills them for food; before the meal he comforts his discouraged companions with words that re-emphasize the certainty of their ultimate escape: "Through chance and change and hazard without end, our goal is Latium; where our destinies beckon to blest abodes, and have ordained that Troy shall rise new-born." But such hope, the poet says, is feigned, and disguises an inner pain and discouragement. The prosaic details of the feast are dwelt upon, again a conventional procedure, and the Trojans discuss the comrades they have lost and mourn their doom.

At this point, when the action has reached a natural standstill, Virgil changes the scene and begins the broad exposition of the love story upon which our attention is fixed for some time. Jove, in heaven, stands looking down upon Africa and musing anxiously; to him comes Venus, divine mother of Aeneas, and complains of Juno's treatment of her son. The king of the gods reassures her, and at the conclusion of his long speech sends Mercury to dispose the Carthaginians to a favorable reception of the Trojans. The poet's manner of introducing this change of scene is characteristic; an early Roman poet, we are told, used this same situation; Naevius, in the third century, had related Aeneas' shipwreck on the coast of Africa and represented Venus as complaining to Jove in the midst of the storm; Virgil does not interrupt the storm by the dialogue between the two divinities, but directs the action of Aeneas and his comrades to a point where we can easily imagine it as continuing through, and alongside of, the conversation between Jove and Venus; during the night Aeneas ponders his many cares (vs. 305); meantime the divinities discuss his fate. The content of the dialogue reiterates the pre-

destined greatness of Rome and Aeneas' assured position as
the founder of its imperial power. The modern reader is already tiring of this theme but he must remember the thrill
that such reiteration gave the Roman reader in the time of
Augustus; nor is it simply repetition; the king of the gods
gives reinforcing detail which is justified by the desire to comfort the anxious mother, Venus. Venus has begun to think
that the divine will has changed; Aeneas is exposed to such
perils that the destined Latin settlement seems to her endangered. But Jove gives the complete future history of that settlement in a passage which illustrates how Roman thought
had expanded, in accord with Italian legends, the Greek version of Aeneas' wanderings; the Roman reader hears that
Aeneas shall wage war in Latium and become its king; that
his son, Ascanius, now called Iulus, shall move the seat of the
kingdom from Lavinium to Alba Longa; that for three hundred years Trojan descendants shall rule here, until Romulus
founds Rome itself and gives his name to the Roman people.
And the king of the gods concludes this compressed statement
of early Roman history with the stirring words: "To these
[Romans] I give no bounded times or power, but empire
without end." So in this full statement of the harmonious
workings of Jove's will and of Fate, not only is the mother
comforted, but the Roman of Augustus' day is filled with pride
and confidence. Nor is the reference to the reader's environment left implicit: "Lo, Caesar comes, whose power the ocean
bounds, whose fame the skies. He shall receive the name Iulus
nobly bore, great Iulius he." Venus shall welcome Julius Caesar to the skies some day, and he shall receive such worship as
the gods. And Augustus, though unnamed, is celebrated in the
announcement of the peace that shall follow Julius Caesar's
reign: "Then shall the world grow mild; the battle-sound
shall be forgot; . . . . the dreadful gates whence issueth
war shall with close-jointed steel be barred impregnably."

To confirm his words to the anxious mother, the king of the gods sends Mercury down to earth to dispose the Carthaginians favorably toward the Trojans.

The poet now returns to Aeneas, who has been anxious all night long and, when morning comes, sets forth with Achates; the poet takes no special pains here or in the earlier preparation of the meal to introduce Achates to us. The two have begun exploring the surrounding country when they meet the goddess Venus, only thinly disguised as a Tyrian huntress searching for her lost sister. Aeneas suspects her of being a goddess and is not much persuaded by her protestations to the contrary. And on leaving him Venus "revealed in each step the veritable goddess." The son, recognizing her, complains of her lack of motherly interest and affection. In her conversation with her son Venus tells the history of Dido and of the building of Carthage.

The manner in which divinities appear in the action of the *Aeneid* is as varied as it is in Homer. They may work invisibly; they may appear to men, either in their divine forms or disguised as human beings, in the latter case revealing their godship on their departure or in the course of the action; and they may appear in dreams. Homer employs no consistent principles in choosing the manner of divine intervention. In Virgil's time it is unlikely that there was any general belief that the appearance of gods to men was possible, though it was common talk that Apollo, in bodily form, directed the victory of Augustus at Actium. Virgil, in any case, uses the appearance of gods in their own undisguised form only when it is inevitable and in order to give special emphasis to impressive events; in general he prefers that they shall appear in human form, if only thinly disguised; and the ultimate revelation, usual in such cases, of their divinity is so managed, again, as to impress the human witness with a sense of the importance of the divine communication. The modern reader resents the intrusion of Venus at this point in the action. Why, he asks, would it not be sufficient to let a real Tyrian or Carthaginian huntress tell the hero the story of Dido naturally, in response to natural inquiries of Aeneas? Why, in the poem, are not human beings allowed to use a normal degree of human initiative in developing the course of action? The answer is partly found in epic tradition; Venus here, as Athena in the *Odyssey*, reveals the history of the people to the hero newly arrived in a strange land; but Virgil as well is giving expression to a profound conviction that no important event in human experience is quite independent of divine influence and positive intervention; and if one charged him with turning his characters into puppets, he would accept the criticism as a compliment, he is simply visualizing what he regards to be the truth of his philosophical creed—in all human actions the godhead is the impelling force.

Yet it will be observed how curiously the poet seems to contradict himself from a modern standpoint. Such a theory of divine influence, we might think, would relieve the poet entirely from explaining on any psychological basis the actions of his characters; on the contrary, no other poet is so careful as Virgil to justify such action psychologically. This scene with Venus begins the accumulation of circumstances which, when Dido and Aeneas meet, inevitably lead them to love each other. The poet, then, dignifies important action by divine intervention, but never abandons the explanation of outer action as due to causes entirely within the soul of the human agent. How variously he manages this combination of divine power with psychological motivation we shall observe in the course of the poem.

The purpose of Venus' narrative, from the poet's standpoint, is to provide the hero with full details of Dido's pathetic history and her masterful energy in overcoming difficulties, so that Aeneas, before he meets Dido, shall feel admiration and no little interested curiosity. Just why Venus should appear at this moment the poet does not explain, except in so far as maternal interest may be implicit in her action. Every detail of her story is important as stirring the emotions of the listener and preparing the reader for later developments. Dido is a Tyrian, not a native African. She was the devoted wife of Sychaeus, a rich Tyrian lord, whom she married in her youth. The king of Tyre was her brother, Pygmalion; he impiously killed Sychaeus at the altars of the gods, but concealed the deed. Dido discovered the truth only through a vision in which her husband's ghost showed his wound, disclosed his murderer, and informed her of buried treasure; with this treasure and trusted friends she has fled to Africa, mere woman as she is; the Tyrians have bought soil, and are building themselves a city. To this Tyrian city Venus bids her son go, incidentally informing him that his fellow-Trojans are not lost at sea, as he supposes. The two heroes, following Venus' directions, journey on, and from a hilltop see the Tyrians at work: "The vast exploit, where lately rose but Afric cabins rude, Aeneas wondered at; the smooth wide ways, the bastioned gates, the uproar of the throng." So Odysseus admired the city of the Phaeacians. The Trojans note each detail of the work, the building of the city wall, the construction of harbor and theater; and if they seem to see or hear the impossible —the people passing laws and electing senators and other magistrates—the poet is developing the reader's imagination as well as his own. Aeneas sees, and (note the Virgilian touch) seeing, he sighs: "How blest of Heaven these men that see their promised ramparts rise." The ruined walls of Troy lie behind him; the walls of the new Lavinium seem, in his present peril, vague and shadowy. But the Roman reader, meantime, glows with pride at the thought that these walls of Carthage were brought to earth by descendants of the very Trojan who now with envy sees them rise.

The goddess Venus has shrouded Aeneas and Achates in a mist which conceals them from view as they pass through the city; they come to a grove in which a temple has been built to Juno; here they await Dido. Why they should wait here, why they should expect Dido to appear at this temple, the poet neglects to tell us. While he waits, Aeneas observes with special interest that this temple is adorned with pictures which show that this queen whom he is about to meet knows the history of the fall of Troy, and even the active part that he himself played in its defense. "He sees old Ilium's well-fought fields in sequent picture, and those famous wars now told upon men's lips the whole world round. There Atreus' sons, there kingly Priam, moved, and fierce Pelides pitiless to both." "Alas," cries Aeneas to Achates, "what far region now, what land in all the world knows not our pain?" And amid plenteous tears "he beheld the citadel of Troy girt with embattled foes," and (note the pathetic detail) "here too was princely Troilus, despoiled, routed and weaponless, O wretched boy, ill-matched against Achilles. His wild steeds bear him along, as from his chariot's rear he falls far back, but clutches still the rein; his hair and shoulders on the ground go trailing, and his down-pointing spear-head scrawls the dust." Aeneas groans to see Achilles' cruel trafficking for the corpse of Hector. "There too [Aeneas] his own presentment" saw surrounded by Greek kings. Moved by the revival of sad memories, encouraged by the knowledge that his story is known to the queen whom he is about to supplicate, Aeneas stands studying these pictures when Dido appears:

> So by the margin of Eurotas wide
> Or o'er the Cynthian steep, Diana leads
> Her bright processional; hither and yon
> Are visionary legions numberless
> Of Oreads; the regnant goddess bears
> A quiver on her shoulders, and is seen

> Emerging tallest of her beauteous train;
> While joy unutterable thrills the breast
> Of fond Latona; Dido not less fair
> Amid her subjects passed, and not less bright
> Her glow of gracious joy, while she approved
> Her future kingdom's pomp and vast emprise.
> Then at the sacred portal and beneath
> The temple's vaulted dome she took her place,
> Encompassed by armed men, and lifted high
> Upon a throne; her statutes and decrees
> The people heard and took what lot or toil
> Her sentence, or impartial urn, assigned.

Aeneas, then, already admiring from his mother's narrative the masculine energy of this barbaric queen, sees her at work surrounded by her royal retinue, with royal dignity performing her functions, dispensing her dooms and impartial justice to her people; he sees the queen in action. And as he looks on, out from the multitude come the very Trojans who his mother has just encouraged him to believe are still alive, to plead for mercy from this queen, shipwrecked strangers as they are. Dido, in her response, promises them safe escort from the land, repeats (what Aeneas already knows) that she is acquainted with the story of Troy and the Trojans, and concludes with the words: "O that this same storm had brought your king Aeneas hither."

It is apparent how perfectly Virgil has prepared this situation; Aeneas, interested and curious through his mother's tale of Dido's history, admiring through his own observation the noble city erected by her efficient direction, conscious from his study of the pictures in the temple of her sympathetic knowledge of his own heroic struggles at Troy, aroused by the queen's own presence and activity to a full realization of her queenly dignity and beauty, her administrative energy, her benevolent grace and mercy toward his shipwrecked comrades, moved by Dido's anxious inquiry after himself, her

concern for his safety, yearns to have the mist which hides
him from her and his dear companions removed: "When suddenly that overmantling cloud was cloven and dissolved in
lucent air. Forth stood Aeneas. A clear sunbeam smote his
godlike head and shoulders. Venus' son of his own heavenly
mother now received youth's glowing rose, an eye of joyful
fire, and tresses clustering fair. . . . ."

It is a dramatic moment; the future founder of Rome's
empire confronts the queen of Rome's worst enemies, but with
far from hostile feelings.

In the succession of events leading to Aeneas' meeting
with Dido and producing interest in, and admiration for, the
queen on the hero's part, none, perhaps, is more effective and
more peculiarly ancient than his observation of the works of
art which adorn the temple of Juno. The poet's elaborate description may surprise the modern reader. Such descriptions
fill a large place in ancient literature, and Virgil's use of the
theme reveals his individual contribution to a long development. Detailed accounts of artistic objects, particularly of
dress and armor, appear in poetry as early as the Homeric
epic, the typical case being the armor of Achilles described in
the *Iliad*. The explanation of these descriptions seems to lie
simply in the enjoyment, of both poet and reader, of works of
art as such. Naturally the art of a given period is reflected
with considerable accuracy in such contemporary descriptions
in the literature, and the development of description from age
to age is nowhere more easily followed than in a comparison
of these numerous accounts in poetry—and later in prose—
of artistic objects. The archaeologist has long busied himself
with reconstructing the shield of Achilles, and Hellenistic poetry is full of descriptions which by their lavish detail and emphasis upon pathetic suggestion clearly reproduce that disregard of proportion and absorption in feeling rather than action which distinguish the plastic art, as well as the literature,

of the later from the classical period. But we are primarily
concerned with the poet's manner of using this theme.

Such descriptions are necessarily, in almost all cases, in
the nature of digressions from the main action; the poet brings
the action to a standstill and describes in the work of art conditions that are themselves primarily stationary. He does not
hesitate, to be sure, especially in Hellenistic poetry, to make
the figures in the work of art move; and he even reads the
minds of the lifeless persons represented on the tapestry or
armor or in the sculpture. Indeed, he is prone to abandon
mere description and to narrate the story which the work of
art depicts. So in Catullus' poem, no. lxiv, the description of
the coverlet develops into a vivid narrative of Theseus' adventure with the Minotaur, his elopement with Ariadne, and
his desertion of her. Even in briefer descriptions, such as that
of the cups in Theocritus' first idyl, the poet animates the
picture of the coquette and the rival lovers; the rivals abuse
each other, and the coquette anon casts a smiling glance at
one lover, and anon—to use the poet's bold phrase—casts a
thought at the other. But in spite of these vivifying touches
the passages remain digressions, decorative episodes.

Virgil often so uses them. His description of Aeneas'
shield in the eighth book is an attempt to match the Homeric
account of the shield of Achilles, and although the Roman
poet succeeds in giving it a tremendous significance and suggestiveness, the description remains purely an episode. And
in the picture which Virgil draws, in the sixth book, of the
doors of Apollo's temple, pathetic as he may make the content, the description halts the action, or, rather, fills an interval of time in the action, without itself contributing to the
action in any way. Our present passage, on the other hand,
marks the highest point which any such description can reach,
and the artistic skill here exhibited cannot be matched in
Greek poetry. Not only does the description fill an interval in

the action before Dido's approach; not only does it convey in the choice of detail a wealth of pathetic suggestion to Aeneas and the reader, noticeable particularly in the elaboration of Troilus' fate—a mere boy pitted against the Greek champion —but in the selection of the general theme the poet has made the description contribute to the development of the inner action: Aeneas is not only moved to tears in the newly awakened recollection of Troy's fall, but he finds in the pictures evidence of the kindly feeling of the Carthaginians and their queen toward himself and his friends; nor is his own interest in the queen diminished by the discovery that she is familiar with his experiences.

Yet in so far as the description is lavish of pathetic detail, it remains Hellenistic. In this respect it contrasts sharply with the severe classic style of the passage immediately following, in which the advent of Queen Dido and her retinue is described. Here there is no emphasis upon anything but the external dignity and beauty of the queen, and her action as judge over her people; the Homeric atmosphere is palpable in the elaborate simile in which Dido and her retinue are compared with Diana and her attendant nymphs; so Homer described Nausicaa and her maiden attendants in the *Odyssey;* Apollonius, like Virgil, appropriated the simile when he came to recount Medea's journey to the rendezvous with Jason. Virgil, unfortunately, has borrowed less skilfully than Apollonius; for the nymphs attending Diana in the simile have a parallel in both Homer and Apollonius in the maidens accompanying Nausicaa and Medea, but in Virgil these nymphs have no counterpart in the retinue of men who escort the queen; Virgil, of course, intends to fix our attention upon the queen supreme in beauty and dignity among her followers, but the reader who knows his Homer and Apollonius is disturbed by the ineptness of the detail in the borrowed comparison.

The Trojan friends of Aeneas emerge from the crowd that attends the queen and are graciously received; the queen herself admits that she is favorably informed of the Trojan story, and craves only the presence of Aeneas himself; at that dramatic moment Aeneas steps forth, free of the mist that hitherto concealed him and endowed with special beauty by his goddess-mother's power. The poet has prepared for this moment with consummate skill; not only have Aeneas' interest in, and admiration for, the queen gradually been aroused by an accumulation of natural incidents, but the queen herself has revealed no little concern, not merely for the Trojans as a company, but for their leader, Aeneas, in particular. Such careful psychological motivation might well lead the reader to expect love at first sight. That is the normal procedure in Hellenistic poetry whenever the sentimental situation is introduced; indeed, a Hellenistic poet would entirely neglect any such careful preparation as Virgil has arranged, and, without the slightest regard for any preliminary internal development, would have hero and heroine fall in love at sight, attracted each to the other merely by physical beauty. Virgil not only motivates the situation, but, after his careful preparation, further postpones the inevitable issue. This postponement, however, is not due entirely to his dramatic instinct. Love at first sight in this case has been made impossible by conditions in the prior experience of both hero and heroine which the poet has described in his narrative. Aeneas brings with him a son, Ascanius; Dido, as Venus' account of her made clear, was married in her youth to Sychaeus, and her devotion to the husband of her youth has been emphasized; neither of them, therefore, is a Jason or a Medea, easily susceptible to first impressions, but both are experienced and matured. Even the poet's elaborate preparation cannot counteract the caution induced by a ripe experience.

Aeneas, stepping forth from the cloud, expresses the emo-

tions of the moment: effusive gratitude for the gracious hospitality of Dido, sorrowful consideration of the weakened
remnant of Troy's now exiled people, in contrast with the
auspicious beginnings of these Tyrian exiles in their new
home. Only the Roman reader appreciated the unconscious
irony of the hero's final words, in which he prays that the
name and fame of Carthage and Dido may abide undimmed
through the ages, while he himself must go "to lands I know
not where." After this courteous speech he welcomes his newly recovered shipmates. "Sidonian Dido felt her heart stand
still when first she looked on him; and thrilled again to hear
what vast adventure had befallen so great a hero." She greets
him in turn, and at last makes known to him and to us whence
she has heard so much about these Trojans even before their
arrival in her land. The praise of their great deeds has come
to her ears from a most trustworthy source: from one of their
enemies, the Greek, Teucer. And she concludes with words
that betray the perfect sympathy that she, an exiled Tyrian,
must feel for him, driven far from his native land: "I also
bore hard fate like thine. I too was driven of storms and after
long toil was allowed at last to call this land my home. O, I
am wise in sorrow, and I help all suffering souls." The frank
expression of such sympathetic feeling marks an advance
toward the swiftly approaching issue.

Dido's promises are realized in generous hospitality. She
sends abundance of food to the Trojans who have been left
behind in the peaceful harbor where they landed after the
storm. Aeneas, Achates, and the lost Trojans, now reunited
to their leader, she welcomes to her palace, and the poet briefly
dwells upon its splendor, perhaps not unmindful of the fact
that its decorations show that Dido is in every way the peer
of Aeneas: "The board had massy silver, gold-embossed,
where gleamed the mighty deeds of all her sires, a graven
chronicle of peace and war prolonged, since first her ancient

line began, from royal sire to son." Aeneas' mind, however, is
not attentive to the rich broideries or the graven chronicle of
peace and war; in this return to safety and homelike surroundings, "love in his paternal heart," the poet says, "spoke
loud and gave no rest." He yearns to share this comfort with
his young son, Ascanius, and sends Achates to fetch him from
the ships with gifts, which the poet, in conventional style,
stops to enumerate, gifts for Dido in return for her courtesy.

But this Virgilian emphasis upon the strength of domestic
ties leads to a situation which the modern reader may naturally regard as unworthy of Virgil. The goddess-mother,
Venus, becomes apprehensive lest Juno, protectress of Carthage and of Dido, and bitter foe of Aeneas, may use an opportunity to harm Aeneas; to anticipate any such guile Venus
determines to inflame Dido with love for the hero by the intervention of the god Cupid; accordingly she steals away the
real Ascanius, substitutes Cupid, and Dido, embracing and
fondling the pseudo-Ascanius, unconsciously lets the secret
fire of love breathe o'er her heart. The modern reader objects
that such divine intervention is superfluous; why superimpose
this mechanical and external agency upon the inner motivation which the poet has exquisitely devised, preparing both
hero and heroine by a natural sequence of events dramatically
arranged to increase gradually the interest of each in the other, and leading to an inevitable issue? The charitable critic,
however, will at least remember the characteristic procedure
of Apollonius in Hellenistic epic; Medea fell in love at first
sight with Jason, and for no convincing reason other than that
Cupid, bribed by his mother at the instigation of two other
divinities, had shot his dart at her. Not only has Virgil justified the love of Dido as a natural inner development, but, in
taking over the symbolic figure of Cupid from Hellenistic
models, he has tried to make Cupid's activity as inevitable as
possible by grounding it on Venus' justifiable apprehension

that Juno is active; only divine forces can cope successfully with divinity. And the playful decorative scene in which, in Apollonius, Cupid is portrayed at length as a mischievous boy cheating Ganymede at dice, gives way in Virgil to a pathetic interview between Venus and Cupid, in which Venus' anxiety and urgency are alone expressed, without the slightest elaboration of the knavish love god whom Hellenistic poets delight to portray in episodic style. Nor does the reader forget entirely that this pseudo-Ascanius is to Dido, at least, a real Ascanius, and to that extent her admiration for him as Aeneas' son increases naturally her interest in the father: "The Tyrian queen, ill-starred, already doomed to her approaching woe, scanned ardently, with kindling cheek and never sated eyes, the precious gifts and wonder-gifted boy." So the poet, yielding to tradition in introducing this symbolic figure, has at least removed as much as possible of the purely ornamental and mechanical aspects of the Hellenistic Eros.

The detailed description of the banquet itself is quite as much Homeric as Hellenistic; the song of the bard, Iopas, recalls the bard, Demodocus, in Homer's Phaeacian episode, who entertained Odysseus when he was hospitably received by Alcinous and Arete; but the theme of Iopas' song is more like the song of creation which Orpheus sings in Apollonius' epic. Demodocus, in the *Odyssey*, may relate the adventure of Ares and Aphrodite, the strife of Odysseus and Achilles, the story of the wooden horse, but Virgil chooses a higher theme: the creation of the universe, the wonders of nature, a theme that Roman, as well as Hellenistic Greek, never tired of hearing. "Dido the while drank both long and deep of love and wine"; she craves to know the story of Troy's fall and of Aeneas' seven years' wanderings. That narrative of "dauntless courage and exploits of war" which the poet lets us hear, too, in Books ii and iii of the poem, provides the final stimulus to Dido's interest, admiration, love. "Now felt the queen the sharp, slow-gathering pangs of love; and out of every pulsing vein nourished the wound and fed its viewless fire. Her hero's virtues and his lordly line keep calling to her soul; his words, his glance, cling to her heart like lingering, barbèd steel, and rest and peace from her vexed body fly." So the fourth book opens after Aeneas' narrative is finished.

But before leaving the first book of the *Aeneid* we must note a few general characteristics. The considerable detail which Virgil gives at the end of the book in his elaborate description of the purple-pillowed couches, the service at the banquet, the heavy-laden board, the symposium after the main feast is over, is not merely a concession to epic convention which demands such detailed account of feast and revelry. Thereby also the poet marks the unity of the book by the striking contrast between its beginning and end; the comfort, the splendid furnishings of Dido's palace, the generous courtesy of the queen, these are the counterpart of the turbulent scene with which the poem opened—storm, shipwreck, and dire peril. But the first book is not merely a well-defined unit by itself; it is an integral part of a larger unit comprised in the first four books of the poem, the tragic story of Dido. This tragic drama proceeds through a regular dramatic development from expository scenes in the first book, where hero and heroine are gradually stimulated to sentimental interest in each other, through the narrative of the hero's exploits and wanderings in Books ii and iii, which develops that interest into passionate love, to a dramatic conflict between love and duty at the beginning of Book iv; this conflict is settled in the dramatic climax of the cave scene; no sooner is the happiness of Dido and Aeneas consummated than their good fortune is reversed by Aeneas' higher call to the performance of his sacred mission; from the climax we move steadily to the catastrophe and to the tragic issue which coincides with the cur-

tain-fall at the end of the fourth book. The last three acts of
this drama remain to be considered.

The opening verses of the fourth book, already quoted,
mark the culmination of Dido's steadily growing love; the
bright light of the morning after the love-compelling banquet
throws into sharp relief the inner conflict between this new
love and her vows of fidelity to her first husband, Sychaeus,
treacherously murdered. The poet does not describe this conflict. It is dramatically revealed in the dialogue between Dido
and her sister, Anna. This sister, unlike Chalciope in Apollonius' story of Medea, is a confidante; so the Roman poet
escapes the monotonous sequence of hysterical soliloquies
with which Apollonius is forced to develop the weaker conflict in Medea's spiritual experience. Dido's words to Anna
present the conflict simply and directly. The queen loathes
the idea of a second marriage, but admits that since the murder of Sychaeus "this man alone has moved me; he alone has
shaken my weak will. I seem to feel the motions of love's lost,
familiar fire." Yet no sooner has she confessed the strength
of the new appeal than she swears a solemn oath binding herself to her first husband: "But may the earth gape open
where I tread, and may almighty Jove with thunder-scourge
hurl me to Erebus' abysmal shade, to pallid ghosts and midnight fathomless, before, O Chastity, I shall offend thy holy
power, or cast thy bonds away. He who first mingled his dear
life with mine took with him all my heart. 'Tis his alone—O,
let it rest beside him in the grave." Such a solemn oath cannot
be broken without subjecting Dido to a not undeserved punishment; the poet has laid the foundation for an error which
justifies the tragic issue; Dido has committed herself to the
pallid ghosts of the other world, where Aeneas finds her in the
sixth book.

But this solemn oath is not merely a necessary link in the
dramatic development, a technical device; nor has Virgil

merely taken over from the tradition about Dido a detail and strengthened it for his artistic purposes. The poet is co-operating with the best endeavor of his own times in making Dido's fealty to Sychaeus a moral and religious obligation; her violation of her oath brings her the pangs of repentance: "I broke faith. I cast the vows away made at Sychaeus' grave," she exclaims later (vs. 552); the complaining call of her husband's ghost greets her when she has made up her mind to die (vss. 458 ff.); and Aeneas, in the sixth book, finds her reunited to her husband in the other world.

Anna's response to Dido's statement of this inner conflict is specious and plausible; she reminds her sister of the injustice done herself in this self-imposed youthful widowhood; not only her personal happiness, but the safety of her state requires a male adviser and protector. Incidentally we learn a detail of value to the later developments. Dido has rejected with scorn the suit of Iarbas and other native African princes. Surrounded by barbarians whom she has scorned, and on far from friendly terms with her home people in Sidon, she needs Aeneas and the Trojans. The sisterly sympathy of Anna, her insight into the true state of Dido's feelings are admirably revealed. Her positive advice is to consult the gods; if the omens are favorable, Dido may safely welcome Aeneas, urge him to tarry with her, and await developments. Dido, accordingly, "her doubting mind infused with hope," sues for grace, sacrifices to various divinities, particularly to Juno, as goddess of marriage; she peers anxiously into the victims' cloven sides and reads the fate-revealing tokens. But the result of her inspection the poet dismisses with a generalization: "How blind the hearts of prophets be! Alas, of what avail be temples and fond prayers to change a frenzied mind?" Dido gives way to the madness of love and ranges up and down the city, desperate.

Modern commentators find a defect in the action here.

They object that we do not learn the issue of the sacrifices, the result of the inspection of entrails. And having made a problem, they undertake to solve it by saying that Virgil simply shirked a difficulty: he could not represent the sacrifices as favorable; otherwise the gods must have deceived her, or the inspector of entrails made a mistake; on the other hand, if Juno herself is immediately to bring about the marriage, the poet can hardly report that Juno showed any disfavor. But there is no difficulty or any violent shirking of difficulty on the poet's part. The poet has not represented any prophets, any inspector of entrails, as present at the ceremony; Dido herself conducts the ceremony; she herself inspects the entrails; the mention of prophets (*vates*) in vs. 65 is part of a broad generalization, and does not imply that any prophet was present save Dido herself; she, as queen, is high priest of the nation. With perfect psychological truth and without the slightest vagueness the poet represents Dido as blinded by the frenzy of love, and so misreading, or failing entirely to see, the ominous signs which the entrails would have revealed to a less blurred vision.

The poet now describes in full the symptoms of love, and in so doing draws on the rich stores of Hellenistic poetry; here are all the pathological phases of the love fever as we saw them in Apollonius' tale of Medea and Jason. There is nothing original save a negative quality; Virgil has at least avoided the cheaper vulgar manifestations which his Greek models, with less refined taste, often included in their descriptions of the situation. Dido's love appears in efforts to impress Aeneas with the wealth and power of her new city; her voice, in the emotion of love, fails her as she tries to tell him of it; so she spends her day. When night comes, she spreads a banquet and begs again for the Trojan story; she yearns to hear him speak; then, when the guests are gone and others sleep, she throws herself upon the couch where Aeneas has sat. Like

Medea, she recalls his voice, his figure, when he is absent from her; and, as Medea could not, Dido clasps to her breast the young Ascanius, as substitute for his father. Meantime the work of building the city is at a standstill.

At this point, when we may imagine Dido's love continuing to express itself as the poet has sketched it for us, Virgil introduces again his divinities; Juno perceives Dido's infection and seeks to turn it to her own advantage; she suggests to Venus that this love be allowed to work out to a natural issue, and that so Carthage and the destined power of Rome be united. The hostile and favoring divinity confront each other, arch-intriguers both of them. Venus questions whether this new plan accords with the decrees of Fate; but Juno, she says, may easily ask Jove and find out. So Venus craftily pretends not to object, though the assurance she has received earlier from Jove makes it clear to her that Juno cannot realize her hope. Nor does Juno ask Jove if her new plan crosses his will. Her purpose, implicit in the action, is to bring about a state of affairs that, as she imagines, will force Jove to change his will. The particular means which she undertakes to use for her purpose are then announced; a hunting party has been arranged for Aeneas' entertainment the next day; Juno will cause the hunt to be interrupted by a storm; in the storm Dido and Aeneas will seek shelter in a cave; there will be consummated a pseudo-wedding under the auspices of Juno, who is herself, in Roman religion, the divinity presiding over marriage. This wedding is, of course, only a pretense of wedlock; in reality it involves a moral error; the goddess hopes, by the complication thus produced, to effect ultimately a real union, and so to thwart Aeneas in his predestined establishment of Trojan power in Latium.

Once the divine plan has been announced, the poet in rapid narrative recounts the execution of it. Nowhere, perhaps, is his art more happily exercised. The cave as the scene

of this pseudo-marriage he may have taken from Apollonius'
account of the marriage of Jason and Medea, made imperative
in the story of the Argonauts as an anticipation of Alcinous'
award of Medea to Jason in the event of his having previously
married her; in Apollonius, too, there were nymphs sent by
Hera with gifts of flowers for the bride; this, however, is all
that the Greek poet furnished toward the situation; the rest is
Virgil's poetic invention. Nowhere, then, may we better see
what his principles of art impelled him to provide. In Apollonius there was no reason for the choice of a cave except the
implied need of secrecy; the marriage as consummated in
Apollonius is a pretty picture, but the details are all decorative. Contrast with this Virgil's careful motivation of every
detail in the action, and the rich ironic suggestiveness of every
detail in the description of the marriage ceremony.

It is noticeable that although almost all this action, as Virgil has indicated, is executed by divine will; yet Virgil insists
on making it all natural as a purely human development.
Dido plans the hunt as part of her natural desire to entertain
her guest, and more particularly as a means of keeping by her
side the man she has come to love. The storm comes into the
action as an accident of the weather, though we know it to be
Juno's work; the storm makes inevitable the resort to the
cave for shelter; the separation of Dido and Aeneas from the
rest of the company is plausible. But along with this careful
development of the action comes a wealth of picturesque detail which a casual reader may easily be misled into thinking
is purely decorative:

> . . . . Aurora rose,
> And left the Ocean's rim. The city's gates
> Pour forth to greet the morn a gallant train
> Of huntsmen, bearing many a woven snare
> And steel-tipped javelin; while to and fro
> Run the keen-scented dogs and Libyan squires.

> The Queen still keeps her chamber; at her doors
> The Punic lords await; her palfrey, brave
> In gold and purple housing, paws the ground
> And fiercely champs the foam-flecked bridle-rein.
> At last, with numerous escort, forth she shines:
> Her Tyrian cloak is bordered in bright hues,
> Her quiver gold; her tresses are confined
> Only with gold; her robes of purple rare
> Meet in a golden clasp. To greet her come
> The noble Trojan guests; among them smiles
> The boy Iulus; and in fair array
> Aeneas, goodliest of all his train.
> In such a guise Apollo (when he leaves
> Cold Lycian hills and Xanthus' frosty stream
> To visit Delos and Latona dear)
> Ordains the song, while round his altars cry
> The choirs of many islands, with the pied,
> Fantastic Agathyrsi; soon the god
> Moves o'er the Cynthian steep; his flowing hair
> He binds with laurel garland and bright gold;
> Upon his shining shoulder as he goes
> The arrows ring;—not less uplifted mien
> Aeneas wore; from his illustrious brow
> Such beauty shone.

No doubt this copious detail describing the youthful beauty of the hero and heroine and the gorgeous trappings of the cavalcade is primarily in accord with epic convention, and especially with the interest of later Greek poetry in ornament, but the Roman reader could hardly have failed to associate it in his thought with the splendor of a bridal procession, with the festal preparations for marriage in his everyday experience. Such an association the poet makes explicit when the scene in the cave itself is described: "Old Mother-Earth and wedlock-keeping Juno gave the sign; the flash of lightnings on the conscious air were torches to the bridal; from the hills the wailing wood nymphs sobbed a wedding-song." The nymphs who in Apollonius were decorative figures, in Virgil take the place of the maiden friends of the bride, and their cries replace the hymeneal song of the Roman ceremony; so the lightning flashes take the place of the torches which were necessary to the regular celebration of the Roman wedding at nightfall; and the goddesses, Mother Earth and Juno, preside here as in Rome itself on the wedding day.

Quite different from the poet's concentrated effort to suggest the marriage ceremony and the bridal procession is the brief digression which he allows himself in the description of the hunt. The relative commonplaceness of the details of the chase he relieves characteristically by dwelling for a moment upon Ascanius, the young son of Aeneas, and by his other name, Iulus, the eponymous hero of the Julian family: "Ascanius, flushed with the sport, spurs on a mettled steed from vale to vale, and many a flying herd his chase outspeeds; but in his heart he prays among these tame things suddenly to see a tusky boar, or, leaping from the hills, a growling mountain-lion, golden-maned." The boyish desire to get at some real sport instead of the African deer is not merely a tribute to the courage and high spirit of the progenitor of the Julian family; it reveals also the sympathetic interest in young men which Virgil exhibits throughout the *Aeneid*, an interest in that younger generation upon which, after the havoc wrought by many years of civil war, the hope of Rome's future depended in the poet's own time.

We have seen that the elaborate detail in the description of the gorgeous cavalcade and of the ceremony conveyed a rich ironic suggestiveness. This scene marks the consummation of Dido's happiness; it is the climax of the drama. But the reader anticipates the sharp contrast between the bright splendor of this wedding day and the gloom of the tragic issue. The poet leaves no doubt of the contrast when he concludes his account with the solemn statement: "Such was that day of death, the source and spring of many a woe." Dido has broken the oath of fidelity she swore to her husband, Sychaeus; she has forgotten her honor and good name; she calls her moral error a marriage, and with phrases veils her shame.

The reversal of fortune follows rapidly upon the dramatic climax. A modern poet would probably let Aeneas' abandonment of Dido develop naturally from the hero's gradually awakened consciousness of his high mission—the founding of a new kingdom of his own in Latium—but Virgil chooses to mark the importance of the event by divine intervention. Jove sends Mercury to remind the hero of his sacred obligation. Jove himself is moved thereto by the barbaric king, Iarbas, the scorned suitor of Dido, who begs the god to drive the Trojan lover from the land. So the action is closely knit. Every step has its impelling cause. Even the god moves not entirely of his own initiative. But the transition to Iarbas' prayer is no easy problem for the poet to solve; the story provides nothing to fill the gap between the cave scene and the determination of Aeneas to leave Carthage. The poet admirably connects the two stages of the action by the famous passage in which Rumor spreads the news that Dido and Aeneas are wasting the winter in revel and voluptuous ease and that a shameless life is diverting the queen from her proper task as city-builder. This rumor reaches the ears of Iarbas. So every scene in the action becomes part of a well-organized whole.

But this rumor, instead of being merely the careless gossip of the community, is given a definite personality and is symbolized concretely; the reader is made to see Rumor and appreciate her potent force:

> In movement she grows mighty and achieves
> Strength and dominion as she swifter flies.
> Small first, because afraid, she soon exalts
> Her stature skyward, stalking through the lands
> And mantling in the clouds her baleful brow. . . . .
> Feet swift to run and pinions like the wind

The dreadful monster wears; her carcase huge
Is feathered, and at root of every plume
A peering eye abides; and, strange to tell,
An equal number of vociferous tongues,
Foul whispering lips, and ears, that catch at all.
At night she spreads midway 'twixt earth and heaven
Her pinions in the darkness, hissing loud,
Nor e'er to happy slumber gives her eyes;
But with the morn she takes her watchful throne
High on the housetops or on lofty towers,
To terrify the nations. She can cling
To vile invention and malignant wrong,
Or mingle with her word some tidings true.

One may call this mere allegory, but the animating force of the poet's imagination has vivified a mere abstraction. One feels that Rumor is as personal and forceful as the barbaric king, Iarbas, to whom she comes with her malicious talk and whom she moves to angry appeal to Jove. This barbaric king, it may be observed, though a mere incidental character, is given a certain individuality in his prayer; he speaks to Jove with little respect, and concludes with veiled threats; he has a savage contempt for the queen who has scorned his suit; and he views with disgust the oriental invader, Aeneas, and his Trojans: "that Paris," he styles him, "with his eunuch crew, beneath his chin and fragrant oozy hair ties the soft Lydian bonnet, ..." So from his barbaric standpoint he abuses the millinery and perfumery of civilization.

The prayer of Iarbas prevails; Jove sends Mercury to Aeneas to remind him that his task is to found an empire in Latium, not to help a woman in the building of Carthage. Similarly, in the *Odyssey,* Zeus dispatched Hermes to Calypso to admonish her to dismiss the hero, Odysseus, and suffer him to continue his homeward journey. And as there Homer elaborates the picture of Hermes and describes with some fulness the journey of Hermes, so here Virgil is generous of detail. In both Homer and Virgil Mercury (Hermes) is the official messenger of Jove (Zeus), but in Homer the messenger visits Calypso, who corresponds roughly to Dido. Mercury accomplishes here what in modern literature Aeneas himself would accomplish by a calm consideration of his moral obligation to establish a home for the Trojan gods in Latium balanced over against his love for Dido.

Mercury finds Aeneas busy building the wall and citadel; Rumor was malicious in implying that love had interrupted the task. But his activity on Dido's behalf only emphasizes the anomaly of his position; he should be building walls in Latium. The effect, therefore, of Mercury's reminder is immediate; Aeneas fain would fly at once and get him gone from that sweet land; only in the adjective "sweet" does the poet suggest the least reluctance to leave Dido; preparations for a secret departure are made at once. The modern reader may resent this situation; it is entirely proper to adopt a twentieth-century attitude and criticize Aeneas for an unchivalrous action in abandoning Dido to her enemies. Probably no other part of the poem has given rise in modern times to more bitter attack upon Virgil. The Dido episode is largely responsible for the depreciation of both poet and poem from the eighteenth century on. But proper as this modern standpoint may be, it is justifiable only when the critic admits that he is indulging a modern prejudice. The Roman reader did not question the correctness of Aeneas' immediate obedience to Jove's orders or the propriety of those commands. Virgil's age was not an age of chivalry; the moral obligation was to follow God, and God is Fate. Nor must the modern reader attempt to explain the situation by assuring himself that Aeneas did not love Dido. It is quite true that Virgil has not, up to this point, explicitly described Aeneas' consuming love for Dido; the earlier scenes of the fourth book dramatically present Dido's passion for Aeneas; not even in the cave scene

does the poet represent the hero as anything more than submissive to Juno's matchmaking devices. Yet there can be no
doubt of Aeneas' strong attachment; the preparatory scenes
of the first book were evidently constructed with a view to
stirring in Aeneas, quite as much as in Dido, an inevitable
love. If the emotional effects have been portrayed only in
Dido's case, that is in accord with psychological truth and artistic fitness; the heroic progenitor of the Roman people may
not reveal on the surface the frenzy of his spiritual experience.
The poet lets the great fact speak for itself; Aeneas has forgotten his sacred mission; he is building Carthage, not Lavinium. That is proof enough of his devotion to the queen.

And, however little Aeneas' feeling has hitherto been
suggested, in the scenes that now follow the poet leaves no
doubt of the hero's true state of mind. Here, too, the modern
reader may find Virgil's answer to modern criticism. The
plans for secret departure are rumored about and reach
Dido's ears; after a frenzied search she finds Aeneas and pathetically complains, reminding him of his obligation to her
and the danger in leaving her exposed to the barbarians, her
enemies. Aeneas, the poet says, "with strong repression
crushed his cruel pain"; his answer is that his destiny is de-
creed; if his will had been free, he would now be in Troy, re-
building the walls of Ilium; as it is, the oracle calls him to
Italy; his heart is there, his fatherland. He reminds her that
she, too, is driven by Fate to find a throne in a foreign country; and he appeals to her human sympathy by recalling his
obligation to his son, Ascanius. He has seen the god; received
his word: " 'Tis not my own free act seeks Italy." And when
her piteous plaint changes to a torrent of wrath, "Aeneas,
faithful to a task divine, though yearning sore to remedy and
soothe such misery, and with the timely word her grief as-
suage, and though his burdened heart was weak because of
love, while many a groan rose from his bosom, yet no whit did

fail to do the will of heaven. . . . ." So the poet justifies the action of the hero in accord with the thought of the age; nor in doing so does he fail to ascribe to Aeneas a tenderness toward, and due consideration of, the suffering victim of fate; this may fall short of chivalry, but it is far in advance of the unemotional separation of Odysseus from Calypso, and of Jason from his Lemnian queen, Hypsipyle. The modern reader who wishes to understand, rather than praise or blame, will join the Roman reader in seeing only the inner significance of the event: long before the Punic Wars the destined greatness of imperial Rome overshadows the claims of Carthage.

Between Aeneas' determination to leave Carthage and the tragic issue, the story provides only the emotional effects upon Dido of her lover's intent to abandon her. The fashion of later Greek poets and of Virgil's contemporaries in such emotional crises is illustrated in Apollonius' treatment of Medea's spiritual conflict under different circumstances. We saw in that case a realistic hysteria, presented in a succession of rather rhetorical soliloquies. Virgil avoids rhetorical devices, or uses them with discretion, and allows his heroine only one genuine soliloquy, and that only at the moment of death. He regulates artistically, but with no loss of psychological truth, her emotion, and develops a gradual progression that issues finally in her plan of suicide. Nor does he neglect to portray, alongside of the inner turmoil, corresponding chapters of external action; each new development in the outer action affects the heroine differently and leads to a new phase of the inner development. So, even where action is somewhat subordinate to feeling, Virgil is true to his dramatic instincts. And this dramatic sense appears also in his so managing the situation that the feeling is not described by the poet, but expressed in the heroine's own words; the poet himself narrates the action that prompts this feeling.

These coherent chapters may be indicated briefly as fol-

lows: Dido, on first learning of the secret preparations for departure, expresses painful surprise at Aeneas' faithlessness,
but still hopes to rouse him to a sense of his duty to her.
When he, in answer, makes it clear that he is determined to
abandon her, she expresses her scornful hatred and bids him
go. But when the preparations are at last carried on openly,
her pride gives way; she seeks her sister Anna, and bids her
humbly supplicate Aeneas at least to defer his departure, "to
give repose and more room to this fever, till my fate teach a
crushed heart to sorrow." Many intercessions, however, on
Anna's part are of no avail; the hero's heart is "smitten sore
by unceasing wail and cry," but "his serene intent abides un-
moved." Dido, appalled, asks only death, and her decision is
confirmed by gruesome omens and dreams. She conceals her
real purpose from her sister, and pretends to be devising a
magic ceremony to win back the love of Aeneas; but the pyre
built for the ceremony is to be her funeral pyre. These preparations made, the poet tells us of a sleepless night that intervenes and reports the words she uttered when, a rush of feeling getting the better of her determination to die, she considers for the moment other ways of escape; ultimately, however, death is the only issue; she is hopeless. Rousing in the
early morning after this sleepless night, she sees the ship carrying Aeneas away from her. The suddenness of the discovery drives her to anger and desire of vengeance; she wishes
she had destroyed them all; she breaks forth into bitter curses.
Dido hastens the preparations for her death, and mounts
the funeral pyre. There, on the pyre, as necessary to the pretended magic ceremony, are the souvenirs of her lover, dumb
witnesses of her short-lived happiness. The sight of them, of
Aeneas' garments and the nuptial couch, brings her the peace
of resignation; she dies reconciled at least to death, though
in her last words praying "from yonder sea may his cold Tro-

jan eyes discern the flames that make me ashes. Be this cruel death his omen as he sails."

The manner in which Dido accomplishes her own death probably required no little invention on Virgil's part. Dido, of course, existed in the historical tradition of Carthage quite apart from the story of Aeneas' wanderings. Only Roman interests brought about the blending of the account of a historical queen of Carthage with the tale of Aeneas' travels; before these two stories were fused together Dido, as queen of Carthage, had a tragic fate, but her tragedy was quite independent of Aeneas. The historical Dido, according to a historian of the third century B.C., was, like Virgil's Dido, a Tyrian, sister of Pygmalion and wife of Sychaeus; the murder of Sychaeus, Dido's flight with her friends and the buried treasure to Africa, her building of Carthage, all appear in the account of the historic queen. But from this point on the Dido of history is different from Virgil's heroine. She is asked in marriage by an African king (compare Iarbas in Virgil's story) and at first refuses him, devoted still to her first husband, Sychaeus. But the citizens of Carthage constrain her for political motives to accept the offer of the African king. Dido, pretending to consent, says that she must first appease the ghost of her husband to whom she has sworn allegiance; for the purpose of making such a conciliatory sacrifice to the dead, she has a pyre erected near her house; then, setting fire to the pile, she throws herself from the roof into the flames, thus remaining faithful to her dead husband.

It will be observed that a poet like Virgil, in developing a love affair between Dido and Aeneas, may easily make over the tragic issue to suit the new story. All that he need do is to substitute some other pretext which shall have reference to Aeneas. Virgil represents Dido as pretending to her sister that she must make one final effort to recover the love of Aeneas; for that purpose she proposes to perform a magic ceremony, and a pyre is built for use in that connection, which she turns into a funeral pyre by killing herself upon it with the sword. But the ingenuity of Virgil (for probably it is his invention) in choosing a magic ceremony as the pretext can only be appreciated by a reader who knows something about the purpose and manner of such magic rites in Virgil's own day; the Roman reader immediately understood Virgil's artistic intention; the modern reader entirely misses the admirable harmony between Dido's real and pretended action on this occasion.

The powers of magic, according to the ancient conception, are part of the functions of the underworld gods; the upperworld gods—Jove, Juno, and others—have no concern with magic; they are gods of light; magic is associated with the world of darkness and death; Hecate combines the function of a goddess of death and of magic power. It is at once clear how neatly Dido's pretended purpose harmonizes with her real purpose; as part of the magic ceremony Hecate and other powers of darkness are invoked, but these same powers are at the same time naturally addressed by the queen, who herself knows that she is about to leave the world of light and become a subject in the realm of darkness and death.

Even more important, however, than this general harmony between the real and pretended situation is the wealth of effective action and emotional detail that Virgil is able to introduce with perfect naturalness simply because Dido represents this magic ceremony to be of a special sort, a magic incantation to recover the love of Aeneas. This special form of magic ceremony has in ancient practice a very definite ritual. The celebrant is undertaking to overcome a stubborn resistance on the part of somebody whom she loves and who refuses to requite her love; for this purpose she employs the peculiar form of magic which we call, technically, sympathetic; that is, the woman takes a number of tangible, concrete objects which are supposed to symbolize the stubborn lover and subjects these to fire, which is itself symbolic of the flame of love. The underlying principle is that as these concrete objects burn in the flame, so the loved one symbolized by them will himself burn with the fire of love. The concrete objects chosen are of various sorts in the usual love ceremony. They are easily inflammable substances such as dry meal or dry laurel branches; or the celebrant, more realistically, may fashion a piece of wax roughly into human form, and melt this in the flame, pronouncing the magic formula, "As this wax melts, so may my beloved melt in the flame of love" (cf. vs. 508). But most potent of all such objects is something that the stubborn loved one has touched or worn, the fringe of his garment, the garments themselves, a weapon that he has handled, the couch he has lain upon (cf. vss. 507–8); such things are most directly symbolic of the person of the loved one himself.

With these facts of the magic ritual in mind, the modern reader begins to understand both the poet's art and the tremendous significance of the death scene.

. . . . Dido (horrorstruck
At her own dread design, unstrung with fear,
Her bloodshot eyes wide-rolling, and her cheek
Twitching and fever-spotted, her cold brow
Blanched with approaching death)—sped past the doors
Into the palace garden; there she leaped,
A frenzied creature, on the lofty pyre
And drew the Trojan's sword; a gift not asked
For use like this. When now she saw the garb
Of Ilian fashion, and the nuptial couch
She knew too well, she lingered yet awhile
For memory and tears, and falling prone
On that cold bed, outpoured a last farewell:
"Sweet relics. Ever dear when Fate and Heaven
Upon me smiled, receive my parting breath,
And from my woe set free. My life is done.

> I have accomplished what my lot allowed;
> And now my spirit to the world of death
> In royal honor goes. . . . ." Her maidens all
> Thronged to obey her cry, and found their Queen
> Prone fallen on the sword, the reeking steel
> Still in her bloody hands.

In other words, Dido kills herself with the sword of her lover, Aeneas—"a gift not asked for use like this"; we may imagine it hung up in their common chamber, a fatal symbol of the hero's abandonment of heroic adventure for lover-like co-operation in the building of Carthage; she throws herself upon the couch which she and her lover have shared, covered by the Trojan garments of Aeneas. These sweet relics which fill her with a flood of sweet memories in her last moments are there upon the pyre properly and naturally as symbols of the lover whom in her pretense of magic ceremony she would win back by consuming them in a symbolic fire. But in her real action their presence and the use she makes of them lend a tremendous emotional effect to her tragic death; her lover's sword becomes the instrument of death, and she falls dead upon their common couch and his familiar garments.

But valuable as the essential conditions of the magic ceremony are for the emotional effects of Dido's death, Virgil, in choosing this magic ceremony, had to guard against a possible danger. Horace has made very clear to us that such magic incantations in Virgil's day were vulgar and far from respectable; witches and sorcerers drove a questionable trade, especially in magic potions for lovers. Virgil, with his usual regard for the dignity of epic treatment, raises a vulgar ceremony to the heroic plane of its new environment. The witch who is called in to conduct the rite is no ordinary sorceress; she has been custodian of the shrine of the Hesperides; she has learned to tame the dragon that guards the priceless fruit of that sacred orchard; her power to stop the downward flow of

rivers and to turn back the stars in their course is more conventional. The preparations for the ceremony are on a grand
scale: not a simple altar, but a pyre surrounded by altars;
and the invocation of the powers of darkness is made solemn
and magnificent; she invokes not only Hecate, but Erebus
and Chaos; three hundred gods of the lower world she calls
upon in a voice of thunder. The queen herself may take part
as a servant in a rite so exalted as this.

The death of Dido has a striking analogy in the death of
Ajax in Sophocles' tragedy; Ajax kills himself with the sword
of Hector, as Dido with that of Aeneas. As in Greek tragedy,
we do not see the death stroke, but only the effect of her death
upon her servants; they rush to her aid; the rumor of her
death spreads through the city; it reaches her sister, Anna,
and through its effect upon her the poet makes us realize the
significance of the issue: "In thy self-slaughter, sister, thou
hast slain myself, thy people, the grave counselors of Sidon,
and yon city thou didst build to be thy throne." Dido has deserved her death; she broke her solemn oath to Sychaeus; but
she may receive a final favor from her patron divinity, Juno.
The modern reader does not immediately understand why
Juno sends Iris down to release the struggling spirit; only the
sixth book elaborates the ancient notion which makes divine
intervention necessary to bring peace to Dido's soul. This
notion is, in brief, that each mortal has a definite term of life
assigned him; if, by suicide, or death on the battlefield, or
court sentence, or any other means, the individual dies a violent death before his term of life runs out, his soul must wander for the balance of that allotted term before it comes to
rest in the other world. Dido has earned a special dispensation: Iris comes and cuts the tresses of Dido; this marks her
final consecration to the goddess of the other world, Proserpine; so her soul finds immediate release and peaceful abode

at once in the realm of the dead, without the usual period of detention from her final resting place.

We have noticed that in this tragic drama Dido, not Aeneas, is in the foreground; it is Dido's story, not Aeneas'; and the modern reader certainly has been warmly interested in the heroine. When, however, we consider the means by which the poet has succeeded in awakening an enthusiastic interest in Dido we are struck by his somewhat novel method. Dido does not correspond to the great heroines of Greek tragedy, or to the lovestricken women who so frequently meet us in the pages of Hellenistic love poetry, and least of all, to the great characters of our modern literature. In the Greek tragedy which Euripides built about this same general theme of the abandoned wife or sweetheart, Medea has a strong and positive individuality; her dominant quality is a half-barbaric cruelty and lust for vengeance, stimulated by a just cause in Jason's neglect of her, and conflicting with the gentler mother-love that prompts consideration for her children. The fair ladies of Hellenistic poetry have no such strong individuality; they are usual passive instruments in the poet's hands; he puts them in pathetic situations and then plays upon them; they respond, sensitive to his touch, and yield various emotional strains. Modern characters are more like Euripides' Medea; they have some one dominant trait—ambition in Macbeth, greed in Shylock—out of which the dramatic issue develops and to which the tragic catastrophe is related. Dido has no dominant characteristic; yet she is far from being a mere passive instrument in the poet's hands, as Hellenistic heroines are likely to be. Virgil has provided her with a number of qualities, no one of which he allows to be developed to excess and to control the issue. He dwells at the outset of his story upon her queenly generosity and human sympathy in the cordial reception of the shipwrecked Trojans and of Aeneas himself. The narrative of events earlier in her history sharply emphasizes the masculine will-power and energy with which, after her husband's death, she took control of her affairs, fled to a strange barbaric country, and founded there a city of her own. Either of these traits a modern poet might have used as a dominant quality to determine the course of action; with modern feeling Virgil might conceivably have chosen her generosity and human sympathy and allowed her at the end to exercise this quality in gentle forgiveness of her enemy. Or he might have developed her masculine energy, her consciousness of her duty as queen of her people; but as a matter of fact that element seems to disappear, and in her dying words she herself shows no thought of her queenly duty or of her people; only Anna suggests that aspect of the situation. These qualities of masculine energy and queenly generosity are at least positive, though neither is dominant. Otherwise Dido can be described only in negative terms; these negative terms show how unlike the lovestricken heroines of Hellenistic poetry she is: she is not naïve and timorous, as is Medea in Apollonius' epic; she is not abject, sly, hateful; she is no rough barbarian, for her threat of physical violence to Aeneas is the result of a mere temporary delirium; nor does she revel in her misery, as do both Euripides' tragic heroines and the ladies of later Greek love poetry; laments, sentimental indulgence in her misfortune, futile regret are quite wanting in her speeches, though they are the commonplaces in monodies of tragic heroines and in soliloquies of the Ariadnes, Phyllises, Oenones, of Catullus and Ovid and their Greek models.

If Virgil has not individualized the character of Dido, one wonders, naturally, just how he has managed to develop the tragic issue, which in modern literature so often is evolved from an excess of one quality, the quality that differentiates hero and heroine from the rest of the world. The answer to the question may readily be found by studying the passages in which Dido's state of mind is revealed before her determination to end her life. We find the poet accumulating motives for this act. Most prominent among them is her thought that she has proved faithless to her first husband; it is remorse for the act of the cave scene that seals her determination; that is in complete accord with the procedure of Hellenistic love stories, where the motive is usually shame over some lawless or humiliating act. But Virgil is not content with this single motive; he adds thereto her mortification: "Shall that departing fugitive make mock of me, a queen?" She mourns the loss of her best title to fame: "Yes, for thee my chastity was slain and honor fair, by which alone to glory I aspired." She fears to be abandoned, surrounded by her enemies now that she has lost the confidence of her subjects: "What refuge now? Shall I invite the scorn of my rejected wooers, or entreat of some disdainful, nomad blackamoor to take me to his bed—though many a time such husbands I made mock of?" Gruesome omens strengthen her apprehension, among them the appeal of her husband's ghost. All of these thoughts crowd upon her; her death is the result of an accumulation of motives. But the poet gives unity to the variety in so far as one act occasions all her misfortune, and one man, Aeneas, makes this act the cause of her ruin instead of her good fortune. Therein lies the peculiarity of Virgil's method; the tragic issue in our modern literary experience is the outgrowth of the conditions of a carefully drawn and consistently planned character; in Virgil's story the poet lets a single situation accomplished by a single act develop naturally in all directions until, by an accumulation of motives, the tragic issue is made inevitable.

Thus the Roman poet gives personality, if not individuality, to the historic queen and inspires enthusiastic interest on the reader's part by a method that shows independence and artistic skill along the general lines of his Hellenistic models. The relation of earlier tradition to his own treatment of the story is not perfectly clear; the Dido of history, as we have seen, provided a dramatic story, but that story concluded about where Virgil begins the action of his drama; Dido in history corresponds to the narrative with which Venus in the first book stimulates the curiosity of Aeneas; she fled from Sidon after the discovery of her husband's murder, founded Carthage, and proved her fidelity to Sychaeus by perishing on the funeral pyre rather than marry the African prince, Iarbas. Out of this story there has been developed a strong dramatic conflict in Virgil's narrative; her devotion to Sychaeus is made the cause of her hesitation, the source of her error in yielding to Aeneas, and the justification (with other motives) of her death. And Iarbas is taken over from history as an incidental character; the scornful rejection of his own suit explains his prayer to Jove that Aeneas be removed from Carthage.

But Virgil was not the first to adapt the historic Dido to the needs of the national Roman legend of Aeneas. Somebody before him had developed the love affair between Aeneas and Dido, and thereby made the Dido story part of the Aeneas legend. This person was a poet, and probably he had handled the love story in the style of Hellenistic poetry, emphasizing the pathetic situation. Who he was, we do not know; what we do know is that Naevius, an epic poet of the third century, in a poem on the first Punic War, in which he had himself played a part, referred in some way to Dido and Anna. It is a plausible conjecture that it was he who had anticipated Virgil in making the Dido of history a heroine of Roman poetic fiction. Naevius himself was certainly a bold original genius; of that his activity as a comic poet is clear evidence; but how far he had forestalled Virgil in the artistic dramatization of the story we shall perhaps never know. It seems unlikely that at the very beginning of Roman literary effort in the third century Naevius could have even approximated the dramatic power of

Virgil's treatment. In Naevius the story probably served to introduce an account of the intimate relations between Rome and Carthage which led in Naevius' time to the Punic Wars. It will be observed that such a use of the story might well have brought out the splendid perspective which marks Virgil's theme: the abandonment of Dido establishes the ground for the undying hostility between Carthage and Rome.

This historical significance, however, was not the only motive that prompted Virgil to include the story in his poetic treatment of the national legend. He saw a technical advantage, which of course Naevius himself may have suggested. The narrative of Odysseus in the *Odyssey* was told to Alcinous and Arete. The narrative of Aeneas' adventures, in part, might profitably be told in the first person to some other character; that other person must be interested in the narration, and, from Virgil's more exacting standpoint, the listener should be more profoundly interested than were Alcinous and Arete, in the *Odyssey*, in the narrative of the Greek hero. The choice of such a person as Acestes, for example, a dignified figure in the Sicilian episode of the fifth book, could not suit Virgil's demands so well as a woman sentimentally interested in the narrator. And to the choice of a woman, and a woman who should love the hero, he was irresistibly drawn by the epic convention of his day. Hellenistic treatment of epic narrative had made the sentimental situation inevitable. Even Homeric epic had initiated the practice. Unless Aeneas had a Circe or Calypso, a Hypsipyle or Medea, his adventures must pale in comparison with those of Odysseus and Jason. In the prosaic historical account of Aeneas there were love affairs; but they were with insignificant women in Delos and Arcadia; once some earlier poet had suggested a love affair with Dido, Virgil's choice of the person to whom Aeneas should tell the narrative of his adventures was predetermined; the meeting of these two great founders, friendly and hostile, contained a significance which Virgil was the last person to overlook. There remained only the close organization of Aeneas' narrative with the love story of Dido, in which, as we saw in our account of the *Odyssey*, Virgil successfully challenged comparison with the loose juxtaposition of the Homeric chapters in a corresponding situation.

The general scheme of the story was suggested by the tradition about Dido. That tradition already contained a tragic issue, the germ of a dramatic conflict in her attachment to her husband, and preliminary dramatic incidents in her adventures before reaching the site of Carthage. Of a sister, Anna, Naevius, perhaps, had made some use. The African king, Iarbas, was easily made a helpful subordinate character after Aeneas became the hero of the story. Virgil's main task was to elaborate the personality of Dido, to develop the incidental action, and to organize the parts into an effective whole. For the general treatment of love he had various literary precedents. The Homeric epic offered the cold unfeeling attachment of an Odysseus to a Circe or a Calypso; this had been continued by Apollonius in his account of Hypsipyle's temporary union with Jason. In all these cases a wanderer was diverted from his main purpose for a season by a woman; to that extent Aeneas' situation was analogous. But in these cases, in the fashion of old epic, the poet did not dwell upon the strong emotion of love; on the contrary, it was a casual and cold incident in the wanderer's journey. Not even the earlier tragedy of the fifth century allowed itself to emphasize love as a strong motive in the drama; Antigone's attachment to the son of Creon in Sophocles' play, though used to strengthen the chain of action, is an incidental link; and Antigone is not allowed to give any full emotional expression to her love, even if the poet himself, in a splendid chorus, reveals the undercurrents of feeling which a sense of propriety kept out of the main action of early tragedy as an efficient motive. The youngest of the three great tragedians, Euripides, on the contrary, had elaborated with all his humanizing power the forceful effect of love as initiating tragic action and issuing in gruesome catastrophe. He had found, particularly in the illicit love of married women, a fruitful source of dramatic complications. Nor had he hesitated in pathetic monodies, in confidential dialogue between heroine and nurse, to exploit all the misery of these lovestricken women. In such a character as Euripides' Medea, Virgil could find an immediate analogy to his own Dido; each was an abandoned queen, though Medea was deserted by her husband instead of by a lover. This special theme of the abandoned sweetheart was cultivated after Euripides by those Hellenistic poets who gave literary form to sentimental legends in elegiac and epic verse. How these poets used the sentimental situation may be guessed from Roman adaptations of their themes in Catullus' portrayal of Ariadne deserted by Theseus and in Ovid's of Oenone and Phyllis abandoned by Paris and Demophoon. Here, in rhetorical soliloquy, all the emotional possibilities were realized, but in a manner quite out of keeping with the dignity of a national epic in Virgil's conception of his task.

In all this literary tradition the conditions of Virgil's own story and the demands of the literary type in which it was to be expressed were best satisfied in fifth century Greek tragedy. It is not strange that in organizing his material he constructed a drama, a tragedy; the stationary emotional figures of Hellenistic poetry, the cold unfeeling heroines of Homeric epic, gave place to a tragic heroine with all the emotional power of a Hellenistic abandoned sweetheart, but with that emotion dramatically regulated; and we have failed in our interpretation of the story if we have not already made clear the complete dramatization of all the chapters of Dido's experience, the careful exposition, the dramatic conflict, the climax, the reversal of fortune, and the tragic issue. And in the

details of the tragic issue we have noted the influence of
Sophocles' *Ajax,* in which, as in Virgil, the victim of the catastrophe kills himself with his enemy's weapon.

Instead of recapitulating what we have constantly emphasized in the course of interpretation, we may better illustrate
further Virgil's special characteristics in the handling of the
Dido story by dwelling upon one feature which we have hitherto dismissed briefly: the rôle of the sister, Anna, in the action
of the play. In Apollonius' story of Medea and Jason we
noted the Greek poet's use of a sister, Chalciope; we saw that
although it would have been a simple matter to make that
sister a confidential friend to whom Medea might have con-
fided in dramatic dialogue her inner suffering and perplexity,
Apollonius had chosen to leave Medea without any intimate
friend, so that all Medea's torment of soul had to be poured
forth in a monotonous succession of soliloquies; Chalciope
was used simply to link together chapters of the external action; to her Jason, through an intermediary, communicated
his desire to secure the co-operation of Medea; she therefore
strengthened Medea's wavering inclination to love and help
Jason. This use which Apollonius makes of the sister is quite
in accord with the procedure of Homeric epic, and at odds
with normal procedure in later Greek poetry when it comes to
tell the love story. Such a love story often provides the heroine with a confidante to whom she confides her suffering and
who serves as a go-between to relieve the distress; it is her
part to carry messages from heroine to lover, to promote clan-
destine interviews; she is regularly a nurse or servant of the
household, and her rôle is often dangerously near the vulgar
part of a mercenary and unscrupulous accomplice. This same
confidante appears in Euripidean tragedy quite regularly;
there, too, she is a nurse or servant, as in the case of Medea
and Phaedra, and the nurse of Phaedra seems, at least to
some interpreters, to anticipate the rather unscrupulous char-

acteristics of the Hellenistic confidante. To Euripides, however, this nurse is a great help in the economy of the drama.
With a chorus present through the play it is difficult, with any
degree of realism and probability, to bring out the emotional
distress of the tragic heroine and its cause; this distress, con-
fided to the nurse, however, is more easily expounded to the
audience; the confidante therefore becomes an important
dramatic rôle, and has not ceased in modern drama to serve
the convenience of dramatists.

Virgil's use of Anna exactly corresponds to the dramatic
rôle which the confidential servant plays in Euripides; to her
in dramatic dialogue Dido conveys her feeling; and Anna
serves also as intermediary between Dido and Aeneas. But
Virgil has carefully avoided any of the possible vulgarity in
the activity of the Hellenistic confidante and the Euripidean
nurse by giving the rôle to a sister, whose relations to Dido
are on a much higher plane than that of a mere servant; so, as
usual, he is careful to lift the action to the grand and heroic,
and avoids the vulgarizing tendencies of both Euripides and
Hellenistic poets. The Hellenistic nurse Virgil uses only once;
she is Barce, nurse of Sychaeus, whom Dido employs just before the tragic issue to summon Anna and give her instructions for the ceremony; this incidental use of Barce provides
for the presence of Anna soon after the death scene. Nor
should we miss the perfect fitness of a congenial sister for the
rôle which Anna plays; through her, with strong effects, the
poet brings out all the pathos of the final scene. Instead of
being forced to tell us in his own words the significance of
Dido's death, by describing its effect upon her sister and confidante he can approximate the dramatic to the very end of
his story. As Dido dies in Anna's arms, the grief of the sister
and her despairing words impress the meaning of the queen's
death upon our minds.

Virgil's methods, then, not only in the story of Dido, but

throughout his poem, may be seen clearly in this small feature of the Carthaginian episode. In Virgil three great lines of Greek literary tradition converge: Homeric epic, Greek tragedy, Hellenistic sentimental poetry. The Homeric epic furnished the outline of a wanderer telling a narrative of adventure to hospitable friends, and a Homeric world of divinities intervening in human action; Greek tragedy provided a dramatic structure and various means of securing dramatic effects; Hellenistic poetry was rich in the details of the sentimental situation, though they often had to be dignified and purified for the new environment of Virgil's epic. If Virgil took the story of Dido and Aeneas and made it over under the influence of these various literary precedents, we are not, in so describing his work, denying him the highest kind of originality. On the contrary, by using all that is best worthy of imitation in his predecessors he has again constructed a new whole that is inimitable. The tribute that time has paid to his accomplishment is clear and indisputable; Greek literature has contributed to modern times a multitude of women who are household words, Penelope, Nausicaa, Medea, Ariadne, Antigone—their names are almost legion; but the whole extent of Latin literature has made just one Roman literary heroine familiar to educated people of our generation. Aeneas' prayer in the first book, in his ignorance of the destined destruction of Carthage by the hands of his Roman descendants, was to the Roman reader unconscious irony; he cried in gratitude to the generous queen: "O while the rivers run to mingle with the sea, while shadows pass along yon rounded hills from vale to vale, and while from heaven's unextinguished fire the stars be fed—so long thy glorious name, thy place illustrious and thy virtue's praise, abide undimmed." Though Carthage fell, the prayer has been answered. Dido has become part of the literature of the world.

V. THE FALL OF TROY

Into the web of the Dido story is woven a narrative by Aeneas himself of his adventures up to the time of his arrival on the coast of Africa; this narrative becomes an organic part of the sentimental episode in so far as the hero's tale stimulates Dido to a fever of love for the narrator. But looked at as part of the larger narrative of Aeneas' wanderings, it illustrates the poet's happy variation in the manner of setting forth to the reader the incidents of action prior to the arrival in Latium; in Books i, iv, v, and vi those incidents are reported by the poet; in ii and iii we have the vivid account in the first person of an eye witness and chief participant. This narrative in Book ii carries us back to the real beginning of the action and supplies the presuppositions which the poet waived temporarily in introducing us to the midst of things in the storm of Book i. The beginning of the story in Book ii is determined by an essential feature of the plot: Aeneas' wanderings and sufferings, as we were told in the prelude of the first book, were a part of his endeavor to bring his fathers' gods to safe abode in Latium. Necessarily we must learn how those gods which he brings with him were first obtained; that explains why the poet must include in the action the story of the fall of Troy; here Aeneas, by divine command, rescued those gods from the Greeks and began his long effort to establish them in a new home.

Were it not that the continuity of Roman and Trojan religious tradition made this beginning inevitable, one might easily suspect that Virgil would have avoided a retelling of such an old theme as the fall of Troy. It is true, of course, that success in literary art is insured rather than defeated by the choice of an old theme; an absolutely novel theme, unfa-

miliar to the audience, often endangers a writer's chance of
immediate approval. But the choice of what might fairly be
called the best-worn story of all literary tradition since the
age of Homer placed Virgil in a rather unenviable position, at
least from a modern standpoint; it may be doubted, however,
whether he or his Roman reader was greatly disturbed by the
triteness of the story; funeral games, descents to Hades, battle scenes were also as old as Homeric epic, but Virgil and his
Roman audience were not only content to find them in the
national Roman epic centuries after Homer, but very likely
would have resented the omission of them. Again the modern
reader must reckon with that conservatism which dominates
ancient literature.

Virgil, however, in choosing an old theme, was forced by
the conditions of his main plot to treat that theme from a relatively novel standpoint. The poetry of an early Greek age had
celebrated again and again the various chapters of the Trojan
story subsequent to the action of Homer's *Iliad*; not only the
epic cycle, but lyric poetry and the drama, from the seventh
to the fourth centuries, had interpreted the mythical history
of Troy; later still, Hellenistic poetry and art—the statue of
Laocoön and his sons strangled by the serpents is a familiar
example—had continued this epic tradition. But all through
these centuries of uninterrupted interest in the Trojan narrative the point of view from which it had been regarded was
Greek; Greek authors and artists had celebrated Greek prowess, Greek strategy, notable Greek achievement. Only in a
few dramatic presentations of the fall of Troy, represented in
several extant plays of Euripides, had the story been told from
a Trojan standpoint, largely with a view to interpreting the
pathetic situation in which the vanquished Trojans found
themselves. Virgil was writing a patriotic epic in which these
vanquished Trojans were progenitors of his own people, of
the greatest military heroes of his time; he was compelled by

the literary tradition to represent the lineal ancestors of the Romans as abandoning their native city to a Greek people whom the Romans themselves in intervening centuries had reduced to the position of humble subjects of the Roman empire; he was forced to put his hero, Aeneas, the forbear of Julius and Augustus Caesar, in a position which only by the most skilful manipulation of detail could appear to the Roman reader worthy of any hero, worthy especially of a hero who embodied the cardinal virtues of the Roman people and of the Julian family.

Although this story had been told in art and literature for centuries, we are in no position to place side by side Virgil's version and the Greek accounts. What is now extant of these Greek versions is fragmentary. But there can be no reasonable doubt that the main problem that confronted Virgil was what we have just stated it to be. In solving this problem he had in the tradition only one helpful resource: though centuries of literary treatment had hardened the main outlines of the story, the multitude of versions no doubt offered the possibility of a choice by which he could at least minimize those features which were discreditable to the Trojans; in the selection of details he might at least guard against the inclusion of anything essentially derogatory to the Trojans. But this was merely a negative precautionary measure. There remained the positive task of preventing in the Roman reader's mind any sense of disgrace, of protecting the Trojans, and especially the hero, from any charges of cowardice or weakness, of spiritless renunciation, of disloyalty toward the fatherland.

To appreciate Virgil's art in this second book we must identify ourselves with the Roman reader; Rome is to him what Troy was to Aeneas. Could a Roman ever be willing to turn his back on his own city after it had been conquered, taking with him his wife and child and friends, instead of falling in defense of it? Could he think of carrying his gods to a foreign land? The answer to this question is happily expressed for us by one of Virgil's own contemporaries, the historian Livy; in the course of his history he has occasion to invent a speech which the old Roman hero, Camillus, is supposed to have made when, in the earlier days of Rome, events led to the proposal to move Rome to the site of Veii; the speech reveals admirably the attitude of Virgil's contemporaries toward any such abandonment of the fatherland:

> This is a fight for my native city, to leave which, so long as life remains to me, would be for others a disgrace, for Camillus impious audacity. . . . . Our state was established by auspices and auguries; there is no spot in it that is not associated with religious rites, in which gods have not dwelt; the regular sacrifices to our gods not only have the days of their offering fixed, but the place. Will you abandon all these gods of our state and families? . . . . We shall be regarded, not as victors who have left their native city, but as vanquished who have lost it; . . . . Should we not better live in herdsmen's huts on our sacred hills than go with all our people into banishment? Does our native land, this earth which we call mother, have so little hold upon us?

That was the kind of Roman feeling that Virgil had to consider in refashioning a story which represented the progenitors of the Roman people as deserting Troy.

After ten years of unsuccessful fighting the Greeks before Troy resort to strategy; they build a huge wooden horse, secrete in it their bravest warriors, destroy their camp, and sail for the neighboring island of Tenedos; they spread the rumor that the horse is a votive offering to a divinity to insure their safe return home. The Trojans, seeing the Greek camp deserted, fancy that the enemy have gone forever, and swarm forth from the city to wander curiously over the scene of their former contests. They find the horse and immediately fall into a dispute over the disposal of it; some favor removing it to the acropolis; others, more suspicious, advocate its destruction in the sea, or by fire, or approve of boring into it to discover its contents. The dispute between the two opposing groups is still undecided when a new actor appears on the scene. The narrator does not stop to tell us how the newcomer heard of the wooden horse, from what vantage-point he discovered it, or through whom he learned of the dispute; he hurried down from the citadel; perhaps that is meant to suggest that he saw the horse and the quarreling disputants from that elevated point; in any case neither Dido nor the Roman reader demanded further explanation; such explanation would have interrupted the rapid course of dramatic action. Our interest is roused by the evident seriousness and urgency of his purpose; his swift pace is the outward mark of uneasiness and earnest intent; his retinue marks him as a man of some prominence, whose advice deserves attention. Laocoön indignantly hails the company about the horse, and declares his assurance that this is only a trick of the Greeks; he reminds them of the notorious wiles of Odysseus, and condemns the whole Greek nation. The end of his speech he punctuates with a firm thrust of his javelin at the horse, which roars loudly from its cavernous depths. The narrator stops at this moment to comment on the situation: "If heaven's decree, if our own wills, that hour, had not been fixed on woe, his spear had brought a bloody slaughter on our ambushed foe, and Troy were standing on the earth this day."

The poet in these words has struck the keynote of the narrative. The Trojans, if they succumb, will yield not to a superior foe, the Greeks, but to an irresistible supernatural force, the will of Fate. Their case is hopeless from the start; Dido, the Roman reader, the modern reader, at once begin to sympathize with the Trojans; no man can withstand the gods.

The narrator's interpretation of the situation interrupts the action; in so doing it sets in sharp relief the scene that follows. The activity of Fate is not apparent to the group of eager disputants about the horse; upon them Laocoön's speech and action must have had no little effect; but just

when Laocoön is turning the balance in favor of the only safe
course of action, the destruction of the horse, there enters a
counteracting force in the person of Sinon. Sinon is a figure
strikingly contrasted with the influential Trojan who has just
denounced the trickery of the Greeks. His pitiful condition—
a captive dragged in by the Trojan shepherds—the narrator
describes only to reveal his true mission as a traitor, and pictures the unsuspecting Trojans mocking their captive; again
the narrator interrupts himself for a caustic comment: "Hear
now what Greek deception is, and learn from one dark wick-
edness the whole." That is, Sinon is not only a rascal himself;
he typifies the treachery of the entire Greek race. Once more,
therefore, Dido's sympathies and ours are diverted from the
Greeks to the Trojans.

The speech of Sinon is admirably adapted to the situation
and the character. Tradition reports that Virgil was in his
youth averse to rhetoric, but here at least he employs to advantage the devices of the art. One may properly suspect that
this masterly speech of Sinon's would find no place in any
Greek version of the fall of Troy. Obviously it is part of a
pronounced effort to minimize the simplicity of the Trojans;
a Greek account would represent Sinon's trick as easily perpe-
trated, and the Trojans as gullible victims. Only in a Roman
version would the author perfect the finesse of Sinon to the
highest degree in order to accredit the success of his scheme
to his own wiliness rather than to Trojan stupidity; the greater Sinon's art, the less our respect for the Trojans is impaired.

His speech falls into four parts, and after each part the
narrator describes its effect upon the emotions of the audience;
this emotion passes from respectful attention to eager interest, from interest to pity and forgiveness, and finally to complete credulity. His first words express well-feigned despair;
everybody, Greek or Trojan, is his foe; but the sly suggestion
that the Greeks are no friends of his, though he is himself a

Greek, stimulates the curiosity of his Trojan audience and begins to dispel their suspicions. They bid him tell his history
and his reason for surrendering himself, a Greek, to his dead-
liest foes. At once he launches upon a story told with all circumstantial detail and apparently springing from a vivid recollection of actual experiences. The facts, as he sets them
forth, are these: he is a friend of Palamedes; Palamedes was
not in favor of the war against the Trojans; this attitude
brought down upon him the ill will of Odysseus and other
Greek chieftains, who conspired to put him out of the way;
Sinon, his kinsman and comrade, after the death of Palamedes
joined in the Trojan war at his father's behest. Once at Troy,
however, he incautiously expressed his desire to punish Odysseus for his conspiracy against Palamedes; henceforth Odysseus became Sinon's bitter foe. At this point in his story, just
when his auditors are anxious to hear how the wily Odysseus
carried out his malicious designs, Sinon breaks off—an artful
self-interruption—exclaiming that it is useless to continue the
narrative, for the Trojans naturally think all Greeks alike; he
himself must not hope for mercy; the Trojans will think him
just as treacherous as Odysseus. But his artful speech has
already won the Trojan ear. They free him from his chains,
and bid him continue. The rest of his tale, in the chronological
sequence of events (which he does not regard), may be reconstructed as follows: The Greeks knew that their only hope of
taking Troy depended upon their winning the favor of the
goddess Minerva, or Pallas; this hope was practically demol-
ished when Odysseus and Diomed stealthily entered Troy and
removed from the citadel the statue of Pallas, the Palladium;
omens and prodigies showed how angry the goddess was at
this desecration of her sacred image. Warned by the prophet
Calchas that they cannot hope to conquer Troy except after a
return to Greece, the Greeks try to appease Pallas before
leaving the Trojan shore by building a huge horse as an offer-

ing to her; it has been made of huge size so that the Trojans, on discovering it, shall not be able to carry it into Troy; for if they do, it will take the place of the stolen Palladium and restore to Troy the divine favor of Pallas. But the building of the horse called forth further omens and portents which frightened the Greeks; on consulting Calchas they learned that they could return home to Greece in safety only if a Greek life were sacrificed as expiation; then, according to Sinon's story, Odysseus' malicious designs began to appear; conniving with the prophet Calchas, he brought about the selection of Sinon as the expiatory offering; Sinon, however, has managed to escape at the last moment, and is now left, a wretched refugee, the rest of the Greeks having sailed home.

The artfulness of this story lies not merely in the wealth of circumstantial detail, but in the insidious nature of incidental phrases. It will be observed how neatly and naturally Sinon has given the Trojans to understand that it will be to their distinct advantage to drag the horse into the city, for it will restore to them the favor of Pallas. Furthermore, there is a vast amount of clever manipulation of Trojan feeling. Sinon starts off with a frank avowal that he will tell the whole truth, no matter what it costs him. He admits that he is a Greek. Then he shrewdly emphasizes the disinclination of Palamedes to join in the war against Troy; Sinon himself, close friend of Palamedes, joined in the war only at his father's command. Incidentally, without undue emphasis, he lets the Trojans appreciate the fact that his present plight is due to his loyalty to his friend, Palamedes; every detail wins sympathy and credence. When he comes to tell of the selection of himself as the expiatory victim, he gives all the incidents of the preparations with dramatic vividness, arousing the human sympathy of his auditors; he reluctantly admits his impiety in running away when he had been chosen the scapegoat; he emphasizes his desolation, and in the same breath his devotion to fatherland and kin, attests his truthfulness with a solemn oath, implores their sympathy and aid, and celebrates the virtuous soul that endures unmerited misery. Only when he sees that the Trojans are completely convinced of his sincerity does he solemnly renounce all allegiance to the Greeks. The poet, or narrator, meantime, in his casual comment after each chapter of the speech, never ceases to emphasize the rascality of the speaker and of the nation that he represents; one is constantly reminded, in these remarks, of the treachery ascribed to the Carthaginians, the *Punica fides,* in Roman authors. The Trojans, on the contrary, are ignorant of all wiles: "Of such Greek guile we harbored not the thought." And in the closing words of the narrator, in which he sums up the result of Sinon's effort, one hears again the appeal of Virgil to the pride of his Roman audience: "Thus Sinon's guile and practiced perjury our doubt dispelled. His stratagem and tears wrought victory where neither Tydeus' son nor mountain-bred Achilles could prevail, nor ten years' war, nor fleets a thousand strong." The Trojans have been tricked, not vanquished; the Roman reader is filled with admiration and sympathy for his progenitors, and with disgust at the faithlessness of Sinon.

The modern reader may naturally feel that the elaborate artifices of Sinon's speech are quite sufficient to produce the desired effect—the complete deception of the Trojans and the removal of the wooden horse to the city. But from Virgil's standpoint human action makes the story credible; only, however, when the serpents appear from the ocean and strangle Laocoön and his sons does this manifestation of divine will translate belief into decisive action. These serpents, after their cruel work, disappear into the shrine of Pallas; so the intervention of Minerva is apparent. Not only does the second Laocoön scene satisfy the need of some god-given assurance that the removal of the horse is advisable, but Dido and the Roman reader are again impressed with the fact that the Trojans are but tools in the hands of a higher destiny. And quite apart from these considerations, the ancient, like the modern, reader would have been unfairly treated if, after his interest had been excited by the action of the sturdy patriot in the first Laocoön scene, he had been left without some further account of the hero who had been brought prominently into the foreground of the dramatic action.

We left Laocoön protesting in word and action against the reception of the wooden horse; he was interrupted by Sinon. What Laocoön was doing during Sinon's speech the poet has not told us; at its conclusion we find him sacrificing, apparently near the seashore, to Neptune; the occasion of the sacrifice is not revealed. The thoughtful reader may miss these details; some of them the Roman reader easily supplied; if Laocoön was sacrificing to Neptune, presumably he was supplicating the god of the sea to destroy the Greeks on their homeward journey; but just why Laocoön, rather than anybody else, should address the sea god would still be left very vague. This vagueness may rightly excite criticism; but the critic should understand at once why Virgil leaves the details undetermined; the poet is constructing a very effective bit of dramatic action; he cannot afford to interrupt the desirable rapidity of that action to answer questions which Dido and the ancient reader would not have stopped to raise in their interest in the drama which was being vividly enacted. Virgil was not writing this poem for the modern editor, often insensitive to the demands of technique. The catastrophe, consequently, comes immediately, with impressive effect. The narrator dwells on the gruesome details, the approach of the serpents, the tragic issue; possibly the gruesomeness may offend some modern readers, but Virgil's choice and amount of detail compares favorably with Hellenistic descriptions of similar tragedies.

With admirable brevity the narrator describes the effect

and subsequent action. The fate of Laocoön is immediately interpreted as punishment for his impiety in hurling his spear at a sacred image. The convincing result of Sinon's speech is now expressed in strenuous action. With nervous eagerness the Trojans move the horse to the walls of the city, dismantling them to accommodate its huge bulk. The joyful songs of the sturdy young helpers who fancy that they are contributing to the salvation of their native city, the disregard of all ominous incidents, of Cassandra's prophecy—as ever, discredited —enhance the pathos of the situation. The final couplet comprehends the pitifulness of it all: "Our hapless nation on its dying day flung free o'er streets and shrines the votive flowers." To appreciate fully the effect secured by this brief sketch of the final result, one should turn to the descriptions of the same event in late Greek epics of post-Christian times, which themselves probably reveal the methods of the Hellenistic poets whom Virgil had before him. There the authors dwell upon the details of the drunken revelry which attended this festal celebration; there the speech of Cassandra, which Virgil dismisses in two verses, is given in full, and the whole constitutes an episode in the midst of the action. Nowhere else is the poet's sense of proportion, his sensitiveness to dramatic organization, more apparent than in this brief and rapid narrative of the issue to which the previous scenes have led with constantly accumulating force.

Indeed, throughout the scenes which we have been discussing, the poet's originality manifests itself in the structure of the action. Others had described the episode of the wooden horse, and had portrayed, in connection with it, the trickery of Sinon and the fate of Laocoön. Virgil may have elaborated the speech of Sinon and emphasized throughout the deceitfulness of the traitor and of the Greek race which he represented. But in other respects the Roman poet attempted nothing more than the effective unifying of the scenes; he accomplished this simply by dividing what was in his Greek sources a single Laocoön scene into two scenes. So far as we can discover from earlier traces of the story, the procedure in Hellenistic versions of the fall of Troy was to represent the Trojans as discovering the horse, then Sinon as appearing and tricking them into acceptance of it, then Laocoön as opposing the action and immediately suffering an apparent punishment for his impiety. Virgil seems to have divided the third scene into two parts; he has Laocoön appear first and oppose the party of disputants who favor taking the horse to the city; then comes Sinon, as a counter-irritant; then a third scene portrays the strangling of Laocoön by the serpents. The advantage secured by this change reveals at once Virgil's artistic purpose. In the Hellenistic account Laocoön's speech, after Sinon's, must weaken the effect of Sinon's artful narrative; but in Virgil's rearrangement a perfect dramatic unit is developed. First, the Trojans split into opposing groups differing over the question of the disposal of the horse; just at the moment when the party that favors receiving the horse is getting the upper hand, Laocoön appears and turns the balance in the opposite direction. No sooner has he almost caused the miscarriage of the Greek stratagem than Sinon appears, convinces the Trojans, and turns the scale again; at this point comes Laocoön's tragic fate to strengthen the conviction of the Trojans. In brief, Virgil, at the climax of the action, introduces opposing action; he brings about a dramatic conflict of opposing forces leading to a tragic catastrophe. In accomplishing this he makes some sacrifice to clearness and plausibility; obviously the Hellenistic versions which put Laocoön's death immediately after his speech and hurling of the spear present a more plausible sequence of action; and Virgil, in dividing the Laocoön scene into two parts, has failed to make perfectly clear to us just why Laocoön, at the beginning of the second scene, is discovered sacrificing to Neptune.

In the narrative up to this point Aeneas has referred to himself only as one of the general company of Trojans. At times he has abandoned the standpoint of the first person. That is, though pretending to state events that he witnessed and facts of which he was cognizant, he has necessarily allowed himself to describe the departure of the Greeks in the opening verses of the book, their destination and purpose, when he could not himself at that point in the action have known anything about such matters. Now, too, he recounts the action of the Greeks after the horse was taken into the city, although he could have learned these details only later in the action; for example, from somebody such as Panthus, who appears presently and narrates to him what has happened during the night. So, temporarily abandoning the narrator's point of view, he gives events in their chronological sequence with great vividness; if he told only what he witnessed, we should get a jerky incoherent account.

In this way we learn that at nightfall the Trojans departed to their homes and slept heavily after their exertions; the Greeks sailed back from Tenedos by moonlight; the ship of Agamemnon signaled to Sinon; Sinon released the Greeks from the wooden horse; they took advantage of the heavy sleep of the Trojans, killed the sentries, and admitted their fellow-Greeks from the ships into the city. From this point Aeneas begins to report his personal experiences, and the action of the rest of the book centers about him.

In this preliminary statement the time is briefly indicated, and it has an important bearing on the scenes that follow: it is night, but the darkness is relieved by moonlight. These two elements of light and darkness are used by turns to suit the exigencies of the later action. Where illumination is needed, the moonlight reappears (vs. 340); where the action requires darkness, as in the confusion of the Androgeus scene, the shadows of night are opportune (vss. 360, 397); this shift from light to darkness is quite plausible in the narrow moonlit streets of the city.

Further illumination is furnished, as the action progresses, by the flames of the burning city. This feature, however, is not devised to lighten the darkness. It is another of the many factors that make the fall of Troy seem inevitable both to Dido and to the reader of the poem. It is impressed upon us that the Trojans are fighting against tremendous odds; not only against fate and a superior foe, but against the uncontrollable force of this natural element. The constant reiteration of this detail (vss. 310–12, 327, 329, 337, 353, 374, 431, 505, 566, 600, 632, 664, 705, 758, 764) is a part of the poet's deliberate purpose to win our sympathy for the vanquished; nor is Aeneas' desertion of his native city so discreditable if Troy is but a mass of smoking ruins.

Similarly, in the scene in which Aeneas' personal experiences begin, the poet's purpose is mainly to provide an efficient motive for the hero's abandonment of Troy. The vision of Hector makes it clear to Aeneas that Troy is doomed, and that he himself, so far from being impelled to defend his native city, has a higher duty to perform in saving the *sacra* and *penates* of Troy, and in establishing a new home for them in a strange land. The scene, then, is not episodic or superfluous, but of the utmost significance in the orgnization of the story: it gives a supernatural sanction to Aeneas' future action, and weakens any charge of cowardice that may be brought against him. As is often the case, however, with scenes in Virgil that are primarily essential to the action, the poet has skilfully made it subserve other artistic purposes. With his customary fondness for pathetic effects he has chosen a situation and a figure that excite sympathy and pity:

> That hour it was when heaven's first gift of sleep
> On weary hearts of men most swiftly steals.
> O, then my slumbering senses seemed to see

Hector, with woeful face and streaming eyes;
I seemed to see him from the chariot trailing,
Foul with dark dust and gore, his swollen feet
Pierced with a cruel thong. Ah me, what change
From glorious Hector when he homeward bore
The spoils of fierce Achilles; or hurled far
That shower of torches on the ships of Greece.
Unkempt his beard, his tresses thick with blood,
And all those wounds in sight which he did take
Defending Troy.

The gruesome apparition and its emphatic and discouraging
admonitions cast about us the gloom that is appropriate to the
calamity celebrated in this book. Not only does Hector speak
with greater authority than any other of the Trojan victims
of the war, but his cruel wounds and bloodstains vividly recall
its greatest tragedy. The poet, however, abruptly turns from
the appeal to our feelings back to the action; Hector makes no
answer but a groan to Aeneas' emotional questions; he gives
instead laconic directions, impressive and decisive in the brevity characteristic of the man of action; he recalls the hero to
his duty and reminds the reader that the real significance of
the scene is contained in the announcement of the foreor-
dained destiny of Troy, and of the divine mission of the hero:

Haste, goddess-born, and out of yonder flames
Achieve thy flight. Our foes have scaled the wall;
Exalted Troy is falling; Fatherland
And Priam ask no more. If human arm
Could profit Troy, my own had kept her free.
Her Lares and her people to thy hands
Troy here commends. Companions let them be
Of all thy fortunes. Let them share thy quest
Of that wide realm, which, after wandering far,
Thou shalt achieve, at last, beyond the sea.

The vision which furnishes divine approval of the mission
of Aeneas as rescuer of the gods of Troy is naturally followed
by the realization of the dream, by the waking reality of Pan-

thus, the priest of Apollo, who comes bringing in his arms "his holy emblems, his defeated gods, and his small grandson." Between the two scenes is a transitional description; Aeneas is awakened by the din of arms and looks from the roof of his house down upon a sea of flames. The sudden revelation of the treachery of the Greeks counteracts in a measure the effect of the previous scene: instead of considering his country's gods and the mission intrusted to him, Aeneas yields to momentary impulse, with reckless heroism seizes his weapons, and yearns to indulge a warrior's craving for strenuous action though it issue only in patriotic self-sacrifice. This apparent neglect of Hector's directions increases the reader's admiration for Aeneas' heroism, and consistency with the previous scene is conserved by the speaker's characterization of himself as unreasonable and of his action as passionate frenzy (vss. 314, 316).

This irrational purpose is stimulated by the news, which Panthus brings, that Troy is in the hands of the Greeks; before this scene Aeneas exclaims, "Wildly I armed me (when the battle calls, how dimly reason shines); I burned to join the rally of my peers, and to the heights defensive gather. Frenzy and vast rage seized on my soul. I only sought what way with sword in hand some noble death to die." And after Panthus has brought him definite news of the plight of the Trojans, Aeneas continues: "By Panthus' word and by some god impelled I flew to battle, where the flames leaped high, where grim Bellona called, and all the air resounded high as heaven with shouts of war." But though the intervening Panthus scene serves mainly this purpose of spurring Aeneas on to the fight in spite of Hector's commands to the contrary, it has probably a higher function in the development of the action. Panthus brings with him "his holy emblems, his defeated gods"; these presumably are the gods whom Hector has just directed Aeneas to save. Apparently Virgil intends us to understand that Panthus leaves these images at the house of Aeneas, whence the hero conveys them later in the book (vss. 717, 747). Unfortunately the poet does not definitely say this. Whether we are to regard the omission as a feature of Virgil's suggestive style or an absolute defect must be left for the individual reader to decide. So far as any explicit indication appears in the narrator's words, the effect of the scene is simply to stimulate to accomplishment the cravings of the hero for the fight; the desperate case of Troy is clearly depicted by an eye witness, and realizes Aeneas' worst fears. Incidentally, one may note further evidence of Virgil's suggestive style in the pathetic reference to Panthus' grandson, whom he brings with him along with the images of the gods. The poet does not tell us what happened to this grandson, but leaves us with a suggestion of the pathetic possibilities; of the death of Panthus himself we learn in the course of the scene that immediately follows.

Aeneas, then, after the Panthus scene, dashes into the general mêlée, and for the next few scenes we are in the midst of the night battle. We shall better appreciate Virgil's art in this part of the story if we briefly review other earlier versions in Greek of this chapter of the action. In these earlier versions Aeneas' rôle was variously managed; in one type of story the hero left Troy immediately after the death of Laocoön; that tragic catastrophe motivated his departure. In our extant remains of the tradition the report of his saving his father and his gods appears somewhat later; this fuller story represents his escape either as miraculous, in which case the goddess Aphrodite-Venus protected him from the flames and the missiles of the Greeks, or as natural and rational. The rationalized form of the escape is in its turn somewhat varied in detail; in one form Aeneas falls into the hands of the Greeks, but is allowed to go free either because of his treachery in behalf of the Greeks or because he had before the war entertained Odys-

seus and other Greek heroes; in its elaboration this type of
story has Aeneas defend the citadel to the very end, surrendering only on condition that he be allowed to depart; the
Greeks offer him the opportunity of taking with him whatever
he chooses; whereupon he chooses his father; in recognition
of his filial devotion the Greeks allow him a second choice; he
chooses the images of his country's gods; then the victors
allow him to take all his possessions, and furnish him a ship
besides. This version is significant: it contains the *pietas*
which Virgil emphasizes in the *Aeneid*. On the other hand, it
represents Aeneas as dependent on the generosity of his foes
in a way that was ill adapted to the taste of a Roman reader.

Still another form of the rationalized story of Aeneas' escape from Troy reports the action as a well-developed series
of military maneuvers in which Aeneas plays the most prominent rôle. He discovers the entrance of the Greeks in time to
occupy a strongly fortified castle; thither the Trojan refugees
resort. When this castle cannot be longer defended against the
attacks of the Greek captain, Neoptolemus, Aeneas sends the
women and the defenseless under escort to Mount Ida, and
then retreats in orderly array with the rest of his forces, meeting the refugees at a rendezvous. There are obvious points of
contact between this story and that of Virgil: in Virgil Aeneas
at once plans to occupy the citadel, gathers a force about him,
plays a part, though somewhat inactive, in the defense of
Priam's palace, and finally arranges a rendezvous on the road
leading to Mount Ida. But Virgil's deviations from the military version are quite as conspicuous as his indebtedness to it.
The palace of Priam in Virgil is not a fortified castle; Aeneas
reaches it, not with a strong force, but almost alone, and is
unable to contribute much to its defense; he returns afterward to his home, and, attended only by his nearest of kin,
escapes in desperate case. The striking difference is that in
the Greek military version Aeneas is the center of the action

and displays all the wisdom and prowess of a true hero, while in Virgil he shows none of the quick and forceful determination, the prudent and persistent bravery, which are ascribed to him in the later books of the *Aeneid*. Virgil's refusal to make his hero heroic in this night battle of the second book is probably another instance of his consistent purpose to diminish the responsibility of the Trojans: it is not in consonance with such a plan to represent a decisive conflict in which Greeks are pitted against Trojans on almost equal terms with an issue disastrous to the latter. On the contrary, as we have seen, the poet throughout the action emphasizes the fact that the fall of Troy is the work of destiny, of which Sinon's perjury is the instrument (vss. 320, 329, 334, 354, 367, 452); the Trojans are vanquished at the start even before Aeneas wakes up from the sleep in which he sees Hector's apparition, and all subsequent efforts are but fruitless attempts of men who are driven to desperation, and, in the madness of despair, essay the impossible (vss. 313, 333, 336, 446).

The account of the night battle, therefore, is not the place to emphasize Aeneas' heroism; incidentally, the hero is thereby relieved from exploiting in his own narrative to Dido any positive achievements. Virgil selects from earlier Greek versions the *pietas* of his hero and some features of the military account of the night battle, but denies to Aeneas a strong and active fighting rôle in the conflict.

Hellenistic accounts of the night battle probably described it from a general standpoint. Virgil concentrates; he must treat it from the point of view of the narrator, Aeneas; we may learn from Aeneas only what he, as an eye witness, saw. The action which Aeneas himself observed includes only two incidents: the stratagem of Coroebus and its failure, and the fight round Priam's palace. As in the battle scenes of the last four books, so here Virgil introduces his account by a brief general description of the mass of fighters: Aeneas gathers a few men about him, stimulates them to action, and we hear how the general conflict raged. From this mass of fighters one suddenly emerges: Androgeus, in the darkness, mistakes Aeneas and his companions for Greeks, and in the confusion pays the penalty of death for his error. The mistake of Androgeus suggests to Coroebus the notion of putting on the armor of the Greeks whom they have slain, and of confusing and slaughtering their Greek foes in this disguise. The stratagem itself was probably suggested to Virgil or some earlier author by historic parallels; it is a legitimate *ruse de guerre*. And the figure selected for the foreground of the action, Coroebus, was not Virgil's invention: in the *Iliad* (xiii. 360 ff.) an ill-fated lover of Cassandra had appeared under a different name; and in Hellenistic poetry the same lover recurred under the name of Coroebus, which Virgil gives him. But neither in Homer nor in Hellenistic poetry, so far as we know, had the action been handled as Virgil constructs it. In the Greek stories Coroebus falls, slain in battle by Idomeneus; his sweetheart, Cassandra, and her captor, Ajax, play no part in the death of the young lover. Possibly Virgil is responsible for the admirable structure of the scene here. Coroebus and the other Trojans make some headway through the neat trick of disguise. Just as their success reaches its height it happens that the Greek Ajax rushes past, dragging Cassandra, daughter of Priam, and loved by young Coroebus: "Her loose hair had lost its fillet; her impassioned eyes were lifted in vain prayer—her eyes alone, for chains of steel her frail soft hands confined." Young Coroebus, crazed at the sight of his sweetheart thus mistreated, forgets entirely the necessity of preserving his disguise and rôle of Greek, and as a heroic young Trojan dashes into the fight to rescue Cassandra. This action easily makes evident to the Greeks the masquerade of the Trojans; in the general conflict that follows Coroebus is slain trying to rescue the Trojan girl.

This small chapter well illustrates again Virgil's artistic purpose. He introduces us to Coroebus in the general description of the Trojans that gather about Aeneas, and in that introduction, with the single adjective, "ill-starred," prepares us for the issue and excites our interest and sympathy in the young lover; throughout the scene it is his pathetic figure that occupies the foreground; we lose sight of Aeneas; the auspicious beginning of the stratagem intensifies the effect of the disastrous issue; Cassandra and Ajax appear just at the climax of success; the young Hotspur who has conceived and carried out the ruse nullifies the result by his own heroic imprudence. Nor should we miss the tragic irony: the Trojans, who have disguised themselves as Greeks to kill their foes, are now in their disguise mistaken for Greeks by their own fellow-Trojans and suffer death at the hands of their own countrymen.

Just as the Coroebus scene, by Virgil's art, becomes a tragic drama in miniature, so the whole action of this second book follows the principles of dramatic composition. We have been moving steadily toward a dramatic climax. That climax is the death of Priam, after which Aeneas gives up his frenzied resistance and resigns himself to the mission imposed upon him by Hector's admonition, which, thus far, in his moment of madness, he has disregarded.

In his first discovery of the perfidy of the Greeks, earlier in the night battle, Aeneas had thought of occupying the citadel; now, as he works his way out from the tumultuous fight that follows the death of Coroebus, accompanied only by two disabled soldiers, he finds the battle raging in front of Priam's palace on the acropolis. Here the Greeks, under the lead of the son of Achilles, who is variously called in the narrative Pyrrhus or Neoptolemus, are assailing the doors, their shields held over them to form a tortoise-back, and are trying to climb up ladders laid against the walls. Aeneas seeks a secret

gate in the rear, which he pathetically refers to as the gate
which Andromache and her young son used in earlier days to
gain access to her father, Priam, and her kinsfolk—so Virgil
not only calls to the reader's mind the famous scene of the
Iliad in which Hector bade farewell to his wife and child, but
perhaps suggests the pitiful issue in the later chapters of the
Trojan story, in which the same Neoptolemus who is now
leading the attack on Priam's palace hurled young Astyanax
from the walls of Troy and forced Andromache to become his
slave-wife. Through this door Aeneas gets access to the roof,
in the hope of aiding in the defense; he assists in hurling
down a tower of the palace upon the Greeks, but by this time
Neoptolemus, at the head of fresh forces of the Greeks, stands
at the threshhold of the outer court; the narrator stops to describe the triumphant Greek in his burnished helmet, and
compares him to a swollen viper just emerging from his winter rest, fresh and strong. Neoptolemus breaks down the
doors and opens the way to the inner courtyard, the hearth
and home of Priam. The household of King Priam is a large
one: he has fifty sons and fifty daughters; the children are
married; it is, then, a panic-stricken crowd of mothers whom
the Greek captain, cruel as his father, Achilles, according to
the narrator's testimony, drives before him. Priam's wife,
Hecuba, and her hundred daughters and daughters-in-law
seek refuge at the altar in the center of the courtyard; the old
king himself, though too feeble for action, insists on donning
the armor of his youth, prepared to make a last stand; but
his wife rebukes him and urges him not to resist vainly, but
to join them at the altar; only in the sanctity of that hallowed
spot is there safety, and then only if the Greeks revere the
gods and refuse to desecrate with blood the altar. Hecuba
succeeds in drawing Priam to the altar by her speech, but just
at that moment Polites, a son of Priam, rushes into the court
pursued by Neoptolemus and, mortally wounded, falls dy-

ing at his father's feet. This tragedy, occurring before the
father's eyes, rouses his anger against Neoptolemus, and in a
bitter speech he taunts the Greek, reminding him how his
father, Achilles, had yielded to Priam the body of Hector,
while he, Neoptolemus, now slays another son of Priam's before the father's eyes. With the weakness of old age Priam
hurls his spear at Neoptolemus, in vain; Neoptolemus, angered by Priam's act, drags the aged king to the altar and
drives his sword into the old man's heart, bidding him carry
to Achilles in the other world the tale of his son's grim deeds.
The narrator concludes with a formal epilogue: "So Priam's
story ceased. Such final doom fell on him, while his dying
eyes surveyed Troy burning, and her altars overthrown,
though once of many an orient land and tribe the boasted lord.
In huge dismemberment his severed trunk lies tombless on the
shore, the head from shoulder torn, the corpse unknown."

This summary reveals how closely knit every chapter of
the action is; each incident inevitably issues from the preceding and into the following incident, and all the closely knit
scenes serve as an accumulated motivation of the final tragedy. Hecuba's speech brings Priam to the altar, the death of
Polites strengthens Priam to resist Neoptolemus, the old
king's resistance drives Neoptolemus to disregard gray hairs
and to butcher Priam even at the sacred altar of the gods.
The final effect upon the reader is pity for the helpless Trojan
king, hatred for Neoptolemus, only slightly qualified in so far
as Priam's bitter words provoked his cruelty. And throughout
the action there is the constant Virgilian appeal to the emotions: the panic-stricken women, the aged queen, the feeble
king, the murdered son and father are pity-compelling characters in sharp contrast with the merciless Greek assailants.

But the poet has not wholly won our approval. What of
Aeneas all this time? He got access to the roof by a rear door
and helped tumble down a tower on the Greeks; did he then sit

on the roof overlooking the courtyard, dangle his legs, and observe with passive interest the cruel butchery of his king by the Greek hero? So the reader may naturally feel; Aeneas certainly seems to be inactive and almost ludicrously isolated. But a more careful reading will show that the poet has mitigated the harshness of this situation so far as possible. Up to the point where the narrative of Priam's death begins (vs. 506) Aeneas declares that he saw with his own eyes all the events; but on beginning the narrative of Priam's murder he carefully introduces the story by saying: "Would ye haply know what stroke of doom on Priam fell?" This phrase, contrasting directly with his previous statement, "My own eyes looked on Neoptolemus," suggests that in reporting Priam's death he is not telling what he himself saw, but what he later heard from others. The poet evidently intends us to picture Aeneas on the roof, not, however, idly watching the butchery of Priam, but shut off entirely from the sight of it by the smoke of the burning palace. Virgil has then done his best to lessen the awkwardness of Aeneas' position; we have already seen why he could not, at any stage of the night battle, make Aeneas a forceful heroic figure.

The death of Priam is the climax of the second book. Up to this point Aeneas, however vain his effort, has joined in the struggle against fate, and despite the instructions from Hector's ghost has tried to save Troy; with Priam's death this vain effort ceases. But such a climax is not truly dramatic; to be dramatic Priam's death should be the death of some strong heroic warrior upon whom the safety of Troy depended; the death of a weak old king may be coincident with the fall of Troy, but cannot cause the fall of Troy. Such climax as there is, therefore, is picturesque and emotional. Any genuine dramatic climax is made impossible by the whole plan of action; if, as we have seen, the poet intends to represent the Trojans as vanquished at the moment when Sinon's trick prevails, he cannot mark the fall of Troy by any real climax in the action later than Sinon's trick. We are not made to feel that because Priam is dead Troy has fallen, but only that Priam's death awakens in Aeneas' mind the thought that further resistance is useless. As there is no genuine dramatic climax, so there cannot be a genuine reversal of fortune, but only a turn in the action; Aeneas, seeing the aged king lying dead at the altar, is reminded of his own gray-headed father and of his father's danger; the fate of Priam seems to the hero symbolic of the fate of his own house. Thus the last chapter of the second book is introduced, the story of the escape from Troy.

We have already noticed that critical action in the *Aeneid* often requires the special stimulus provided by divine intervention: Sinon's speech convinced the Trojans; but only the serpents of Minerva strangling Laocoön and his sons brought about decisive action. So here, before Aeneas' thought of father, son, and wife becomes a determination to provide for their safety, his divine mother furnishes definite proof of the futility of further opposition to the Greeks by revealing to him a splendid panorama, the picture of the gods actively at work in behalf of the Greeks. Thereby again the poet diminishes the responsibility of the hero and his countrymen; the gods, not the Greeks, are the real enemies of the Trojans.

The presence of divine beings, as of Venus here, is not in Virgil always caused by the urgency of the situation; so, in the first book, she appeared without any special reason save only to tell Aeneas Dido's early history; there the poet did not feel obliged to establish any other cause for her appearance. Such unexplained appearance of divine beings is fully in accord with their supernatural character, which places them quite above any laws of cause and effect. In the present case, however, Virgil felt moved to justify by a special situation the intervention of Venus; she appears because her son,

Aeneas, is tempted to lay violent hands on Helen, the cause of Troy's trouble, whom he happens to see clinging in dumb fear to the altar of Vesta. This momentary indignation and inclination to take vengeance on the woman who first brought the Greek troops against Troy threatens to interrupt Aeneas' original purpose of returning home to save his own people. Venus stays his murderous hand, and by the vision of the gods recalls him to his important duty.

The three chapters—the Helen scene, the vision of the gods, and the scene at Aeneas' home—are thus indissolubly linked together. But the first of the chain, the Helen scene, is far from perfect in its general situation. The adverse criticism of it is as old as the Latin commentary of Servius in the fourth century; the objections which he raises are not without some validity; he notes that in the sixth book of the poem Helen is represented at this stage of the action as very differently employed; there it is she who, when the horse had been brought into the city, signaled to the Greeks on the ships; after the Greeks entered the city she continued her activity against the Trojans by stealing away the weapons of her new Trojan husband, Deiphobus, and leaving him thus defenseless to the mercies of the Greeks; it is clear that such hearty co-operation with the Greeks would be quite inconsistent with her dumb fear of the Greeks which leads her in the second book to hug the altar of Vesta. A second, purely aesthetic objection which Servius raises is not so important: he remarks that it is unseemly for a brave man to be angry with a woman, as Aeneas is here; obviously, as long as Aeneas' anger does not issue in any violent treatment of Helen, there is nothing unheroic in his temporary aberration. Similarly, at the beginning of the twentieth book of the *Odyssey,* Odysseus is angry at the women who consort with the wooers of Penelope, and plots their death; and there, though the Greek hero restrains himself, the goddess Athena, as Venus here, has to

come down to stay his hand. But though the action is justified
by the Homeric scene, which may have suggested it to Virgil,
the inconsistency with the sixth book is rather serious. Virgil
himself seems not to have been satisfied with it, and his literary executors, in publishing the *Aeneid* after his death, left
out the scene, probably because of the poet's own discussion
with them of its weaknesses. Yet the soliloquy of Aeneas in
which he bitterly arraigns Helen is worthy of the situation:
"For though there be no glory if I smite a woman's crime, nor
conqueror's fame for such a victory won, yet if I blot this
monster out, and wring full punishment from guilt, the time to
come will praise me, and sweet pleasure it will be to glut my
soul with vengeance and appease the ashes of my kindred."
This blind tumult of his soul is happily contrasted with the
clear vision of his mother: "(never had I seen her presence so
unclouded) I beheld in golden beams that pierced the midnight gloom my gracious mother, visibly divine, and with that
mien of majesty she wears when seen in heaven." Venus rebukes him with the reminder that it is not Helen or Paris who
is causing the fall of Troy, but the unaided gods. She takes
away "the barrier cloud that dims [his] mortal eye," and
shows to him the gods in action. This situation is, of course,
borrowed from similar revelations in the *Iliad*, but Virgil has
skilfully chosen the details and recombined them. It is not a
mere panorama of the fight, stationary and apart from the
action, such as Homer gives, but a moving picture and an integral part of the action. The poet's imagination conceives
details in the revelation that are far grander than Homer's;
indeed, almost too grand for the human eye to witness: Neptune shaking Troy from its foundations, Juno at the Scaean
gate calling the Greeks from the ships (a curious anachronism
at this stage of the action), Pallas seated on the acropolis
wrapt in a cloud, and last, as most potent of all, Jupiter himself inspiring the Greeks and inciting the gods against Troy.

Aeneas is indeed rash if after such a vision he continues to resist the god-directed devastation of Troy.

In her final words Venus bids her son fly: "The war's wild work give o'er. I will be always nigh and set thee safe upon thy father's threshold." She reiterates Hector's advice, given much earlier in the action; so far as there is anything heroic about Aeneas in this book it is his reluctant concession to this divine assurance that resistance is useless. Aside from the repeated command to leave Troy, Venus promises her protection, but with a peculiar limitation—she will set him safe upon his father's threshold; considering the dangers that beset him even after he leaves his home, in the next scene, we might expect her to extend her protection further. Certainly in some older versions it was Venus who diverted the missiles of the enemy and the flames when her son was escaping from Troy; why should she so particularly assume no responsibility, in Virgil's story, beyond the threshold of his home? The poet has rather weakly allowed us to see his manipulation of the action. Creusa, the wife of Aeneas, must disappear in the final scene of the departure from Troy; if Venus protects Aeneas in that scene, the disappearance of Creusa will be difficult to arrange. In other respects, as we shall presently see, this disappearance of Creusa puts the poet in an awkward position.

But the scene at the house of Anchises is free from all blemishes. In it Virgil's personality, his environment, his art are fully expressed. We cannot be sure how elaborate a rôle was given Aeneas in Greek versions of the fall of Troy; at least some earlier stories made him prominent. But this scene at the house of Anchises has exclusively Roman elements; it contains a full presentation of the Roman method of taking the auspices, which no Greek story could have included. And the intimate domestic picture which it reveals has Roman features. It is not impossible that the entire scene is one of the few chapters in the action which the Roman poet developed himself without his usual dependence upon Greek models. If so, it gains in significance and interest.

Aeneas threads his way through the maze of foes and fire, under Venus' protection, to his own home. The ultimate issue of his visit there is that he carries with him his father, son, and wife and gods toward a place of safety. But that final issue of the scene is long deferred. Aeneas finds every obstacle in the way of his cherished plan of rescue. At the outset his aged father stoutly refuses to go; Anchises thinks he is doomed to perish; he has had signs from Jove which convince him it would be crossing the will of God to attempt escape. Aeneas protests without avail; in despair he turns back to the fight, refusing to escape without his father, but his wife clings to his knees and lifts up to him their infant son, appealing for protection. At this pathetic moment Anchises receives a further sign from heaven that changes his mind; a flickering flame appears above the head of the child, Iulus; it is interpreted to indicate Jove's consent to the departure of Anchises; he yields, and the little party starts forth. All through this action Aeneas is in the foreground as the initiating force; father, wife, and child appear upon the stage effectively grouped; in the background is the chorus of servants of the household, referred to once or twice throughout the scene. Again, in brief, we have a play before us, with all the rising and falling action of the drama: the obstacles to be overcome, the climax of Anchises' refusal, the turn of action in the sign from heaven, all the picturesque grouping and dramatic accessories. This reiteration of dramatic composition in Virgil's art may be growing wearisome, but therein lies Virgil and his great contribution to the development of epic narrative.

The scene, however, is peculiarly rich in content, quite apart from the dramatic form. Primarily, of course, it serves to throw full light upon the hero's dominant quality of *pietas*, of which hitherto we have had only glimpses; here that quality is revealed in dramatic action. It is well known that *pietas*, in the Roman sense, involves not merely piety, but the full performance of one's duties to one's family and fellow-men, as well as toward the gods. It is important for the general course of action that in this scene Aeneas take with him the images of his gods, but reference to that action is purely incidental; the main emphasis is thrown upon the hero's devotion to his father; strong as Virgil's religious interest may be, his human sympathy is paramount to any regard for civic or religious duty. The purely domestic side of piety reappears in the action of the wife and mother, Creusa, in demanding to share the fate of her husband: "If thou wouldst rush on death," she says to Aeneas, "O, suffer us to share thy perils with thee to the end. But if this day's work bid thee trust a sword, defend thy hearthstone first. Who else shall guard thy babe, Iulus, or thy reverend sire? Or me, thy wife that was— what help have I?" This temporary prominence of Creusa wins our sympathetic interest in the character who is to be prominent in the final scene of the second book; and in general the action introduces us to Anchises and the young Ascanius-Iulus, both of whom, in the subsequent chapters of the poem, are more immediately interesting to us after we have made their acquaintance in this domestic setting. This picture of family life with the rich warmth of filial, paternal, and wifely devotion is, of course, not peculiarly Virgilian; the parting of Hector and Andromache in the *Iliad* and the pathetic figure of the infant Astyanax in that scene, the interrelation of Odysseus, Penelope, and Telemachus in the *Odyssey*, the constant emphasis in Apollonius' Hellenistic epic upon various phases of family life—all these emphasize the sacredness of that essential unit in ancient life, the family. And here, too, the inclusion of the gods, if somewhat inciden-

tal, makes the scene an epitome of the social life of ancient
times in which the individual members of the family, the families bound together in larger units, and the whole organized
with common privileges and duties in the greater corporation
of the state, constitute a thoroughly welded social body quite
different from our modern organization. The virtues, the moral
obligations, which are the mainsprings of action throughout
the poem, though in many respects modern, are fully appreciated only as they issue from the conception of the body poli-
tic which this scene dramatizes into actual and real sacrifice
of the individual to the interests of family and state. Paramount in the action is the hero's devotion to his father as head
of the family; this, at least in so emphatic a form, is thoroughly Roman. And both the patriotic and religious service
of Aeneas in rescuing his gods and perpetuating his national
religion in a new country is peculiar to the ancient conception
of society in so far as such religious service is prompted by the
individual's sacrifice of personal interests to the demands of
the great corporation of which he is himself an infinitesimal
part. Nevertheless, Virgil's portrayal of a social concept is
more or less accidental; the reader is impressed, not by any
theory of government that may underlie the scene, but by the
simple and natural compliance of the hero with duties and
obligations that are pervasively human; as dutiful son, father,
and husband, Aeneas is revealed to us for the first time, and
as such he stirred the admiration, not only of Dido, but of all
readers of the national epic.

Moved as Aeneas is by the action of Creusa in confronting him with their child just as he is on the point of returning
to the fight, desperate at the stubbornness of Anchises, it is
consideration for father, rather than for son and wife, that is
dominant in this scene. To that extent there is at least a
possible suggestion of the paternal authority which was more
binding in the Roman than in the Greek home. So, too, in the

concluding incident of the scene—the sign from heaven—the poet's immediate environment, the peculiarly Roman institution of taking the auspices, supplies the general setting and details. It is part of the poet's patriotic and artistic purpose, as we have already seen, to include in his national epic real or pretended explanations of the customs and institutions of the nation whose achievements he was celebrating; those customs and institutions gained in sanctity if they were carried back to a remote past, and the continuity of Trojan and Roman tradition was specially strong if a Roman institution appeared to have upon it the impress of a Trojan prototype. This general practice in epic had been thoroughly established in the Hellenistic period; we have already noted in Apollonius his constant interest in linking together present and past; in Virgil's case the spirit of his age, as we saw it in an earlier chapter, demanded this transference of the present into the past; with Virgil it was a matter of reinvigorating the lost forces of old Roman tradition by emphasizing the venerableness of Roman institutions. There are, however, artistic problems raised by any effort of this sort. It is easy for an unskilful artist to intrude inartistically such explanations of contemporary rites and customs; so, for example, Apollonius, like other Hellenistic poets, is prone to tell a story in explanation of some contemporary practice and then conclude with the mechanical footnote: "Hence it is that from that time on we have always done so and so." Such an epilogue is a frank admission of the poet's purpose, and inevitably violates the general illusion created by the context. Obviously it is a much higher artistic achievement if without any such mechanical addendum the poet can develop, as a natural part of the narrative, a setting and details which will immediately impress the reader as being the historic anticipation of a rite with which he is familiar in his daily experience, and if the poet then leaves this impression upon the reader's mind without mechanically thrusting upon him the obvious interpretation of the action. This Virgil has done; there is not the slightest indication in the text that we are witnessing the first formal taking of the auspices in history; Virgil simply presents the action and leaves inferences to the reader; nor could any Roman reader fail to draw the proper conclusions; but we, as modern readers, in order to appreciate Virgil's art, must first place ourselves in the position of the Roman reader, thoroughly cognizant as he was of every detail in the elaborate ritual of the auspices.

The particularity of the ritual itself is characteristic of the Roman people and of their religious forms; and the accuracy with which Virgil reproduces the details is necessary to the effect upon the Roman reader. The rigid observance of ceremony, however, makes the poet's artistic task all the heavier; the mechanical regularity of the technical procedure must in all its details issue naturally and inevitably from the situation in the scene which the poet represents as the origin of the ritual. The ceremonial requirements were somewhat as follows: The observer of the omens was one high in authority and represented the head of the state; he took his observation early in the morning, usually before daybreak; he sat during the observation; the omen, which was supposed to come from Jupiter, required confirmation to assure the observer that it was certainly a sign from heaven; such confirmation was supplied by a second sign which the observer solemnly called for and which normally took the form of lightning; as soon as this second confirmatory sign appeared the observer immediately rose from his seat; for otherwise another sign might appear and confuse his reckoning. In the action of the scene the nature and succession of the incidents closely parallel the essentials of the ritual, but they are the natural outgrowth of the situation created by the poet. The action of the book up to this point has covered an entire night; it is now just before

dawn (cf. vs. 801). Anchises has declined to accompany
Aeneas; the old man is sitting down, as an aged cripple would,
and shows his obstinacy by refusing to stir: "He still cried
'No,' and clung to where he sate" (vs. 654). The final reason
that he gives for his refusal is that Jove had previously indicated his displeasure and doomed him, as he believes: "For
many a year gone by, accursed of heaven, I tarry in this world
a useless burden, since that fatal hour when Jove, of gods the
sire and men the king, his lightnings o'er me breathed and
blasting fire." Under these circumstances when "there seemed
upon Iulus' head to glow a flickering peak of fire," Anchises
naturally wonders if this is a further sign from Jove, and calls
on the god to "ratify this omen thou hast given." Confirmation of the divine sign is furnished at once, not by lightning,
to be sure, but by a novel manifestation, to give greater sig-
ificance to the occasion: "Scarce ceased his aged voice, when
suddenly from leftward, with a deafening thunder-peal, cleav-
ing the blackness of the vaulted sky, a meteor-star in trailing
splendor ran, exceeding bright. We watched it glide sublime
o'er tower and town, until its radiant-beam in forest-mantled
Ida died away; but left a furrow on its track in air, a glittering long line, while far and wide the sulphurous fume and ex-
halation flowed." After this second sign Anchises rises at once
to address the gods and obey their will: "My father strove
not now; but lifted him in prayer to all the gods, in holy awe
of that auspicious star." Here and there the poet makes use
of the technical language of augury, but in every case the
phrase is a simple and natural expression of the thought.
Thus the Roman reader was convinced that this was the first
observation of the auspices, and on the sacred soil of Troy.

The family leaves the house of Anchises in the fashion
made familiar to the Roman by many pictures current in his
own day, some of which have come down to us: "Haste,
father, on these bending shoulders climb; this back is ready
and the burden light; . . . . close at my side let young Iulus

run, while, not too nigh, my wife Creusa heeds what way we
go." The servants are directed to meet them, and Anchises is
bidden to carry the images of the gods, which Aeneas himself
may not touch, defiled as he is by the fresh blood of those
slain in the fight. These gods may easily be taken in the context as the family gods of the household, but if our interpretation of the earlier scene in which Panthus appeared was correct, they should be the images brought by Panthus from the
acropolis and left by him at the house of Aeneas. They became the gods of the Roman state, as they were of Lavinium
and Alba before Rome was founded; the Roman regarded
them as the state gods of Troy, not merely household gods of
Anchises; so Hector in the earlier scene distinctly says: "Her
Lares and her people to thy hands Troy commends." And in
that same scene Hector was described as bringing forth from
the inner shrine the fillets of Vesta and the undying hearth
fire.

The details of the following scene are in the main skilfully
managed. Aeneas is naturally anxious: "I who once had
viewed undaunted every instrument of war and all the gathered Greeks in grim array, now shook at every gust, and heard
all sounds with trepidation, fearing both for him I bore and
him who clasped my hand." While he is thus perturbed, his
father suddenly announces the approach of the Greeks;
Aeneas turns from the path to avoid them; when he has
reached a place of safety he discovers that Creusa has not followed them; in dismay and anguish he leaves Anchises and
Iulus with the attendants and returns to the city to look for
her. The narrator's account of his fruitless search gives the
poet a final opportunity to picture the complete desolation of
Troy; the house of Anchises is now in flames; Priam's palace
is stripped of its contents; booty and captives are collected
under the guard of Greek chieftains. "Yet oft my voice rang
dauntless through the gloom, from street to street I cried with
anguish vain; and on Creusa piteously calling woke the la-

menting echoes o'er and o'er." In answer to his cries at last
the ghost of Creusa appears, but her apparition is larger than
she had been in real life; so the poet suggests she has lost her
human existence and attained to some higher form of life.
She consoles Aeneas with strange news: it is all destiny, the
will of the gods; she herself is safe, caught up by the mother
of the gods. In her new existence she has prophetic power,
and foretells his wanderings, his safe arrival, his new kingdom, and his new bride: "Long is thy banishment; thy ship
must plough the vast, far-spreading sea. Then shalt thou
come unto Hesperia, whose fruitful plains are watered by the
Tiber, Lydian stream, of smooth benignant flow. Thou shalt
obtain fair fortune, and a throne, and royal bride." She comforts him with the thought that she is in no danger of captivity
and slavery, and contentedly bids him farewell, reminding
him of their son and a father's responsibility. The hero, vainly trying to embrace her, at last returns to his companions.

In this scene, then, the wife of Aeneas is prominent, as
was his father in the previous scene. This wife, variously
named, played a changing part in Greek versions before Virgil's time. Even the scanty evidence now extant discloses not
only a story in which, as in Virgil, the wife is saved from
slavery by the mother of the gods (and Aphrodite), but another that represented her as accompanying her husband on
his travels. There may have been still other variant accounts.
From all of these Virgil could make a choice according to the
needs of his own plot; that choice was dictated by the hero's
future action in the poem. Dido and Lavinia made the presence of Creusa in the wanderings impossible. Indeed, the sentimental affair with Dido could hardly take place if Anchises
were present to recall his son to his main duty. The poet obviously must remove both the father and the wife of the hero
from the action before the Carthaginian episode; it becomes
desirable to remove Creusa before they leave Troy, and to

avoid the monotonous duplication of deaths in the course of the wanderings.

We are not given a very clear notion of Creusa's experience, nor do we require it; the suggestion that she is detained by the mother of the gods is sufficient, and was easily interpreted by the Roman reader to mean that she had joined the goddess' retinue. But there are some peculiarities in the management of her disappearance. Twice in the narrative the poet refers to Creusa's being behind the others; this position is natural enough; for, as one of the weaker sex, she may not keep pace with the hero; and as a matter of gallantry the male members of the party may properly put themselves between Creusa and the Greek foe. But the thoughtful reader is somewhat conscious of the fact that Creusa falls behind to suit the convenience of the poet; so placed she may more easily be lost without the knowledge of Aeneas; it is a rather crude and obvious device.

Another question that arises in the reader's mind may be answered with less discredit to the poet. One might fitly ask, If it was Creusa's fate to disappear, why such pains to provide for her disappearance? Why should she not disappear on the road before her husband's eyes? The obvious answer to this query reveals the poet's art and his main purpose in the structure of the scene. Such a disappearance would rob the scene of all its dramatic possibilities, of all its rich content; thus arranged, the hero's devotion in searching for his lost wife would be impossible, her own reappearance impossible, and thereby the prophecy less effective; and in general all the suspense arising from retarding the action would be lost. There are tremendous gains in structure and in subsidiary effects through the simple device of having Creusa fall behind and disappear without Aeneas' discovering his loss; his futile search, the account of the desolation of Troy, her dramatic reappearance and prophecy are all made available by this means.

This prophecy from Creusa's lips is a distinct and manifest conclusion to the second book, and gives it a unity of its own; again, it relieves the gloomy tragedy of Troy's fall by a brighter outlook into the future; the reader is given in outline the ultimate issue of the tragic events previously narrated. Creusa's statement of the destination of their journey as Italy, with the precise mention of the Tiber, seems to have fallen on deaf ears, or else Hesperia and the Tiber were unfamiliar terms to the Trojan listeners. For in the next book we find the hero in a quandary as to where his course lies, whither he is to take these gods of Troy to a new home. Whether the poet is inconsistent or not is a moot question, which each reader must answer for himself.

Aeneas, setting forth to found a kingdom, must have more of a retinue than is furnished by his kinsfolk and the family servants. The poet has neatly provided a company of followers sufficient for the later action of the story. When Aeneas returns after his vain search for Creusa he discovers that Trojan refugees, making their way out from the city, have fallen in with Anchises and the attendants; so, to his surprise, the hero finds his following considerably increased. The quick departure of the company is a necessity: "Now above the crest of loftiest Ida rose the morning-star, chief in the front of day. The Greeks held fast the captive gates of Troy. No help or hope was ours any more. Then, yielding all, and lifting once again my aged sire, for refuge to the distant hills I fled." At the beginning of the next book they are compelled by many an augury and sign to leave the land; they build a fleet in the harbor near Mount Ida, and when summer comes, spread all sails "on the winds of fate." "Through tears I saw recede my native shore, the haven and the plains where once was Troy. An exile on the seas, with son and followers . . . . and Troy's great guardian-gods, I took my way."

VI. THE WANDERINGS OF AENEAS

In his second book Virgil was dealing with a theme which had been treated for ages by innumerable poets. The third book, forming the second chapter of Aeneas' story to Dido, covers a large part of his wanderings; here the poet was thrown back upon the Greek stories of Aeneas which had been given currency by historians and antiquarians, by prose writers, not by poets. In the story of Troy's fall he had only to adapt what was already poetry to the special needs of a Roman national epic; in the third book he had to make poetry out of the baldest prose. His success with this more difficult problem is not conspicuous. The second book deals with one great event; the third, with a loose succession of adventures. Nor does it contribute to his own artistic success that Homer had given poetic value to a similar loose succession of adventures in the *Odyssey*; the very existence of the *Odyssey* spoiled Virgil's chance of notable achievement. The conditions of the Aeneas legend forced him into a competition with Homer on unequal terms, and he must have been discouraged at the very outset of the contest. The story of Aeneas' wanderings, as we have seen, was a hopelessly monotonous patchwork of fictitious history; not a single poet, to our knowledge, had ever treated the material which Virgil used in this book, so far as the six stopping places of Aeneas are concerned. Inferior as the result is, there is no little interest in studying Virgil's attempt to solve his artistic problems; for this study we are fortunate in having in the history of Dionysius of Hallcarnassus a fairly full statement of the wanderings of Aeneas in the prose form which was current in Virgil's own time; by comparing Virgil's story with the historian's narrative we can discover what the poet accomplished, and discern his aims and methods.

The Trojans make their first stop in Thrace, northwest of the Troad; here Aeneas founds a city, bequeathing his name to the inhabitants, Aeneadae. But in the course of sacrifices there he is frightened away by portentous happenings at the grave of Polydorus, a son of Priam sent to Thrace early in the Trojan War with treasures of the Trojan kingdom, and murdered by the greedy king of the Thracian country. They leave Thrace for Delos, the island of the god Apollo, in the Aegean Sea far south of Thrace and east of Attica. At Delos Aeneas asks directions from the god Apollo, and receives the usual ambiguous oracular response: "Seek out your ancient mother. There at last Aeneas' race shall reign on every shore, and his sons' sons, and all their house to be." Anchises attempts to explain the oracle; he maintains that the island of Crete is their ancient mother, the cradle of the Trojan race. Accordingly they sail farther south, to Crete; they attempt to settle in Crete, but are convinced that they have been mistaken in identifying Crete as the end of their wanderings by the approach of a pestilence which attacks the crops that they have planted and the members of the company. They must question the god Apollo again, but a return for this purpose to Delos is made unnecessary by a vision. The Trojan gods whom Aeneas has brought with him from Troy appear to him in a dream and inform him that the land he seeks is called Hesperia, or Italy; there is the real cradle of the Trojan race. Creusa had already told Aeneas as much, but he seems not to recall it, and Anchises, when informed of this announcement from the gods, remembers only a discredited prophecy of Cassandra which had foretold that Hesperia and Italy was to be the home of the Trojans. They are overtaken by a storm in leaving Crete, and after the storm subsides, make the islands called Strophades, the abode of the Harpies. These uncanny monsters, part bird, part women, have large herds of cattle which excite the cupidity of the Trojans; they slay them for food, but are no sooner enjoying the meal than the Harpies swoop down on them; the Trojans are forced to fight them, and drive them off, but not until Celaeno, leader of the Harpies, perched on a crag, delivers an ominous curse: she tells them they shall reach Italy in safety, but shall never found their city until they have been forced by hunger to eat their tables; this in punishment for their attack upon the Harpies. Leaving the Strophades, they skirt the southern coast of Greece proper and journey up the west coast, past the islands off the outlet of the Gulf of Corinth, near the home of Odysseus; they stop at Actium, on the mainland of Greece, just north of the gulf; this was the scene of the famous battle of Actium in Virgil's own day, in which Octavian defeated Antony and put an end to the ambitious designs of Antony and Cleopatra. There Aeneas celebrates athletic games and dedicates a shield on the temple door with an inscription describing it as Aeneas' spoil, won from triumphant foes. Sailing farther north, they pass the modern Corfu, which the ancients identified with Phaeacia, the home of Alcinous, to whom, in the *Odyssey*, Odysseus told the story of his wanderings, and skirt the coast of Epirus, landing at Buthrotum. Here they learn, to their surprise, that a son of Priam, Helenus, is king of the Greek cities in the vicinity and has married Andromache, formerly wife of Hector, and since Hector's death, the slave-wife of the Greek Pyrrhus, or Neoptolemus, who played a rôle in the second book. This situation gives rise to much pathetic detail. Aeneas comes upon Andromache making offerings to her dead husband, Hector; she tells the story of her own life since she last saw Aeneas, inquires for Ascanius, herself recalling her own son, Astyanax. At this point Helenus appears; as priest of Apollo he is competent to give specific direction for their journey, and not only repeats the familiar reference to Italy as their goal, but warns them of dangers to be avoided, gives them the route of their course to Italy, and urges them to seek further directions from the Sibyl at Cumae in Italy. And incidentally, as an offset to the table prodigy which they received from the Harpies, Helenus encourages them by telling of another prodigy which shall indicate to them the site of their new city: they shall find a huge white sow, surrounded by a litter of thirty pigs. Helenus' directions are very full; following them, the Trojans soon sight the southeast coast of Italy. Stopping only to sacrifice to Minerva and to appease the wrath of Juno, against whom Helenus has warned them, they hurry past the coast towns of Southern Italy which, as Greek settlements, are to be avoided, and reach Sicily, safely passing Charybdis; the eruption of Mount Aetna frightens them and they seek cover for a night; the next morning Achaemenides appears on the shore as they are sailing off and begs to be taken with them; he is a Greek survivor of Odysseus' adventure with the Cyclops, Polyphemus, and the episodic scene which Virgil here inserts as a faint reflection from the *Odyssey* we have already discussed. Taking Achaemenides aboard they sail by many towns of Sicily until they reach the harbor of Drepanum; here Anchises dies. Thence they intended to sail north along the coast of Italy, but the storm of Book i drove them off to Africa. Aeneas' narrative to Dido, then, ends with the mention of Anchises' death. The fifth book resumes the story of Aeneas' wanderings after the Carthaginian episode, but in the poet's words, not Aeneas'; that resumption of the narrative begins with the departure from Carthage for Sicily, which accordingly is touched twice in the journey. In Book v they land in Sicily, near Eryx, at the home of Acestes, a Sicilian of Trojan descent, and celebrate here the funeral games in honor of the first anniversary of Anchises' death; the destruction of the Trojan ships at the conclusion of the games leads Aeneas to establish a city of refuge for the women and men who do not wish to continue the journey; of this city Acestes is made king. From this point on they sailed straight to their destination in Latium, except for the visit to Cumae near Naples, where Aeneas consults the Sibyl and visits the other world. Such, then, is the course of their journey from Troy, and the main incidents of that journey. Though we are concerned mainly with the third book, a general knowledge of the wanderings as contained in Books v and vi is essential to our discussion.

In this long journey the poet, of course, mentions many places which the Trojans pass in transit, but the stopping places in the third book are few in number; there are, in fact, only six. This is in direct contrast to the historical narrative in Dionysius, whose account includes not only all the stopping places in Virgil's story, except Crete, but adds many others. This historical record in Dionysius brings together into a connected narrative the numerous traditions about the settlements of Aeneas on the coast of the Mediterranean, his establishment of cults and temples. Aeneas stops to revive old connections, or contrary winds compel him to land, as favorable winds lead to a departure for some new destination. The only unifying factor in the historical narrative is the general westerly course of his journey; this general direction is determined in advance by an oracle received from the Sibyl of Erythrae before they leave Troy, or else, in a variant form of the story, from the shrine of Zeus at Dodona in Epirus later in the journey. The end of the wanderings is to be recognized by the table prodigy. This historical narrative, therefore, has no unity except in the westerly direction of the course; all the separate episodes are only accidental, welcome or unwelcome interruptions, postponements of the final arrival without relation one to another, and diminished or increased at will without affecting the action. Virgil's first task was to organize this prose narrative, to give it an inner unity, and to make the constituent parts inevitable; a loose succession of foundings of cities, of landings, and friendly greetings could not satisfy his artistic sense.

This inner unity is secured, if somewhat imperfectly, by choosing from the traditional account of Aeneas' wanderings six of the many stopping places and arranging at least five of them so that they become progressive stages in the hero's effort to reach his destination in Italy. Aeneas leaves Troy in response to auguries which bid him seek a new home in a foreign land; in Delos he receives an oracle describing that new home as his "ancient mother"; seeking Crete as his ancient mother, he learns that he is mistaken, and finds out from the Penates that Italy is meant; in the Strophades he receives an ominous warning in the table prodigy that defines the time when he shall found his new city; from Helenus in Buthrotum he gets specific directions how to reach Italy, he is given the sow prodigy by which he may identify the place where he is to found his city, and he is instructed to seek further light from the Sibyl at Cumae. So gradually he learns his goal and is enlightened as to the means of recognizing his destination when he reaches it. Nor would he fail to reach it immediately after leaving Helenus, were it not that the storm sent by Juno diverts him to Africa. It should be observed that all the chapters in this progress were suggested by tradition; tradition told of an Erythraean Sibyl who directed him westward; the table prodigy of the Harpy, Celaeno, was in tradition delivered to Aeneas either by this Erythraean Sibyl or by the oracle at Dodona, but in tradition it indicated the end of the journey and it came from a friendly, not a hostile, source; the sow prodigy appeared in tradition, too, but in a different context; there the white sow referred to the name of Alba Longa, the long white city, and the thirty pigs alluded to the thirty years after which Alba Longa was to be settled; here, it will be observed, Virgil has used this prodigy simply to indicate the site of Lavinium, and in so doing has awkwardly kept the white

sow and thirty pigs which have no bearing at all upon the mere
building of Lavinium; the meeting with Helenus appeared in
tradition as one of the incidents at Dodona in Epirus, but Virgil has brought Helenus down from the inland town or shrine
of Dodona to the coast of Epirus at Buthrotum and has eliminated the oracle of Jove at Dodona and given Helenus a prophetic power which takes the place of Jove's oracle in the tradition; the directions from the Penates at Delos were also in
the traditional account. So there is almost nothing absolutely
invented by Virgil, though he has exercised the utmost freedom in making over in various ways the motives employed in
the historical narrative; in the main he simply modified and
rearranged these chapters in a progressive development.

The gradual revelation of the destination is effected
through divine agency, and that divine agency is one god,
Apollo; in tradition Apollo played almost no part at all; but
in Virgil it is Apollo who speaks in Delos; Apollo who bids the
Penates speak in Crete; from Apollo the Harpy received her
information; Helenus is Apollo's prophet; and at Cumae the
Sibyl is inspired by Apollo. To some extent the fact that
Augustus regarded Apollo as the patron god of his family perhaps influenced Virgil to put this god in the foreground of the
action. But a more compelling reason was that in Greek legend Apollo was the colonization god, and it was from these
Greek legends which described the supernatural guidance of
Greek colonists in the earlier centuries of history that Virgil
probably got the idea of unifying his narrative of Aeneas'
wanderings. Aeneas becomes a heroic colonist, and the story
of the foundation, ultimately, of Rome is made over into a
colonization legend on the analogy of the numerous stories
explaining the founding of Greek cities. A single example of
these Greek legends will illustrate how closely they resemble
Virgil's manipulation of the Aeneas legend in the matter of
progressive action and of Apollo's prominence. The founding

of Cyrene in Africa is related in Herodotus (iv. 140) as follows: The king of the island of Thera in the Aegean Sea received directions from the oracle of Apollo at Delphi to found
a colony in Libya, but he did not know where Libya was;
accordingly he neglected to send out the colonists. Immediately a drought broke out in Thera (analogous to the pestilence in Aeneas' experience in Crete), and the king hastily
consulted the oracle again; the god simply referred them to
Libya. They determined to make an attempt, and under the
escort of a Cretan, set out to find Libya, but the Cretan guided
them to an island off the coast of Africa; they settled this
without success, and again consulting Apollo, they were informed that they had not yet reached Libya; then, finally,
they crossed over to the mainland and founded Cyrene. Similarly, in Virgil's making over of the sow and the table prodigies in the Aeneas legend he has clearly been influenced by
stock features of these Greek stories; Greek legends, for example, tell of Cadmus' asking Apollo where he shall settle,
and the oracle responds: "Wherever a cow meets you that has
never borne the yoke"; or Greek colonists locate their settlement "wherever they lose their anchor and their goddess," or
wherever they see rain from a clear sky; in this last case there
is an ambiguity similar to the tables of the table prodigy as it
is realized in Book vii, for "clear sky" in the Greek is also the
name of a mountain at the foot of which the colonists are
caught in a shower.

The prominence of Apollo as a colonization god directing
the wayfarers by omen and oracle brings a certain disturbance
into the general plan of the poem. This third book contains a
large part of the wanderings; in the introduction of Book i we
learned that Aeneas was driven about by the angry Juno; yet
in Book iii we hear little of Juno's activity except through
Helenus' warning that she is dangerous and must be ap-
peased; Aeneas attempts to appease her as soon as he reaches

Italy, but her intervention is not mentioned before the storm that drives them to Carthage. Similarly, Venus, who in the first book and elsewhere is the protecting divinity and whom naturally we should expect to appear in Book iii, where, if ever, her help is necessary, does not intervene at all; so complete is Apollo's control of the action in this book. But the Roman reader probably found no inconsistency in this sudden disappearance of the hostile and the friendly divinity when the action seemed most to require their presence. In fact this was precisely the general situation in the Homeric *Odyssey*. There, at the outset of the action, Poseidon and Athena, as hostile and friendly divinities, are clearly set before us; but when we reach the books in which Odysseus tells his wanderings there is almost no mention of either Poseidon or Athena; the reader knows that they are both active, but the hero is not aware of their activity.

In organizing the traditional narrative Virgil reduced the extant material considerably. He selected such stopping places as fitted into his scheme of unity. When he came to the later stages of the journey, the second visit to Sicily, and the consultation of the Sibyl in Books v and vi, he could afford to treat the incidents elaborately; for Sicily and Cumae were well within the range of the Italian reader's interest. But the stopping places of Book iii, being mainly in the Greek world and relatively uninteresting to the Roman, had to be briefly dismissed with just enough of incident to give the various stops proper distinction. In his choice of motive and incident the poet aimed to avoid monotony; tradition made a very dry and repetitious narrative; it gave a dull succession of foundings of cities, of temples, of dedications of votive offerings; the same things happened in various places on the route; Virgil, in his artistic handling of the story, could not admit any such monotonous reiteration of events.

All of the six stopping places save one, Actium, subserve

the controlling idea of the book—the gradual revelation of the hero's goal. This revelation necessarily comes from supernatural agents, and as one follows the narrative one perceives the poet's concern to vary the means by which this revelation is made. In establishing a city in Thrace, Aeneas innocently supposes that any place will do as the new home of his gods; the portents at the grave of Polydorus drive him away and he seeks enlightenment from Apollo at Delos. There the god himself makes it clear that a definite destination is fixed for the Trojan settlement; positive direction, however, is furnished only in the equivocal reference to their ancient mother. In Crete they receive a negative and positive expression of divine will; the pestilence makes clear that Crete is not the intended goal, and Apollo, no longer in his own person, but through the Penates, announces Hesperia as their destination. Here it will be observed that the poet has, in the pestilence, simply taken over a familiar incident of colonization legends; in the divine assurance from the Penates he has transferred an incident from a later stage of the Aeneas legend and made it serve a new purpose; in the prose tradition this utterance of the Penates was made after the Trojans had arrived in Latium; when Aeneas and his army were encamped opposite the Latins, the Penates, in a dream, advised him to make peace with the Latins; Virgil has introduced it into the account of the wanderings as a means of varying the manner of divine revelation. The adventure with the Harpies is a further variation; here only are the Trojans exposed to danger, and receive from a divine source a discouraging prodigy instead of enlightenment; and it is expressed by a novel mediator, the Harpy, Celaeno. The prophecy of Helenus at Buthrotum offsets this ominous incident; Helenus is a human prophet, unlike Celaeno and equally unlike either Apollo or the Penates· as a human prophet his directions may be more explicit; in tradition Virgil found at this stage of the journey the oracle

of Jove at Dodona enlightening the hero; this did not serve
his purpose, for Apollo alone controls the sources of divine
communication in this book; Helenus in tradition was an incidental character in the Dodona episode; Virgil transfers the
action to the seacoast of Epirus, makes Helenus the spokesman of Apollo, and so recomposes the incidents of tradition
for his special purposes. Thus we have various personal
agents, Apollo, the Penates, Celaeno, Helenus; various imper-
sonal factors, the prodigies at the grave of Polydorus, the
pestilence in Crete, the table prodigy in the Strophades, the
sow prodigy announced by Helenus; omens, prodigies, divine
utterances vary the form of prophetic direction and announcement. This artistic striving for variety would be even more
apparent if we could consider all the many motives and incidents of tradition which Virgil abandoned; one example may
illustrate this negative aspect of his work; in tradition a Sibyl
at Erythrae, near Troy, played a considerable rôle by giving
Aeneas instructions before he left home; this character is
completely eliminated from Virgil's story, obviously because
the poet wishes to make use of a Sibyl at Cumae in his sixth
book, and refuses to duplicate the rôle.

Yet when the poet has reduced the material of tradition,
organized it into a definite unity by providing a gradual revelation of the goal of the journey through Apollo and his various agents, and introduced a variety of motives to avoid the
monotony of the prose tradition, he has achieved hardly more
than a framework, a dry skeleton of the action. The task still
remained of giving to this skeleton substance and movement
and of providing incidents that would interest the reader and
arouse his sympathy.

One of the six stopping places disturbs somewhat the
unity of the plan. At Actium Aeneas learns nothing of the
future; he stops there to celebrate his escape from the perils
of his journey. The celebration takes the form of thankoffer-

ings to Jove, of games, and of the dedicatory offering of a shield. There is no attempt to enrich the content of the action here, and we may well suspect that Virgil's main purpose in this brief reference to Actium, which, even in tradition, was included among Aeneas' stopping places, was simply to perpetuate the memory of the scene of the famous battle between Octavian and Antony, which took place only just before the poet began his work upon the *Aeneid*. Tradition recorded that Aeneas dedicated a temple here; this dedication of a temple Virgil saves for a locality which was more closely identified with the religious interests of Rome, the temple of Venus of Eryx, in Sicily (v. 760); the games and dedication of a shield serve to distinguish Actium from other stopping places.

But in the other five cases the poet has enriched the content by a variety of incident. In developing these incidents he did not depend upon his own imagination, nor did he draw from the traditional story of Aeneas or from Greek colonization legends; he simply drew upon the vast stores of epic tradition contained in the *Odyssey*, in the story of the Argonauts by Apollonius, and in the stories of Troy subsequent to the action of the *Iliad*. By composition and expansion of lesser incidents in earlier epic narrative he made each stage of the journey stimulate various emotions in the reader, and in so doing, of course, he shows no little originality and power.

The story of Polydorus which Virgil weaves into the action of the stop in Thrace is characteristic of his general method. In Thrace the Trojans begin the building of a city, apparently assuming that this is to be their new home. Virgil does not make very clear how far the building of the city got; we might suppose that they had only begun the foundation when the prodigy warned them off, but the description of their time of sailing (vss. 69 ff.) rather points to a winter's sojourn in Thrace; nor are we certain whether this attempted foundation left any permanent traces; whether, for example, their interrupted colonization survived as the town of Aenus or Aeneia, both of which towns play a part in the prose account of Aeneas' wanderings; all that the poet tells us is that Aeneas called the people Aeneadae, after his own name. In general there is a neglect of that antiquarian detail about the founding of the city which the prose historian and even the Hellenistic poet would certainly have dwelt upon. This very vagueness, however, is characteristic of Virgil. He does not care about the historic town which, probably, Aeneas started in this Thracian region; he gives us hints about it out of respect for the historic tradition. But his main interest is in the pathetic detail which he himself as a poet has interwoven into the prosaic story of Aeneas' journey. This pathetic incident at the grave of Polydorus is essential to the action in so far as it motivates their departure from Thrace; seeing the gruesome signs they realize that the gods do not favor their sojourn in this spot. But the story of Polydorus Virgil found, not in the account of Aeneas' wanderings, but in that body of saga which dealt with the history of Troy after the death of Hector; in this legendary material Priam was represented as having made special provision for the safety of a very young son, Polydorus, and also of his royal treasury; he gave the boy the family wealth and sent him to a neighboring Thracian king who was to be the lad's guardian and protector during the days when Troy was exposed to the cruel and greedy Greeks; the Thracian king, however, betrayed his trust; tempted by the gold which Polydorus brought, he killed the boy and possessed himself of the money; this incident appears in Euripides' *Hecuba,* a tragedy which Virgil may have used for some of his detail. But in the manner of the death and the fate of the body Virgil could hardly have been influenced primarily by any account of Polydorus' tragedy; it would be hazardous to say whether Virgil or some earlier author is responsible for the details, but it is at least clear that the details do not fit at all the circumstances of Polydorus' death, but are chosen entirely with reference to the special needs of Virgil's narrative; in other words, not only has Virgil gone outside of the Aeneas story for this incident, but he has probably invented detail which he hardly found even in Trojan saga attached to the death of Polydorus. According to Virgil's account this helpless young fellow was killed by spears thrown at him from a distance; these spears then took root and grew up into a grove of myrtle and cornel; Aeneas, preparing a sacrifice in connection with his dedication of the town, pulls up some of these trees to serve as altar-boughs; blood flows from the roots; a second attempt yields the same result; "but when at a third sheaf of myrtle spears I fell upon my knees, and tugged amain against the adverse ground, a moaning and a wail from that deep grave burst forth and murmured in my listening ear: 'Why wound me, great Aeneas, in my woe? O spare the dead, nor let thy holy hands do sacrilege and sin. I, Trojan-born, was kin of thine. This blood is not of trees. Haste from this murderous shore, this land of greed.'" Polydorus then tells of his fate. Aeneas, at all these ominous events, is frozen with fear, tells the prodigies to his mates, and is advised to leave "that land of sin where foul abomination had profaned a stranger's right." So they take advantage of the first fair winds and leave Thrace. Now it will be observed that these incidents have no special appropriateness in connection with the death of Polydorus. He was a helpless lad; but according to Virgil he was killed with spears thrown from a distance; such a death is appropriate only to an invincible hero whom his antagonists do not dare to approach in hand-to-hand conflict; nor is there any explanation offered for the transformation of the spears to myrtle and cornel bushes; this transformation in the normal run of such stories is effected by some divine agency by which the victim is protected after death; finally, the bleeding of the tree properly appears in stories of the metamorphosis of human beings into plants; such plants, when bruised, reveal their original human nature by bleeding. In brief, it looks very much as if Virgil, needing some prodigy to motivate the departure from Thrace, had chosen the bleeding, which, as a shower of blood or as appearing in springs or in the sea or issuing from the statues of gods, is common enough in ancient prodigies, and had then brought about the bleeding by a manipulation of the Polydorus story which, though awkward and involving quite improbable and unexplained incidents, serves his main purpose of frightening away the Trojans and at the same time of arousing the interest and sympathy of the reader in the pathetic fate of this helpless son of Priam. The bruising of the corpse of Polydorus after he has already suffered so cruelly at the hands of the Thracian king is just short of the horrible; it may be gruesome, but it stirs sympathy, rather than horror, as Virgil handles it.

Similarly, in the action of the Helenus scene in Buthrotum the poet has introduced from the later Trojan saga incidents which appeal primarily to the emotions of the reader instead of contributing directly or exclusively to the action. The meeting with Helenus was in the traditional account, though he played no prophetic rôle in the Aeneas legend. Virgil, however, once having brought Helenus into prominence, enriches the scene by including Andromache, his wife. The story of Andromache after the death of Hector and the fall of Troy brought her into the power of Neoptolemus, the cruel murderer of Priam in the plot of Virgil's second book; as slave-wife of this son of Achilles she lived a pitiful existence in northern Greece; she bore Neoptolemus a son; her husband, however, soon abandoned her for Hermione, daughter of Menelaus and Helen; the new wife attempted to murder the son of Andromache and Neoptolemus; Orestes, however, the lover of Hermione, slew her husband, Neoptolemus; so Andromache was released. This was the tragic story as told in Euripides' tragedy, *Andromache*. But Virgil's Andromache is not the Euripidean heroine except in so far as she is a pathetic figure. She is rather the Andromache of the *Iliad,* former wife of Hector and mother of Astyanax, and still sorrowfully looking back to those happier days, even after her misery as the slave-wife of Neoptolemus has been relieved by her new marriage to her fellow-Trojan, Helenus. The poet gives much space to the prophecy of Helenus, but it is evident that his own main interest is in the pitiful experiences of Andromache. When Aeneas meets her she is bringing offerings to the shade of Hector:

> She saw me drawing near; our Trojan helms
> Met her bewildered eyes, and terror-struck
> At the portentous sight, she swooning fell
> And lay cold, rigid, lifeless till at last
> Scarce finding voice, her lips addressed me thus:
> "Have I true vision? Bringst thou the word
> Of truth, O goddess-born? art still in flesh?
> Or if sweet life be fled, is Hector here?"

Her first thought is of Hector. In answer to Aeneas' questions she tells the story of her life since she left Troy, and concludes with the affecting question: "Tell me of the boy, Ascanius? Still breathes he earthly air? In Troy she bore him—Is he mourning still that mother ravished from his childhood's eyes? What ancient valor stirs the manly soul of thine own son, of Hector's sister's child?" Helenus appears, the prophecy follows, and the Trojans prepare to continue their journey; Helenus sends them rich gifts:

> Likewise Andromache in mournful guise
> Took last farewell, bringing embroidered robes
> Of golden woof; a princely Phrygian cloak
> She gave Ascanius, vying with the king
> In gifts of honor; and threw o'er the boy
> The labors of her loom, with words like these:

"Accept these gifts, sweet youth, memorials
Of me and my poor handicraft, to prove
Th' undying friendship of Andromache,
Once Hector's wife. Take these last offerings
Of those who are thy kin—O thou that art
Of my Astyanax in all this world
The only image. His thy lovely eyes;
Thy hands, thy lips, are even what he bore,
And like thy own his youthful bloom would be."

The emphasis is upon the same domestic ties which made significant the scene in the house of Anchises in the second book, but the effect upon the reader is even more stirring than the picture of Aeneas' own devotion to father, wife, and child. Seldom has Virgil succeeded better in compelling the sympathy and pity of his readers; so out of the prosaic instructions of Helenus develops a situation that enriches the dry content of the Aeneas legend.

The poet's construction of the adventure with the Harpies is altogether different. These uncanny creatures had no part in the Aeneas legend. Virgil found them probably in Apollonius' epic on the Argonauts; in that poem the Greek heroes in their wanderings fell in with Phineus, a blind prophet, punished for his disloyalty to Zeus; the Harpies snatch his food from him before he can carry it to his mouth. Taking pity on him, the sons of Boreas, who, as children of the north wind, are winged, undertake to rescue him from the Harpies and, drawing their swords, drive the Harpies before them through the air as far as the Strophades; the Harpies finally give in and take up their abode in the island of Crete. Virgil represents them as residing in the Strophades, and the Trojans are led to attack them somewhat as the sons of Boreas do. But otherwise the situation is very different. The Roman poet represents the Strophades as their ancestral kingdom; here they have rich herds of oxen and goats, which the hungry Trojans seize upon and thus excite the wrath of the grim monsters. It

is likely that these herds of cattle and goats and the greed of
the Trojans in seizing the property of supernatural creatures
were suggested to Virgil by the scene in the *Odyssey* in which
the Greek heroes got into trouble by slaying the cattle of the
sun god. Virgil seems to have fused these two different stories.
And the dovetailing of the two stories has left traces in the
Virgilian narrative. For the Roman poet, following Apollonius or the general conception of the Harpies, has made them
hungry scavengers: "Ghastly lips they have, with hunger
pale." But at the same time he provides them, from the story
in the *Odyssey*, with herds of oxen and goats which are quite
inconsistent with their nature as hungry scavengers. All of
this scene provides a setting for the table prodigy, which alone
of the details was found in the Aeneas legend, though there
serving a different purpose and proceeding from a friendly
source. The action of the Trojans excites the attack of the
Harpies and leads to the hostile declaration of the prodigy;
Virgil's invention or recomposition of earlier material, therefore, is mainly intended to lead up to this prodigy, and in this
case the invention is not altogether happy. But it will be observed to his credit that, having chosen characters that are
uncanny and gruesome, he has done his best to dignify them
and make them suitable for the new context. The Harpy,
Celaeno, from whom the announcement of the table prodigy
comes, is described as eldest of the furies and mouthpiece of
Apollo's oracle; so she is raised to the higher plane of Virgil's
epic. The adventure, along with the portent in Thrace and
the pestilence in Crete, provides hindrances which vary the
succession of prospering hopeful indications received at the
other stopping places.

Virgil's general indebtedness to the *Odyssey* we have
already discussed. We found him in this third book adorning
the poetic geography by passing allusions of varied extent to
Scylla, Charybdis, Phaeacia, the Sirens, and, in a later book,

to the island of Circe. We discussed at length the episode of
Achaemenides, in which, at the end of this third book, he pays
tribute to the adventure of Odysseus with the Cyclops, Polyphemus. It will be remembered that in his new invention of
this single survivor of Odysseus' company, accidentally left
behind on the island of the one-eyed giants, Virgil again threw
all the emphasis upon the pathetic details; the miraculous
achievements of Odysseus are neglected; all the light is
thrown on the grim one-eyed giants and the hunger-wasted
misery of the unkempt Greek who appeals not in vain to his
deadly enemies, the Trojans, for rescue from his dangerous
environment. In this case, however, Virgil was not enriching
the content of adventure at one of the stopping places in the
traditional story, but rather inserting an episode which relieved the somewhat prosaic enumeration of notable places in
Sicily which the Trojans passed in their journey. Again, however, he remodels and expands what the Trojan saga had
transmitted.

In all these travels the Trojans are not exposed to any
serious danger. They are discouraged by the portent in
Thrace, by the pestilence in Crete, by the table prodigy, and
in the last case they have their one occasion to draw swords
against an enemy; outside this book their wanderings are not
perilous, except in the storm at sea in Book i, where Aeneas
is saved without much effort on his part. All this is in striking
contrast with the wanderings of Odysseus, which gave every
opportunity to test the heroism, the resourceful energy of the
Greek hero. It is not surprising that Virgil's Aeneas has not
excited much admiration in the modern reader, however absorbed Dido may have been in what she calls his dauntless
courage and exploits of war. This is sentimental exaggeration.
But the poet without question regarded Aeneas as a true
hero. If the sufferings of Aeneas during his wanderings do not
bring out the courage and strength of the sufferer as do those

of Odysseus, if they are not overcome at the risk of constant danger to life and limb, it is not that Virgil meant to make the lot of his hero an easier one. The suffering which Virgil makes Aeneas undergo is mental and spiritual, a kind which the poet himself felt more keenly than physical pain and danger; the loss of home, the bitterness of exile, constantly disappointed expectation, the search for years after an unknown goal— these are the trials of Aeneas. His title to fame and heroism is that in spite of all he is faithful to his duty, imposed upon him by God, the duty which he owes to the gods of his native city. Such mental and spiritual suffering and action admit of description much less easily than the visible outward manifestation of physical strength and courage; they are specially difficult to portray in the hero's own narrative of adventure; the poet counts upon the reader's so vividly transposing himself into the situation of Aeneas that he will experience anew, himself, the feelings that must have stirred Aeneas; upon this, perhaps even more than on the effect of the various adventures, depends the pathos of the wanderings of Aeneas which the poet aims to produce. Nor should the Christian reader, at least, complain of Aeneas' character in this third book; he represents the Stoic ideal of Virgil's day; his chief effort is to find out the will of God and to obey it; that Stoic ideal is the nearest approach that paganism makes to Christian ideals of conduct.

VII. THE DESCENT TO THE LOWER WORLD

The burning of the Trojan ships after the funeral games[1] is the work of the hostile divinity, Juno; she sends the goddess Iris, disguised as a Trojan matron, to stimulate the women, already filled with loathing for the long laborious sea; recognizing the goddess in spite of her masquerade, the women are the more ready to assume the responsibility for their desperate act. The news is brought to Aeneas at the funeral games; the young Ascanius, on horseback just after finishing the cavalry maneuver, rushes to the Trojan camp, with the older Trojans close behind. Aeneas prays Jove to save the ships. A shower of rain drowns the fire, and all but four ships escape. These hardly suffice to convoy all the Trojans to Italy; the old man, Nautes, whose matured wisdom and experience make him the Nestor of the *Aeneid*, advises founding a settlement in Sicily and making Acestes the ruler of it. While Aeneas is pondering this advice it is confirmed by the ghost of Anchises, who appears to his son in a dream, counsels him to select his best warriors and go to Italy, leaving the rest in Sicily: "Only with warriors of dauntless breast to Italy repair; of hardy breed, of wild rough life, thy Latin foes will be. But first the shores of Pluto and the Shades thy feet must tread, and through the deep abyss of dark Avernus come to me, thy sire; for I inhabit not the guilty gloom of Tartarus, but bright Elysian day, where all the just their sweet assemblies hold. Hither the virgin Sibyl, if thou give full offerings of the blood of sable kine, shall lead thee down; and visions I will show of cities proud and nations sprung from thee." These instructions in part repeat what the prophet Helenus had told Aeneas at Buthrotum; but Helenus

[1] For the analysis of the funeral games of Book v, cf. pp. 206 ff.

had referred only to the Sibyl; Aeneas should seek her and learn the future from her oracles: "Her rede shall tell of Italy, its wars and tribes to be, and of what way each burden and each woe may be escaped or borne." Helenus sa:d nothing of a visit to the other world; but his advice came before the death of Anchises. The apparition of the dead father gives a new purpose to the visit to the Sibyl; she is not only to prophesy the future, but to escort the hero through Hades to the Elysian Fields, where his father shall show him a vision of the future power of Rome. Thus the action of the sixth book is completely motivated, and it should be observed that the meeting with Anchises, according to this admonition from his father's ghost, becomes the main purpose of Aeneas' visit to the other world. Having carried out the plan of Nautes, Aeneas sails for Italy; Venus, meantime, has secured the help of the sea god, Neptune, against any possible further injury from Juno; the fleet has an easy passage, safely skirting the island of the Sirens, and at the beginning of the sixth book they land at Cumae. In this voyage only one mishap has befallen them: their pilot, Palinurus, fell asleep and slipped overboard; so the landing at Cumae is effected not without tears for the unburied Palinurus, though otherwise the long-deferred arrival in Italy must have brought relief to the wearied Trojans.

The action of this sixth book is a distinct chapter in the poem; it covers the time of their stay in this Campanian town; at the beginning of the next book we find them reaching their destination, farther north in Latium; Cumae is the last stopping place in their long wanderings before the goal is reached. The sixth book bridges over the two main portions of the poem, the story of the wanderings and the narrative of the war in Latium; it marks a critical point in the action; before it lie discouragement and hardship, patient submission on the hero's part, a constant struggle to ascertain the will of the gods, a painful effort to endure the sufferings to which an exiled wanderer is exposed, a vague unrest as long as the future seems shadowy and perilous. After this book come new obstacles and dangers in the war between a handful of Trojans, assisted by a few allies, and a host of native Latins and Rutulians; but these new dangers the hero meets not with mere patient submission and increased discouragement; on the contrary, he faces the new vicissitudes with a vigor and forcefulness quite in contrast with the frequent discouragement that he exhibited in the lesser perils of his wanderings over the long laborious sea. The sixth book, standing between these two main portions of the poem, explains the different attitude of the hero toward the shocks of fortune, and as such an explanation, justifies its existence. Aeneas receives a vision seldom granted to mortal man; he sees the unborn souls of the future statesmen, warriors, benefactors of the Roman empire. Such a vision immediately removes all doubt and discouragement; he has seen the great issues of his wanderings that now lie behind him, and of the struggle in Latium through which he has yet to go; no wonder, therefore, that after Anchises "quickens in his mind hunger for future fame," he leaves the world of death and returns to his own task a new man, refreshed and inspired by the knowledge that his reluctant abandonment of Troy, his painful uncertainty in the laborious wanderings, and the strenuous effort to establish a new home in Latium, all have a glorious and inevitable issue—the Roman empire, far surpassing as a worldpower the humble city of Troy, and assimilating even the Greek conquerors who forced Aeneas to desert his home in Troyland. From this point on the patient Aeneas of the first five books gives place to the forceful hero of the Latin war.

But though this is a function of the sixth book in the development of the action, the poet, in elaborating the details of this notable vision of the after-life, has made it a depositary of much that the paganism of his day had contributed toward a definite conception of the immortality of the soul, of the life after death, and of pre-existence. These ideas that he conveys are not a beautiful harmony, a logical unit; on the contrary, they are the interwoven, rather the intertwined, strands of popular fancy and enlightened theory; and among the ideas are some that faintly foreshadow modern conceptions. To the modern reader, therefore, the book must ever have an added significance in that it bridges over the gap between Paganism and Christianity. For the present, however, we must confine ourselves to a consideration of Virgil's literary craftsmanship.

The Greek versions of Aeneas' wanderings assigned a prominent rôle to a Sibyl; but this Sibyl belonged in the Troad, and gave Aeneas directions for his journey before his departure from Troy. Any part that Cumae, in Italy, may play in Virgil's story is likely to have been introduced into the narrative of the hero's wanderings after the Romans had taken over the legend and molded it to suit the needs of their national pride; whether it was Virgil who was the first to elaborate this chapter of the story we do not know; he may have been anticipated by some earlier Roman poet. In any case the substitution of the Cumaean Sibyl for the Trojan prophetess of the Greek legend was natural; for many generations before Virgil the Sibylline oracles had been held in special regard by the Romans; soon after the poet's death they were deposited in Apollo's temple on the Palatine; these oracles were in Greek, and were commonly believed to have come to Rome through the Greek cities of Southern Italy; of these Greek cities Cumae was most intimately connected with prophetic Apollo and with a prophetic Sibyl. The temple of the god, the grotto of the Cumaean Sibyl, were familiar to every Roman visitor to Campania.

But the choice of the Cumaean Sibyl as an active character, and consequently of Cumae as a stopping place, was determined not merely by contemporary interest in the region and in the person of the Sibyl. The calling up of the shades by Odysseus in the eleventh *Odyssey* constrained Virgil to include in his poem a similar adventure. The scene of this bit of action in the *Odyssey* had been definitely localized in Virgil's day as Lake Avernus, near Cumae; naturally, when the rôle of Odysseus was transferred to Aeneas, the accepted scene of the action, too, was taken over, and Cumae necessarily furnished the setting of the incidents. The temple of Apollo at Cumae, and the Sibyl serving as his prophetess, harmonize with the poet's general plan of the wanderings in which Apollo and his ministers are consistently the exponents of the divine will in determining the hero's movements during his search for the site of a new Troy. The Sibyl, however, is not merely priestess of Apollo; the poet has made her as well a priestess of Hecate, the goddess of the underworld; by this means he links together two otherwise separate chapters of the action; the Sibyl whom Aeneas consults at Cumae and from whom he receives comforting assurance becomes also his guide in the descent to the underworld. It is evident that the poet's desire to include this visit to the other world, suggested by the *Odyssey*, largely explains the appearance of the Sibyl and her functions.

In addition to the Homeric epic, the prose account of Aeneas' wanderings supplied one incident that Virgil incorporated in the story of events at Cumae; the death of Misenus, whose fate explained to Italians the name of a promontory near Cumae, was a somewhat regular feature of the legend; the location of this incident made it naturally, in Virgil's story, part of the happenings in the stop at Cumae.

Briefly, then, the sixth book owes its framework to the *Odyssey*, just as the games in the fifth book were suggested by the *Iliad;* with this theme of the *Odyssey* the poet has combined the Sibyl, suggested by the Aeneas legend but much modified to suit her new position in the story, and the fate of Misenus. These three elements Virgil has organized into a new whole, with some defects, but with no little skilful modification, particularly of the Greek material.

The landing at Cumae is described in the opening verses with some detail, most of which is devoted to the somewhat prosaic task of building a fire and getting water. Such matter-of-fact detail is conventional in epic, and Virgil is content simply to idealize in his diction the trivial nature of the action; so fire becomes "the seed-spark hidden in the veins of flint," and firewood is dignified as "the shelter where the woodland creatures hide." In these trivial tasks the other members of the company are absorbed, but the hero himself has a commission to perform which brooks no delay. He seeks at once the temple of Apollo on the hill at Cumae, attended only by Achates; the poet is somewhat vague at this point, and we must discover for ourselves the topography. Today, at least, this hill at Cumae rises in two peaks, on one of which is the temple of Apollo—some remains of it are still visible. The hill itself is honeycombed with grottoes. The situation which Virgil has in mind seems to include a temple structure, sacred to Apollo, and near it a grotto from which the Sibyl presently speaks; this grotto, however, may be distinct from another grotto near Lake Avernus to which later Aeneas brings the golden bough and in which sacrifices preliminary to entering the lower world are performed. If this is the case we are to imagine the Sibyl as using the first grotto for her function as priestess of Apollo, and residing in the second grotto near Lake Avernus as the servant of Hecate. However this may be, it is clear that when Aeneas reaches the temple he sends Achates after the Sibyl, possibly to the distant grotto at Lake Avernus; meantime the hero himself fills the interval of waiting by observing the ornamentation of the temple doors.

The part played by such descriptions of works of art in epic poetry we briefly sketched in discussing the passage in the first book in which Aeneas studies the decorations of Juno's temple at Carthage while awaiting the arrival of Dido; here, as there, the description fills an interval of waiting; but there, as we saw, the scene contributed directly to the action by stimulating Aeneas' interest in the queen; here there is no such added justification, and the action, which elsewhere in this part of the story moves with desirable rapidity, is somewhat inexcusably retarded. It is none the less interesting to note the characteristics of the Virgilian description; the poet informs us first that Daedalus, mythical architect and aviator, landed here at Cumae when he was trying to escape on wings from his enemy, Minos of Crete, and here built this temple of Apollo and fashioned these doors. The doors are then described. Whether Virgil is describing what he had actually seen, or is indulging his own fancy, is immaterial; in either case it is easy to recognize the symmetrical grouping characteristic of contemporary art. The doors have two panels, with balanced pairs of pictures on each panel; the scenes are chapters from Daedalus' own experiences in the island of Crete; it was he who designed the labyrinth and won the enmity of Minos by helping the queen, Pasiphae, in her strange amour. On one door are the scenes in Attica which led to the sacrifice of Athenian young men and maidens to the Minotaur; above, perhaps, the killing of Minos' son by the Athenians; below, the drawing of lots at Athens to determine the seven youths and seven maidens who shall be sent as tribute to the Minotaur; on the other panel are scenes in Crete; above, Pasiphae and the Minotaur; below, the labyrinth. But however the pictures are arranged, the poet's interest is clearly in the pathetic situations; he dwells upon the pitiable fate of the young Athenians, upon the tears of lovelorn Ariadne, and with true Virgilian feeling represents the artist, Daedalus, as wishing to portray the fate of his own rash son, Icarus, who, attempting to fly with artificial wings from Crete with his father, flew too near the sun, melted the wax that bound the wings to his body, and sank into the Icarian Sea. The artist-father, however, is overcome with emotion; twice he strove to fashion the picture of his son's fate, but his fingers strove in vain.

At this point the Sibyl arrives with Achates and demands the sacrifices as a necessary preliminary to her prophetic utterance; all through the religious observations which mark these early scenes of the sixth book Virgil is careful to adhere to all the scrupulous requirements of contemporary religious ritual; the priestess demands these sacrifices before the worshiper has a chance to offer them; the sacrifices include male and female animals, because Apollo and Hecate, male and female divinities, are involved, and there are to be seven of each kind, seven being the sacred number. The Sibyl summons them into the temple; we are to imagine, probably, a subterranean passage leading from the temple to the grotto, whence presently the priestess utters her prophetic words; Aeneas and the Trojans stand without at the threshhold; the Sibyl enters the grotto; her voice is heard through the hundred apertures that cover the side of the cavern. As the Trojans pause at the entrance the Sibyl begins to feel the god taking possession of her. This possession was something very real to the ancient reader, however fanciful it may seem to us; the god was supposed actually to enter into her, producing that condition which the Greeks call *enthousiasmos*, or the state of having a god within one, a divine frenzy or enthusiasm: "From her face its color flew, her twisted locks flowed free, the heaving breast swelled with her heart's wild blood, her stature seemed vaster, her accent more than mortal man's.

as all th' oncoming god around her breathed." All this is the outer manifestation of the presence of the god within her; it is Apollo himself who speaks through her lips. In effective contrast with the frenzied priestess is the hero, Aeneas, who now, self-contained and dignified, prays for assurance of a permanent home in Latium, promising in return, again according to the ritual, a temple to Apollo, festal games, and careful preservation of the Sibylline oracles in the promised temple. In these vows Virgil is representing Aeneas as promising what Augustus had already established or planned; the temple of Apollo was dedicated on the Palatine in the year 28, just before Virgil began the *Aeneid;* the secular games sacred to Apollo and Diana were celebrated soon after the poet's death, and the Sibylline oracles were deposited in the temple beneath the god's statue at about the same time; so Virgil is transferring the present into the past. The hero's final request that the Sibyl shall not intrust her oracles to leaves reflects the caution of Helenus in the third book, who warned Aeneas to urge the Sibyl to utter her oracle by word of mouth, instead of committing it to leaves, as she often did.

The ecstasy of the prophetess now becomes a struggle between the god and the woman whom he seeks to control; though prophetic power is a divine gift, the prophetic trance is an act of force which the human agent resists; so the Sibyl struggles, according to Virgil's description, like an unbroken colt against its rider: "The virgin through the cave, scarce bridled yet by Phoebus' hand divine, ecstatic swept along, and vainly strove to fling her potent master from her breast; but he more strongly plied his rein and curb upon her frenzied lips, and soon subdued her spirit fierce, and swayed her at his will." The prayers of Aeneas have a magic effect upon the hundred apertures of the grotto; hitherto closed by doors, these now swing open, and the Sibyl, submitting at last to divine power, becomes the mouthpiece of Apollo and responds to the questions of the worshiper. Her response is in oracular form; indeed, it is not impossible that its content was derived by Virgil from actual Sibylline oracles to which he had access. She speaks in jerky sentences appropriate to her frenzy, and uses the ambiguous language of oracular wisdom: she sees "war, red war" in store for Aeneas; the Tiber is stained with blood; "Simois, Xanthus, and the Dorian horde thou shalt behold; a new Achilles now in Latium breathes"; so she employs terms taken from the Trojan War to describe the new war in Latium; Simois and Xanthus are Trojan rivers intended to suggest corresponding streams in Latium, and the new Achilles is Turnus, the chief antagonist of the Latin War. She bids Aeneas not to yield to his misfortunes, but rather to face fortune boldly; and she concludes with a mysterious reference to a Greek city which shall bring him help, meaning the city of Evander, which Aeneas later visits and from which he gets auxiliaries. So, as the poet says, she "commingles truth with ecstasies obscure." "Apollo as she raged flung loosened rein, and thrust beneath her heart a quickening spur." At last her madness ceases, and again the hero speaks with a calmness and solemn impressiveness in contrast with her ecstatic frenzy; the balanced speeches are noteworthy; they are in contrasted pairs. But the second pair of speeches which now begins is abrupt in the introduction of a new theme; Aeneas has asked for assurance as to his future and received it; yet, instead of expressing any joy and gratitude, he practically asserts that he is quite indifferent to the fortune which awaits him in Latium; he wants really only one thing: the privilege of going to the other world and seeing his father. The Sibyl may guide him hither if she will; other mortal men of divine descent have had the privilege—Orpheus, Hercules, Pollux, Theseus—why should not he go, too? The abrupt introduction of this new theme reveals the poet in the act of combining in his own poem what had hitherto been

two unconnected themes. A Sibyl as prophetess assuring
Aeneas of the future had existed in the Aeneas legend; Virgil
wished to add a visit to the other world suggested by the
Odyssey; the first pair of speeches is part of the theme of the
Aeneas legend; in the second pair Virgil is making over the
prophetess of legend into a guide to the other world necessary
to his organization of the material of the *Odyssey* with the
theme of the Aeneas legend.

The Sibyl's answer is introduced with some very inappropriate commonplaces. It is, of course, true in general that the
descent to Avernus is easy, and the return, difficult; this is
the usual condition of things when mortal men die and go to
the other world; they go to the bourn whence no traveler returns. But this rhetorical commonplace is entirely pointless
in connection with Aeneas' request and with the unusual visits of living demigods like Hercules, Pollux, and the rest; for
in their cases the descent is not easy, but difficult, and the
return to the upper world not difficult, but a very simple
matter. Aeneas' own experience later in the book flatly contradicts the Sibyl's generalizations; Aeneas confronts on his
way down grim monsters and makes his way through them
with drawn sword, but his return to the upper world is easily
accomplished. The poet has allowed the Sibyl to declaim like
a thoughtless rhetorician. Nor is there any force in the Sibyl's
warning that only demigods have been allowed to visit the
other world before death, so long as Aeneas himself has just
shown that he knows this fact and has justified his own request by pointing out that he, too, is a son of a goddess. Having unburdened herself of these inappropriate truisms, the
priestess lays down three conditions which are fulfilled in the
subsequent action: Aeneas must find the golden bough and
bring it as an offering to Proserpine, goddess of the underworld; he must bury with due ritual the body of a friend of
whose death he is not aware (the reader understands, of

course, that if such a friend remains unburied, the gods of the underworld to whom the soul of the corpse belongs will not show favor to Aeneas); and finally, he must offer special sacrifices to the gods of the other world.

These three conditions, it should be observed, again reveal Virgil organizing his narrative. The condition which imposes the burial of Misenus is Virgil's means of bringing over into his story the Misenus episode from the legend of Aeneas; the golden bough is a motive from folk-lore of which we get no trace elsewhere in ancient literature; the sacrifices to the gods of the underworld are taken over from the *Odyssey*, where Circe, corresponding to the Sibyl, directs Odysseus to perform certain rites essential to calling up the spirits of the dead.

Of these three themes that of the golden bough has a mysterious fascination. It adds nothing to our appreciation of the motive to know definitely the underlying idea, or to identify the bough; indeed, such an obvious bit of folk-lore is best left unsolved; for popular fancy easily eludes all the learned efforts to bring it down to earth and relate it to anything concrete and tangible. The Sibyl describes the bough as hidden in a tree; the bough is sacred to Proserpine; nobody can pass to the underworld without it; when plucked, another immediately grows in its place; nor may it be plucked unless fate ordains; neither mortal strength nor strong sharp steel avails to rend it from the tree. Later in the action, birds guide Aeneas to it; it is found near Avernus; the poet compares it to the mistletoe: "Through green boughs flames forth the glowing gold's contrasted hue. As in the wintry woodland bare and chill, fresh budded shines the clinging mistletoe, whose seed is never from the parent tree o'er whose round limbs its tawny tendrils twine—so shone the th'outleafing gold within the shade of dark holm-oak, and so its tinsel-bract rustled in each light breeze." Of course this simile may contain the clue to the folk-notion; nothing is commoner than the identity of the object compared with that to which it is compared, at least in mythology. The mistletoe had magic properties, according to ancient authorities; such magic power was easily suggested by the fact that it seemed to grow without seeds and to have no connection with the earth; and its fresh green and gold in winter when other plants were asleep would have easily made it symbolic of life in the midst of death. In European mythology the plant plays a rôle not altogether at variance with its function in Virgil: closest to the Virgilian theme are passages of the older Edda in which Loki breaks off a bough of mistletoe near the entrance of hell and the gates of hell open before it. But modern students of folk-lore are not agreed, and we must not press the point. We do not know where Virgil got the idea; it is quite unlikely that he invented it; the most plausible theory is as old as the Latin commentator, Servius, who refers to writers on the mysteries of Proserpine as the source; without much doubt it was a mystical emblem in the mysteries of the Greek goddess Ceres, who, as goddess of vegetation and of death, would find in such a bough her own powers happily symbolized.

On leaving the Sibyl, Aeneas and Achates are lost in thought. Who can this unburied friend of theirs be? Such a perplexity is hardly justified by the preceding action of the poem. The end of the fifth book related in some detail the death of Palinurus, their pilot, who fell overboard in their trip from Sicily to Cumae. Clearly they ought to identify him as the unburied friend, but they never think of him. Instead, they suddenly stumble upon the body of Misenus. This situation discloses an awkwardness in the structure. Virgil has blundered in an effort to combine material from different sources; the death of Palinurus corresponds to an incident in the *Odyssey*—just before Odysseus visited the other world he lost a companion, Elpenor, who appears to him as soon as he

calls up the shades and asks Odysseus to bury his body that
his soul may have rest. So Palinurus will meet Aeneas in the
other world and ask for burial. But Virgil wished also to include in the action the story of Misenus, from the Aeneas
legend. By attempting to use both these themes he has
brought into his story a doublet; there are two cases of unburied friends, and much awkwardness results.

Virgil has, however, very neatly arranged the fulfilment
of the Sibyl's conditions; instead of having the hero carry
them out in a mechanical one-two-three order, the poet represents Aeneas as discovering the golden bough while he is gathering the firewood from a grove for the funeral pyre of
Misenus; more mechanically, the performance of sacrifices to
the underworld gods is added to the account of Misenus' cre-
mation.

Equally neat, of course, is his device of bringing the
story of Misenus into the action by making the burial of the
corpse one of the conditions preliminary to the visit to Hades.
The story of Misenus is an aetiological myth, that is, a bit of
fiction invented to account for the name of Cape Misenum,
near Cumae; and Virgil handles the legend much in the style
of Hellenistic poets by concluding it with the prosaic statement that the cape henceforth was named after the victim of
the tragedy. The story itself is a familiar theme; it is one of
several which narrate the fate that overtakes mortal men who
dare to compete with gods; the most familiar similar anecdote
is the legend of Marsyas' competition in music with Apollo;
so the trumpeter, Misenus, rashly boasts of his superiority in
blowing the shell-shaped horn; Triton, expert upon the conch
shell, hurls Misenus into the sea in angry jealousy of his mortal rival.

Virgil, however, is more interested in the funeral rites
than in the story of Misenus' death. The elaborate description which he gives of the building of the pyre and of the

details of the ceremony is part of the same purpose which moved him to describe the auspices in the second book; and here he does not hesitate to disclose that purpose in the parenthetical comment which reminds us that the rites are performed according to ancestral custom. The passage becomes, therefore, our chief source of knowledge of the Roman funeral ceremony. The pyre is built of pines and funereal cypresses; the weapons of the hero are burned with him; they bathe and anoint the corpse, place it on a couch, and the couch on the funeral pyre; over the corpse are thrown purple garments; the fire is lighted with face averted, that the escaping soul may not be seen by the living witnesses when it leaves the body; incense, food, and olive oil are burned with the corpse; the fire is put out with wine; the ashes are then gathered in an urn; the witnesses are purified with lustral water sprinkled from an olive branch; the formal last words are spoken; the grave is built; and the rounded top of the grave still survives in the peculiar formation of the cape to which Misenus' name was given. No doubt this accidental resemblance of the cape to a grave gave rise to the story. The lavish detail may prove tedious to the reader, but the Roman found satisfaction in the venerable antiquity which this scene established for the customs of his own day; the details of the rites are, however, Greek as well as Italian, and the general situation, though not the details, was suggested by the funeral of Patroclus in the *Iliad;* not every incident of the action is paralleled in what we learn elsewhere of Roman ceremony in Virgil's time.

The transition to the fulfilment of the third condition is abrupt. Nor is the condition itself quite inevitable; the golden bough seems in itself to be sufficient to secure access to the other world; Virgil is rather obviously adding a feature from the *Odyssey.* But again the details of the rite do not correspond to Circe's directions to Odysseus; for in the *Odyssey* the ceremony simply enabled Odysseus to call up souls to the side of a trench. In Virgil the rite is made exciting and emotional; it is much in the style of the magic ceremony practiced by the witches of ancient days. Hecate is conjured up by blood-offerings; the ritual of the underworld gods is carefully observed; the animals sacrificed are black, to accord with the sable powers of Hades, or they are barren, in harmony with the unfertile nature of the world of death. The ceremony comes just after midnight: "At dawn's dim earliest beam began beneath their feet a groaning of the ground; the wooded hilltops shook, and as it seemed she-hounds of hell howled viewless through the shade . . . . 'Aeneas, on! Begin thy journey! Draw thy sheathèd blade! Now all thy courage! Now th' unshaken soul!' She spoke, and burst into the yawning cave with frenzied step; he follows where she leads, and strides with feet unfaltering at her side." So, after their night vigil, amid the reverberations of the earthquake and the howls of hell-hounds, the journey begins.

If the reader's nerves are somewhat overwrought by this realistic picture of the powers of darkness, the poet quiets him by a solemn and dignified prologue which marks the significance of the approaching chapters of the action: "Ye gods, who rule the spirits of the dead. Ye voiceless shades and silent lands of night. O Phlegethon, O Chaos, let my song, if it be lawful, in fit words declare what I have heard; and by your help divine unfold what hidden things enshrouded lie in that dark underworld of sightless gloom."

The journey, therefore, is to a world beneath Cumae and its environs, and the entrance to it is found through one of the yawning caves that a volcanic region such as Campania easily supplied. Virgil may have been inspired by the *Odyssey* to include a visit to the other world in his poem, but it is clear that his conception of that world and the situation into which he puts Aeneas are entirely different from the setting of the eleventh book of the *Odyssey*. In the Greek poem the hero sails across the sea to the river Ocean, evidently westward; he reaches the city of the Cimmerians shrouded in mist and cloud, a sunless country; there is no indication of any descent to Hades; the world of death is apparently at the western edge of the world of life; Odysseus, in accordance with Circe's directions, digs a trench, and into it pours the blood of the victims; the shades of the dead gather about the trench, by which Odysseus remains, ultimately conversing with whomsoever he chooses to allow to drink the blood. Virgil has transformed this passive situation into active movement; his hero must move from stage to stage through an underworld, each stage bringing him nearer to his father, Anchises, in the Elysian Fields. The idea of such a descent the Roman poet derived from a stock theme of Greek mythology which Aeneas has already referred to in an earlier scene; the journeys of Orpheus, of Heracles, of Theseus to an underworld Hades were commonplace in myth and literature; nor is there much doubt that in some of the narratives the living visitor was guided by some competent cicerone through the dangers of the region which popular fancy had peopled with grim monsters. It was from such tales that Virgil got his idea of a descent, rather than a mere calling up of ghosts, and of the Sibyl as a guide for the hero; she, as priestess of Hecate and a former visitor in Hades, may escort him safely to his father.

The purpose of Odysseus in calling up the shades was to learn from the prophet Teiresias of his future fate; this function in the *Aeneid* the Sibyl has performed in her first prophetic utterance; the visit to the underworld in Virgil is justified by a special motive which finds no place in the *Odyssey*; the vision of Anchises has directed his son to seek him out in the other world; in his visit Aeneas has a definite goal, and whatever he sees by the way is retarding him in his eager purpose to reach his father in the Elysian Fields. So again Virgil has abandoned the *Odyssey* and refashioned the action in such a way as to provide, not only movement, but progressive movement toward a goal; the reader knows the goal at the outset; every scene, therefore, before the goal is reached heightens the reader's suspense, and when the hero meets his father, a climax in the action and in the reader's feelings occurs which the noble revelation of Rome's future greatness resolves into peaceful enjoyment of an assured favorable issue to the hero's labors. Into this region of death the hero and his guide enter, shrouded in the darkness appropriate to the place; every word in the opening verses casts about us the gloom of these halls of death which will ultimately open into the radiant abodes of the blest in sunlit Elysium: "They walked exploring the unpeopled night, through Pluto's vacuous realms, and regions void, as when one's path in dreary woodlands winds beneath a misty moon's deceiving ray, when Jove has mantled all his heaven in shade, and night seals up the beauty of the world."

A poet's topography is naturally vague, and never vaguer than when it concerns so fanciful a region as the other-world Utopia. Virgil seems to conceive of Hades as an extensive region with a spacious courtyard; leading to the court is a narrow entrance way; beyond the court are doors leading into the main quarters, and ultimately to the palace of Pluto.

Before the courtyard and in the narrow entrance stand grim monsters. So popular fancy in Egypt and in Germanic countries peoples with demons the approaches to hell. In the court itself are other demonic creatures, and in the center of the open space is a huge elm tree, the description of which sets apart the two different categories of demons that occupy these forehalls of Hades. The first of these is a group of personified abstractions: "Sorrows and vengeful Cares on couches lie; there sad Old Age abides, Diseases pale, and Fear, and Hunger, temptress to all crime; Want, base and vile, and, two dread shapes to see, Bondage and Death." Just within the court "Sleep, Death's next of kin; and dreams of guilty joy. Death-dealing War is ever at the doors, and hard thereby the Furies' beds of steel, where wild-eyed Strife her snaky hair with bloodstained fillets binds." These abstractions are, many of them, regarded by the vitalizing fancy of common folk and of poets as the children of darkness and chaos; so they appear to us at the threshold of Greek literature in Hesiod's mythic genealogies; as the children of these parents they have a natural home in the underworld, where darkness and chaos are supreme. Yet in the choice of such abstractions Virgil may well have been affected by the history of his own day and generation. Discord and war are prominent in his catalogue, and many other evils mentioned are natural issues of the civil strife that disrupted Rome in Virgil's youth.

The other category of demons springs ultimately from no poetic fancy, but from the cruder conceptions of a people still raw and unrefined: "Strange prodigies of bestial kind: Centaurs are stabled there, and double shapes like Scylla, or the dragon Lerna bred, with hideous scream; Briareus clutching far his hundred hands, Chimaera girt with flame, a crowd of Gorgons, Harpies of foul wing, and giant Geryon's triple-monstered shade." The casual reader of ancient literature or the reader of modern poetry, with its frequent intrusion of ancient mythology, is not familiar with these creatures as denizens of Hades; their grotesque forms have contributed to the weird uncanny effects of many a Greek myth; they bring to our minds the stories of Heracles, of Perseus, of the blind prophet, Phineus, of Bellerophon, but to few of us do they bring any inevitable association with the world of death. Yet Virgil is no innovator in making them residents of Hades. Aristophanes, the writer of Greek comedy, in his playful account of Dionysus' trip to Hades in search of a good tragic poet, after the deaths of the three great tragedians of the fifth century, has the god meet similar grim monsters and serpents, among them the variformed Empusa, a bogey with misshapen legs. Not only, however, are such monsters as a class properly at home in Hades; the individuals here selected, even if we are more familiar with them quite apart from Hades, are primarily and fundamentally hounds of hell when once we consider their names and their functions in the stories in which they play common rôles. The winged women, for example, whom we identify as Harpies, malevolent creatures who snatched the food from the lips of the blind prophet, Phineus, are not exclusively food-snatchers; their name in its Greek form means snatchers in a general comprehensive sense, and primarily in the sense of soul-snatchers; and Greek tombstones marking the graves of children that are victims of a premature and violent death are regularly adorned with grim pictures of these fiendish women as the agents of underworld demons who have stolen the souls of infants.

Separating these two groups—the personified abstractions and the grotesquely formed monsters—is a brief description of the mystic tree in the center of the courtyard; it is a shadowy elm, and "in its leaves deluding visions ever haunt and cling." Virgil's tree of dreams is as unique in classical literature as his golden bough. But the general idea behind it is easily comprehended. Sleep, he has told us above, is next of kin to death; sleep and dreams, therefore, abide in the same world with death, and the beautiful epilogue that concludes this book, in suggesting Aeneas' exit from this underworld, describes the two gates, not of Death but of Death's brother, Sleep, whence issue true and false dreams; the latter, the false dreams, are sent forth from this world below by the spirits of the dead; and here in a mystic tree these false dreams nestle like so many winged birds awaiting flight to the upper world. This description of the tree is an interlude, resting the reader as he passes from the dread abstractions to the awesome monsters. But Virgil's emphasis is upon the grim shapes that haunt the courtyard and entrance; they deepen the gloom and terror of the initial stages of the journey: "Aeneas, shuddering with sudden fear, drew sword and fronted them with naked steel; and, save his sage conductress bade him know these were but shapes and shadows sweeping by, his stroke had cloven in vain the vacant air."

From this forehall, Virgil vaguely says, runs the road that leads to the river Acheron. This river divides the remaining region through which Aeneas passes into two significant districts; this side of Acheron he moves through the ghosts of dead who have been left unburied; beyond Acheron he sees the shades of those who, properly buried, are resident either between Acheron and the interior of Hades or, farther beyond, in the interior of Hades itself. The group of persons whom he now meets before crossing the river is determined by the ancient notion that funeral rites duly performed are essential to the restful abode of the soul in its after-life. Without such proper consignment to the gods of the underworld the soul is restless, and wanders, in Virgil's expression of the idea, in a precinct outside of Hades; in other statements of the general notion this wandering soul may have malevolent purposes and cause trouble to those connected with the deceased; but Virgil states the case somewhat differently; if the unburied at any time obtain burial, they may be immediately admitted to Hades; but failing burial, they wander for a hundred years in this outer precinct. Such an idea seems to be a step beyond the simple folk-notion of the malevolent power of roving souls that linger near an unburied corpse; this period of a hundred years marks the arbitrarily estimated length of a normal human life which will meet us in other forms in the theory underlying this account of the soul's existence; this precise and rather humane provision for the unburied, whose condition is clearly no fault of their own, may represent an accommodation of the cruder folk-notion to the speculation of somewhat advanced thinkers, to more refined theological ideas; in any case the arbitrary estimate of human life as a hundred years is an incidental feature of speculation regarding the soul's history which will slowly emerge as we follow Aeneas through his experiences in Hades.

Into his description of the outer precinct, and in connection with these unburied souls who hover anxiously by the river bank hoping for passage to the more peaceful quarters across the river, Virgil naturally brings a conventional figure, the ferryman, Charon. He, like the grim monsters and the unburied souls, comes to Virgil by way of the many accounts of mythical descents by Heracles and others to these regions. Like all such details, he is a product of popular fancy rather than rational theory. Properly he was the sentry, the guard, who collected the toll from those who desired to cross to Hades; but the collector of harbor dues, *portitor*, easily became a ferryman, so that even the Latin word *portitor* itself took on the meaning of ferryman, as if it were *portator;* this older idea of Charon as collector of dues and guard Virgil may be echoing when he describes him as keeping ward upon these waters. The details of his appearance and action are conventional; he is "foully garbed, with unkempt, thick gray beard upon his chin, and staring eyes of flame; a mantle coarse, all stained and knotted, from his shoulder falls, as with a pole he guides his craft, tends sail, and in the black boat ferries o'er his dead; old, but a god's old age looks fresh and young." These are the stereotyped features of generations of poetic treatment of the ferryman, the spooky details that long before Virgil had intensified the awesomeness of descriptions of the underworld; some of them are merely picturesque; others express crude superstitions; his garment is fastened over his shoulder by a knot instead of by the pin which living men used; for metal is a pet aversion of these demonic powers.

The group of souls that flocks to the river bank at Charon's approach includes not only the souls of the unburied dead, but of course also the souls of the duly buried who are entitled to cross into Hades; from the eager assembly Charon selects only those who, their bodies properly interred, are rightful claimants for his services. The general assemblage Virgil sets before us in phrases that he had already used in the *Georgics*, but with the simple natural feeling which expresses his own individuality: "Husbands and wives, and pale unbreathing forms of high-souled heroes, boys and virgins fair, and strong youth at whose graves fond parents mourned." The crowd is numberless as the leaves that fall in autumn, and the leaves to which they are compared suggest as well the fragile nature of these lifeless forms, mere shadows. In sharp contrast to the pathetic figures reaching out pale hands in passionate yearning for the distant shore stands the grim boatman, unpityingly taking some aboard his black boat and thrusting others back from the stream which they may not yet cross.

In traversing the region of Hades Aeneas *sees* groups of ghosts and *talks* with individual shades; the poet must introduce us both to masses and to individuals; nor may he separate the two without injury to the organization of his material; so, regularly, we shall find him giving us first a comprehensive picture of the mass; then from that mass will slowly emerge individuals, one of whom becomes the prominent figure in the scene. Thus, on the banks of Acheron the poet's description and the Sibyl's words present the general account of the shades seeking passage across the river; presently from this larger company Aeneas distinguishes Leucaspis and Orontes, each briefly described, then Palinurus, who becomes the central figure of the next scene.

The full story of Palinurus is left somewhat vague by the poet's implicit style. The famous pilot—his name became a synonym of "pilot," so famous was his story—had been as-

sured by Apollo that he should reach the shore of Italy in
safety; but the god was ironical; ambiguity is the privilege of
oracular utterance. Palinurus did reach the shore of Italy,
but, as the narrative of the fifth book set forth, he fell overboard, and swam to land, as we learn here, only to be butch-
ered by the savage natives. His corpse, cast ashore and left
unburied, brought trouble upon the Lucanians, the people on
whose coast the body drifted; a pestilence attacked the country; the Lucanians sought the god for an explanation, and,
enjoined to bury the body of Palinurus, they carry out the
god's instructions, not only burying the body, but celebrating
an annual festival at the grave; the cape near which these incidents occurred is named after Palinurus. The story in its
conclusion, then, is a replica of the Misenus story; both the
promontory of Misenum and Cape Palinurus were landmarks
in the voyage of an Italian from Latium to Sicily, and the stories, consequently, were familiar and dear to Virgil's contemporaries. The final chapters, of course, appear here only in the
Sibyl's prophetic words, and somewhat vaguely stated. The
poet emphasizes the pathetic details of the earlier chapters.

But in so far as Palinurus asks for the burial of his corpse
by Aeneas, and is the first shade to converse with the hero
after his arrival in Hades, the poet has, clearly, not only intended to interweave neatly into this action a chapter of the
Aeneas legend which before Virgil's time had probably not
appeared in this special context, but in connection with other
experiences of the hero; he has also obviously been influenced
by the corresponding scene in the *Odyssey* in which the ghost
of Elpenor is the first to meet Odysseus and asks for burial,
having met with an accidental death (like Palinurus) just before Odysseus calls up the shades. Virgil, however, has Palinurus ask for burial as only one of two alternatives; failing
burial, Palinurus seeks a special dispensation which shall allow him to cross Acheron without burial; Aeneas cannot, like

Odysseus, go back and bury Palinurus; and the Sibyl answers the second alternative by prophesying a burial at the hands of the Lucanians. Virgil, however neatly he has interwoven the story into the new context under the influence of the *Odyssey*, has offended the reader by repeating the theme of the unburied corpse; Misenus and Palinurus should not appear so near together in the story.

All through the narrative of the descent Virgil happily varies the style of presentation; one moment we have description in the poet's words; presently dramatic dialogue. Palinurus comforted, Aeneas and the Sibyl approach the ferryman, Charon, and in conversation with him justify their claim to passage across the river; so the story of Palinurus is interleaved between two chapters of action in which Charon is the main figure. Charon objects at first; he has had trouble with other living visitors to his underworld—with Hercules, Theseus, and Pirithous but the golden bough is a potent passport, and it is no mischievous mortal such as Theseus or Hercules, but Aeneas, "famed for faithful prayer and victory in arms," a pious, as well as militant, hero who seeks his father in "the gloomy deep of death." The living body imperils the frail skiff of Charon, used only to unsubstantial ghosts; as Aeneas boards it, it groans and strains at every seam, and lets in the foul waters of Acheron; this is a conventional theme, commonplace, like so much of the detail in these parts of the narrative, in various earlier accounts of descents to Hades.

Once the river is safely crossed they reach sea-green sedges and a formless mire; beyond this lies a new precinct, still short of the interior of Hades proper, still a sort of purgatory preliminary to the real inferno. But it is near enough to the real Hades to require a special sentry; here in his cave lies the dog Cerberus; it is a manifest contradiction of the statement in Charon's remark to Aeneas in the previous scene that other visitors to Hades had stolen Cerberus away from the throne of Pluto; the throne of Pluto lies in the interior of Hades in Virgil's story, but Cerberus is placed before the entrance to the interior and remote from Pluto's throne; to such small contradictions Virgil is indifferent; they are due to the divergencies in detail of earlier accounts of such descents from which he draws indiscriminately without interest in consistency. The dog Cerberus is ultimately of a piece with the grim monsters, the Harpies, Scyllas, Centaurs, and what not, that met Aeneas before they crossed the river; Cerberus, too, is properly a grotesquely formed soul-snatcher, but his dog-like form easily led to his function as watchdog before the entrance. The details of description are again commonplace and conventional; the poet at least dismisses them briefly; new as they may be to some of us, the ancient reader must have found them trite—Cerberus' triple throats, the serpents writhing round his neck, his roar, even perhaps the medicated cake with which the Sibyl stills his clamor.

The shades that meet Aeneas after Cerberus is quieted and safely passed, and before they reach the actual interior of Hades, are described in five groups. The reader is hardly conscious, unless he is forced to unwelcome reflection, that these five groups are bound together by a common characteristic; once this common quality is discovered, we become aware that Virgil must be presenting in poetic form a fairly well systematized doctrine; yet he has certainly withheld any explicit statement of any such dogma; as a poet he has no interest in the arbitrary or rational views of theologians in their systematic form. Indeed, as we shall presently see, clear as his dependence upon a religious theory is, he has not hesitated to exercise a poet's freedom in introducing details into the midst of this presentation of dogma which sharply violate the logical unity of the theory. In fact, the content of this whole account of the other life has ever been a subject of fruitful discussion which has only recently reached any very satisfactory issue, and which still, in some details, may arrive at better conclusions. In general the situation may be described, in comparison with the Homeric description of the life after death, somewhat in these terms. Homer's account of the after-life is simply and purely mythological; it represents fairly well, and with reasonable uniformity, the views of the people either of Homer's age or of a period slightly earlier than Homer. Virgil, on the contrary, presents, not a uniform mythological account, but a blend of popular mythology and of religious-philosophical theory; contradictions, at least from a logical standpoint, are bound to result; to such contradictions, especially when they affect unimportant details, Virgil is quite indifferent; he is interested in appealing to the emotions rather than to the intellect; as to larger, more essential, conflicts, we may not all agree as to his point of view, but there again we should at least remember that he is a poet primarily, and not a systematic philosopher.

The five groups of ghosts that meet Aeneas in this limbo just outside the entrance to Hades proper are of infants, of persons who have been condemned to death unjustly by sentence of court, of those who have committed suicide, of those who have pined away for love, and of those who have been slain on the field of battle. A moment's thought makes it clear that all these groups are composed of those whose death is either premature, as in the case of infants, or premature and violent, as in the other four cases. Nor are we offered any explanation of the reason why the victims of a premature death should be thus detained outside the inner precincts of Hades. This explanation we get explicitly only from an author centuries later than Virgil, who remarks upon a belief that those who die before their time must wander until they have reached that age which they would have attained but for their premature death; when we recall that Virgil himself, in describing the fate of the souls of the unburied, stated that they must wander for a hundred years (vs. 329), and that the Roman commentator, Servius, in his note upon this verse, says this period of a hundred years was an arbitrary estimate of the length of a natural lifetime, we can easily supply the missing dogma that underlies Virgil's grouping of these five classes of souls; they evidently were doomed, according to some religious theory, to wander for the remainder of the life assigned them by fate, and the length of that life was, for administrative purposes, set at one hundred years; so the implication is that these souls, after they have fulfilled this requirement outside of Hades proper, are ultimately admitted to the inner precinct and seek Tartarus or Elysium according to their deserts. But once granting this underlying principle as controlling Virgil's grouping of these souls and their location in this outer limbo, we must immediately recognize an inconsistency; among the members of two of the five groups there appear certain heroines who died for love's sake and certain warriors slain on the field of battle; some of these individual heroines and warriors perished centuries before Aeneas' visit to Hades; for so far as mythical stories have any chronological relation one to another, the deaths of such a heroine as Pasiphae or of those warriors who perished in the fight of The Seven against Thebes took place many generations before the time with which legend associated Aeneas and the fall of Troy; these persons, then, according to this dogma, should have finished their period of wandering and should now be in the inner precincts, instead of in this outer limbo. But the apparent contradiction is explained by the fact that in introducing individual heroes and heroines into these scenes Virgil has followed popular mythology; these are such heroes and heroines as appear in Homer's account of the other world; Virgil has brought them in from the popular mythology, disregarding the fact that, introduced into such a classification, they contradict the principle that logically links the five groups together. Nor should we emphasize the contradiction and blame Virgil; on the contrary, it must be remembered that *we* have forced the contradiction; Virgil himself *says* nothing of the wandering or of the theory which we have brought out to explain the grouping; in other words, Virgil has carefully avoided any contradiction by withholding an explicit statement of the theory which certainly underlies his segregation of these five groups.

Such a classification was well established long before Virgil, and the individual groups in Virgil's account may be easily paralleled in authors before and after his time; the authors who report this classification may include fewer groups or may increase Virgil's categories, but the unity is the same; the view that premature death involves a preliminary residence outside of Hades is the obvious principle in all such classifications. Plato, for example, in the vision of the afterlife at the end of his *Republic*, makes special provision for infants; Lucian, two centuries after Christ, has all of Virgil's groups, adding thereto usurpers and adulterers; even fuller and more specific lists are found in later authors than Lucian; and from such later sources one gathers the general idea that prompts the special provisions made for such persons: fate assigns a definite lifetime to each mortal, and the soul is not fully released until that time elapses; in cases of violent and unnatural death, therefore, the soul cannot immediately secure its final abode in the world to which death consigns it. Such souls, like those of the unburied, are detained for a season, after which they are admitted to the inner quarters of the realm of the dead.

But Virgil's indifference to the rigidity of such a logical scheme is apparent as soon as we turn to the details of his description; here he finds an outlet for his real interest in the elaboration of pathetic incident, of purely emotional circumstance. The souls of babes greet Aeneas with piteous lisping cries: "Them ere they took their portion of sweet life, dark Fate from nursing bosoms bore, and plunged in bitterness of death." The phrasing may be conventional so far as it echoes the words that we find on many a tombstone, Greek and Roman, but the poet, with due brevity, has given the group its differentiating trait. In making a group of those "unjustly" condemned to death there is a further conflict with the logical consistency of the theory; for clearly it makes no difference whether the court sentence is just or unjust; in either case the death is premature and violent; but again it is the pathetic aspect of the "unjustly" sentenced that determines the poet's description; those who were justly condemned would not excite the reader's sympathy, and the poet abandons fact for his poetic purpose. Following the single verse referring to the unjustly sentenced comes a general description of Minos and his activity as a judge in the lower world: he "holds assembly of the silent shades, hearing the stories of their lives and deeds," and assigns them to their proper abode in Hades after due legal procedure. This account of Minos is often wrongly referred to the previous verse, as if only the unjustly sentenced in the world above were tried in the world below. Though this is part of the meaning, the activity of Minos is much more general; he stands in this outer precinct to hear the cases of all souls; if they are victims of premature death, he allots to them this outer region; if they have died natural deaths, he decides by a formal judicial process whether they belong in Tartarus or Elysium, beyond this outer precinct. The description is parenthetical, and inserted here rather than elsewhere in the account because the mention of the *unjustly* sentenced in the world above suggests the *infallible* legal procedure of the underworld; and the poet uses some of the technical words of Roman law to make the legal process more real to his Roman reader. Close by are those who have committed suicide, now willing enough to bear the burdens of life from which they sought relief, but confined by the nine winding coils of the sad unlovely Stygian river.

These three groups are briefly dismissed; but the next group is too full of pathetic possibilities to admit of brief discussion. Virgil elaborates the account of the lovers—"All whom ruthless love did waste away wander in paths unseen, or in the gloom of a dark myrtle grove; not even in death have they forgotten their griefs of long ago." To the region in which the lovers wander Virgil gives the name Fields of Sorrow; such a precinct is quite unknown to other extant writers on this common theme of the after-life, but it probably found a place in some lost Hellenistic poem; for in such poetry a sentimentalizing pathetic fallacy would most easily have led to the invention of a special precinct for the victims of love. In Virgil's mind these sufferers are all women; not only is this limitation to one of the sexes another contradiction of the facts of story and experience for the sake of emotional appeal, but the individual heroines presently introduced by name furnish an artistic contrast to the individual male warriors in the next group.

At this point in his narrative the Roman poet begins to reveal his indebtedness to the *Odyssey;* Odysseus, in calling up the shades, after first performing his main errand by interviewing the prophet Teiresias, conversed with his mother, Anticleia; then with certain heroines of mythology, whose lineage the Greek poet described; then with three great heroes of the Trojan War, Agamemnon, Achilles, and Ajax; and finally catalogued the stock figures of the other world, Minos, Orion, Tityus, Tantalus, Sisyphus. In this Homeric account, as we said in an earlier chapter, our admiration for Homer's splendid conception of the three scenes in which Odysseus converses with the three great heroes of the Trojan War is somewhat qualified by the commonplaceness of his dry listing of the stock heroes and heroines of mythology. Virgil's relation to the Homeric account is clear: his sentimental heroines correspond to the heroines in Homer, though the latter are not exclusively sufferers from love; Virgil's general group of warriors corresponds to the Greek heroes in the *Odyssey;* and the victims whom we meet presently in Tartarus are the Virgilian counterpart of Homer's conventional figures—Tantalus, Sisyphus, and the like. Furthermore, in choosing individuals with whom Aeneas shall converse, Virgil has obviously been influenced, in his choice of Dido and of what she does, by the Homeric scene between Odysseus and Ajax, and in the choice of Deiphobus, among the warriors, and of what he says, by the scene between Agamemnon and Odysseus. But having once yielded to the charm of Homer's general conception of the action, the Roman poet proceeds to refashion both the structure and the detail. The heroines in Homer are an isolated class; the dialogue with Ajax, upon which Virgil models the attempted conversation with Dido, is in a scene quite apart from the heroines. Virgil, following his regular practice of massing his groups and letting individuals emerge from the several groups, gives a general description of sentimental heroines—and so far as they are forlorn lovers they differ from Homer's heroines; then enumerates individual heroines stricken by love, Phaedra, Procris, Eriphyle, Evadne, Pasiphae, and others, several of whom appear in Homer; and finally allows Dido to come into the foreground. Nor is the imitation of Homer's Ajax scene inferior to the Greek model, admirable as that is. Odysseus vainly attempts to conciliate his former enemy; Ajax stands apart, sulking, utters not a word, and passes on to Erebus. Virgil's scene has the added effect of furnishing an effective epilogue to the tragedy of the fourth book. "Dido, her wound unhealed, roamed through a mighty wood. The Trojan's eyes beheld her near him through the murky gloom, as when in her young month and crescent pale, one sees the o'er-clouded moon or thinks he sees. Down dropped his tears. . . . ." Aeneas admits his guilt, but declares he left her not of his own will, and craves a last farewell. "Thus though she glared with fierce relentless gaze, Aeneas with fond words and tearful plea would soothe her angry soul. But on the ground she fixed averted eyes. For all he spoke moved her no more than if her frowning brow were changeless flint or carved in Parian stone. Then, after pause, away in wrath she fled, and refuge took within the cool dark grove where her first spouse, Sychaeus, with her tears mingled his own in mutual love and true." Her reunion with Sychaeus is the natural and just issue of the dramatic conflict in the fourth book, but the curious reader may discern the love for Aeneas still lingering, if her averted eyes and the pause she makes before her final flight are a tribute to the Trojan's power over her.

Similarly, out from the next group emerges the hero's kinsman, Deiphobus. Virgil, in choosing the individuals with whom Aeneas communes, has made consistent use of a suggestion which he found in Homer less uniformly followed. Homer makes the dialogues with Odysseus' mother and with the Greek heroes yield more pathos than any of the other chapters of the account; that pathos comes largely through the close personal interest which Odysseus feels in his mother and in his former comrades-in-arms. Virgil makes this personal interest uniform; he allows Aeneas to converse at length in these later scenes only with Dido, Deiphobus, and Anchises, a sweetheart, a kinsman and comrade-in-arms, and his father; so the conversations seem inevitable and natural, and the common bond of affection and kinship increases the possibilities of natural emotional expression. The warriors as a group include, first, the heroes of the famous war of The Seven against Thebes, familiar from Aeschylus' tragedy, then the heroes of the Trojan War, and finally the Greek participants in the same war, who, recalling Aeneas' prowess, tremble with amaze to see him, living, in the world of the dead, and shrink from him in terror. As in Homer, the shades are represented as still possessing in weaker degree the feelings, muscular power, and even the physical appearance which were theirs in the life on earth. So these frightened Greeks "raised aloft a feeble shout, or vainly opened wide their gaping lips in mockery of sound." And Deiphobus, son of Priam, who now comes into the foreground, bears still upon him the marks of Greek cruelty: "With body rent and torn . . . . his mangled face, his face and bloody hands, his wounded head of ears and nostrils infamously shorn." Thus Hector's apparition appeared in the second book, and stirred, as Deiphobus does here, the reader's sympathy and no small degree of horror.

In the dialogue with Deiphobus Virgil was less fortunate than in the Dido scene. Any attempt to parallel the dialogue between Agamemnon and Odysseus was doomed to partial failure, for that scene is one of the finest in all Homeric epic; in it the Greek poet chose wisely the splendid figure of the leader of the Greek hosts; and having chosen him, with exquisite art adapted speech to character, and portrayed feeling through speech. The tragic pathos of this speech and the grandeur of Agamemnon in contrast with his pathetic inquiries can hardly be matched by Virgil in choosing an inferior hero, such as Deiphobus. The treacherous rôle of Helen in betraying Troy to the Greeks and putting her defenseless husband at the mercy of her former countrymen is an intelligent effort to parallel the cruelty and faithlessness of Clytaemestra, but the bitterness of Deiphobus is less intense, nor can it be softened by any such pitiful inquiry for a son and heir as Agamemnon makes. Deiphobus, in conclusion, naturally asks the reason for Aeneas' appearance in this lower world. But the Sibyl intervenes, and prevents Aeneas from answering the question. ". . . . The crimsoned car of Morn had wheeled beyond the midmost point of Heaven on her ethereal road. The princely pair had wasted thus the whole brief gift of hours; the Sibyl spoke the warning: 'Night speeds by, and we, Aeneas, lose it in lamenting. Here comes the place where cleaves our way in twain. Thy road, the right, toward Pluto's dwelling goes, and leads us to Elysium. But the left speeds sinful souls to doom, and is their path to Tartarus th' accurst!'" This intervention of the Sibyl has an economic purpose in the narrative. An answer to Deiphobus' question would only tell the reader what the reader already knows, and the Sibyl's remarks neatly include a suggestion of the time; the first half of the day they have spent in the outer precincts of Hades; the remaining afternoon and night is left for the distant view of Tartarus and the visit to the Elysian Fields; so the narrative of the action is symmetrically disposed. And finally, the Sibyl's urgent request reminds Aeneas and the reader of the essential purpose of this journey; we are moving with Aeneas toward a definite goal, and that is the meeting with his father, Anchises, in the Elysian Fields and the revelation of the future which splendidly consummates the whole. Aeneas, moved by his feelings and natural sympathy with these groups of souls, lingers and momentarily forgets his main purpose in this visit to Hades. The Sibyl sharply reminds him and us of his mission and of the artistic purpose of these scenes as retarding stages in the rapid movement toward the climax, the meeting with Anchises: a structural unity of which Homer in the *Odyssey* had no conception. We leave, then, the outer precincts of Hades, and pass within to the palace of Pluto and the Elysian Fields. But we are at the crossroads; as we take the turn to Elysium we discern off to the left the spreading rampart and the adamantine gate of Tartarus; that region Aeneas does not visit, but the Sibyl whiles away the time as they pass along the other road to Elysium by telling him what she once saw in a former visit to

Tartarus. So the poet, neatly varying the style, changing narrative of action to description in the Sibyl's words, and without unduly delaying the action by a special visit of the hero to Tartarus, succeeds in presenting to the ancient reader what he craved as essential to any account of this other world: the punishments of criminals in Tartarus as well as the blessed existence of the pure in heart in the radiant fields of Elysium.

In the Homeric picture of the after-life the shades appear to Odysseus from Erebus, the world of darkness, and retire to Erebus; Odysseus himself, though he makes no descent to an underworld region, at least seems to see not merely the shades that gather about his trench, but various mythological heroes actively engaged in the house of Hades, as the poet calls it. The judge, Minos, for example, whom we have met in Virgil, Odysseus also saw sentencing the dead; and the hunter, Orion, was engaged in hunting, his favorite pursuit on earth; Tantalus and Sisyphus, on the other hand, were suffering torment, though the Greek poet does not fully explain the reason for the suffering. In brief, the Homeric picture is not clear and definite; at one moment we think of shades rising from below before Odysseus at the trench; presently Odysseus seems to have a view into the other world. But in any case Homer gives no hint of any distinct division of the world of death into districts, one of which is occupied by sinners suffering torment for their crimes committed on earth, the other an abode of the righteous. Yet elsewhere he reveals a knowledge of the folk-conception of a special abode for heroes destined to immortal life; in the fourth book of the *Odyssey* (vss. 563 ff.) the sea god, Proteus, prophesies for the hero, Menelaus, a blessed existence: "Thou, Menelaus, son of Zeus, art not ordained to die . . . . but the deathless gods will convey thee to the Elysian plain and the world's end, where is Rhadamanthus of the fair hair, where life is easiest for men. No snow is there, nor yet great storm, nor any rain; but always ocean sendeth forth the breeze of the shrill West to blow cool on men." A special abode is here provided at the world's end; it seems to be an abode of gods and heroes; its equable climate is characteristic of the home of the gods. This, therefore, is our earliest evidence of a special precinct for the peculiarly blessed, a sort of garden, a paradise; and in subsequent literature this garden, variously described and located, frequently recurs, sometimes as an island or islands of the blessed. It is ultimately a popular idea, a folk-notion. Of a similar precinct for the sinners condemned to punishment Homer gives no clear suggestion; yet the Homeric epic definitely conceives of furies who punish men specially for their breaking of oaths. The Virgilian picture, with its definite provision for sinners in Tartarus chastised by furies and variously tortured, and for the holy in Elysium leading an ideal life in radiant sunshine and amid all the pleasures of a Christian heaven, marks the end of a long development between Homer and Virgil. Early and vague ideas of an after-life at the world's edge have at last become incorporated in a clearcut theory of an after-life below the earth; there in that underworld, at least so far in Virgil's narrative, we find a spacious region divided first into two main precincts; the region this side of the river Acheron, mainly the temporary abode of the shades of the unburied, and the region beyond Acheron, where the souls of the properly interred abide. This second region is again divided into two main quarters: an outer precinct, the temporary residence of those who have suffered premature and violent deaths, and the inner region of Hades proper, composed of two precincts, Tartarus, the prison house of those condemned to eternal punishment, and Elysium, where abide the eternally blessed.

In his account, therefore, of Tartarus and Elysium Virgil is quite independent of the *Odyssey;* he is rather in the current of tradition later than Homer, when an underworld and a systematic theory of penalties and rewards in the after-life were fully developed.

We have already observed the skill with which the poet at this point varies his manner of presenting his theme. Aeneas takes a road to the right leading to the palace of Pluto and Elysium; off to the left, on another road, he sees the walls of Tartarus and hears the cries of the tortured sinners; in answer to his query the Sibyl tells him what is taking place in Tartarus; so, without a visit to that region, and consequently with less detail than might otherwise be necessary, he learns, and the Roman reader learns, what is essential to the completeness of the account of this after-life. For this description involved any narrator of Virgil's time in the elaboration of one of the most trite and commonplace themes of poetry, the punishment of sinners in Tartarus; Tantalus, Sisyphus, Ixion, and others could not be described in any novel fashion; their sufferings were absolutely stereotyped by centuries of poetic treatment. Virgil must have shrunk from repeating the well-worn commonplaces; but convention made it imperative to include them. He saves detail by having the Sibyl describe, instead of having the hero see, this special precinct; thereby, incidentally, he spares himself the unpleasant necessity of dwelling upon the horrible and gruesome; the Sibyl gives us just enough of the grim aspects of Tartarus to make effective the contrasted picture of Elysium.

Tartarus is not only part of the underworld; it slopes down below the level even of Hades proper, and its uttermost limit is twice as far below the surface of the earth as Heaven is above the earth. So poetic phrasing had described it long before Virgil. The precinct is surrounded by huge ramparts, and the ramparts themselves are further confined by the flaming waters of the river Phlegethon, which encircles the walls. The fury, Tisiphone, guards the portal, arrayed in blood-stained garments; within, Rhadamanthus lays bare the guilt of the sinners and forces confession. Tisiphone and her sister furies then scourge the guilty. When the sinner has confessed and the punishment has begun, the doors open and the Hydra with her fifty mouths is revealed; Tisiphone guards the door without; the Hydra stands guard within, and behind her yawns the abyss of Tartarus.

The residents of this abyss the Sibyl now describes in a formal speech so symmetrically arranged that one may easily imagine that she has been taught the art of exposition in some rhetorical school of Virgil's day or in a modern university. In orderly fashion she passes from descriptions of punishments to descriptions of crime, so that her speech from this standpoint falls into three chapters, each chapter covering the two topics of penalty and sin. But another line of thought helps to determine her arrangement of the facts: she neatly alternates sinners of mythology and sinners of real life. This orderly arrangement not only shows Virgil's interest in artistic symmetry, but illustrates an important aspect of the content of this account. Virgil's description of the sinners of mythology is hardly more than a selection from the catalogue of such sinners which many poets before him had fixed as part of the conventional account of Tartarus; every Roman reader had read again and again of the giants, of the Aloidae, of Tityus, the Lapiths, Ixion, Pirithous, Theseus, and Phlegyas; even Salmoneus, though a novel figure in extant accounts, was hardly original with Virgil. But on the other hand, mythological poetry did not, probably, furnish the sins of real life which Virgil interweaves in the midst of his account of these mythical figures. Such sins come from a theological system of pains and penalties in the other life, not from a popular fancy which creates the mythical figures of a Tantalus or Sisyphus. These sins, therefore, interest us particularly as suggesting the characteristic moral weaknesses of ancient life in contrast or comparison with our own, and to that extent

they relieve the commonplaceness of the catalogue of purely
mythical sinners. "Here in a prison-house awaiting doom are
men who hated, long as life endured, their brothers, or mal-
treated their gray sires, or tricked a humble friend; the men
who grasped at hoarded riches, with their kith and kin not
sharing ever—an unnumbered throng; here slain adulterers
be; and men who dared to fight in unjust cause, and break all
faith with their own lawful lords." Then, passing back to the
mythical figures, the Sibyl describes Theseus and Phlegyas,
the latter of whom is represented as warning others in these
words: "O, ere too late, learn justice and fear God. Yon
traitor sold his country, and for gold enchained her to a
tyrant, trafficking in laws, for bribes enacted or made void;
another did incestuously take his daughter for a wife in lawless bonds. All ventured some unclean prodigious crime; and
what they dared, achieved." In brief, the sins include hatred
of brothers, maltreatment of parents, defrauding of clients in
the technical Roman sense, avarice, adultery, inciting of civil
war specially on the part of slaves against their masters (a possible allusion to the Servile War in Italy), treachery toward
the state in betraying the government into the hands of a
tyrant, graft in the passing and annulment of laws, and violation of the laws of marriage. Now to some extent this list of
sins may be the issue of a long tradition; some of these sins
are of course concretely realized in early Greek history; the
treacherous dealings with usurpers and tyrants, for example,
is characteristic of early periods of Greek history, and tyrants
themselves are familiar figures in the Tartarus of earlier accounts of the after-life than Virgil's; avarice, too, was a weakness of society in the latter Greek period, as the preachments
of late philosophers attest. But though some of these sins
may be conventional and traditional, one easily detects that
many of them are peculiarly Roman; so, for instance, the defrauding of a client by his patron presupposes Roman, rather

than Greek, conditions; nor can anybody familiar with the
history of the first century—Virgil's own time—fail to see
that the sins here enumerated are peculiar to the poet's own
environment; family dissension, civil war, a pretty clear allusion to the war of slaves against their masters which took
place early in the first century, and the mention of adultery
and incest and the general disregard of domestic purity, point
almost inevitably to the influence of the poet's own surroundings in the selection of these special crimes. So Virgil has relieved the triteness and commonplaceness of the mythological
figures by a bit of real life, of the actuality of his own surroundings, and the Roman reader, deadened to all interest in
Sisyphus, Ixion, and the rest, was enlivened by this drastic
record of the social weaknesses which had sapped the vitality
of his people and made imperative the intelligent reforms of
Augustus, the poet's friend and patron.

The same urgency which the Sibyl showed in hurrying
Aeneas away from Deiphobus she now repeats as they move
toward the palace of Pluto. There is a task to be fulfilled.
The golden bough must be hung on the door of Pluto's palace.
This bit of action is briefly dismissed and forms an interlude
between the larger chapters devoted to Tartarus and Elysium.

Virgil is sensitive to the need of variation, to the desirable
contrast of light and shade. The gloom of Dido's tragedy in
Book iv and of the descent to the world of death in Book vi
was relieved by the joyous festival of athletic sports in the
fifth book; so, with similar contrast of light and shade, in
the sixth book itself the grim, forbidding picture of Tartarus
is immediately followed by the description of a precinct where
light and joy are supreme, the Elysian Fields:

> An ampler sky its roseate light bestows
> On that bright land, which sees the cloudless beam
> Of suns and planets to our earth unknown.
> On smooth green lawns contending limb with limb,

Immortal athletes play, and wrestle long
    'Gainst mate or rival on the tawny sand;
With sounding footsteps and ecstatic song,
    Some thread the dance divine; among them moves
The bard of Thrace, in flowing vesture clad,
    Discoursing seven-noted melody,
Who sweeps the numbered strings with changeful hand,
    Or smites with ivory point his golden lyre.

This is the first description in Latin of the abode of the blessed, but for many centuries in Greek literature it had been celebrated as a delectable land; Virgil has shown restraint in selecting its characteristic features; he gives enough to excite the imagination without overwhelming it. Even before this pleasurable country became part of an underworld Hades it existed in the fancy of the Greeks as an abode of gods and heroes, and in that function acquired many of the qualities which remain attached to it after it becomes a home of the blessed souls of men in the after-life. As a garden of the gods it was a favorite haunt of the sun god, and when popular fancy transferred it to the underworld, his radiance gave it a supernatural light that isolated it from the surrounding realm of darkness; as such a divine garden it contained a mystic river that has here developed into an underworld Eridanus; and in general it shares with all Utopian countries that Greek fancy created many features that anticipate the heaven, the New Jerusalem, of Christian doctrine. The song and dance and Orpheus' lyre are the pagan prelude to the harps of the New Jerusalem. Only the immortal athletes contending in athletic games are distinctively Greek; and even there the underlying idea is common to pagan and Christian conceptions of heaven; both creeds find the joys of the life hereafter in a continuation of the pleasures of this earthly life without its pain. As early as the Greek poet, Pindar, in the sixth century, the islands of the blessed had been invested with almost all the charm that Virgil gives them here: "For them," says Pindar, describing the place and its inhabitants, "the light of the sun shines down below while in our world it is night, and in rosy meadows their precinct is wreathed with frankincense and laden with golden fruit; and some find delight in horses and in gymnastic games; others, in dice play or in the music of the lyre; and ever by them is a wealth of flowers, and a lovely fragrance diffuses through the place as they ever mingle with fire all kinds of incense on the altars of the gods." Thus early in Greek thought had a paradise been created for those who had lived righteous lives on earth. Into this paradise the great musicians, Orpheus and Musaeus, were admitted as early as Plato, if not earlier. Nor is Virgil an innovator in placing here the groups of souls whom he describes after the mention of Orpheus. The great-hearted founders of Troy with their horses and chariots, the chorus of ghosts singing victorious paeans on the fragrant air of laurel groves, the brave "who for their native land fell wounded on the field," the priests and poets, and "all who found new arts to make man's life more blest or fair" (by whom he means philosophers, primarily), and "all those dead whose deeds bequeath deserved and grateful memory to their kind." Of these many groups the patriots, the priests and poets, the philosophers, and the general benefactors of the human race are regularly provided in Greek poetry and philosophy with an eternal home in the abode of the blessed. From these groups Aeneas discriminates Musaeus, the mythical father of poets, and asks him the way to Anchises, his father; Musaeus directs him to a neighboring hill, and from there they behold Anchises below, opportunely engaged in surveying thoughtfully "a host of prisoned spirits, who there abode awaiting entrance to terrestrial air. And musing he reviewed the legions bright of his own progeny and offspring proud—their fates and fortunes, virtues and great deeds."

We have reached the climax of the action; Aeneas has fulfilled his father's command and found him in the Elysian Fields. From this point on the narrative of movement from one stage to another of this lower-world journey changes to a splendid revelation of the great truths of human existence. Following an effective but brief conversation with his father, Aeneas hears the doctrine of transmigration and sees the mustering of souls who in their rebirth are to become the great benefactors of the Roman people and promoters of the Roman empire. The introductory dialogue, though brief, suffices to revive in the reader's mind the many pictures in earlier books of the poem which portrayed the reciprocal devotion of son and father; Anchises welcomes his son with tears, remembering the exertions which have preceded his safe arrival; Aeneas vainly seeks to embrace his father, thought of whom has inspired and impelled him to the arduous task of visiting this underworld. Turning from Anchises he is

> . . . . Aware
> Of solemn groves in one deep distant vale,
> Where trees were whispering, and forever flowed
> The river Lethe, through its land of calm.
> Nations unnumbered roved and haunted there;
> As when upon a windless summer morn,
> The bees afield among the rainbow flowers
> Alight and sip, or round the lilies pure
> Pour forth in busy swarm, while far diffused
> Their murmured songs from all the meadows rise.

Aeneas inquires what this river of forgetfulness may be, and who are these souls crowded by its banks. Anchises answers that they are the souls about to be reborn, reincarnated; they include the posterity of Aeneas, whom he will shortly review for his son's encouragement; and they stand by the river to drink its waters, which dispel care and induce forgetfulness of all that they have witnessed in this other-world existence. Aeneas' surprise that souls rise again to the upper air and once more return to cumbering flesh leads Anchises to unfold the theory of transmigration.

This theory, set forth with the elevated diction of the poet, Lucretius, but in content a sharp contrast with the Epicurean doctrine of that earlier poet, brings into relief the great contradiction in the thought of this book. Hades has hitherto been divided into a neutral region, where five classes of spirits temporarily reside, a precinct, Tartarus, permanently tenanted by the spirits of the wicked, and Elysium, the abode of the righteous. This conception presupposes that departed spirits remain in a fixed state, each preserving its own individuality. The theory of transmigration, on the contrary, takes all spirits alike as soon as they have been separated from the body, puts all of them through a period of purgation, and commits a majority of them to a further existence in new bodies; nor do we hear, in this new theory, of good or bad lives, of sin, but only of the stains which an ethereal soul contracts from being imprisoned in an alien element, the body. A paraphrase of the passage in which Virgil states the theory may clarify the immediate meaning of it, though its deeper significance must be deferred for consideration in the next chapter. What Anchises says, in effect, is this:

The four elements, fire, water, air, earth, are animated and nurtured by the spirit, which, permeating the whole and mixed with it, moves the universe, as if it (the universe) were a living organism, and generates the living creatures on earth, in the air, and in the sea. The seeds of things, being fiery by nature and akin to the deity, are weakened by being confined in corruptible and torpid bodies as in dark prisons, and from contact with these bodies acquire the emotions of fear, desire, pain, pleasure. And not even when the souls are freed by death from the bonds of the flesh are they rid of pollution which is fixed and resident within them from long contact with the body. Because of this evil condition of the souls dread punishments await them first of all; and one soul punished by fire, another by water, another by winds, they pay the penalty for the long defilement according to the demon which has fallen to the lot of each. Then, crossing to the so-called Elysian Fields, a few

souls who have lived more seemly lives abide in that place until, after
the revolution of a cycle of ten thousand years, their impurity is removed and the spirit is left of the finest possible texture and becomes
pure fire; but the majority of souls must be purified in a recess of
Elysium, whence, after a cycle of one thousand years, they pass into
other bodies, having lost their recollection of what has happened to them
through drinking the water of the river Lethe before leaving Hades for
their new life in the upper world.

This paraphrase, difficult as it is to follow, may be expanded in a more intelligible form:

The universe is composed of soul and body, just as the individual
man is composed of soul and body; the world-soul and man's soul are
made of the same material; and the world-body and man's body are
made of the same materials. The world-soul and man's soul are made of
fire of the finest and purest texture; this fire, which is the soul both of
the universe and of man, is the animating reasoning principle, the deity,
which gives life and motion to the world and to man. The body, both of
the world and of man, is made of four inferior elements: fire of a
coarser grade than the soul-fire, earth, air, and water; the world, and also
man, are made living organisms by the union of this fire-soul with the
body; the fire-soul permeates the body and supplies animating generative
power. But the spark of pure fire that emanates from the world-soul
and becomes the individual man's soul is polluted when it comes into
contact with the four elements that constitute the body; there is a
certain amount of pollution that is common to all souls; but in addition to this common quantity of pollution, individual souls have a further varying degree of defilement according to the extent to which
during life they have yielded to the emotions of fear, desire, pain, pleasure. Consequently, after death, when the man's soul is released from the
body, there is a certain common measure of punishment and purification
provided, and in addition, a special individual provision to cover the
various degrees of defilement in individual cases; so all souls are first
exposed to one of the elements of air, water, fire; then all souls pass to
Elysium; at this point a discrimination is made into two classes; one
class, a minority, continues for ten thousand years in Elysium, until the
fire of the soul is completely purified and it may rejoin the world-soul
whence it came; but the majority are too corrupt for any such purgation; they stay for one thousand years in a recess of Elysium, after
which they again enter into bodies and live a second life.

This bald statement of the case will, I hope, make clear the unity of the thought, though I have purposely omitted one or two details and have intentionally withheld for the present the deeper significance of the theory.

In accordance with this theory Aeneas sees before him, near the river Lethe, the souls awaiting rebirth after their thousand years of purification in a recess of Elysium; Anchises, it will be observed, in contrast to these souls, probably belongs to the favored few who are to remain for the long cycle of ten thousand years in Elysium without rebirth. Now it will be noted that the souls of future Romans whom Anchises presently reviews are not, all of them, selected in perfect accord with this theory. For instance, it is clear that the early Romans, such as Silvius, might be now awaiting rebirth; but that Augustus, who is to be reborn about a thousand years later than Aeneas' visit to the other world, should already be at the river bank awaiting reincarnation is quite at odds with the theory; but this apparent contradiction will trouble only the logically minded; the poet allows himself a reasonable license for the purpose of his splendid mustering of Roman heroes, the consummation of Aeneas' descent to Hades. This realizes Anchises' promise in the vision of the fifth book: "Visions I will show of cities proud and nations sprung from thee."

The long muster-roll of names is to the modern reader tedious; the modern student resents the imperative demand upon his dictionary of biography, and forgets, as soon as he has learned, the identity and the achievements of the heroes paraded before him. But it would be a pity not to enter into the spirit of the Roman reader and not to allow ourselves momentarily to be infused with his patriotic interest in this anticipatory hall of fame.

The artistic problem that confronted Virgil in this scene was no simple one. How was he to prevent a monotonous

cataloguing of names, a prosaic abridged history of his people
in chronological sequence; how vary the handling of individual heroes; how secure the symmetry desirable to clear exposition and artistic effect without the monotonous mechanical
listing of innumerable Roman Washingtons and Lincolns?
He obviated the dangers of his task by a variety of means.
First, he skilfully employed the fiction of a long procession in
which persons pass in review in groups accidentally formed;
being accidentally formed, they do not always include all the
possible constituent members of a given group, and the poet
is able plausibly to eliminate some of the famous men of history; so, for example, Regulus and Marius are missing from
the enumeration, though they may easily be imagined as
somewhere in the procession. This same accidental mustering
in groups enables the poet to neglect in a measure chronological sequence: only the large groups as wholes are chronologi-
cally arranged; Alban kings are followed by Roman kings,
and Roman kings by republican heroes; but within these
three groups only the Roman kings appear in chronological
order; in the other cases, by neglecting chronology, the poet
has accomplished the effective juxtaposition of Romulus and
Augustus; Augustus, thus placed, appears as a second Romulus. In general Virgil avoids the sequence of prose history;
the order of republican heroes is an artistic disarray; if there
is any effort here to group, the principle of grouping varies;
Brutus, the Decii, Drusi, Torquatus, Camillus may come together as men who sacrificed their own welfare for their country; in opposition to them, possibly, stand Caesar and Pompey, who turned against their country; and finally, a group of
heroes who served their nation in the broadest sense, arranged
in pairs. Thus a sort of architectural symmetry is provided,
a happy variation, without impairing the clearness of presentation.

This artistic form is permeated by a noble spirit; the language itself of the passage, by its sublimity and noble pathos, increases the impressiveness of the situation. And the poet has made of Anchises' speech, not a mere formal introduction of future heroes, somewhat as Helen, on the walls of Troy, introduced to aged Priam the unfamiliar Greek heroes, but rather an urgent expression of patriotic admonition; nor does Anchises praise, exclusively, the progeny of Aeneas; prohibition is mingled with admonition; these heroes are mainly exemplars, but, like the concrete examples which the father of the poet, Horace, pointed out to his son, there are some warning examples, as well as models, to be observed by the audience for whom Virgil is writing.

The more elevated passages naturally dignify the appearance of the greater heroes, Romulus and Augustus; but there is a simple noble pathos in the brief characterization of Brutus: "He first the consul's name shall take; he first the inexorable fasces sternly bear. When his own sons in rash rebellion join, the father and the judge shall sentence give in beauteous freedom's cause. . . . ." In contrast with such praise stands the stern appraisal of civil war in the picture of Caesar and Pompey: "Who are these in glorious armor clad, and equal power? In this dark world of cloud their souls in concord move; but woe is me, what duel twixt them breaks, when by and by the light of life is theirs, and forth they call their long-embattled lines to carnage dire. . . . . Forbear, my children. School not your great souls in such vast wars, nor turn your giant strength against the bowels of your native land. But be thou first, O first in mercy, thou who art of birth Olympian. Fling away thy glorious sword, mine offspring and mine heir." So the mere review of a parade is elevated to prophecy and to exhortation.

In the epilogue to the scene the tendency to admonish and exhort, previously restrained, is freely indulged; though Anchises speaks, the reader feels that the scene and situation

have been abruptly abandoned; the poet's voice is heard in an
immortal appreciation of the two great cultures of antiquity.
The modern reader may well be conscious of the Roman pride
that finds expression here, but it is militarism tempered with
mercy; Greece stands for the life of the intellect; Rome for
action:

> Let others melt and mould the breathing bronze
> To forms more fair, aye, out of marble bring
> Features that live; let them plead causes well;
> Or trace with pointed wand the cycled heaven,
> And hail the constellations as they rise;
> But thou, O Roman, learn with sovereign sway
> To rule the nations. Thy great art shall be
> To keep the world in lasting peace, to spare
> The humbled foe, and crush to earth the proud.

This famous passage is the epilogue of the great scene
with which this book concludes; but it is peculiarly placed;
for though an epilogue, it is followed by a further review of
heroes; these heroes are, however, only two in number, and of
the same family; the older Marcellus, hero of the wars with
Hannibal, and the younger Marcellus, the ideal youth of Virgil's own day, whose early death in the year 23 B.C., when he
was twenty years old, cut short a life of great promise. The
nephew and son-in-law of Augustus, he was buried with great
ceremony while Virgil was at work upon the *Aeneid*, and the
Emperor himself delivered the eulogy. This passage, therefore, is a compliment to the Emperor as well as a touching
tribute to the young fellow, who evidently had endeared himself to the people of Rome. Coming as it does after an obvious
epilogue, and so distinctly separable from the preceding
action, the passage is often said to be a later insertion after
the rest of the book was finished. Such a possibility cannot be
denied. But a modern reader, at any rate, may indulge his
own feelings in appreciating the effect of this pathetic scene,

coming as it does immediately after the proud celebration of
Rome's immortal achievements. Whether Virgil was fully
conscious of this effect we can hardly say. But in any case as
modern readers we may express our satisfaction that the
scene does not end in a spirit of conscious pride and in the
assertion of national achievement. Anchises' speech has been
marked by blame as well as praise; Rome's history has passed
through perilous stages, and the greatest perils have arisen in
the age of Virgil, when anarchy threatened order and civil
strife endangered the very life of the great empire which
Roman energy and efficiency had created. There must have
been in many a Roman's mood in Virgil's day a strong strain
of pessimism, of fatalism, which seriously qualified any proud
confidence in the assured permanence of Roman power. The
death of young Marcellus was a serious blow to the Emperor's
own hopes; Marcellus typified that strength and probity upon
which, as realized in the younger generation, Augustus was
endeavoring to build a new Rome, linking it to the great traditions, the higher ideals, of a remote past. As the death of
Marcellus chastened the Emperor's hopes and ambitions, so
this pathetic eulogy, the lilies and the purple blossoms on
Marcellus' grave, concludes the scene, softening the arrogance
of the self-assertive epilogue with a serious outlook upon the
vicissitudes of human and national fate.

The book, as well as the scene, must have its conclusion.
The gates of sleep, through one of which Aeneas finds an exit
to the upper world, mark the end and round out the unity of
the whole with a picturesque description: "Now Sleep has
portals twain, whereof the one is horn, they say, and easy exit
gives to visions true; the other, gleaming white with polished
ivory, the dead employ to people night with unsubstantial
dreams." Through this ivory gate of false dreams Anchises
releases Aeneas to his own world above. What further significance these gates of sleep may have has long been disputed.

Possibly the poet thereby neatly indicates the time spent by his hero in this underworld. The journey began at early dawn; when they approached Elysium it was already afternoon; it is a general idea in ancient thought that false dreams come to the sleeper before midnight; Aeneas issues from the gate of ivory, the exit of false dreams; like these false dreams, then, he leaves the lower world before midnight. So the epilogue of the book is more than merely ornamental; it conveyed poetically to the ancient reader a definite suggestion of time in accord with other similiar indications throughout the action.

But more important is the new mood with which Aeneas rises to his new task in the conquest of Latium; Anchises has quickened in his mind hunger for future fame. Nor must we forget the Roman reader; he too was as discouraged by the labors, the toils, and struggles of the first century as any Aeneas by wanderings over the long laborious sea; he, like Aeneas, had a troubled future before him, made quite uncertain by the ravages of the Civil War. To such a Roman reader, as well as to Aeneas, this great prophecy, these solemn admonitions, expressed the ideals of the greatest days of Roman history; it was these ideals exemplified in the lives and actions of old Roman worthies that Augustus was striving to revive and to realize in the young Romans of his day; this was the ancestry of which Rome in Virgil's day must show herself worthy. The poet missed his great patriotic purpose if he failed to stimulate, not only in his hero a desire to start the great movement toward high achievement, but in his Roman reader an eager passion to finish worthily that triumphant progress which Aeneas was about to begin.

VIII. THE LIFE AFTER DEATH IN POPULAR FANCY AND SPECULATIVE THEORY

Simple folk-notions of an existence after death seem to be determined very largely by experience with dreams; so far as the living have any knowledge of the dead it is through the vision of the dead in sleep; in such visions the dead appear as ghosts, shadowy replicas of the living person, reproducing the features and general forms of the living, but voiceless or shrill-voiced, weak, unsubstantial. The popular imagination peoples with these ghostly figures the region of Hades, the invisible world of death. There is in such a conception no real notion of immortality, no clear idea of a soul; the ghost is simply a shadow of the living person, a sort of second self; after death it has no real life, any more than a reflection in a mirror; this ghostly figure retains all the features of the living person. Immortality is the privilege of gods; the great differentiating characteristic that distinguishes men from gods is that man dies, gods live forever; any clear notion of immortality for man is impossible for the Greeks so long as god and man are thus sharply separated.

It is, however, possible for man to approximate god, and as a half-god he may have divine privileges. That thought underlies the early conception of the Elysian Fields to which we found Proteus, in the fourth book of the *Odyssey*, consigning the hero Menelaus; Menelaus, the poet clearly said, was not ordained to die; he was to be removed just as he was in life, body and all, to the miraculous garden of the gods; that is true immortality, but in the Homeric conception it is not open to all, but is the special reward of a few mortals who are thereby properly deified and partake of immortality as part

411

of godship. This place to which they are removed is a divine garden; all the features ascribed to it are the regular characteristics of the abode of gods; it has an ideal climate, a special light and radiance—in fact, it is often identical with the home of the sun god; mystic rivers, golden fruits, rich odors add to its attractiveness. But in early Greek thought it is the heaven of a privileged few; gods and a few heroes live there.

Along with this notion of the Elysian Fields there existed ideas of Utopian countries, variously located, where lived people who were peculiarly blessed, who, as singularly just and virtuous, enjoyed the riches of a land of great fertility. Such countries, too, are clearly the homes primarily of gods and a few select mortals; the land of the Hyperboreans is Apollo's special abode; he has, however, a sacred priestly people resident with him in this mystical country. These Utopian regions are developed in later Greek literature with a considerable variety of miraculous features; they are nothing more than elaborations of the simpler notion of the Elysian Fields as homes of the gods and heroes; but they have a special significance for us because there is so regularly emphasized the justice, the uprightness, of denizens of these Utopias, and the unruffled peaceful existence of their lives. No essential trait of the Christian heaven is missing from these Greek Utopias; in these regions are heard continual song, the music of flute and harp; not only is the air singularly bright and radiant, but the inhabitants have a radiant beauty; they wear garments of finest texture, as white and clear as the air of their ideal homes; here abide the few, the chosen, the just and virtuous.

Popular fancy in early times provided also a home after life for the shadowy ghosts of the dead, for the great majority; Homer located it at the western edge of the world; but it must in very early times have been placed below the earth's surface. This conception of the home of the dead is likely to appear as early as burial becomes a regular practice, and most of the details of this underworld Hades develop naturally from the knowledge that the buried body eventually disappears, gradually consumed by some unknown powers. Popular fancy gives a definite concreteness to these unknown agents that consume the body. They are conceived as flesh-eating monsters. Ultimately these monsters become inhabitants of a definitely arranged underworld, spacious and conveniently divided into districts under the influence of various theological and generally religious notions; and when a different line of thought posits a soul in contrast with body, the flesh-devourers become easily soul-snatchers. The early stages of such development are only vaguely visible in Greek literature, but Cerberus, the Harpies, and Gorgons, and Chimaera of Virgil's underworld are crude survivals of even cruder beginnings: Cerberus is a flesh-rending dog, and the Harpies, as gaunt fiends stealing food, perhaps reveal their earliest function as body-snatchers, which later is elevated slightly into soul-snatchers. Once these cruder ideas have been weakened or refined, these cruel monsters continue in the world of death as guardians, watchdogs, or generally awesome creatures, the bugaboos and bogeys of the nursery; and some of them, originally barbaric devourers of the flesh of dead bodies, may easily become punishing demons in the after-life so soon as any general conception develops of the life after death as involving rewards and penalties for the life on earth.

These fancies, pleasant and grim, of gardens of the gods and of special heroes, and of a world of death peopled with ghosts of the living and with grotesque monsters, once body-renders and soul-snatchers, may turn up anywhere; they are not peculiar to the Greek people. Theology, religion, themselves often mere refinements of popular fancy, slowly develop and change these cruder notions. Homer puts the shadowy ghosts of the dead off in a dim western land which is quite devoid of grim monsters, and reckons with punishment after death only in the case of a few mythical figures like Sisyphus and Tantalus; possibly the eleventh *Odyssey* is without the grim monsters because the body is burned, not buried, in the Homeric epic. But elsewhere Homer seems to know of punishing demons and of punishments that take place underground, for in the *Iliad* (iii. 276, xix. 258) he refers to the furies who punish, underground, men who have broken their oaths. These furies originally were angry souls avenging themselves for wrongs done them; only later did they become spirits of hell concretely representing the anger of the souls. Once they flew through the air, where souls are supposed to reside, pursuing their victims; only later are they demoted to an underworld Hades as punishing agents, when souls, too, are transferred from residence in the air to a new home below ground. They become generalized in function; once the soul of a murdered man punished the murderer; but this punishing soul, as a fury in an underworld Hades, punishes the murderer's ghost, and eventually it develops into a multitude of furies punishing various sinners. As time goes on—if we may briefly cover many centuries—these furies are replaced by demons, souls of the departed, who may be good as well as bad, avenging souls, like the earlier furies, or as semidivine beings, servants of the gods, carrying out divine commands in punishing men after death; it is these demons, perhaps, themselves surrogates of the earlier furies, who appear as the good and bad angels in early Christian doctrine.

The Virgilian picture of the after-life presents an underworld with provision for sinners punished by furies and other means, and saints resident in Elysian Fields. Long centuries before Virgil, souls once denizens of the air had been brought down underground, and punishment for sin once wreaked by souls themselves in the air became an underground system of pains and penalties effected by definite agents—the furies—

now personal, though once themselves nothing but disembodied souls; into this underworld Hades had been brought the Elysian Fields, with all the brilliant radiance which they had acquired in the happy fancy of the folk when they were no part of a general theory of after-life, but only a visionary garden of the gods set apart for divine beings and a few select mortals; these few select mortals, having won the favor of the gods, partook of the divine nature, and with it, of immortality. How did all this come about?

Greek theology supplied certain underworld divinities quite superior to the grim monsters and avenging furies of popular fancy. These underworld gods were worshipped as devoutly as the gods of the upper world; their favor was even more essential than that of the gods of Olympus, for mortal man is in the domain of these underworld divinities much longer than he is subject to the sway of the upper-world gods. One of the most significant cults of these chthonic deities was devoted to the worship of Demeter at Eleusis, near Athens, and in the Homeric *Hymn to Demeter* in the seventh century we read these words: "Blessed is the man who has seen the mysteries; but whoever is uninitiated and without part in the mysteries, he shall not have a pleasant lot in the dark swamp of Hades after death." Here for the first time we find a distinction between the blessed and the accursed, the initiate and uninitiate, and a precise distinction implied between those who are rewarded and those who are punished after death. From all that we hear of the dramatic presentation at Eleusis of the so-called "mysteries," the abode of the blessed in the after-life was invested with all the features of the Elysian Fields: with wonderful light, lovely meadows, melodious songs and dances. Entrance into this blessed life was insured only to those who joined the church, who became members of this special cult; the eternally blessed and the eternally condemned are synonymous with the initiated and the uniniti-

ated. The closeness with which such mystic cults of underworld divinities approximate Virgil's picture of the after-life
is best illustrated by the *Frogs* of Aristophanes, a Greek comedy which is admittedly affected by the beliefs and practises
of the cult of Eleusis. In this play Dionysus, the god of tragedy, goes down to the underworld to seek a good tragic poet;
since the deaths of the three great tragedians there is a dearth
of them in the upper world; Dionysus sees a great lake, bot-
tomless, a region full of serpents and innumerable grotesque
monsters, including the bogey Empusa with her misshapen
legs, the dogs of Cocytus, hundred-headed Echidna, and Gorgons; he finds mud and ever flowing filth, and in it lies whoever has wronged a guest, or abused his mother, or broken his
father's jaw, or sworn a false oath—obviously the antecedents
of Virgil's criminals from real life, as distinguished from
mythical figures such as Tantalus and Sisyphus. But beyond
lies a different precinct, where is the sound of flute music and
a beautiful radiance like that of the upper world, and myrtle
groves, and companies of blessed men and women, and loud
clapping of hands; later in the play the chorus, made up of
initiates in the mysteries, sing of the delights of this precinct,
its flowery meadows, and the dances there celebrated, of the
bright sunlight which only the initiates enjoy who have lived
righteous lives in their dealings with strangers and with their
own community. Here in this fifth-century picture, therefore,
are most of the essential details of Virgil's Hades, its Tartarus
as well as its Elysium.

But the full background of Virgil's account is not so
clearly provided by the mystical doctrines of Eleusis as by
other mystic cults of ancient Greece. Immortality is synonymous with divinity. The ecstasy and enthusiasm of worship-
ers of the Thracian god, Dionysus, presupposes that the
devotee is capable of uniting with the deity and practically
identifying himself with the god; in this divine frenzy the

worshiper becomes the god and is called by the god's name; so the women possessed by the god Bacchus are themselves Bacchae. This Dionysus plays an important rôle in the most significant mystic religion of ancient Greece, so-called "Orphism." The sect of Orphics was somewhat apart from orthodox Greek religion, and at best only tolerated by the state; it was peculiar in having a very definite body of dogma that was presented in written form and constituted a code, or various codes, of religious principles and practice which the worshiper should follow to attain the highest purposes of the cult. The chief center of Orphism seems to have been Southern Italy, but it was introduced into Athens by the second half of the sixth century; its influence upon religion and philosophy was considerable. The name of the sect seems to be taken from the mythical Thracian singer, Orpheus, who was the reputed author of the various writings in which the theology and ritual of the sect was fully and somewhat variously revealed.

In these theological writings the Orphics seem to make over the myths of Hesiodic poetry into a symbolic presentation of their theory of the creation and early history of the world. There is the genealogical sequence of gods, much as Hesiod relates it, until at last we reach, as the son of Zeus and Persephone, a new god, Dionysus, surnamed Zagreus, to whom Zeus has turned over his royal power. This god is approached by evil demons called Titans, who overcome him and rend him in pieces; these fragments of Dionysus-Zagreus are swallowed by the Titans, except his heart, which is rescued and given to Zeus; Zeus swallows the heart, and there is born a new Dionysus in whom the old Zagreus still lives. Zeus had destroyed the evil Titans by his thunderbolt; from the ashes of the Titans arose the human race; inasmuch as these Titans had swallowed the god Dionysus, the human race thus created was, naturally, a compound of two elements: a good element, the god Dionysus, and an evil Titanic element. This strange composition determines the end and aim of man's existence; man must continually strive to free himself from the evil Titanic element, and return absolutely pure to the god of whom he has within him a vital part. This part of the god within him is his soul; the Titanic element is the body; the good divine element is resident in the body like a prisoner in a dungeon, and the release from this prison is a long and difficult process; the soul cannot itself break loose from the prison; even death provides only a temporary release; for when death lets the soul escape from the body, the soul hovers in the air only to be sucked into some new body. So it passes, sometimes free and unencumbered, sometimes incorporated and imprisoned, through what the Orphics called a cycle of generation; the wheel of fate, as they expressed it, revolves incessantly.

There is, however, one way of escape from the cycle, one final and absolute release from the wheel of fate. This is afforded by Orpheus and initiation into the rites of Dionysus; join the church and you shall be saved; man himself cannot be his own liberator; the revelations of Orpheus must be known and followed. One must live an Orphic life to restore the god within him to its pure form; and this Orphic life is not a life devoted to the practice of civic virtues or to the development of high moral character, but simply an asceticism which has for its sole object absolute aversion to everything carnal and earthy; so one must not eat flesh; one must do everything to keep the soul pure of the body and its defiling power; the residence of the soul in the body is an unnatural condition; life on earth and in the body is the soul's death; the main effort should be to get free of the body, purify the soul of its pollution; only the Orphics attain to such purity. The reward of pious devotion to the principles of the sect is manifested in the intermediate existence that follows an

earthly life; then the uninitiated who have been sinners are
punished in the depths of Tartarus; those who are not
Orphics lie in mire and slime; a grim fate is in store for those
who have scorned the mysteries. But the initiates and the
purified abide in community with the gods; they enjoy the
meal, the symposium of the pure and holy, and a pleasant in-
toxication. But this is only a temporary existence. The punishment in Tartarus is not eternal; the uninitiated are born
into new lives; in the new life they suffer what in their former
life they inflicted on others. The initiates, too, enter into new
bodies, and are rewarded in these new lives for their virtues
in a previous existence. But initiates may be thoroughly purified; in that case they escape from the cycle of generation;
they are relieved from a new birth; they need not suffer again
the death that comes from residence in the body; they have
eternal life as does the god who contributed the divine element, the soul, to the compound of Dionysus and the Titanic
element of which man was made.

This sect, therefore, is committed to the belief in an immortal soul which is defiled by contact with the body; existence on earth and after death is a continual penalty and purification in which Orphic initiates have an advantage; and a
theory of continual rebirth is essential to the doctrines of the
sect; only the Orphics themselves may escape rebirth and
unite with the god without fulfilling the complete cycle of
generation. The significance of this doctrine for the interpretation of Virgil's sixth book lies not merely in its theory of
immortality and transmigration, but in the fact that it oper-
ates with all the popular notions of a Tartarus and Elysian
Fields and provides penalties and purification, rewards and
special privileges, in the intermediate existence that succeeds
the death of the body and precedes rebirth into a new body.
Such a revelation of this intermediate existence as Virgil gives
was in its general form and content, and in many details, no

doubt, anticipated in one of the Orphic presentations of the theories of the sect; for we hear of a book called the "Descent of Orpheus," which probably represented just such a descent to Hades as Aeneas accomplishes, with similar pictures of Tartarus and Elysium, and such a descent of Orpheus may well have culminated in a formal pronouncement of the speculative theory of the sect, corresponding in general form to the theory of purification and transmigration which Anchises sets forth in the *Aeneid,* though of course differing in detail. And such contradictions as may appear in Virgil between a punishment of morally guilty in Tartarus and a theory of the soul which does not reckon so much with moral guilt as with defilement of the soul by the body must have been as prominent in Orphic preachments; for they describe the sufferers in Tartarus in moral terms and anticipate Virgil in his categories of sinners from actual life. The only essential difference in Virgil is in the possible implication that suffering in Tartarus is eternal; that would perhaps hardly appear in Orphic doctrine, nor does it fit with Virgil's theory of transmigration; but it should be noted that this idea of eternal punishment is not explicitly stated in Virgil except in the case of Theseus.

In another important respect Orphism anticipates Virgil's account: both theories seem to provide for three classes of persons, not only a specially sinful class, but a further division of the relatively good into an average good and a superlatively good, the former subject to rebirth, the latter released permanently from the body and ultimately joining the god.

Orphism has obvious points of contact with the theories of Pythagoras. So close is the relation between the two that it is difficult to say whether Pythagoreanism was influenced by the Orphic doctrines or vice versa. I have chosen to recount in some detail the views of the Orphics rather than of Pythagoras simply because it is somewhat easier to give a relatively complete statement of Orphism; but the school of Pythagoras stated some facts in close accord with the Orphic doctrine, and the later influence, especially upon Greek philosophy, of such views must be loosely described as the combined influence of Pythagoreanism and Orphism. This influence is peculiarly apparent in the beautiful myths in which Plato in several of his dialogues seeks to express his notions of the after-life; he represents himself as unable to utter his thoughts in the usual language of philosophical discussion, and resorts to myths to suggest as well as he can these thoughts which strain the powers of ordinary expression. In such myths he obviously reflects much of the doctrine of Orphism and Pythagoreanism, but with the further fusion of moral purity and guilt which these mystical doctrines could hardly have emphasized primarily. Such points of contact as there obviously are between Virgil and Plato may suggest the common background of both, the mystical doctrines of special cults.

So, in the myth of the *Phaedo*, the souls are divided according as they have lived righteous or unrighteous lives. Those who have lived an average life go to Lake Acheron and, abiding there, get themselves cleansed, and paying the price of their evil deeds, are acquitted from the guilt thereof, and for their good deeds receive each the reward that is meet. A second class of incurable sinners is doomed to eternal punishment in Tartarus. A third class of curable sinners stay in Tartarus a year, and may get out to Lake Acheron if the persons they have wronged will let them. A fourth class, of the godly, is released from these places in the earth, and departs from them as from a prison house and comes unto the pure mansions which are above, and dwells upon the earth. And of these, whoso have cleansed themselves thoroughly by wisdom live without fleshly bodies forevermore, and come to yet fairer mansions, whereof it is not easy to tell. Here we have the average, the incurable sinners, the curable sinners, the godly who are reborn, and the superlatively good who are released from rebirth; the last two clearly correspond to the two classes in Virgil's doctrine of transmigration, the many who are reborn after a thousand years of purification, and the few who abide in Elysium without rebirth, becoming pure fire after ten thousand years. These same cycles that Virgil gives appear in the Platonic myth in the *Phaedrus:*

> Now into the same place from whence each soul cometh she return-eth not again until ten thousand years have been accomplished. . . . . The souls of such men, when the third course of a thousand years is fin-ished, if they have chosen this life three times in order, ... do then depart. But the other souls, when they have ended their first life, are brought before the judgment seat, and when they have received sentence, some go to the prisons under the earth, and there pay the penalty; and some by the sentence are exalted, and go into a certain place of the heavens, where they fare as beseemeth the life which they spent when they had man's form. But in the thousandth year both sorts, being come to the casting of lots and to the choosing of the second life, choose, every soul, the life which pleaseth her.

This provides for the superlatively good exemption from re-birth after they have passed through three lives, including one thousand years of purification after each life; the average soul and the ordinarily good soul are obliged to pass through rebirth with a thousand years of purification after each life, but are differentiated in Hades by their place of residence, the average suffering penalty under earth, the ordinarily good better off in a certain part of the Heavens, the two places roughly corre-sponding to Tartarus and Elysium. Similarly, in the *Repub-lic,* the myth of Er refers to a thousand years as the period of punishment under earth. In general, then, in these Platonic myths we have a similar doctrine of purification and rebirth, with similar cycles, and of course in Plato the purification, the penalties, and the rewards emphasize moral virtues and de-fects; the types of sinners correspond to a considerable extent to the types enumerated in Virgil; in other words, this combi-nation of moral purification with a theory of transmigration which in Virgil's theory seems not to fit his account of the soul as polluted chiefly by contact with the body appears in Plato without vital contradiction, since Plato's theory of the soul does not represent it to be of fire and degraded by contact with inferior elements. Plato, however, like the Orphics, regards the soul as imprisoned in the body and suffering from its earthly existence.

His notion of the fiery soul Virgil took from the contemporary school of Stoic philosophy, the doctrines of which pretty thoroughly permeate the *Aeneid;* the idea of fate, as well as this theory of a fire-soul, Virgil owes to the Stoics. The Stoic view of the soul, in turn, is a development from earlier views. Early Greek philosophers, abandoning the religious and mythical explanations of the formation of the world and of man, endeavored to find a more rational account. They saw order in the universe, yet, along with it, constantly changing phenomena; how were they to explain the orderliness in spite of the many visible changing aspects? Many of them found the explanation in developments which they saw taking place in their daily experience; some of them, for example, saw, in watching fire burn, a certain orderly development, a constant change as the fire itself burned steadily. There was the fuel constantly feeding the flame, the flame burning steadily, the flame giving forth a vapor, and the vapor, under certain conditions, apparently changing to water, and so on; the flame seemed to them the essential thing, and other elements seemed to issue from it and pass back into it. Such observations led to the idea that fire was the soul, the deity of the universe; this fire, by natural processes, developed other elements which made the body of the world in which the fire-soul resided as the intelligent principle; but ultimately, at the end of a world-cycle, these other elements resolved back into the fire-soul, and every ten thousand years there was a grand conflagration, after which a new world-cycle began, the other elements again developed from the fire, another world was created, and this process kept on indefinitely in an unending series of world-cycles, each of ten thousand years. In this world, composed of a fire-soul and a body made of inferior elements developed from the fire, man existed as a minute copy of the universe. Man, like the world, had a fire-soul, a spark, as it were, of the world-soul; man's body, like the world's body, was made of inferior elements; man's soul had an affinity for the world-soul, and was imprisoned in the body, tainted by contact with inferior elements and, after such residence, requiring purification before it could rejoin the world-soul of which it was a part. From this standpoint man's life is a sort of living death; the only real life is death, for death makes possible release from the defiling body and reunion with the world-soul. It will be observed how close this is to the Orphic view, in which man has a soul, a bit of the divine Dionysus-Zagreus, and a body, composed of the evil Titanic element; from this prison of the body the soul seeks escape to reunite with the divine. But as in the Orphic, so in the Stoic, theory, the individual soul has to pay the penalty for its defilement by the body; that penalty involves purification as much as punishment; in Stoic theory the fire-soul was always contaminated by the mere contact with the body, but the degree of pollution in individual cases might vary according as the soul had yielded to, or resisted, the emotions, or commotions, which are necessary consequences of the union of the soul with the body. Hence, when death releases the souls they have to go through a general and a special purification. The details of this purification, as certain Stoics of Virgil's day conceived it, involve notions which Virgil himself, for obvious reasons, does not explicitly state; this fire-soul of the world is of very fine texture and the lightest thing in the universe; as such it naturally abides at the top of the world, where its lightness raises it above everything else; but the other inferior elements are denser, and sink nearer the bottom; the fire-soul in the individual man is naturally as light as the world-soul, and, when released from the body, would properly rise immediately to the top of the universe and join the world-soul, but contact with the body has polluted the man's soul, increased its weight; it rises slowly when released from the body, and lingers first just above the surface of the earth, where the air is thick and condensed, where clouds, rain, and winds are massed together; contact with these removes some of the pollution from the soul; it is this stage of the purification which Virgil refers to in saying "one soul punished by fire, another by water, another by winds, they pay the penalty for the long defilement." Having passed this first stage of purification, the soul is somewhat lightened and may rise higher; here, in a second stage of its upward progress, it reaches the rarer air beneath the moon, where further purification takes place; at this point some souls are too thoroughly defiled to be successfully purified, and after staying a thousand years here, they drop again to rebirth; these constitute the majority of souls, and they are subject to constant rebirth after each life on earth and after the thousand years of purification near the moon; this region near the moon is the recess of Elysium to which Virgil refers and where the souls are mustered for rebirth. But a few souls are curable and may be entirely purified; they go beyond the recess of Elysium, beyond the air beneath the moon, to the moon itself, which is Elysium; here they abide ten thousand years, after which, completely purified and restored to the fire of finest texture, they may rise to the last station and rejoin the world-soul itself at the top of the universe. This is the complete story. Virgil carefully omits any reference to these four stations of purifying ascent in an upward progress toward the world-soul, but he covers all four as stages of purification; all pass through the fire, water, winds, which, in the Stoic theory, are above the earth; all reach the recess of Elysium where a discrimination is made: the majority, after a thousand years, are reborn; a few dwell in Elysium for the great cycle of ten thousand years and are restored to pure fire. Obviously Virgil has omitted all reference to an upward movement through the air because it would conflict too manifestly with Aeneas' descent to an underworld Hades, but the Stoic reader of this book without doubt filled in the upward progress, which was inevitable in the Stoic conception and which is essential to the perfect harmony of their views. Even Virgil himself has shown his real meaning in at least one place; for in verse 887, after this theory has been set forth and after Anchises has reviewed the souls of future heroes, the poet says: "So far and wide through spacious fields of air they wander free, witnessing all"; how could they wander free through fields of air except in accord with the Stoic theory in which Elysium was the moon, and the recess of Elysium, from which souls are reborn, the rarer air beneath the moon?

But though Virgil has avoided flat contradiction with his main situation, with the descent of Aeneas to an underworld Hades, there still remains the apparent contradiction between a purifying of the soul from the pollution of contact with the body and a religious notion of sin for which criminals are punished in Tartarus; this contradiction is purely logical, and existed long before Virgil. Similarly the Orphics included Tartarus in their accounts of the after-life and provided punishment for typical sinners, though their general theory regarded the chief sin as being simply a failure to live the Orphic life, and the typical sinners were so many examples of persons who scorned the mysteries of their sect. There is some evidence that Stoics, on occasion, reckoned with a Tartarus, though it may have been with them a mere figure of speech. Plato certainly uses all the machinery of the Tartarus and Elysium of popular fancy in combination with an upward and downward movement of the soul: downward to rebirth, upward to a region of purity in Heaven. It is quite unlikely that Virgil is responsible for such a blending of logically inconsistent ideas.

Thus we have followed a long development from crude popular fancy through mystical religious belief to philosophical reasoning; in Virgil's conception of the after-life the result is many intertwisted strands, the other ends of which run far back into the earlier stages of Greek thought. The modern student will hardly fail to observe the constantly increasing approximation to Christian doctrine; to the Orphic the soul was a divine element in a corporeal prison; death was really life; the soul enjoyed an immortal life, more peacefully attained if one joined the church and lived the Orphic life of struggle for purification from all the defilement of earthly existence. The Christian heaven, with its harps and angels and heavenly choirs and bright raiment, was long anticipated by popular fancy, though in early times placed at the edge of the world or, later, beneath the world as part of an underworld Hades. But the Stoic theory of a fiery soul elevated that heaven to an upper world above the earth, the abode of the world-soul, toward which each man's soul struggles and strives, by purifying punishments (in which hell-fire is not omitted), through stations in a constant upward progress toward the fine ether of heaven itself. One may easily see, therefore, how this pagan world, by a natural development and refinement of its conception of the soul and of the after-life, had prepared itself, unconsciously, for the reception of Christian doctrine, and, indeed, in some important respects was ready to contribute to that doctrine out of its own sublime intimations of immortality. In that sense Virgil's sixth *Aeneid* is a bridge between paganism and Christianity.

IX. THE WAR IN LATIUM

The last six books of the *Aeneid* are relatively unfamiliar to the modern student of literature. A rigid school curriculum for its practical purposes has confined attention to the first half of the poem; so, while the descent to Hades, the fall of Troy, the tragedy of Dido, are more or less known to at least a few of the present generation, the events of the war in Latium and the characters of these later chapters of the poem are much less familiar to us than they have been to earlier generations of the English people. Yet it may well be doubted if the second half of the poem is inferior to the first six books. In the first six books the poet is intent upon Aeneas; only for a brief interval, in the fifth book, have we met any considerable number of other heroes; now there is presented to us a greater variety of characters whose portraiture tested the poet's capacity. Even Aeneas himself has changed under the stimulus of his vision of the other world, and emerges to his new task no longer a patient observer of the decrees of Fate, but a militant hero. The passive endurance of long wanderings before Latium is reached now gives place to a forceful occupation of the territory promised the Trojans by divine assurances in the earlier action. The perils of travel through unknown seas and countries become the more pressing dangers of war in a strange land with a strange people. The first six books are an *Odyssey;* the last six, an *Iliad.* Whatever special charm the *Odyssey* may have for a modern reader, the ancient world, with its militant spirit, found in the *Iliad* the masterpiece of Homer. Virgil and Augustus may have felt greater pleasure in the relatively peaceful pictures of the earlier portions of the *Aeneid,* but the poet must have known that the average Roman reader would find more satisfaction in the record of Trojan conquest; here, in the tale of a successfully prosecuted war, lay the incontestable guaranty of Rome as a world-power; these skirmishes with Latins and Rutulians were so many initial steps in the ultimate conquest of all Italy and of the great world of Augustus' generation; here the Roman reader found his ancestors possessed of all the virtues of the heroes of the later republic.

Virgil himself was conscious of the different and larger task that confronted him in the second half of his epic; his prologue (vii. 37 ff.), calling for special inspiration from the muse, declares: "Dread wars I tell, array of battle, and high-hearted kings thrust forth to perish, when Etruria's host and all Hesperia gathered to the fray. Events of grander march impel my song, and loftier task I try."

The story of these last six books is briefly this: From Cumae the Trojans sail farther north, stopping at Caieta and passing the land of Circe until at last they reach the promised Latium; they sail up the Tiber to Laurentum, or rather, near it. Aeneas builds a fortified camp near the Tiber. Latinus, the king of the surrounding country, has a daughter, Lavinia, much wooed and half-promised to a young prince, Turnus, leader of the Rutulians, a neighboring people. King Latinus, however, has been warned by various omens not to betroth his daughter to a native prince, for a stranger is coming to be her husband; when he hears of the arrival of the Trojans, and later receives the envoys of Aeneas, he is convinced that Aeneas is the intended bridegroom, and immediately offers Lavinia in marriage to the Trojan leader. While the envoys carry this offer back to the Trojan camp, the hostile divinity, Juno, renews her activity against Aeneas. She instructs the fury, Allecto, to stir up war. The fury accomplishes this by exerting her power in three different directions; she inspires the queen, Amata, mother of Lavinia and wife of Latinus, and already predisposed in favor of Turnus' suit, with a mad

resentment and aversion to the union with the Trojans;
Allecto then approaches Turnus and fills him with a furious
eagerness to resist Latinus' purpose, even to the extent of
fighting with the Trojans; finally Allecto uses the accidental
killing, by Ascanius, of a pet animal belonging to one of the
rustic families to inspire in the country folk hostility toward
the Trojans. King Latinus is overwhelmed by the general
demand for war against the Trojans; knowing from the omens
that his daughter should marry Aeneas rather than Turnus,
but unable to stem the tide of war, he renounces responsibility
and relinquishes control of affairs. Juno herself opens the
gates of the temple of war, the formal indication of hostile
activity. The Rutulians and Latins are consequently joined
against Aeneas and the Trojans; Turnus is the chief antagonist; King Latinus drops into the background; the implication is that the war is to decide who shall obtain the hand of
Lavinia in marriage. The seventh book concludes with a catalogue of the troops marshaled under the banner of Turnus.
Aeneas finds himself and his Trojans pretty well isolated, and
begins to look about for possible allies with whose aid he may
meet his enemies on more nearly equal terms. These allies he
finds, first, in Evander, a Greek settler in Latium who has
established himself on the site of what is to be Rome; then,
through Evander, he also gains the help of the Etrurians.
These Etrurians have driven out a tyrant king, Mezentius,
who has sought refuge with Turnus and is now joined with
Turnus against Aeneas; the Etruscan people, therefore, more
readily combine with Aeneas against their former king. The
eighth book is taken up with Aeneas' visit to Evander and to
the Etruscans; as an incident in this book comes the description of the marvelous armor which Venus has persuaded her
husband, Vulcan, to make for Aeneas. The absence of Aeneas
leads Turnus to open hostilities by an attack on the Trojan
camp, which occupies the ninth book. In the tenth book

Aeneas returns by sea with his new auxiliaries, and the last three books are taken up with successive battles leading up to the final duel between Aeneas and Turnus, which decides the issue, makes Lavinia the bride of Aeneas, and effects the amalgamation of Trojans and Latins under Aeneas' leadership. The building of a new city (named Lavinium, after the bride), the home of the new kingdom and of the Trojan gods, is indicated as the outcome.

This story is Virgil's artistic refashioning of a mass of variant accounts of the experiences of the Trojans in Latium. It will be remembered that the legend of Aeneas developed primarily as a Greek story; in its Greek form the emphasis was laid upon Aeneas' wanderings before he reached Latium, upon his experiences in the Greek world outside of Italy. But when the Romans took over this Greek tale and used it to dignify the beginnings of their own history the elaboration of events after the arrival of the Trojans in Latium became an obvious task; such an elaboration had to reckon, not only with general probability, but with an already existing mass of Italian legends which accounted for early conditions in Latium, the existence of old settlements, cults of divinities, early customs, and what not; for several centuries before Virgil historians and antiquarians had worked over this theme, and the particular way in which, in a given century or period, the story was elaborated could hardly fail to be affected by current events and by national policy. During the previous centuries Rome was in close contact with other parts of Latium and of Italy; it conquered Latium and Italy; presently the conquered peoples claimed and merited not merely merciful treatment, but a delicate handling, a consideration which was their due as helpers of Rome; they were entitled to, and received, certain rights and privileges; they needed to be conciliated. In the course of such experiences the Romans, in developing a national legend in which a Trojan progenitor was represented as coming into close friendly and hostile contact with various Latin and Italian settlements, had to be careful to manipulate the story so as not to give offense to persons who, at the time the story was being elaborated, required tactful treatment. So, to some extent, the development of the Aeneas legend in respect to the adventures in Latium reflects, as we follow it through the centuries, the effect of contemporary history. Unfortunately our evidence of the gradual development is incomplete; we can, however, at least get glimpses of the changes from the third century on.

Of older versions of the story we know only that of Cato, at the beginning of the second century. In his account the Trojans, on their arrival, are given a piece of land, but they engage in predatory incursions into Latin territory and a war arises in which the Rutulians and Latins fight against the Trojans; King Latinus falls in the first battle. The war is then renewed by Turnus, king of the Rutulians, aided by Mezentius, the Etruscan king; in this campaign Aeneas disappears and Turnus falls on the field of battle. A third campaign follows, in which Ascanius kills Mezentius. The characteristics of this version are, first, the hostility between Latins and Trojans, and the three distinct campaigns in each of which a prominent foe falls—Latinus, Turnus, Mezentius, in that order—and second, the omission of any reference to Lavinia and a marriage alliance. The change that two centuries between Cato and Virgil made in this legend may be illustrated by the story as told by a contemporary of Virgil, the historian, Dionysius: Without Latinus' permission Aeneas settles on the site of what was later Lavinium, but Latinus enters into pleasant relations with him; Aeneas marries the king's daughter, Lavinia, and vanquishes the Rutulians in co-operation with the Latins; Lavinium is built. After two years the Rutulians revolt under the lead of Turnus, but both Latinus and Turnus fall in battle, so that Aeneas rules over

Latins and Rutulians. Three years later war breaks out again
with the Rutulians, who are now supported by the Etruscans
under Mezentius; in this war Aeneas falls and Ascanius succeeds him on the throne. Ascanius conducts the war successfully, and Mezentius concludes peace after the death of his
son, Lausus. In this account we have again a succession of
wars in which heroes successively fall—Turnus and Latinus
at the start—but this story includes the marriage of Lavinia,
and from the outset represents the Latins as siding with the
Trojans agains the other Italians. This new feature of friendly relations between Trojans and Latins is probably the issue
of events in Roman history in the early part of the first century, when the Latins were enabled to secure considerate
treatment from the Romans and the Romans were anxious to
represent them as, historically, allies of the Roman people.
But there is common to both Cato's and Dionysius' account
the series of wars and the death of Turnus early in the series;
nor in the second account is there any indication that the
marriage with Lavinia was an important issue of the campaigns; on the contrary, it precedes the first war and simply
marks the friendly relations between Latins and Trojans.

In spite of the prosaic nature of the facts it is not uninteresting to observe the changes which a poet makes in order to
refashion them into artistic form. Virgil immediately concentrates and condenses. He secures unity of time and unity of
action. Out of the three or four campaigns of tradition he
makes a single war with four battles, thereby compressing
events of many years into a few days. So the poet of the
Iliad, according to one modern view, had taken events of a
ten years' war before Troy and compressed them into a few
days in the poetic version of the epic. Along with this concentration goes a desirable unity of action. The historical narrative scattered the successes of the Trojans; first the Latins
were defeated, and Lavinium built; then the Rutulians beat-

en, and Turnus killed; finally, the Etruscans vanquished, and
Mezentius slain or forced to yield. But Virgil, by unifying
these campaigns, represents Aeneas as having Latins, Rutulians, and the Etruscan king against him, all at the same time.
And more significant than this, tradition always puts the conquest of Mezentius last, and the death of Turnus early, in the
disasters. Virgil has changed the whole sequence: the death
of Turnus becomes the final catastrophe, and the death of
Mezentius is only a prelude to the duel between Aeneas and
Turnus; only after that duel does Aeneas marry Lavinia, and
is Lavinium founded. So we get a definite goal toward which
everything else moves, and the story becomes a dramatic
progress toward the duel between two chief antagonists, in
which Lavinia is the prize of victory. In these points Virgil
is absolutely unique; here the poet and artist shows his skilful
hand; for such unity of action the historian had no regard.

But to obtain this unity Virgil has been involved in some
difficulty. Wishing to make Lavinia the prize of victory, he
could not bring about any conflict without establishing a dis-
agreement over the question of marriage between Aeneas and
the princess. He has consequently been forced to represent
the Latins as opposed to the match, and as enemies of Aeneas;
in that respect he has gone back to the old version of Cato, so
far as the Latins are not friendly to the Trojans. But the hero
could not very well obtain his bride in defiance of her father
or by killing him; so Virgil has been driven to represent Latinus himself as favoring the match and as refusing all responsibility when the war breaks out; here Virgil departs from
Cato. Accordingly, in Virgil the king, obeying the omens, offers Aeneas his daughter, and Aeneas is justified in defending
his claim to her by force of arms. But Latinus is left in a
rather awkward and vague position, and as we read through
the last six books watching the action of Latinus or his general attitude we cannot be fully content with the poet's at-

tempt to make the king's position clear and consistent. Primarily the general situation is not a plausible one; it is hardly likely that a whole people would make war in opposition to their king and without his participation. And in working out the later action the poet seems to be making some distinction between Latinus as an individual and Latinus as king; for from time to time Latinus is charged with responsibility for the war, though in other places he emphasizes his own blamelessness. So, in the earlier chapters, he calls the gods to witness that he yields only to violence; he puts the responsibility upon the others; he shuts himself up in the palace and, the poet says, relinquishes the reins of government. Juno declares the war, not Latinus. But later (xi. 113) Aeneas charges him with breaking his word, a charge which is true only in so far as Latinus represents his people. When the time comes for peace, Latinus calls a council of state, submits proposals, and regrets that he has not called the council earlier, just as if he had never given up his control of affairs. He even assumes responsibility for the war (xii. 29), in apparent contradiction of his earlier statement, and says expressly: "I have taken up impious arms" (xii. 31); this can be made consistent only on the assumption that, for the moment, he is speaking as representative of his people. But we are not concerned primarily with emphasizing Virgil's defects in this matter; rather, with indicating how his difficulty was forced upon him. It would have been much simpler to make Latinus opposed to the match from the outset; then consistent speech and action would have resulted easily; but the poet could not easily make his hero obtain his bride in opposition to her father, and once the father is on Aeneas' side, that circumstance separates king and people and brings about an awkward situation.

Thus far we have observed Virgil condensing his material with great advantage to unity of action. But over against this compression stands an equally notable expansion. The poet had a patriotic, as well as artistic, task to perform. Here were the progenitors of the Roman people engaged in war with various Latin tribes; the opportunity of celebrating various old towns, historic peoples of early Latium and Italy with whom the history of Rome itself was intimately concerned, could not be neglected. Virgil justifies the introduction of such material by a very simple device. He has both Trojans and Latins draw upon every possible resource in the way of auxiliaries and allies. It was natural for Latins and Rutulians to seek help of their neighbors; Aeneas and his Trojans would be quite helpless in the face of superior numbers if they did not find allies in the vicinity; so the poet manages to interweave many tales of early colonizations and origins. The modern reader, wearied by the catalogue of forces at the end of the seventh book, with its abundance of local legend and personal allusion, must remember the enthusiasm of the Roman reader for these bits from the archives of early Italian history.

The poet's art, however, is shown in so far as he not only satisfies the demand of his audience for local coloring, but employs this material to enrich the artistic effects. A few examples will illustrate this aspect of his work. Primarily, Aeneas' visit to Evander, which occupies the eighth book, serves to inspire the reader's patriotic interest; here is a Greek refugee settled on the site of what is later to be Rome; Aeneas, seeking recruits, is, by a sort of irony, led to seek assistance from this Greek, though Greeks are natural foes of Trojans; Evander has ever been at odds with the Latins and is easily persuaded to help the Trojans against the Latins. The Roman reader followed with interest Aeneas' visit to Evander's home above the Latin settlement and on the Tiber; when he read of the cattle browsing in what was later the Roman forum, his pride was stirred, much as is the Bostonian's in recalling the

days when Boston Common was a cow pasture. The legend of
Cacus and Hercules, the details of the rites of Hercules familiar to every Roman, the settlement of Pallanteum, which became the Roman Palatine, an abundance of local allusion to
persons and places and customs, make this eighth book a depository of early Roman legend, and peculiarly dear to the
Roman patriot, however it may drag in our perusal of it today. But Virgil is not content to let it serve this purpose only;
immediately the situation yields further benefits to the structure and content of the poem. Aeneas, to obtain Evander's
help, sails up the Tiber, leaving his Trojans in their encamp-
ment by the river; at once the enemy, under Turnus, take
advantage of the hero's absence and attack the camp; in the
engagement that follows the poet is enabled, by the absence
of Aeneas from the scene, to introduce to us a number of
other heroes whose prominence in the action would be less
natural if Aeneas himself were on the scene; thereby we get a
full account of the prowess of Turnus, the chief antagonist,
and our interest in, and admiration of him is aroused in the
ninth book so that we follow his adventures to the end with
sympathetic appreciation; and a number of lesser chieftains
on both sides are made familiar to us in this book, and consequently appear as old friends in the action of the later books.
All this is made possible by Aeneas' visit to Evander; that
absence of the hero serves an artistic purpose comparable to
the anger of Achilles in the *Iliad;* Homer, by letting Achilles
sulk in his tent, gives himself an opportunity to set before us
other Greek chieftains as men of prowess; if Achilles were in
the midst of the fray, their bravery would necessarily be
diminished by the greater achievements of the Greek champion. Again, not only the structure of the action, but the
pathetic content, is affected by the visit to Evander. Evander
is represented as an aged man, too old for active co-operation;
he sends his troops to help Aeneas, but puts in charge of them

his young son, Pallas. Pallas was in tradition a grandson of
Evander, and history supplied the suggestion of pathos by recounting his premature death. Virgil, emphasizing the connection of his name, Pallas, with Pallanteum, and so with the
later Palatine, and making him a son of Evander and a Sabine
mother, of Greek and native Italian origin, suggests to the
Roman reader that Pallas is an ideal type of the later Roman
youth, and the premature and tragic death of the young fellow in the war, which Aeneas views with special indignation
and horror because of his responsibility as a sort of guardian
over this young heir of the aged Evander, is made to enrich
the pathetic effects of the battle scenes even up to the duel at
the very end of the poem. In this respect, then, the trip to
Evander is used to contribute a specially pathetic figure to the
action and to enrich the content of the later books.

A second auxiliary force is furnished Aeneas by the Etruscans, to whom Evander refers Aeneas and whom Aeneas visits
after leaving Evander. Again, primarily, the Etruscan allies
serve to increase the Trojan forces and to make plausible the
fact that Trojans and Latins are evenly matched. Secondari-
ly, the Etruscan alliance gives Virgil a chance to symbolize
neatly future developments in the relations between Rome
and Etruria; the Etrurians are without a king; the Etruscan
allies, therefore, by divine will, as explained by the seers, are
committed to the leadership of Aeneas; thus we have reported
as a decree of Fate in ancient times what actually was to be
attained only after centuries and with great difficulty—the
subjection of Etruria to Roman power. But important as this
primary and secondary purpose of the Etruscan alliance may
be, the modern reader is more impressed by the subsidiary
artistic contribution which the Etruscan material makes to
the poem. From it develop the picturesque catalogue of Etruscan forces which, as a catalogue of ships, reflects the famous
catalogue in the second book of the *Iliad;* the journey of

Aeneas by sea from Etruria, which relieves the monotony of the narrative; but, more particularly, several significant characters who add to the interest of the battle scenes. One of these is the bold, determined cavalryman, Tarchon; but more especially, the unique figure of the Etruscan king, Mezentius: he is an ally, not of Aeneas, but of the Latins, alienated from his own people by his tyrannical government of them. Thus a striking situation is introduced, made even more striking by the peculiar force of Mezentius' character. In the current tradition of Virgil's own time, Mezentius co-operated with his people against Aeneas, but an earlier story contained some hints of a visit of Aeneas to the Etruscan city of Agylla or Caere, and of some connection between the Trojan hero and the Etruscan captains, Tarchon and Tyrrhenus. So far as we can see, Virgil combined the two versions, left Mezentius isolated from his people and on the side of Turnus, and made the Etruscans as a people the friends of Aeneas, not as allies on an independent footing, but only as subordinate to Aeneas' leadership. By this means Mezentius, whose tyranny and impiety were well-known facts of history, is put in a situation where his traditional characteristics are greatly vivified and strengthened; his traditional arrogance is increased by the situation which brings his own people into direct and active hostility toward himself; and the one soft spot in his hard nature, his passionate love for his son, Lausus, probably already suggested in the historical account, is made even more pathetic by the peculiar isolation of the Etruscan king from his own subjects.

So, in expanding his material, Virgil considered not merely the patriotic interests of his readers, but the artistic needs of his poem. This expansion was even more necessary in the treatment of the four battle scenes; here history was content with a bare outline; Virgil had to make effective and varied scenes. His method is characteristic. His energy was directed simply toward selecting from the *Iliad* the main motives in Homer's descriptions of the battles before Troy and adapting them to the situation of his own poem. Only occasionally, as in the cavalry battle of the eleventh book, with the unique figure of the young Amazon, Camilla, did he venture to depart from his Homeric model.

Having condensed and expanded the material of tradition, Virgil confronted the task of distributing, of disposing this newly molded mass through the six books which were to balance the first half of the poem. His artistic aims in this distribution may be comprehended in the two words, symmetry and variety. One may well suspect that his interest in these two effects was stimulated by a consciousness that Homer, to whom he owed much of his material, was singularly oblivious of the need of any artistic form or of any relief from monotonous repetitions. The poet of the *Iliad* has no conception of short unified chapters of action organized into a unified whole, and Homer's public never resented the monotonous recurrence of battle scenes with their reckless repetition of motives; Virgil's audience was surfeited; it required the variety which nerves tired by centuries of experience naturally crave, and Virgil himself, apart from his audience, was too sensitive to the artistic advantage of well-constructed narrative to indulge in Homeric repetition and monotony.

Symmetry was probably not very difficult to secure. The first two books contain action preliminary to the active warfare; the last four are devoted each to a significant chapter, an important engagement, of the war. Book vii describes the outbreak of the war; Book viii, the trip of Aeneas to Evander and to the Etruscans; Book ix, the fight between Turnus and the Trojans in Aeneas' absence; Book x, the return of Aeneas and the first main engagement; Book xi, the truce and cavalry fight; Book xii, the decisive duel.

But the danger of monotony was a serious one, and most

threatening in the last four books devoted to the battles of the war. Virgil's dramatic sense devised easily the main outline; Turnus was given the rôle of chief antagonist; once that was determined, the end of the action was inevitable: it must be marked by the death of Turnus; nor could his death come, as it did in tradition, in the general mêlée; he must meet death at the hands of Aeneas; no doubt the critical conflict between Hector and Achilles in the *Iliad* forced itself upon Virgil's attention. Once this conclusion was determined, all that preceded, according to Virgil's principles of art as we have seen them constantly realized in the first six books, could serve only as retarding factors delaying the main issue; these retarding chapters must be made significant and richly varied. Such a structure necessitated a further departure from tradition: the death of Mezentius must precede the fate of Turnus. But otherwise the poet was quite free. He uses the absence of Aeneas to set the figure of Turnus in a halo of splendid achievement in Book ix; here Turnus plays the rôle of Hector; the attempt to burn the ships, the battle at the wall, the fight in camp—these are the three essential phases of the fights in Books xii–xv of the *Iliad,* where Hector is protagonist; in throwing all the light upon Turnus the description of the fight of the two armies as large wholes is limited; such mass fighting is deferred to later books. Into this description of Turnus' feats the poet weaves the episode of Nisus and Euryalus, suggested by the tenth book of the *Iliad;* the feats of Turnus bracket this episode. In Book x, before the fight begins, we have rest and relief in the assembly of the gods, a theme which similarly introduces five books of the *Iliad;* there follows in this book the first general massacre, in which, on the Trojan side, Pallas falls by the hand of Turnus, an incident which is ultimately responsible for Turnus' death at the hands of Aeneas; so Hector's greatest achievement, in Book xvi of the *Iliad,* is ultimately the cause of his death; on the Latin side Lausus and his father, Mezentius, are the important victims of the fight; the duel between Aeneas and Turnus is deferred by the phantom Aeneas sent down by Juno, the theme of *Iliad* xxi. Book xi opens with peaceful scenes again, in camp and city; then a second day of fighting, from which the protagonists Aeneas and Turnus are absent; the unique figure of Camilla stands in the foreground, the cavalry battle is fought in a fashion peculiar to itself, the influence of the *Iliad* is not apparent. Book xii also opens without any active hostility; there are the preparations for the duel, the solemn compact, and the violation of it, all suggested by the third and fourth books of the *Iliad;* then another general fight, modeled on Books xx–xxii of the *Iliad*, leading to the duel and final catastrophe, itself affected by the duel between Hector and Achilles.

This summary sketch will suffice to show both the general relation to the *Iliad* and the poet's success in minimizing repetitions; if there are any similar incidents in the battle scenes, they are carefully separated from each other by scenes of a different sort. And such similar incidents are few; in the main there is great variety; individual achievement varied with mass fighting; a cavalry contest to relieve the monotony of the more frequent infantry engagements; peaceful scenes interrupting active hostility; and above all, the constant dramatic progress toward the catastrophe. In all of this choice and arrangement of motives there is the frankest and fullest dependence upon Homer, but in each chapter of Homeric material Virgil's characteristic remodeling is apparent.

The induction of the war in Latium is managed in a succession of scenes of great power which intentionally recall corresponding scenes at the opening of the poem, the storm at sea in which Aeneas found himself involved at the beginning of the first book. There the action began with a monologue in the mouth of the hostile divinity, Juno, explaining her enmity toward the Trojans and deep-seated aversion to the apparent good fortune of the hero, Aeneas; then she sought the help of Aeolus, the god of the winds, who willingly released the storm winds; Aeneas and the Trojans found themselves engulfed and exposed to critical danger, from which Neptune saved them. Here, in the seventh book, Juno beholds with the same angry surprise her enemy, Aeneas, after all the perils of his journey safely landed in Latium at last; here in this book, as in the first, she turns to a divine power under her control to accomplish the destruction of her enemy; and here again her commission is immediately carried out and the injury effected. Virgil intends this apparent repetition; it sharply emphasizes the symmetry of the poem, the perfect balance between the first six and the last six books. But desirable as the repetition may be, he cannot allow it to be mere recurrence of the same theme, of the same situation. His art requires that such a return to the old theme of the first book must be marked by greater force and deeper pathos; this second and last attempt of Juno at vengeance must in every respect be an intensification of the first. This intensification is patent in Juno's monologue of the seventh book as compared with that of the first; hatred of the Trojans, disappointment caused by the mishap to her former plans, mortification, and humiliation—all appear with increased force; just because she foresees the inevitable disaster to her plans, her desire to avenge herself as well and as long as she can knows no bounds. In her own words she contrasts in a splendid antithesis her action in the first book with her new intention:

> . . . . Behold me now
> Outdone by this Aeneas. If so weak
> My own prerogative of godhead be,
> Let me seek strength in war, come whence it will.
> If Heaven I cannot move, on Hell I call.

So she intimates the renunciation of her former agent, the god of the winds; in place of a peaceful ruler, the guest of Jove at Olympian banquets, there comes the terror of the lower world, the fury, Allecto, who drives men to madness; in place of the elements of nature, the storm winds let loose by Aeolus, comes the passion of mortal men let loose and kindled to raging madness by Allecto, the frenzy of human beings that accomplishes more than the elements of nature ever can. Virgil and his contemporaries knew what war meant; they had lived through a century which taught them that war is hell, that its power could be concretely visualized only in the person of one of the direful agents of the underworld; all the bitterness of an age cursed by civil war breathes in the poet's description of Allecto, Juno's newly chosen agent:

> Allecto, woeful power, from cloudy throne
> Among the furies, where her heart is fed
> With horrid wars, wrath, vengeance, treason foul,
> And fatal feuds. Her father Pluto loathes
> The creature he engendered, and with hate
> Her hell-born sister-fiends the monster view.
> A host of shapes she wears, and many a front
> Of frowning black brows viper-garlanded.
> Juno to her this goading speech addressed:
> "O daughter of dark night, arouse for me
> Thy wonted powers and our task begin. . . . .
>   . . . . Thou canst thrust on
> Two loving brothers to draw sword and slay
> And ruin homes with hatred, calling in
> The scourge of furies and avenging fires.
> A thousand names thou bearest, and thy ways
> Of ruin multiply a thousandfold.
> Arouse thy fertile breast. Go, rend in twain
> This plighted peace. Breed calumnies and sow
> Causes of battle till yon warrior hosts
> Cry out for swords and leap to gird them on!"

Only one who understands the utter aversion to war in Virgil's time can appreciate Virgil's reason for representing it as the

work of Allecto; it is an act of madmen to violate the sanctity
of peace. The issues that the fury's activity engenders justify
the choice of her as a competent agent of Juno's intensified
anger and vengeance. She directs her power against three
different individuals; the queen, Amata, is her first victim:

> From her Stygian hair the fiend
> A single serpent flung which stole its way
> To the queen's very heart, that, frenzy-driven,
> She might on her whole house confusion pour.
> Upon Turnus next she hurls her firebrand.
> . . . . Thrusting deep
> Beneath his heart her darkly smouldering flame.
> Then horror broke his sleep and fearful sweat
> Dripped from his every limb. He shrieked aloud
> For arms; and seized the ready arms that lay
> Around his couch and hall. Then o'er his soul
> The lust of battle and wild curse of war
> Broke forth in angry power, as when the flames
> Of faggots round the bubbling cauldron sing,
> And up the waters leap, the close-kept flood
> Brims over, streaming, foaming, breaking bound,
> And flings thick clouds in air.

So in the innocent killing of the pet deer by Ascanius the mischievous fury blows the horn to summon the countryside to
witness the wrong thus done to one of their pets, and the
sturdy rustics throng to battle inspired by the fury who
crouches in the silent forest. The mad tumult breaks out in
three places at once; from the unconnected sequence of three
different events the poet forms a unity by means of the single
figure of the fury, Allecto; behind her, re-emphasizing the
unity of the action, is the will of a single divinity, Juno. The
fury has achieved her task; she has "dyed the day with deep
ensanguined hue"; in proud insolence she flies skyward to
report to Juno her duty done: "See, at thy will, their strife
full-blown to war and woe." The poet could not have more
grandly conceived or more splendidly executed the induction

of his new theme, war, its hell-inspired beginnings; he knew its torments by his own bitter experience.

The details of Allecto's activity in carrying out Juno's orders are managed with equal skill. Her first victim is Amata, the queen, in whom Allecto infuses madness by flinging at her a snaky lock of hair; the deeply venomed sting spreads poison through the queen's body. Amata wanders crazed through the public ways from town to town after first vainly attempting to influence the king against the marriage of Aeneas and Lavinia by a casuistical explanation of the oracle which seems to support the king in his determination. As the madness of the queen increases like a consuming fever, she becomes a Maenad, raging through the woods and carrying her daughter, Lavinia, with her. She hides her daughter in the woods, apparently intending to dedicate her to the service of the god Bacchus. The frenzy of the queen is communicated to the other women of Latium; they, too, fly to the forests: "They leave behind their desolated hearths, and let rude winds o'er neck and tresses blow; their voices fill the welkin with convulsive shriek and wail. . . . ." The general result is that Lavinia is removed from the king's reach, and the women of the whole country are aroused against the marriage; later we learn that this mad fury of the women is communicated to the men. So a suitable means has been found to spread the war fever through all Latium.

Allecto has begun her demoniacal work with the action that can have the least immediate effect and requires the longest time for its development; once started, however, the slow movement of the general frenzy is sure and far-reaching; for the time being it simply delays the carrying out of Latinus' intention to marry Lavinia to Aeneas. Allecto now turns to the real and immediate motive of the war, the Rutulian prince, Turnus, Lavinia's rejected suitor. To him the fury appears in his sleep, assuming the form of a priestess of Juno; she flatters

him with words excellently devised to rouse his manly pride
and sense of honor, mentioning Juno herself, under whose
orders she is working. Turnus rejects her counsel; then the
fury, in anger, appears in her true form and thrusts a torch
into his breast; he starts up from his sleep, bathed in sweat,
and from that time on the demoniacal fire burns within him.

Turnus calls his Rutulians to arms with the immediate
purpose of emphatically dissuading Latinus from the new
alliance with the Trojans. A peaceful arrangement would still
have been possible. Allecto knows that the breach is made
permanent only if blood flows, and so she crowns her work by
a third attack of frenzy. Trojans and Latins must fight together, but it is desirable that the beginning of the fight start
on the Trojan side. For if the Latins fancy themselves injured
they can drive King Latinus to war; but if they themselves
begin the fight, they can hardly appear before the throne of
the king with a just cause. Again, tradition had already represented the Trojans as the offending party in the conflict; their
predatory incursions into Latin territory, according to the historical narrative, had been the direct cause of the war. The
action, however, that is now developed has always been severely criticized; even as early as the centuries immediately
following the publication of the *Aeneid* Roman critics abused
the poet for devising incidents that were in themselves trivial
and puerile. This criticism has a certain validity, but such
objections show a lack of sympathy with the poet in meeting
his problem; it must be remembered that he felt obliged, for
the reasons we have stated, to make the Trojans the aggres-
sors; on the other hand, the Trojan offense had to be made as
mild and innocent as possible so that they, as the heroes of the
action, should not be put entirely in the wrong, though at the
same time they must give their Latin foes a reasonable justification for resentment and a proper desire for vengeance.
Under these conditions Virgil very skilfully makes the fault

of the Trojans as slight as possible, but motivates successfully
the exasperation of the Latins. The madness of Amata has
stirred the city folk; the undisciplined hordes of the countryside, who follow the momentary impulse of passion without
mature deliberation, are now aroused to action. The wrong
which incites them to take the offensive is not robbery or audacious violence, but simply mortification, in which the apparent offender, Ascanius, is quite guiltless. Allecto causes
him to wound mortally in the chase a tame deer, the pet of an
estimable family, the family of Tyrrhus. It is significant that
Allecto does not inspire Ascanius with any such frenzy as she
has inspired in Amata and Turnus; the young son of Aeneas,
dear to the gods and to the Roman people, cannot be pictured
as the victim of the fury; it is the hounds of the young hunts-
man who are maddened by Allecto to attack the deer; Ascanius, passionately interested in the hunt as were the Romans
generally in Virgil's time, catches sight of the animal, and
stimulated by a desire to win distinction, gives chase. The
young daughter of Tyrrhus is the first to see her pet wounded;
she bursts into violent lamentation and calls the country people to her aid; the impulse, therefore, again comes from a
woman, recklessly giving vent to her grief; Allecto takes care
that the excitement spreads; she blows a signal on the shepherd's horn "out-flinging her infernal note so far that all the
forest shuddered and the grove throbbed to its deepest glen."
The poet insists that it is no mere rustic brawl with charred
oak-staff and cudgel, but a true fight with naked steel in which
the Trojans from the camp join heartily, rushing to the aid
of the young offender. The victims are chiefly Latins, among
them Tyrrhus' eldest son. The scantily equipped country
folk are no match for the expert Trojans; the shedding of
blood calls for revenge.

Thus, with gradual intensification of the theme and action, in highly artistic fashion, Allecto achieves her design;

now that the trouble is started there is no further need of the demon's help; once discord has sprung up among men it grows into war by an inner necessity. The three distinct streams of the war-craze unite in the palace of King Latinus; in vain the weak old man tries to stem them; the poet sees to it that Latinus is left isolated in his opposition to the war; the waves of the tumultuous frenzy for revenge sweep over him. The real outbreak, however, requires some concrete visualization. An earlier poet, Ennius, had figuratively referred to the opening of war as Juno's opening of war's iron-bound temple doors; this figure Virgil makes over into an actual occurrence, all the more vivid to the Roman reader of Virgil's day because at that time an actual opening of the gates of such a temple was a regular and solemn procedure at the beginning of a war. And the action here becomes the dignified prototype of the regular custom in Virgil's time in so far as the goddess Juno herself, instead of the still reluctant king, opens the gates with her own hands. So at the end we are reminded that all this action issues from a single and divine source, the hostile divinity intent upon Aeneas' destruction: "Then from the skies the Queen of gods stooped down, and her sole hand the lingering portal moved; Saturnia swung on their hinges the barred gates of war."

War once declared, the poet completes his seventh book with a catalogue of the prominent Latin leaders, doubtless suggested by the catalogue in the second book of the *Iliad,* but happily lacking the dryness of the Homeric list. Mezentius heads the list, as Moloch the pageant of devils in Milton, and the warrior-virgin, Camilla—the purple folds of her royal scarf, her dark hair caught in a golden clasp, her quiver and spear—surrounded by admiring youths and grave matrons, rounds out the book in a peaceful and picturesque conclusion. Virgil was describing the enemies of his hero, but these enemies were the friends and allies of the Romans of his own day.

He succeeds in presenting them as stalwart warriors, whose defeat redounds to the credit of his hero; at the same time he wins for them the respect and admiration of his readers, who know them as essential elements in the organization of the Roman empire. Incidentally he uses the list to relate local legends and in every way to arouse pride in the resources of early Italy.

The same patriotic appeal is the burden of the eighth book. Technically it provides the absence of Aeneas, and makes possible the ninth book as a full exploitation of the prowess of Turnus. But in itself it stands quite apart from all the other books of the poem in being devoted to a celebration of early conditions in the eternal city. It calls up constantly associations dear to every Roman, details of topography, legend, and cult. It may be implied, in the elaborate genealogy which Evander furnishes, that this Greek settlement on the future site of Rome symbolizes the incorporation of Greek power in the developed Roman empire, though this intention is not strongly emphasized. If this implication is part of the poet's conscious purpose, it would harmonize with the equally implicit suggestion of the latter portion of the eighth book and the beginning of the tenth book, in which the readiness with which Aeneas is constituted the leader of Etruscan forces doubtless anticipates the later absorption of Etruria under Roman domination.

But in the main the Roman reader was interested in the details. From an artistic standpoint the poet has no such opportunities for dramatic organization into effective units as he enjoyed and employed elsewhere in his epic. His skill lies in the variety of ways in which he manages to bring before his Roman reader the facts that will stir his patriotic feeling. Aeneas finds Evander engaged in celebrating a festival in honor of Hercules' destruction of Cacus, the cattle thief. The procedure of the festival and the story of the heroic exploit

arise naturally from the situation. The king escorts Aeneas
to the palace, and in natural converse relates the early history
of the region. An interlude introduces Venus and Vulcan, the
forging of armor for Aeneas, and vigorous description of Vulcan's workshop. The narrative returns to Evander, who, in
dialogue, prepares Aeneas for the trip to Etruria and promises
Pallas and meager forces as allies to Aeneas. A sign from
heaven announces the panoply of armor that Vulcan has devised. The heroes depart for Etruria, and the armor descends
from heaven just before they meet their Etruscan friends.
The ornament upon the shield reveals the future history of
Rome down to Virgil's own time, and through the description
of it the poet, varying his technique, obtains another opportunity to rejoice his readers with stories of Roman exploits.
To Aeneas these were "destined mighty deeds of all his sons."
To the reader they were achievements of a glorious past.

These achievements are even more clearly foreshadowed
in the four following books of the poem, in which Virgil's
audience found their ancestors initiating the long succession
of successful wars that issued in the foundation of the Roman
empire. Of the four battles here presented, two, those of the
ninth and the twelfth books, were adaptations of Homeric
battle scenes in the *Iliad,* and we have analyzed them above[1]
in the discussion of Homeric epic. The fight *en masse* in the
tenth book and the cavalry battle of the eleventh book are
Virgil's own creations.

The battle of the ninth book centers interest in a single
hero, Turnus. It provides a relatively simple structure, like
that of a drama with a single plot; a drama with a double
plot, with major and minor action, complicates an artist's
problems. This complex structure differentiates the battle of
the tenth book from that of the ninth. In the tenth book
Aeneas returns from Evander and his visit to Etruria with

[1] Cf. pp. 191 ff., 196 ff.

his new Arcadian and Etruscan allies, and the engagement becomes a more general one. The battle becomes in part an exploiting of Aeneas' achievements as a warrior; he is the hero of the book but Turnus is still more or less in the foreground; the poet tries to keep them both prominent without bringing them together in a decisive duel, which, as the climax of the action, has to be postponed to the final book. But there are other significant and critical phases of the action of this second engagement: the death of Pallas, son of Evander, and Aeneas' special protégé; and on the Latin side, the death of Mezentius, the sturdy Etruscan tyrant. Again the poet constructs a dramatic narrative tending toward the death of Mezentius, as the main catastrophe of the book, and with irregular rise and fall of action in the intervening chapters. In this case, however, the stricter unity and coherence that were possible in the ninth book, by making all the action issue from, and lead up to, Turnus, are no longer available; the poet has to invest Aeneas as well as Turnus with distinguishing qualities, and at the same time interest us in a number of minor heroes, without whom the action of the battle scene would be unrealistic and monotonous.

Virgil starts with the renewal of the attack on the camp and with a description of the critical condition of its few defenders; then he recounts Aeneas' homeward journey, inserting a catalogue of the Etruscan ships, allies of Aeneas; this catalogue balances the enumeration of Latin auxiliaries at the end of the seventh book. The fleet is met by the nymphs, into whom the ships of the Trojans burned by Turnus at the beginning of the ninth book had been transformed, and one of them, Cymodocea, informs Aeneas of the plight of his Trojan forces on land; through her we learn also that the Arcadian cavalry and part of the Etruscan allies of Aeneas have already landed from the ships and taken up a definite position. At this point the poet diverts our attention from Aeneas to the

Trojan camp; from this new point of view we witness the
landing of Aeneas. The purpose in so shifting our attention is
to visualize better the impression which Aeneas' landing
makes upon the Trojans; we see it through their eyes. The
Trojans catch sight of Aeneas; their shouts of joy and renewed courage cause the Latins to turn round and see the
ships of Aeneas' new fleet turned toward the shore. Turnus,
undismayed by this situation, faces his troops toward the
newly arrived forces. The landing follows, and an account of
the battle at the landing. In this account there comes at first,
properly enough, a succession of feats of arms in which
Aeneas is prominent. Naturally Aeneas would seek out Turnus, his main antagonist, but that conflict is the ultimate catastrophe of the entire poem; the poet has to arrange events
so that this catastrophe shall be postponed; sometimes his
motivation of the postponement is forced. While Aeneas is at
the full tide of success three minor leaders of the enemy appear and check his advance, Clausus, Halaesus, and Messa
pus; the fight comes to a standstill; the poet then transfers
us to another part of the battlefield, where the Arcadian allies
of Aeneas under Pallas are in full retreat before the onset of
the Latins; here begins that action which in its logical issue
leads to the final catastrophe of the poem. It is the death of
Pallas which stimulates Aeneas against Turnus; for Pallas, as
the young son of Evander, in charge of the Arcadian troops,
has come to the aid of the Trojans under Aeneas' special tutelage; when Turnus kills him Aeneas is infuriated. At this
stage of the action Pallas is given a chance to exhibit his
bravery and skill. The immediate effect of his exploits is to
turn the retreat of his Arcadians into a successful forward
movement against the Latins; this, however, is checked by
the forces under Halaesus, whom we met among the three
Latin leaders that stopped Aeneas' advance; after Halaesus
has accomplished enough to prove his worth as an antagonist,

Pallas meets and kills him, thus crowning his own achievements. Pallas' success is again checked by Lausus, the son of Mezentius, who is briefly introduced to us that we may later appreciate his own tragic fate; Lausus cannot hold out against Pallas for any length of time; Turnus comes to his assistance, and now slays Pallas at the height of his success. The exultant victor despoils Pallas of his belt, and the poet marks the critical nature of the action by an epilogue which indicates the effect of the incident upon the future action: "O heart of man, not knowing doom, nor of events to be! Nor, being lifted up, to keep thy bounds in prosperous days! To Turnus comes the hour when he would fain a prince's ransom give had Pallas passed unscathed, and shall bewail such spoil of victory." It is this belt of Pallas, worn henceforth by Turnus, which Aeneas catches sight of in the final scene of the twelfth book; it then revives the memory of Turnus' killing of Pallas, and stops Aeneas in his momentary impulse to spare Turnus' life.

The news of Pallas' death kindles the wrath of Aeneas, whom we left fighting a drawn battle elsewhere in the field; now he presses on victoriously; the second series of his exploits is contrasted with the first by an increased intensity of action, and culminates in a detailed description of the death of two brothers, Lucagus and Liger. The result of Aeneas' heroism is that the besieging party of Latins, who stand between Aeneas' forces and the camp of the Trojans, is broken through. Ascanius and the men in camp are relieved by the arrival of Aeneas and his allies. But Aeneas' immediate purpose was the punishment of Turnus; the meeting between the two antagonists is inevitable so long as both are on the scene; the poet, unable to allow the duel at this point in the action, takes over a theme from the *Iliad* and removes Turnus from the scene; the goddess Juno sends down a phantom Aeneas whom Turnus pursues; thus the main antagonist is temporarily eliminated, and Mezentius comes into the foreground as the chief opponent of Aeneas. Mezentius, by a series of exploits, turns the tide of battle; his feats are crowned by the slaying of Orodes, over whom Mezentius sings a paean of triumph; the poet appends a brief description of the general massacre in which the victors are mostly Latins. So the previous success of Aeneas is counterbalanced by the intervention of Mezentius. The poet in an interlude celebrates the drawn battle: "Thus Mars relentless holds in equal scale slaughters reciprocal and mutual woe; the victors and the vanquished kill or die in equal measure; neither knows the way to yield or fall." The time has come for the final contest of the engagement, the conflict of Aeneas and Mezentius; the poet marks the importance of it by a description of the awe-inspiring Etruscan king:

> On strode Mezentius o'er the gory plain,
> And swollen with rage waved wide his awful spear
> Like tall Orion when on foot he goes
> Through the deep sea and lifts his shoulders high
> Above the waves; or when he takes his path
> Along the mountain-tops, and has for staff
> An aged ash-tree, as he fixes firm
> His feet in earth and hides his brows in cloud—
> So loomed Mezentius with his ponderous arms.

The action of this final contest is again arranged with dramatic rise and fall, and in this case also with enriching pathetic effects that make the scene as a whole one of the finest in the *Aeneid*. Mezentius, confronting Aeneas, threatens to strip his carcass of armor and hang it upon his own son, Lausus. Aeneas, undismayed, hurls his spear and wounds Mezentius. The son, Lausus, whom we met in an earlier scene, the poet celebrates in a brief interlude: "O storied youth, if olden worth may win believing ear, let not my song now fail of thee to sing, thy noble deeds, thy doom of death and pain." Lausus, seeing his father in danger, rushes into the fray, and when Aeneas raises his sword to strike Mezentius, Lausus "faces the thrusting sword and gives the hero pause." The father makes a safe retreat, thanks to his son's intervention. Aeneas, angered, turns upon the son, and in spite of Lausus' mad defense drives his sword into the young fellow's side, "through the tunic fine his mother's hand had wrought with softest gold," as Virgil pathetically adds. Aeneas, touched by the filial devotion which, the poet says, matches his own loyalty to Anchises, groans aloud at his necessary but cruel deed. The body of young Lausus is carried back to where Mezentius stands, staunching his own wound and apprehensive of the danger to which his son is exposed. Lausus' death brings the father back to the fight in a mingled flood of sorrow, wrath, and shame; with gloomy forebodings, tired of life, he mounts his faithful war horse, which carries him forth unharmed through the midst of the deadly shower of weapons hurled by his foes. Aeneas receives spear after spear in his shield, thrown by Mezentius in impotent fury; at last the Trojan hero, wearied of the struggle, plants his spear in the forehead of Mezentius' war horse; the animal rears and plunges, and pins Mezentius beneath him. "Where now is fierce Mezentius," exclaims Aeneas exultingly, "and his soul's wild pulse of rage?" With this splendid effect the tenth book is brought to a conclusion; nothing further is said of the course of the battle; the reader is left to infer that after the most prominent Latin leaders, Turnus, Halaesus, Lausus, Mezentius, are out of the way, the beleaguered Trojans are completely relieved and the fate of the day is decided.

In strong contrast with the complex structure of this general engagement in the tenth book stands the simple movement of the cavalry interlude in the eleventh. It is preceded by descriptions of the burning of the dead on both sides, but with special elaboration of the ceremony over the young Arcadian hero, Pallas. In response to a request from the Latins a twelve days' truce is granted. On the Latin side discontent finds expression in the thought that rightfully the issue of the contest should be decided by a duel between Turnus and Aeneas; thus the theme of the twelfth book is introduced. The demand for peace, or for a decisive duel, Turnus meets with rash confidence and leads his troops to face the oncoming forces of Aeneas with the assertion that he craves the duel with the Trojan hero. The Trojans have sent their cavalry ahead, and when Camilla suggests to Turnus that he withdraw, and let her Volscian cavalry meet the Trojan horse, Turnus readily consents, planning an ambush for the Trojan troops who follow behind the cavalry. Thus the poet leads up to the main engagement of this book; its novelty as a cavalry skirmish is enhanced by the prominence of the young Amazon, Camilla. After the withdrawal of Turnus the poet diverts us to a scene on Olympus, where the goddess Diana in conversation with Opis, one of her attendants, acquaints us with the history of Camilla, with Diana's interest in her, and suggests the tragic issue of the action; Opis is sent to avenge the coming death of Camilla. The advance of the two armies is then described, and the background of Camilla's achievement is provided in an account of the gradual inception of the contest; the action of the masses issues, as usual, in individual achievement; Orsilochus on the Trojan, Catillus on the Latin side are the prominent individuals; from them the transition is made to Camilla, the heroine of the scene. First we get a general description of the young Amazon as she strides through the mêlée; then an account of her separate exploits, concluding with the boldest and strongest achievement, reported in great detail; this is the climax of her success. At once the counteraction sets in; on the Trojan side, Tarchon, the Etruscan cavalry captain, revives the courage of his followers by bold speech and action; one of them, Arruns, conceives the plan of wounding Camilla without meeting her face to face. Camilla's imprudence, neatly motivated by her womanly admiration of the resplendent armor of Chloreus, gives Arruns his opportunity; Camilla falls. Then we pick up the theme of the earlier scene between Diana and Opis; at this point Opis, commissioned to avenge the death of Camilla, shoots Arruns with her arrow. Turnus rushes back to the fight, abandoning his plan of ambuscade, and the retreat of the Latin cavalry is fully described; the book concludes with the statement of the new position of the opposing forces; the Trojans are no longer in their camp by the river, but both forces have pitched their camps before the city walls of Laurentum. The structure of this battle scene is noticeably different from that of the two preceding contests; here we do not conclude with a striking catastrophe, such as the death of Mezentius or the safe escape of Turnus from dire peril. The main action is the prowess and death of Camilla; this is bracketed by scenes which symmetrically correspond; Turnus' withdrawal from the action at the beginning is balanced by his return after the fate of Camilla; the scene between Diana and Opis is resumed in Opis' wounding of Arruns; the description of the advancing hosts just before Camilla's prowess is matched by the retreat of the Latin cavalry at the end. So we get a symmetrical grouping, with the climax and catastrophe in the middle and balanced scenes on either side of the central action. The ultimate effect is that the Trojans are no longer beleaguered in their camp, but assume the offensive outside the walls of Laurentum. The scene is therefore set for the action of the last book; the duel between Aeneas and Turnus may be fought before the city walls in the presence of the two armies, as was the duel of Hector and Achilles in the *Iliad*.

The last book begins with Turnus' agreement to fight with Aeneas and ends with the duel and Turnus' death; the poet's art aims to retard the final issue and thereby to keep in

suspense the reader's expectation. The first hindrance to the
duel comes from Latinus and the queen, Amata, but is quickly
removed; the duel is agreed upon, and the two people gather
to exchange oaths; a new obstacle sets in through Juno's conversation with Juturna, the divine sister of Turnus; the goddess instructs Juturna to avail herself of every opportunity to
prevent the conflict. Already Turnus is losing courage; the
Rutulians are affected by their leader's disinclination; Juturna foments the general discontent; it spreads to the other
detachments of the Latin army; a confusing sign from heav-
en, misinterpreted, leads the augur, Tolumnius, to shoot his
spear into the Trojan forces; it hits one of nine brothers; the
surviving brothers clamor for vengeance; the Latins oppose
them; the brothers are supported by the Trojans and their
allies; a tumult arises about the altar where the oaths are
sworn; Aeneas' sense of honor leads him to check the uprising, but a chance wound removes him from the scene; the
fight begins. The removal of Aeneas revives the courage of
Turnus. So, dramatically and with constant emphasis upon
the psychological content of action, the poet defers the duel
and heightens our interest in the outcome. During Aeneas'
absence Turnus has a new series of exploits more intense than
any in preceding books: in Book ix he fought on foot against
a superior number of his foes; in Book x he was victorious in
a duel with Pallas: now he courses over the field in his chariot,
a veritable god of war, striking down everything before him.
While the main action is thus progressing the poet may return
to Aeneas and the healing of his wound; this, too, is dramatized; Iapyx strives in vain to draw the arrow from the
wound; all the resources of the surgeon's art fail; the din of
battle approaches, clouds of dust darken the air, the enemies'
missiles fall into the camp; then Venus intervenes, not with
her own hand, but by dropping a miraculous liquor into the
water with which the wound is being washed; Iapyx, unsus-

pecting, washes the wound; the arrow follows his hand easily; the blood is stayed; the pain disappears; Aeneas returns to the fight. His arrival changes the course of events. He is bent on meeting Turnus, but somewhat deterred by his sense of honor from stimulating the general contest. The duel seems imminent; again Juturna intervenes with retarding action; she tries to save Turnus; Aeneas, anxious to preserve the terms of the compact, is finally driven by the attack of Messapus to disregard the agreement. The poet now gives us an account of the prowess of Aeneas and of Turnus in common until at last they approach each other. So, through these last four books, the poet has successfully created the illusion of a magnetic attraction which draws closer together the main antagonists; in Books viii and ix both were active in very different situations; in Book x they fought on the same battlefield without collision, though mutually desirous to meet; in Book xii, so far, we have heard of them alternately only at considerable intervals; now one deals blow on blow upon the other in the inevitable collision to which all the previous action has been tending. The poet directs the action so that Turnus is spared the pain of being overtaken by Aeneas and forced into the conflict. The queen, Amata, no longer seeing Turnus active, and discouraged by the turn of events, commits suicide; this throws the Latins into turmoil; the news of the death of the queen (which the reader will note is a clever way of getting rid of a character who must be eliminated before the final issue that she has steadfastly opposed) and other discouraging details arouse Turnus to action; he voluntarily faces his enemy; the last great scene of the poem begins.

The duel is fought in the same three phases as those of the Homeric duel between Achilles and Hector, but skilfully rearranged by the Latin poet. First he describes the general attitude of the spectators; then, after one shot with spears, a

longer indecisive sword fight; then an interlude, with change
of scene to Olympus, where the lots of the two heroes are
weighed by Jupiter. The second phase begins with the breaking of Turnus' sword; nothing is left for him but flight, which
protects him for a long time, since Aeneas is hindered by his
wound from close pursuit; while Aeneas vainly strives to pull
his spear from the trunk of a tree, Juturna hands Turnus his
sword; so they face each other, newly armed; the result is
again uncertain. Once more the poet transfers us to Olympus;
there Jupiter, stimulated by Juturna's interference, intervenes and persuades Juno to renounce her hatred of Aeneas;
peace is concluded in heaven. Thus the only remaining obstacle is removed; the poem began with Juno's anger; it can
be removed only at the latest possible moment; Turnus' death
is only the expression on earth of Juno's renunciation; as a
reward for Juno's submission Jupiter promises that Latium
shall come to its rights in the new alliance; Juno's labors and
struggles have not been entirely in vain. Jupiter despatches
the fury, Dira, to fly, birdlike, in Turnus' face and indicate to
him and his sister Juturna the ill will of the gods. So the third
phase of the duel is introduced; Turnus is dazed with fear;
Juturna abandons her brother; both know the gods are against
them. Turnus gives up fighting with the sword and makes a
last frantic effort with a stone; his strength is not equal to the
throw; he looks about him in despair; Aeneas' spear strikes
him down. To the very end Virgil maintains his regard for
dramatic suspense. A feeling of pity arises in Aeneas' breast;
there is a glimmer of hope for Turnus; but that rising feeling
is quickly extinguished when Aeneas sees upon Turnus the
belt stolen from the body of young Pallas. "In this thy mortal
wound 'tis Pallas has a victim; Pallas takes the lawful forfeit
of thy guilty blood."

The succession of four books, one-third of the entire
poem, is thus relieved from monotony by the infinite variety

of the poet's artistic aims and achievement. Homeric as many of the situations may be, the art is Virgilian. There is none of the looseness and incoherence, the touch-and-go of Homeric battle scenes, but everywhere concentration, dramatic structure, compactness, and clearness. This structure of action, however, is the merest mechanism; the machinery of drama, setting in effective motion the normal peaceful narrative of epic, may be—undoubtedly is—Virgil's great contribution to the development of epic poetry; but such machinery only changes epic narrative from a dead level to a shifting gradation of rise and fall ending in climax and catastrophe. Without the interplay of strong human characters, of rich emotional incident, the result would be mere mechanical perfection. We have yet to see the poet's art in visualizing for us the warriors of these dramatic scenes; here neither Homer nor tradition could stimulate his imagination, though tradition occasionally furnished some inspiration; Pallas, Nisus, Euryalus, Lausus, Mezentius, Camilla, as well as the two chief antagonists, are Virgil's creations; we may fitly conclude our account of the poet's art with the consideration of what he has accomplished in the making of characters suited to the heroic action of the battle scenes of his epic.

X. THE CHARACTERS OF THE AENEID

Any discussion of character treatment in ancient literature is likely to mislead a modern reader unless at the outset certain conspicuous differences between modern and ancient practice and theory are made perfectly clear. Generally speaking, the subtlety and delicacy of modern character drawing were not realized by ancient writers; nor did they interest themselves in character development. Modern literature delights to present the evolution of character, to watch the effect of outer action upon the inner self; we desire to see each step of a gradual development, and in the drama, for example, we are accustomed to a complete change in the inner self of the hero and heroine wrought by dramatic action; normally the practice today is to represent an individual as possessing at the outset some one quality in excess, ambition, for example; that dominant quality differentiates that individual from the rest of the world; the literary artist, then, by the contact of that individual with other persons and with events, represents a change, sometimes a regular evolution, in the character of the individual; so, if it be a tragedy, the dominant quality of ambition may be stimulated by outer events and lead to a dramatic climax and tragic catastrophe; or if it be a novel, outer action and the free interplay of the individual with other persons and with the vicissitudes of life may discipline the individual and mitigate his dominant quality. This modern interest in character growth has brought with it the refinements of characterization in our modern literature; we have come to demand that each character shall be differentiated by individualizing traits, and our modern speculative tendency has led to an increasing fondness for careful psychological study of character in play and story which not infrequently is exalted above the coherent structure of action; character, as well as action, is important in the realization of the modern artist's aims; broadly speaking, ancient literature exalts action; it does not neglect character, but such individualizing of persons as there may be is on broad and simple lines.

This relative neglect of individualization in ancient literature is mainly a reflection of contemporary social conditions. The so-called "city-state," contrary to most modern organizations, emphasizes the complete absorption of the individual in the large corporation. In such an atmosphere, if humanity ever becomes an object of study and thought, the first emphasis will be upon the race as a whole, or upon large groups and classes, rather than upon the individual man. But if the city-state ever changes to an organization which gives freer play to individual initiative, the study of humanity will begin to emphasize the individual man. This change from the city-state to a less circumscribed form of government actually took place in ancient life, notably in Greece, when Alexander conquered the city-states and established a monarchy; then individualism began to develop; and in the art of that Hellenistic period we see the inception in literature of a greater interest in the individual; individualizing of characters is frequent, the delineation, for example, in comedy, often delicate, but it still remains rather elementary, particularly in the older and more sublime literary types such as tragedy and epic. Virgil is in the current of this later Greek tradition; we shall not be surprised to find in his treatment of character a certain amount of skilful delineation of some individual traits combined with a broader and simpler characterization. He represents, on the whole, a rather high degree of accomplishment if one considers the artistic ideals of his day.

These generalizations are sound, but for fear of misrepresentation they may be qualified by a few remarks on the practice of various poets. The old Homeric epic well illustrates the complete subordination of character, of psychology, to action; it is perfectly clear that Homer in general has his eye upon the outer action, upon what is achieved upon the battlefield or in the midst of perils on land and sea. His relative indifference to character as the mainspring of action is often illustrated by his employment of stereotyped epithets; so, for instance, he is quite capable of calling a hero great-souled in the midst of some action which reveals that hero as anything but magnanimous. Yet, generally true as this is, there are traces of fine characterization even in Homer; nothing could be better than the delineation of Agamemnon, Ajax, and Achilles in the eleventh *Odyssey*. It is so good that some modern scholars deny that Homer could have done it. In Greek tragedy of the fifth century, though supernatural forces are very visible as ordering man's destiny, it is a mistake to say that individual freedom, and consequently individualization of character, are entirely obliterated by this superiority of fate. On the other hand, though strong and consistent characterization is found in Greek tragedy, the moral qualities and emotions are of a broadly human, rather than of a distinctly personal sort; again the city-state is shaping literary art; religion, the state, the family were the real things in the experience of fifth-century Athens; the tragedy of that century is content to make patriotism, devotion of wife and sister, simple elementary emotions, impel characters to action. The terrible inner discord, the purely personal passions, of modern literature are missing except in Euripides, who anticipates to some extent later developments. Only in the subsequent centuries just before the birth of Christ do we get, consistently, intimations of the consuming modern interest in the inner life; introspection now becomes more of a habit; Hellenistic poetry delighted in the portrayal of lovestricken men and women, though this was mainly an emotional disturbance without any artistic regulation; moral qualities, too, were emphasized in Hellenistic comedy, though there becoming rather stereotyped in typical forms; the conceit of soldiers, the dishonesty of slave dealers, the deceitfulness of slaves, the simplicity of old men are regularly recurring traits defining trades, professions, social classes, and issuing in action; there is still in these cases general, rather than specific, characterization.

The point which literary art had attained before Virgil's day may be further illustrated by two academic discussions of character treatment: the comments of Aristotle in some of his essays, and Horace' poem on the art of poetry. Aristotle evidently regards character as involving moral qualities, and distinguishes between general and individual characterization, emphasizing the latter; Horace, on the contrary, enlarges upon general characterization and disposes of individualization very briefly. What these authorities mean by general and special characterization is clear enough. General characterization amounts simply to representing, for example, old men and young men as being different from each other without distinguishing one individual young man from another; so women must have qualities different from those of men, and Greeks must not resemble Italians.

It is from the standpoint of this ancient theory, with its emphasis upon general characterization, that we may best understand Virgil's achievement in the delineation of persons in his poem. The sum and substance of what we shall now illustrate in some detail is that Virgil, in portraying his characters, emphasizes general traits of character rather than individual qualities; there lies his weakness from a modern standpoint; yet within this broad description of his art we must leave room for a certain amount of clear individualism, and notably in the cases of several of the warriors of the last six books.

To illustrate his emphasis on general traits we may briefly

consider the young men, the old men, the women, of the *Aeneid*. Virgil's sympathetic interest in young men is notable; he loved them; and, like Augustus, saw in them the hope of Rome's continued greatness. Ascanius, Pallas, Nisus, Euryalus, Lausus—they are among the most attractive figures of an epic mainly devoted to the achievements of matured heroic warriors. These five young fellows are in the main alike: they are all ideal types of hopeful, ambitious youth, ready to expose themselves to dangers to which they are not equal. Within this general likeness there is slight individual differentiation. Ascanius has lost his mother at an early age; he has been exposed to hardships in the voyage over sea and land; he has acquired a maturity beyond his years, proficiency in the hunt and on the battlefield; we see him grow from boyhood to youth, and in his final appearance in the ninth book his shot at Numanus marks the beginning of matured power, the god Apollo comes down to admonish him: "Such dawn of glory great Apollo's will concedes . . . . but, tender youth, refrain hereafter from this war." It is this tenderness of youth which Euryalus embodies; he is old enough to compete in the foot race of the fifth book and to participate in the bold enterprise of the sally through the Latin camp in the ninth, but in the fifth book, like a child, he bursts into tears at being threatened with loss of a prize which he has won by Nisus' unsportsmanlike maneuver, and his childish delight in a shining helmet and his general imprudence ruin the effect of the bold sally with Nisus through the Latin camp. Lausus and Pallas have the same terrible thirst for achievement, but they are steadier, less reckless, than Euryalus; Pallas' bravery is exhibited in determined and consistent heroism; Lausus', in filial sacrifice of his life for his father's sake; but the difference is due to situation rather than to any essential variation of character.

Prominent old men are Ilioneus, Nautes, Evander, and

above all, Anchises; speech and action, in their cases, are calm, well-considered, dispassionate, in sharp contrast with the impetuosity of the youngsters. They are directors, admonishers, prone to give others the benefits of their ripe experience and easily led to talk about the good old times; they are endowed with a deeper insight than others into the divine will and the decrees of Fate; Nautes has received this power from the goddess, Minerva; Anchises interprets omens, plays the rôle of prophet on occasion. All these old men are lineal descendants of Homer's Nestor, with all his wisdom and eloquence. Slightly differentiated is the aged king of the Latins, Latinus; he is an ideal king, pious, discreet, generous, gentle, upright; he has one conspicuous defect: he lacks the stiff backbone of consistency and determination; up to old age he has ruled over a peaceful folk; suddenly, when his physical strength is weak, he is exposed to a complicated situation; his family and people oppose him and demand war; he is not equal to the emergency.

The women of the poem are strikingly like one another; their common and almost exclusive trait is excitability; with them every feeling issues quickly in frenzy and passion; passion destroys their balance; when one of them is so affected, the frenzy quickly spreads to others. This emotional excitement is often justified; our present interest is simply in the general attribution of the quality to the sex as its distinguishing trait. Virgil's oft-quoted description of woman as mutable and shifting is exemplified in most of the women of the *Aeneid*. The Trojan women, exhausted by long journeys and perils, are easily stimulated to set fire to the ships in the fifth book, but no sooner do they see their husbands rushing to extinguish the flames than they repent of the deed and begin to loathe life; the women of Latium, supporting the queen, Amata, in her demand that her daughter marry Turnus, rather than Aeneas, and infected with her frenzy for war, join in

bringing about the conflict; but after the first serious defeat
they loudly exclaim against the horrors of war and berate
Turnus and his suit for Lavinia's hand; he should fight a duel
with Aeneas instead of embroiling the whole people. Amata
herself, to be sure, is consistent in her devotion to Turnus'
cause, but it is all a woman's wrath and fear that first inspire
her; she is differentiated only in so far as perhaps every
woman might not be driven to extremes by the fury's goading.
Her supplication of the king, her casuistry in explaining away
the oracle, her insinuation that Aeneas is a faithless adven-
turer the poet himself describes as characteristic of fond
mothers rather than any individual trait of her own. Camilla,
the young Amazon, is not a woman, but a masculine heroine;
yet even in her case the poet motivates her death by a quality
common to her sex; it is a woman's love of finery that leads
her to imprudence. These common limitations of the sex in
Virgil's conception are redeemed, in his portrayal, by a single
virtue: unswerving devotion to family and to kin. This feeling the woman shares, of course, with the virtuous man of the
household, but with him it is a matter of duty; with her it is
part of her being; Euryalus is a tenderly loving son, but his
devotion to his mother cannot keep him from sharing the dangers of a bold exploit with his friend, Nisus; Evander is a
type of the loving father, but he devotes his son, Pallas, to the
service of Aeneas. This love of woman for her kin is variously
manifested; as mother-love in the goddess Venus ever solicit-
ous for her son's safety; in the mother of Euryalus, who forgets all care and anxiety in her work for her son, and in his
loss, loses life itself; in Andromache, who sees in Ascanius the
image of her own Astyanax, and prays that he may miss his
mother, Creusa, for, she thinks, her Astyanax would in like
case have missed her; in Creusa, the wife of Aeneas, whose
last words to her husband remind him of their son, Ascanius;
as sisterly love in Dido and Anna, those sisters with a single

soul between them; Anna's first thought at Dido's death is of the sister dearer than life itself, and her first desire that she might have died with her; in Juturna, the divine sister of Turnus, who finds her immortality a burden as soon as her brother is doomed. The love of wife for husband is exemplified in Dido's devotion to Sychaeus and her reunion with him in the after-life, and in Andromache's loyalty to Hector in spite of her matrimonial vicissitudes. And the immutable loyalty of the entire sex the poet pictures in the ninth book, when, as the Trojans press hard upon the city walls of Laurentum, "above in conflict wild even the women, who, for faithful love of home and country schooled them to be brave, ... rained weapons from the walls, ... as if, well-armed in steel, each bosom bold would fain in such defense be first to die."

This sketch of the general characteristics of young men, old men, and women perhaps does sufficient justice to that aspect of Virgil's art which is most open to criticism. It may be granted that he is intent in these cases rather upon qualities common to groups, and distinguishing age and sex, than upon precise individualization. But when we consider the warriors whom he created for the action of the battle scenes in the last six books, there is discernible in several instances a specific characterization which gives to each a differentiating trait. In general these warriors, at least in contrast with the Homeric heroes of the *Iliad*, are conspicuously individualized. Homer's warriors may differ one from another in respect to strength or dexterity or agility or bravery, and these qualities may determine the issue of a contest. But Homer is not concerned with distinguishing the man as an individual; he is content to distinguish him by martial qualities, physical excellence; Virgil, on the contrary, emphasizes the purely human and moral element, even on the battlefield. Nor should we fail to note, however briefly, the manner of his characterization, as well as the content of it; he seldom indulges in direct description of character, though occasionally the action may demand such direct treatment as in Evander's account of Mezentius; he does employ characterizing epithets in Homeric style, but seldom without confirming them in subsequent action; and in general it is through action that character is revealed in the *Aeneid,* or through the speech of the person characterized.

Camilla, the only woman on the field of battle, appeals to the imagination more readily than any other of Virgil's characters. She revels in the fight, is swift of foot, tireless, determined, with easily offended pride, without suspicion of treachery, even in death undismayed and devoted to duty. Her prowess is best shown by the fact that her enemies do not dare to meet her in open combat; one seeks to escape her by treachery, the other kills her from behind and does not venture to approach her even after she has been struck down. But in all her heroism she remains a woman, and a woman's weakness brings on her death, in her desire for the splendid trappings of Chloreus she forgets everything about her and falls a prey to her hidden foe, who had long sought in vain a vulnerable spot; so blinded is she by the object of her pursuit that she alone does not see the fatal spear hurled at her; her faithful Volscians see the harm coming and cannot protect her; she falls into the arms of her companion.

Pallas, the son of Evander and leader of the Arcadian allies of Aeneas, is the ideal youth of the poem. We see his deeds, see how, by word and example, he induces his wavering forces to hold their ground; we recognize in what he says his sense of honor and his piety, which trusts to providence; we admire and regret the youthful daring with which, though conscious of his inferiority, he refuses to avoid the challenge of Turnus, easily his master. To him the life of the blessed on earth is not the highest reward; victory or a glorious death is his highest hope; with the expression of this thought he confronts the Latin champion, Turnus, "glancing up and down that giant frame, and with fierce frowning brows scanned him from far, hurling defiant words." He prays to Hercules before the duel; Hercules intercedes with Jove; but Jove again consoles Hercules with the same thought: "To each his day is given. Beyond recall man's little time runs by; but to prolong life's glory by great deeds is virtue's power." The elaborate description of Pallas' funeral rites at the opening of the eleventh book is not a mere waste of sentimentality on the poet's part; Pallas comes from the site of future Rome; he is the first great victim sacrificed on Italian soil for the sacred cause of Rome; his death is the prototype of the sacrifices of young lives through later Roman history; often in the future, with the same pain and pride, was Rome to mourn her fallen sons.

The pathetic possibilities of such tragic situations are differently realized in Nisus and Euryalus. Here Virgil's interest in character as motivating conduct is more apparent than elsewhere, because the Homeric model of the action in the tenth book of the *Iliad* so entirely neglects the inner impulse and concentrates attention on the mere achievement of the night sally. In Homer, to be sure, the heroes are brave and cautious, but Virgil, from start to finish, relates action to human qualities; the plan of making the bold sally through the Latin camp springs from the ambitious soul of Nisus; Euryalus, his young friend, is determined to accompany him, and his determination overcomes Nisus' consideration for his younger friend. But just this ambition, the motive-power of their bold undertaking, brings disaster upon them; once they are well started on the exploit, desire for spoil tempts to rashness; Nisus restrains the childish imprudence of Euryalus, but is not strong enough to deny him the boyish delight of adorning himself with the spoils of the dead. This gleaming helmet on the head of Euryalus betrays him to the enemy; Nisus forgets everything in his desire to save the life of his friend; both fall, Nisus sacrificing himself for his imprudent companion. The cause of both deaths is the passion of each of the two young heroes; they failed because they subordinated obvious duty to other considerations, but their mistake sprang from noble motives.

Much as character is elaborated in the action of Camilla, Pallas, Nisus, and Euryalus, it is not so sharply individualized as in the case of the maturer warriors, Mezentius, Turnus, and Aeneas. These three are sharply contrasted one with another. The dominant trait of Mezentius was suggested to Virgil by historical tradition; history told of his demanding from the Rutulians the first fruits of the harvest, which were properly dedicated to the gods; whereupon the Rutulians prayed to Jove to grant them victory over Mezentius if he, Jove, wished to receive the offering that belonged to him; in this same tradition the son of Mezentius, Lausus, fell in battle, and it was his death which induced the father to make peace with the Rutulians. The impiety thus suggested by tradition Virgil employs, deftly making over the situation. In Virgil Mezentius is primarily contemptuous of the gods; his only deities are his own right hand and spear; and in his final speech he maintains that he has no fear of death, and would not refrain from attacking the gods themselves if it were necessary. From the historical tradition about his son, Lausus, Virgil developed a particularly close relation between father and son; the affection of Mezentius for Lausus is the only vulnerable spot in his otherwise hard nature; the son returns this affection, and his death becomes in Virgil a voluntary sacrifice in defense of his father; to heighten sympathy for his self-sacrifice, Lausus is made a bright ideal figure, in sharp contrast with his stern and gloomy father: "Worthy he to serve a nobler sire," the poet says, "and happier far if he had ne'er been born Mezentius' son." But, departing entirely from tradition, Virgil has represented Mezentius, king of the Etruscans, as separated from his own people in the war; the Etrus-

cans fight on the side of Aeneas; Mezentius is himself an ally
of Turnus; to explain this separation the poet adopts the fiction that Mezentius, as a grim tyrant, was expelled from his
own land for his violent acts; in this regard Virgil apparently
has used a traditional characteristic of early Etruscan kings,
who are regularly supposed to have been savage buccaneers.
The antagonism between Mezentius and his own people becomes an effective means of setting in sharp relief his isolation
and defiant spirit; his fierceness in the battles is motivated by
his fury at being surrounded by the anger and hatred of his
own people; from this situation develops the splendid picture
of the tenth book:

> .... The Tuscan ranks
> Meet round him, and press hard on him alone,
> On him alone with vengeance multiplied
> Their host of swords they draw. As some tall cliff,
> Projecting to the sea, receives the rage
> Of winds and waters, and untrembling bears
> Vast frowning enmity of seas and skies, so he.

Then, after relating Mezentius' exploits, the poet continues in
another simile, derived from Homer:

> As when a wild boar, harried from the hills
> By teeth of dogs. ....
> Falls in the toils at last, and stands at bay,
> Raging and bristling, and no hunter dares
> Defy him or come near, but darts are hurled
> From far away, with cries unperilous;
> Not otherwise, though righteous is their wrath
> Against Mezentius, not a man so bold
> As face him with drawn sword, but at long range
> They throw their shafts and with loud cries assail;
> He, all unterrified, makes frequent stand,
> Gnashing his teeth, and shaking off their spears.

These fights reach a climax in Mezentius' outburst of grief
over his son's death; in this he recognizes the punishment of

his own acts, and rues them, for the first time, because they
bring disgrace and ruin on Lausus:

> "O son!" he cried, "was life to me so sweet
> That I to save myself surrendered o'er
> My own begotten to a foeman's steel?
> Saved by these gashes shall thy father be,
> And living by thy death? O wretched me!
> How foul an end have I! Now is my wound
> Deep, deep. 'Twas I, dear son, have stained
> Thy name with infamy—to exile driven
> From sceptre and hereditary throne
> By general curse. Would that myself had borne
> My country's vengeance and my nation's hate!
> Would my own guilty life my debt had paid—
> Yea, by a thousand deaths. But see, I live!

Clear as the grimness and brutality of Mezentius are, Virgil
has avoided the manifestation of these qualities in any brutal
action; such brutality in action is not in accord with the poet's
notion of epic propriety; he does allow Mezentius to put his
foot on a fallen foe, and to prop himself against the spear
which pierces the dying man, but in general the poet brings
out the characteristics of Mezentius by speech and situation,
by implicit contrast with other characters, not by cruelty in
action. Thus it is an intentional contrast when Aeneas mer-
cifully allows Lausus to retain his weapons instead of despoiling him, while Mezentius threatens to have his horse carry
away from the fight not only the bloody spoils, but the severed
head of Aeneas. Another effective contrast, left implicit, is
that between the nervous activity of young Turnus and the
hard immovable composure of this gray-haired long-bearded
Etruscan giant, who, like a rock in mid-ocean, holds his own
against the knocks of the opposing forces, who awaits Aeneas
undismayed, whom only his son's death can move from his
equipoise. While Turnus expresses a desire for life and is willing to purchase it by admission of defeat, Mezentius com-

mands his enemy to deal the final blow; he may not survive defeat; even his war-horse would scorn to serve the Trojans.

Similarly, Turnus is sharply contrasted with Aeneas; Turnus is the peer of Aeneas in strength and courage, but Turnus' strength is not supported by reason and moderation; Aeneas' is controlled by wisdom, by perfect balance, and self-restraint. Turnus fights not, as Aeneas, for his people and for his future, but, as he is justly reproached with doing, for his own claims; to stir up a war for selfish interests is criminal. The fury has driven him to it; under her influence he loses reason and self-control, without which bravery becomes reck-lessness; and all to the advantage of the Trojans, as is spe-cially clear when Turnus, in his mad desire to slaughter his foes, shuts himself up in their camp and forgets to open the gate to his own followers. A lively sense of honor inspires him, but this, too, finds expression in morbid excess. In contrast with the well-chosen words which manifest the self-conscious-ness of Aeneas stands the loud boast of Turnus, his glorifica-tion of his strength and heroism. Like Aeneas, he shows con-sideration for a fallen foe, but he has not the moderation to refrain from despoiling the enemy, and his joy in victory be-comes cruelty when he cuts off the head of the dead and decks his chariot with it, dripping with blood. He does not hesitate to attack Aeneas, and declares himself ready for a duel as soon as it is desired; and when he is taken at his word, he sticks to it, in spite of the supplications of Latinus and Amata; not however, with quiet determination, but in mad violence he prepares for the fight; and it is a finely marked trait that immediately after this feverish excitement his cour-age fails him at the critical moment. Hardly is the danger of the crisis over than he breaks out again in eagerness to fight, but half-consciously and willingly allows himself to be re-moved from the action by his sister, until slowly the old sense of honor is aroused at the sight of his struggling followers, and stimulated by the speech of Saces, he is finally brought face to face with Aeneas; now again the poet emphasizes the fury and violence with which he enters upon the duel. His final act in the contest is symbolic of his whole career; he picks up a huge bowlder to hurl at his foe, but the burden is too heavy; his knees totter; the blood congeals in his veins; the missile falls short of the mark; he attempts a task too great even for his gigantic strength. As he did not enter the decisive fight quietly, so he cannot face death composedly; he does not humble himself so far as to beg for life, but he expresses in his last words a strong desire to live, a willingness to give up Lavinia in return for this privilege; such a man, the poet means to suggest, was never worthy of her and of the crown.

Aeneas, as the hero, is of course an ideal warrior, without the limitations of Turnus and Mezentius; but even in the battle scenes the poet presents him as an ideal man as well as warrior; Aeneas comprehends in himself the cardinal virtues of the Roman citizen in peace and war; he appreciates the magnanimity of his foes, is merciful to his worst enemy; he is self-controlled; good faith, justice, and piety are manifested in various ways—in his effort to keep the oaths sworn preliminary to the duel, in his loving protection of Pallas and grief over his death, in his poignant suffering when he is forced to kill Lausus, and when he celebrates Lausus' filial devotion in the agony of his own remorse; only in a temporary vengeful mood is he hard in feeling and even scornful toward an enemy; the thought of revenge annihilates the instinct of mercy when Turnus makes his last appeal; pity in that case would have been weakness in the performance of duty.

But the Aeneas of these battle scenes is only part of the whole hero; the earlier books of the poem have often presented other aspects of his character; the two-fold nature of his virtue he himself, with the usual Roman pride and self-confidence, asserts in the words with which he greets young

Ascanius before entering the final contest with Turnus: "He clasped Ascanius to his mailèd breast, and through his helmet grim tenderly kissed his son. 'My boy,' he cried, 'what valor is and patient toil learn thou of me; let others guide thy feet to prosperous fortune. Let this hand and sword defend thee through the war and lead thee on to high rewards. Thou also play the man.'" Playing the man, in Aeneas' and Virgil's estimation, means not only valor, but patient genuine toil; prosperity is an easy matter; the real test comes in adversity. It is the Aeneas of adversity, in the first half of the poem, that completes the ideal hero. In large measure, of course, this emphasis upon the patient endurance of adversity in the *Aeneid* and relative contempt for the easier virtues manifested in prosperity is a commonplace in human experience and ethical doctrine. But the concrete realization of the thought in the character of Aeneas throughout the poem gains in significance when we discover that this idea was a cornerstone of philosophical theory in Virgil's day. The same Stoic school which determined the content of Virgil's theory of purification and rebirth of souls in the sixth book preached also the necessity of submission to an all-wise Fate. The words of the philosopher, Seneca, a generation or more after Virgil, seem like an elaboration of Aeneas' admonition to Ascanius. Seneca says (*Dial.* i. 4):

Prosperity falls to the lot of the common herd and ordinary natures; but to o'ercome the calamities and disturbing vicissitudes of life is the peculiar privilege of the great man; . . . . whom god approves and loves, he hardens, trains, disciplines . . . . Fate lashes and bruises us; we should submit to it; it is not cruelty on the part of Fate; it is a good fight, and the oftener we face it, the stronger we grow. The strongest part of the body is that which frequent use exercises; we should submit to Fate that we may be hardened against the shocks of fortune by fortune herself. Gradually Fate makes us a match for herself. We learn to scorn danger by being constantly exposed to it. . . . . Why are you surprised that worthy men are knocked about by life's vicissitudes to get strengthened by them? No tree is firm and sturdy unless the wind often beats against it. By the very shock it is bound fast and fixes its roots more firmly in the ground. The fragile trees are those that grow in sunlit valleys.

This Stoic doctrine is obviously the key to the interpretation of Aeneas' character as Virgil conceived it. The hero of the first six books is schooled by adversity; his virtue there lies in patient genuine toil, in submission to misfortune; thence he rises, stimulated especially by the vision of Rome's future heroes in the sixth book, to a career of positive achievement, to the valorous exploits of war in Latium.

Aeneas, therefore, is not merely an ideal Roman; he is an ideal Stoic; he is an offspring of the ethical thought of the poet's day. This leads to two interesting considerations. The Aeneas of the first half of the poem is not only submissive to Fate; he sometimes resists Fate; and what is far worse to our modern feeling, he not only resents his misfortune, but on occasion he almost snivels. The facts are indisputable: in the second book, for instance, after being informed that Fate decrees the fall of Troy, he persists in rash endeavor to frustrate the Greeks even at the expense of exposing to risk his own family; and in his talk with Venus in the first book he complains bitterly of his hardships and of Venus' unmotherly conduct; not infrequently he is perplexed by the cares and anxieties of his strenuous wanderings. Modern critics have been displeased by these deviations, as they seem to be, from consistency and from the truly heroic. But it might be observed that without such occasional reversion to the weakness of humanity, Aeneas would become a pattern of Stoic virtue, about as real and interesting as patterns usually are. Virgil was wise enough not to devitalize his hero by simply transferring the Stoic abstraction to his pages; Aeneas approximates, as well as human being can, the Stoic ideal; his defects are sufficient to keep him human without making him unheroic, and such apparent inconsistency as there may be is simply the touch of unheroic realism that vitalizes Virgil's ideal portraiture.

Even more important to the student of literary form is the obvious question whether we have in Aeneas a unique case of character development in ancient literature. For, clearly, the Stoic theory provides for a possible development of character and its gradual strengthening by the shocks of fortune; and certainly the Aeneas of the battlefields is a very different person from the Aeneas of the wanderings; indeed, one may detect a distinct gradation from patient genuine toil to positive martial achievement, this gradation marked by the turn of events in the sixth book. I see no reason to doubt that such a development is made possible in Stoic theory and is concretely visualized in Aeneas' experience as Virgil portrays it. But as a feature of literary technique I suspect that this development is accidental; Virgil did not, with conscious poetic art, set about the careful delineation of a development of character; rather, thoughtless of any artistic advantages and moved only by his Stoic convictions, he represented an evolution which might well have led to the artistic use of similar character growth had he or later artists been sensitive to the advantages of such portrayal; but, so far as I know, the unique example did not become an object of imitation.

In conclusion, it should be observed that so far as Aeneas represents a Stoic ideal and so far as his deviations from the pattern are merely such defects as any human being is liable to, the character remains typical and general rather than fully individual. He stands for the typical evolution of a chosen favorite of the gods. Virgil's inspiration is not an actual living contemporary; his imagination is stimulated by an ideal. In general this applies to most of his creations. Dido, whose character we studied earlier at some length, we found possessed, not of one distinguishing quality, but of several qualities, all of which were characteristic of an ideal heroic queen; so Camilla is an ideal young Amazon; Latinus, an ideal king. More sharply individualizing traits are not wanting in Turnus and Mezentius. But in the main we are still well within the range of generalized character rather than of specific individualism. Whatever its limitations, such portrayal of character emphasizes implicitly universal truths; Virgil's epic is innocent of the eccentricities and feverish perturbations, the terrible inner turmoil, which modern analysis has cultivated in the literature of the present day.

INDEX

INDEX

RICHARD HEINZE

Professor an der Universität Leipzig

VIRGILS EPISCHE TECHNIK

---

3. *Auflage. Geh. RM.* 16.-, *geb. RM.* 18.-

Der Verfasser analysiert im ersten Teile grössere zusammenhängende Partien der Aeneis auf ihre Technik hin, während der zweite Teil die so gewonnenen Resultate zusammenfasst und sie zu einem systematisch angelegten Bilde der epischen Technik vervollständigt. In der Neuauflage blieb die Anlage des Buches unverändert, doch war der Verfasser darauf bedacht, die neuesten Forschungsergebnisse im alten Rahmen nach Möglichkeit zu verwerten und, wo nötig, kritisch zu ihnen Stellung zu nehmen.

Aus Urteilen über das Werk:

"Für das Verständnis des Vergil ist durch Heinzes vortreffliches Buch sehr viel erreicht, eben weil es die genaue Analyse des Epos zur Grundlage hat. Keiner wird es aus der Hand legen, ohne den Eindruck von der ungeheuren Gedankenarbeit Vergils gewonnen zu haben, ohne gesehen zu haben, wie künstlerisches Empfinden und wohl überlegte Intentionen hier dauernd zusammenwirken."

(Berliner Philologische Wochenschrift.)

"This work has now become a classic in criticism. Such good and well-tested wine as Heinze's needs no bush." (The Classical Journal.)

"Heinze hat irrige Urteile über V., die festgewurzelt schienen, durch seine meisterhaften Darlegungen berichtigt und dem vielgeschmähten römischen Epiker zu einer gerechten Würdigung seiner Verdienste verholfen. Referent ist überzeugt, dass H.'s Werk, das sich auch durch seine formvollendete, sprachliche Darstellung auszeichnet, auf jeden unbefangenen Leser die gleiche starke Wirkung ausüben wird."

(Zeitschrift für die oesterreichischen Gymnasien.)

"Das Buch ist, soweit ich die Literatur kenne, das Beste, was bisher über Vergil geschrieben worden ist. Es hat allgemeine Bedeutung als durchgeführtes Beispiel der Analyse und wissenschaftlichen Würdigung eines der grossen literarischen Kunstwerke."

(Deutsche Literaturztg.)

". . . . R. Heinzens Buch ist eine bahnbrechende Leistung im wahrsten Sinne des Wortes. Indem der Verfasser sich mit streng durchgeführter Zurückdrängung jedes subjektiven Gefühles in die Absichten des Dichters versenkt hat, ist ihm ein prächtiger Wurf gelungen: die erste wirklich gerechte ästhetische Würdigung der Äneis."

(Allgemeines Literaturblatt.)

VERLAG VON B. G. TEUBNER IN LEIPZIG UND BERLIN